Patent Law Injunctions

Patent Law Injunctions

Edited by

Rafał Sikorski

Published by:
Kluwer Law International B.V.
PO Box 316
2400 AH Alphen aan den Rijn
The Netherlands
E-mail: international-sales@wolterskluwer.com
Website: lrus.wolterskluwer.com

Sold and distributed in North, Central and South America by:
Wolters Kluwer Legal & Regulatory U.S.
7201 McKinney Circle
Frederick, MD 21704
United States of America
Email: customer.service@wolterskluwer.com

Sold and distributed in all other countries by:
Air Business Subscriptions
Rockwood House
Haywards Heath
West Sussex
RH16 3DH
United Kingdom
Email: international-customerservice@wolterskluwer.com

Printed on acid-free paper.

ISBN 978-90-411-9457-2

e-Book: ISBN 978-90-411-9458-9
web-PDF: ISBN 978-90-411-9459-6

© 2019 Kluwer Law International BV, The Netherlands

All rights reserved. No part of this publication may be reproduced, stored in a retrieval system, or transmitted in any form or by any means, electronic, mechanical, photocopying, recording, or otherwise, without written permission from the publisher.

Permission to use this content must be obtained from the copyright owner. More information can be found at: lrus.wolterskluwer.com/policies/permissions-reprints-and-licensing

Printed in the United Kingdom.

Editor

Rafał Sikorski is a Professor of Law at the Faculty of Law of the Adam Mickiewicz University in Poznań, Poland where he teaches Intellectual Property, Civil and Private International Law as well as European Union Law. In 2000 he completed an LL.M. course in International Business Transactions at the Central European University in Budapest, Hungary. In 2005 he obtained his PhD from the Adam Mickiewicz University. His major research areas include: patent remedies, intersection of intellectual property and competition law, standardization and standard essential patents, as well as private ordering in patent law. He has published on patent pools, SEPs and standard-setting, patent remedies, conflicts-of-law rules for IP contracts and IP infringement as well as copyright law.

Contributors

Piotr Andrzejewski has graduated from the Law Faculty at the Adam Mickiewicz University in Poznań, Poland. He works for SMM Legal Maciak Mataczynski, one of the leading Polish law firms. He specializes in intellectual property law.

Jorge L. Contreras is a Professor of Law at the University of Utah (Salt Lake City, USA). Before entering academia, Professor Contreras was a partner at the international law firm Wilmer Cutler Pickering Hale and Dorr LLP, where he practiced transactional and IP law in Boston, London and Washington DC. His research focuses, among other things, on the development of technical standards and the use, dissemination and ownership of scientific data generated. He is the author of more than 100 scholarly articles and chapters which have appeared in scientific, legal and policy journals including *Science, Nature, Georgetown Law Journal, Harvard Journal of Law and Technology, Antitrust Law Journal* and *Telecommunications Policy*. He is the editor of five books relating to technology law and technical standards, including the *Cambridge Handbook of Technical Standardization Law*, 2 vols. (2017, 2019 forthcoming). He has been quoted in the *NY Times, Wall Street Journal, Economist, Washington Post, Korea Times*, has been a guest on NPR, BBC and various televised broadcasts, and his work has been cited by the U.S. Federal Trade Commission, European Commission and courts in the U.S. and Europe. He currently serves as Co-Chair of the Interdisciplinary Division of the American Bar Association's Section of Science & Technology Law, and as a member of the National Institutes of Health (NIH) Council of Councils and the IPR Policy Committee of the American National Standards Institute (ANSI). He has previously served as Co-Chair of the National Conference of Lawyers and Scientists, and as a member of the National Academy of Sciences (NAS) Committee on IP Management in Standard-Setting Processes. He is an honors graduate of Harvard Law School (JD) and Rice University (BSEE, BA).

Trevor Cook is an English solicitor with forty years experience in intellectual property, and notably global patent litigation, who has acted in many of the leading patent infringement cases before the English courts, and also in several leading European cases regarding data exclusivity. In 2014 Mr Cook joined WilmerHale in New York from

Bird & Bird LLP in London, where he had been a partner since 1981. He is chair of the British Copyright Council and was for several years president of the UK group of the International Association for the Protection of Intellectual Property (AIPPI). He is on the World Intellectual Property Organization (WIPO) list of arbitrators. In addition to numerous articles and book chapters Mr Cook has authored the following books: *A User's Guide to Patents* (Butterworths 2002; Tottel 2007; Bloomsbury 2011, 2016); *Pharmaceuticals Biotechnology and the Law* (Macmillan 1991; LexisNexis Butterworths 2009, 2016); *EU Intellectual Property Law* (Oxford 2010); *The Protection of Regulatory Data in the Pharmaceutical and Other Sectors* (Sweet & Maxwell 2000); and *A European Perspective as to the Extent to Which Experimental Use, and Certain Other, Defences to Patent Infringement, Apply to Differing Types of Research* (Intellectual Property Institute 2006). He is a co-author of *Practical Intellectual Property Precedents* (with Audrey Horton) (Sweet & Maxwell 1998 to date); and *International Intellectual Property Arbitration* (with Alejandro Garcia) (Kluwer 2010). He is one of the general editors of *The Modern Law of Patents* (LexisNexis Butterworths 2005, 2009, 2014, 2018) and is editor of *Sterling on World Copyright Law* (Sweet & Maxwell 2015, 2018), *Trade Secret Protection – A Global Guide* (Globe Law & Business 2016) and *The Patent Litigation Law Review* (The Law Reviews, 2017). He contributes to the *Chartered Institute of Patent Agents European Patents Handbook* (Sweet & Maxwell), to the *Chartered Institute of Patent Agents Guide to the Patents Act 1977* (Sweet & Maxwell) and to *Vaughan & Robertson's Law of the European Union* (Oxford University Press).

Matt Heckman has been teaching European law and economics of European integration for thirty years at various universities in the Netherlands. He was Director of International Affairs for fourteen years at a Dutch University and is currently teaching at various graduate programs (both MBA and MA) in the Netherlands, Finland, UK and the USA. Presently he works as senior researcher and principal lecturer graduate programs. He was external examiner at DIT Dublin for four years and still acts as a consultant to both public and private companies. He is also a founding member of the research center on innovative entrepreneurship and risk management at the Zuyd University for Applied Sciences. He is also a senior researcher at a Research Center for International Trade. At Maastricht University he teaches at the Center for European Studies and is an external fellow of the Institute for Globalization and International Regulation (IGIR).

His recent activities also include the involvement in university knowledge transfer. He supports start-ups in relation to the intellectual property aspects of bringing new university research to the market. Mr Heckman studied at the University of Maastricht, the University of Lancaster and the Vrije Universiteit Brussels. He holds a bachelor degree and a master degree in International and European Law and gained working experience at the Commission of the EU. His main research interests are in the field of intellectual property law and competition policy. His PhD-dissertation discussed the strategic use of patents in standardization in relation to US, European and Chinese competition law. Recent publications focus on legal aspects of standardization, artificial intelligence and technology licensing, comparing the jurisdictions of the USA, EU and China.

Contributors

Yoonhee Kim is a licensed Korean patent attorney and currently an Associate at Finnegan, Henderson, Farabow, Garrett & Dunner, LLP. He received a JD magna cum laude from American University Washington College of Law and a Bachelor of Science in Chemical Engineering from Seoul National University. His experience includes working as a Dean's Fellow to Professor Jorge Contreras at American University Washington College of Law, where he researched patent and competition issues surrounding the standard-setting process and FRAND commitments. While in law school, Mr Kim also worked in the Office of Policy Planning at the U.S. Federal Trade Commission where he assisted the staff with the policy projects involving standard-essential patents and patent assertion entities. Mr Kim regularly writes and has been published on international and comparative patent law and on the topics at the intersection of patent and competition laws, including the Korea Fair Trade Commission's investigation of FRAND licensing practices (co-author, published in *CPI Antitrust Chronicle*) and the comparative aspects of a patent law doctrine in the United States, Korea, and Japan (published in *Journal of Patent & Trademark Office Society*).

Amandine Léonard obtained her Master of Laws with a specialization in business law (cum laude) in 2012 from the University of Liège. In 2013 she completed the LLM program of the Liège Competition and Innovation Institute (LCII) in European Competition law and Intellectual Property (magna cum laude). Since October 2013, Amandine is a legal researcher at the KU Leuven Centre for IT & IP Law. In January 2015, she obtained a PhD Scholarship from 'Flanders Innovation & Entrepreneurship' (VLAIO) to work on the topic of '*Abusive patent litigation in Europe – The prohibition of abuse of rights and patent trolls*'. During her PhD she will investigate patent litigation strategies adopted by patent holders both in the currently spread patent litigation system of Europe, and in the future Unitary Patent Package system. From January to April 2018 Amandine was a visiting researcher at Stanford Law School (US) for which she received an FWO travel grant.

Her particular fields of research are as follows: the fundamental rationale and objective of intellectual property laws (patent, copyright and trademark), the approach adopted by the United States and European countries regarding intellectual property laws and their limitations and exceptions, as well as the interface between competition law and intellectual property law.

Yogesh Pai is an Assistant Professor of Law and Co-Director of the Centre for Innovation, Intellectual Property and Competition (CIIPC) at the National Law University Delhi. He teaches and writes on issues relating to intellectual property law and policy. He was the Thomas Edison Innovation Fellow (2017) at the Antonin Scalia Law School at George Mason University, Washington DC. He has previously worked with the South Centre in Geneva; CENTAD, New Delhi; and was an Assistant Professor of Law and Coordinator of the Ministry of Human Resource Development Chair on IPR at the National Law University, Jodhpur. In 2012, Yogesh was a short-term Visiting Scholar at the Asian Law Center of the University of Washington School of Law, Seattle. Since 2014, Yogesh is on the roster of consultants for the World Trade Organization, where he facilitates as a resource person for TRIPS component of the Regional Trade

Policy Courses (RTPC) in the Asia-Pacific Region. He also facilitates as a tutor to the WIPO Academy Programs. He has contributed on committees constituted by the Government of India on compulsory licenses and utility models and has published in journals of national and international repute, including Cambridge University Press, Oxford University Press, Edward Elgar, etc. Yogesh is interested in reforms in Indian legal education.

Christoph Rademacher has been appointed as associate professor for international business and IP law at Waseda University School of Law in Tokyo in 2014. In addition, he is an off-counsel at the Tokyo office of Baker & McKenzie. Christoph Rademacher is the first foreigner who has been appointed as a tenured law professor at Waseda, where he teaches a number of courses at graduate and undergraduate level in the field of business and IP law, both in Japanese and English. His research focuses on the protection of technical innovation by means of patents and other rights. He is a member of the directorate of the Waseda University Research Centre of the Legal System of Intellectual Property (RCLIP), a regular speaker at IP conferences in Asia, Europe or the US and, amongst others, a co-author of the treatise 'Patent Enforcement in the US, Germany and Japan' (Oxford University Press, 2015), and a co-editor of the Japanese interdisciplinary volume 'The Legal System of Design Protection: Current Situation and Issues through the Perspective of Jurists and Designers' (Nippon Hyoron Sha, 2016). Professor Rademacher is admitted as an attorney-at-law in New York and as a solicitor in the Republic of Ireland. He has obtained his first degree in business and law as well as his doctorate degree in law at the University of Siegen, Germany, and an LLM degree at Stanford Law School.

Arno Riße is a highly respected practitioner and an attorney-at-law. He specializes in intellectual property law, particularly in patent and trademark law. Arno Riße graduated from University of Münster. He holds an LL.M. in commercial law from University of Auckland, New Zealand. Arno Riße received his PhD degree from University of Münster where he worked as a research assistant at the chair of Prof. Dr Ingo Saenger. Prior to joining Arnold Ruess Law Firm, he practiced at Freshfields Bruckhaus Deringer.

Piotr Ruchała is a PhD Candidate at the Faculty of Law and Administration of Adam Mickiewicz University in Poznan (Chair of European Law), working on a thesis on European copyright law. Piotr is an attorney-at-law at one of the leading Polish law firms SMM Legal Maciak Mataczynski. He is also an author of publications on intellectual property law, unfair competition and civil law.

Hui Jin Yang is a partner at Lee & Ko, a Korean general practice law firm. She concentrates on patent litigation. She has represented and advised pharmaceutical, biotechnology, medical device, food, cosmetic and tobacco product manufacturing companies. She represented Samsung in the *Samsung v. Apple* case before the Seoul Central District Court. Prior to joining Lee & Ko in 2010, Ms. Yang served as a judge at the Seoul Central and Seoul Western District Courts, where she presided over a variety of medical, pharmaceutical and intellectual property matters. She has bachelor's degree in biochemistry and master's degree in law.

Liguo Zhang is a researcher at the Center for International Intellectual Property Law Studies at Xihua University in Chengdu, China. He was a postdoctoral researcher at the Faculty of Law, University of Helsinki, Finland. He received his LLD from University of Helsinki in 2013 and his LLM in intellectual property and competition law from Munich Intellectual Property Law Center, Germany in 2006. His research focuses on innovation-related legal issues, with special focus on patents and standards. He has published several articles in this area in IIC and QMJIP.

Summary of Contents

Editor	v
Contributors	vii
Preface	xxiii

PART I
US Law 1

CHAPTER 1
Injunctive Relief in US Patent Cases
Jorge L. Contreras 3

PART II
EU Law and Law of the Member States 29

CHAPTER 2
Patent Injunctions in the European Union Law
Rafał Sikorski 31

CHAPTER 3
Injunctions Against Patent Infringement under English Law
Trevor Cook 51

CHAPTER 4
Injunctions in Germany
Arno Riße 63

CHAPTER 5
Injunctions in French Patent Law
Amandine Léonard 87

Summary of Contents

CHAPTER 6
Patent Injunctions in Dutch Law
Matt Heckman 117

CHAPTER 7
Injunctive Relief in Polish Patent Law
Rafał Sikorski, Piotr Andrzejewski & Piotr Ruchała 135

PART III
Asia 153

CHAPTER 8
Injunctive Relief in China's Patent Law
Liguo Zhang 155

CHAPTER 9
Patent Injunction Heuristics in India
Yogesh Pai 179

CHAPTER 10
Patent Injunctions in South Korea
Yoonhee Kim & Hui Jin Yang 207

CHAPTER 11
Injunctive Relief in Japan
Christoph Rademacher 223

PART IV
Conclusions 237

CHAPTER 12
Between Automatism and Flexibility: Injunctions in Twenty-First Century Patent Law
Rafał Sikorski 239

Table of Contents

Editor	v
Contributors	vii
Preface	xxiii

PART I
US Law   1

CHAPTER 1
Injunctive Relief in US Patent Cases
Jorge L. Contreras   3

§1.01	Equitable Remedies and Injunctive Relief under US Law	3
	[A] Equitable Relief under the Common Law	3
	[B] Merger of Law and Equity	4
	[C] Irreparable Harm and the Grant of Equitable Relief	5
§1.02	Permanent Injunctive Relief in US Patent Cases	6
	[A] Before eBay: Presumption of Irreparable Harm	7
	[B] eBay and the Four Factor Test	8
	[C] Determining Irreparable Harm After eBay	9
	[D] Balancing Hardships and Equities	10
	[E] The Public Interest Factor After eBay	11
	[F] Multicomponent Products and Causal Nexus	12
	[G] Empirical Studies of Injunctive Relief	13
	[H] Scope of Injunctions	14
	[I] Compulsory Licensing and Ongoing Royalties After the Denial of Injunctive Relief	15
§1.03	Preliminary Injunctions in Patent Cases	17
	[A] Preliminary Injunction Overview	17

Table of Contents

	[B]	Likelihood of Success on the Merits	17
	[C]	eBay and Preliminary Relief	18
	[D]	Posting Bond	19
	[E]	Empirical Data: Preliminary Injunctions	19
§1.04	Injunctive Relief and FRAND Commitments		20
§1.05	Exclusion Orders At the International Trade Commission		22
	[A]	The ITC and Patent Exclusion Orders	22
	[B]	The ITC's Public Interest Test and FRAND	23
	[C]	Position of Other US Governmental Agencies	23
§1.06	Antitrust Enforcement, FRAND and Injunctive Relief		24
§1.07	Voluntary Commitments Regarding Injunctive Relief		26
§1.08	Conclusions		26

Part II
EU Law and Law of the Member States   29

Chapter 2
Patent Injunctions in the European Union Law
Rafał Sikorski   31

§2.01	Introduction			31
§2.02	Injunctive Relief in Directive 2004/48			32
	[A]	Introduction		32
	[B]	General Framework of the Directive 2004/48		33
	[C]	Permanent Injunctions and Alternative Measures		34
		[1]	Permanent Injunctions	34
		[2]	Alternative Measure	36
	[D]	The Meaning of the Proportionality Principle		37
		[1]	Balancing under the Principle of Proportionality	37
		[2]	Factors Relevant When Applying Proportionality Principle	39
		[3]	Tailoring Injunctions	41
		[4]	Burden of Proof	42
	[E]	Preliminary (Interlocutory, Interim, Provisional) Injunctions		43
§2.03	Standard Essential Patents, Injunctions and EU Competition Law			44
	[A]	Introduction		44
	[B]	The Decision of the CJEU in *Huawei v. ZTE*		45
		[1]	Facts of the Case	45
		[2]	Competitive Harm in SEP Cases	46
		[3]	Framework for Negotiating SEP Licenses	47
§2.04	Conclusions			49

CHAPTER 3
Injunctions Against Patent Infringement under English Law
Trevor Cook   51

§3.01	Introduction	51
§3.02	Interim Injunctions Pending Trial on the Merits	53
§3.03	Injunctions After Trial on the Merits	56
§3.04	Injunctions and Standards Essential Patents	60
§3.05	Summary	61

CHAPTER 4
Injunctions in Germany
Arno Rißwe   63

§4.01	Overview				63
§4.02	Substantive Requirements				64
	[A]	Right to Sue			64
	[B]	Capacity to Be Sued			64
	[C]	Infringement			65
		[1]	Direct Infringement		65
			[a]	Broad Interpretation of Acts of Infringement	66
			[b]	Infringement on German Territory	67
			[c]	Equivalent Infringement	68
		[2]	Contributory/Indirect Patent Infringement		69
	[D]	Threat of Infringement and Danger of Recurrence			70
		[1]	Threat of Infringement		71
		[2]	Danger of Recurrence		71
	[E]	Scope			71
	[F]	Defences			74
		[1]	FRAND Defence: Background		74
		[2]	Applicability		75
		[3]	Infringement Alert		75
		[4]	Willingness		76
		[5]	FRAND Offer		77
		[6]	Counter-Offer		78
		[7]	Security and Rendering of Account		79
§4.03	Procedural Aspects				79
	[A]	Proceedings on the Merits			79
		[1]	Competent Courts and Instances		79
		[2]	Course of Infringement Proceedings		79
		[3]	Bifurcation		80
		[4]	Evidence		81
		[5]	Enforcement		81
	[B]	Preliminary Injunctions			82
		[1]	Competent Courts and Instances		82

Table of Contents

		[2]	Course of PI Infringement Proceedings	82
		[3]	Urgency	83
		[4]	Validity of the Patent	83
		[5]	Weighting of Interests	84
		[6]	Prima Facie Evidence	84
		[7]	Enforcement	85

CHAPTER 5
Injunctions in French Patent Law
Amandine Léonard 87

§5.01	Introduction		87
	[A]	Legislative Framework	87
	[B]	Competent Court	87
	[C]	Patent Litigation in France	88
	[D]	Remark on Recent Developments	89
§5.02	Injunctive Relief: Conditions and Flexibility		89
	[A]	Preliminary Injunctions	89
	[B]	Permanent Injunctions	92
	[C]	Enforcement Directive and TRIPs Agreement	95
§5.03	Exceptional Circumstances		96
	[A]	Competition Law	96
	[B]	Abuse of Rights	98
	[C]	Somewhere Between Competition Law and Abuse of Rights?	99
§5.04	Standardization and FRAND		100
	[A]	Case Law	101
	[B]	FRAND Pledges and Requirement to Act in Good Faith	104
	[C]	Royalty Rate and FRAND Terms	106
§5.05	Exploring New Territories		108
	[A]	On Acquiescence (Tolerance), Legitimate Expectations and Estoppel '*à la française*'	108
	[B]	The Complex Product Issue	110
§5.06	US Concerns		111
	[A]	The Impact of eBay on Injunctive Relief in France	111
	[B]	Patent Trolling Scenarios under French Patent Law	112
§5.07	Conclusive Remarks		116

CHAPTER 6
Patent Injunctions in Dutch Law
Matt Heckman 117

§6.01	Introduction to Dutch Patent Law	117
§6.02	General Overview of Remedies and Procedure in Patent Infringement Disputes	118
§6.03	Preliminary (Interim) Injunctions	119

	[A]	Patent Validity	120
	[B]	Urgency	120
	[C]	Likelihood of Infringement	120
	[D]	Complexity of the Case	121
	[E]	Balance of Interests	121
	[F]	Standard of Proof and Other Procedural Requirements	121
	[G]	Judicial Discretion	122
§6.04	Permanent Injunctions		122
§6.05	Cross-Border Injunctions		123
	[A]	*Roche v. Primus*	123
	[B]	*GAT-LuK*	124
	[C]	*Solvay v. Honeywell*	125
§6.06	Injunctive Relief for Standard Essential Patents: Analysis of the Relevant Case Law		126
	[A]	*Philips v. SK Kassetten*	126
	[B]	*LG Electronics v. Sony*	127
	[C]	*Samsung v. Apple*	128
	[D]	*Archos v. Philips*	131
§6.07	Flexibility and Equitable Concerns in Granting Injunctive Relief		131
	[A]	FRAND Licensing	131
	[B]	Patent Trolls	133

CHAPTER 7
Injunctive Relief in Polish Patent Law
Rafał Sikorski, Piotr Andrzejewski & Piotr Ruchała   135

§7.01	Introduction	135
§7.02	Permanent Injunctions and Alternative Measures	137
	[A] Permanent Injunctions	137
	[B] Compensation in Lieu of Injunction (Alternative Measure)	140
§7.03	Abuse of Right Doctrines	144
§7.04	EU Competition Law/National Competition Law Defense	147
§7.05	Enforcement of Permanent Injunctions	148
§7.06	Interim (Preliminary, Interlocutory) Injunctions	149
§7.07	Conclusions	151

PART III
Asia   153

CHAPTER 8
Injunctive Relief in China's Patent Law
Liguo Zhang   155

§8.01	Introduction	155
	[A] Remedies for Patent Infringement in Chinese Law	156

Table of Contents

	[B]	Who Awards an Injunction in China: A Court or Administrative Entity		157
		[1] Judicial Institutions		157
		[2] Administrative Authority		158
§8.02	Preliminary Injunctions and Permanent Injunctions: Procedure and Conditions			158
	[A]	Preliminary Injunctions		158
	[B]	Permanent Injunction		161
§8.03	Defenses Against an Injunction			162
	[A]	Public Interest Defense		162
	[B]	Good Faith		166
		[1] Patentee Violating the Principle of Good Faith		166
		[2] Infringer Using a Patent in Good Faith		166
	[C]	Compulsory License		167
		[1] Procedure to Apply for a Compulsory License in China		168
		[2] Compulsory License Procedure and Injunction		168
§8.04	Injunctions for SEPs and FRAND Commitments			169
	[A]	In re Qualcomm by the NDRC		169
		[1] Qualcomm's Dominant Position in the Relevant Markets		170
		[2] Licensing Offers Violating the ALM		171
		[3] Licensing Offers Violating the AML as a Defense Against an Injunction		172
	[B]	*Huawei v. InterDigital*		172
	[C]	*Huawei v. Samsung*		175
§8.05	Conclusions			177

CHAPTER 9
Patent Injunction Heuristics in India
Yogesh Pai   179

§9.01	Introduction		179
§9.02	Situating Patent Injunctions in India in the Current Debate		181
§9.03	Statutory Foundations of Patent Injunctions in India		188
§9.04	Standards for Granting Patent Injunctions		191
	[A] Interim Injunctions		191
		[1] Prima Facie Case	192
		[2] Irreparable Injury	194
		[3] Balance of Convenience and Public Interest	196
	[B] Ex Parte Injunctions		199
	[C] *Quia-Timet* Injunctions		201
	[D] Permanent Injunctions		203
§9.05	Conclusion		204

CHAPTER 10
Patent Injunctions in South Korea
Yoonhee Kim & Hui Jin Yang   207

§10.01	Injunctive Relief under Korean Law		207
	[A]	Preliminary Injunction	207
	[B]	Permanent Injunction	209
§10.02	Abuse of Rights Defenses to Claims for Injunctive Relief		210
	[A]	Civil Law	210
	[B]	Patent Law	210
	[C]	Competition Law	211
§10.03	Samsung v. Apple: The Korean Court's Perspectives on SEP Injunctions		212
	[A]	FRAND Commitments from a Contract Law Perspective	212
	[B]	The Duty to Negotiate in Good Faith and Abuse of Rights Defenses	213
	[C]	FRAND Negotiation under Scrutiny	215
§10.04	The IPR Guidelines: The KFTC's Perspectives on SEP Injunctions		218
	[A]	SEP Injunctions and FRAND Negotiation	218
	[B]	NPEs and Jurisdictional Reach	219
	[C]	The 2016 Amendment: Distinctions Clarified Between SEPs and "De Facto" SEPs	220
§10.05	Conclusion		221

CHAPTER 11
Injunctive Relief in Japan
Christoph Rademacher   223

§11.01	Legal Framework and Court System			223
§11.02	Remedies			224
	[A]	Permanent Injunctive Relief		224
		[1]	Requirements	224
		[2]	Scope	225
		[3]	Compulsory Enforcement of Injunctions	226
	[B]	Preliminary Injunction		226
		[1]	Requirements	226
		[2]	Procedural Overview	228
		[3]	Damages for Wrongful Injunctive Relief	229
§11.03	Defences Against Injunctive Relief			229
	[A]	Compulsory License		229
		[1]	Lack of Practice	230
		[2]	Dependent License	231
		[3]	Public Interest License	231
	[B]	Abuse of Rights Defence		232
§11.04	Concluding Thoughts			235

Table of Contents

PART IV
Conclusions   237

CHAPTER 12
Between Automatism and Flexibility: Injunctions in Twenty-First Century
Patent Law
Rafał Sikorski   239

§12.01 Patent Exclusivity and Injunctive Relief: Two Sides of the Same Coin 239
§12.02 Cases for Flexibility   242
        [A]   Standardization and Standard Essential Patents   243
        [B]   NPEs, PAEs, Patent Trolls and Privateering   245
        [C]   Complex Products   246
        [D]   Public Interest   247
§12.03 Legal Framework   247
        [A]   International Law Framework – The TRIPS Agreement   247
        [B]   Permanent Injunctions at National Level   248
        [C]   Preliminary Injunctions   249

Preface

Patent law injunctions have attracted a lot of attention in the aftermath of the U.S. Supreme Court decision in *eBay v. MercExchange*. This interest has been genuinely global. Much of that interest results from vast litigation in the ICT markets concerning access to standard essential patents, operations of patent assertion entities, trolls and patent privateers as well as complex products. To grant or not grant an injunction is the dilemma lying at the very centre of patent and smartphone wars fought on all continents and in all major jurisdictions.

These developments have clearly shown that remedies and injunctions in particular play a crucial role in delineating the boundaries of patent protection. Prior to the patent and smartphone wars on the ICT markets, IP lawyers – both practitioners and academics – have largely underestimated the role of patent remedies in determining the effective scope of protection. Criteria of patentability, scope of exclusive rights or the limitations and exceptions attracted more attention than remedies.

Today, when so many patent wars have already been fought, it becomes clear that injunctive relief may overcompensate, undercompensate or enable the patentee to obtain reward commensurate to the value of his invention. For the patent system, whose primary role is to provide incentives to innovate, finding a proper approach towards injunctions is absolutely crucial. Comparative analysis should be very helpful. Indeed, though jurisdictions differ, the problems faced by a trial judge in the U.S. District Court and a judge sitting in London, Delhi or Dusseldorf, are not very different.

It is fascinating to see that judges from different jurisdictions indeed look at the practice in other countries. It is not uncommon that a decision to grant an injunction in Delhi might well inspire a federal judge in California, or a method of calculating FRAND royalties applied by English judges may inspire a German judge deciding a similar case in German courts.

Recognizing that patent disputes have become truly global disputes, the book looks at injunctive relief in major patent jurisdictions around the world. Unsurprisingly, the journey starts in the United States with a chapter written by a leading world expert in this field – Jorge Contreras. It is followed by chapters on EU law written by Rafał Sikorski and selected jurisdictions of EU Member States. Again, unsurprisingly we begin with chapters on Germany and the United Kingdom. Both have been written by outstanding practitioners – Trevor Cook and Arno Riße. The EU section ends with chapters on French, Dutch and Polish law written respectively by Amandine Leonard, Matt Heckman and finally Rafał Sikorski, Piotr Ruchała and Piotr Andrzejewski.

The third part of the book is dedicated to Asian jurisdictions. It begins with a chapter on China written by Liguo Zhang. It is followed by a chapter on India, South Korea and Japan. These were written by respectively Yogesh Pai, Yoonhee Kim and Hui Jin Yang and finally Christoph Rademacher. The book ends with a concluding chapter by Rafał Sikorski.

This book is a result of a research project financed by Narodowe Centrum Nauki on the basis of the agreement signed by the NCN and the Editor (contract no. UMO-2014/15/B/HS5/02698).

Part I US Law

CHAPTER 1
Injunctive Relief in US Patent Cases

*Jorge L. Contreras**

The law of injunctive relief in United States patent cases presents a puzzling set of contrasts. On one hand, it is grounded in venerable common law principles of equity that have been applied by the courts for centuries. On the other hand, it reflects the unique complexities of massively multicomponent products and advanced technology standards. This chapter provides an overview of the US law of patent injunctions, both generally and specifically as applied to standards essential patents. It also addresses, briefly, considerations surrounding the issuance of exclusion orders by the US International Trade Commission (ITC), a non-judicial federal agency that has recently become an important venue for patent litigation.

§1.01   EQUITABLE REMEDIES AND INJUNCTIVE RELIEF UNDER US LAW

[A]   Equitable Relief under the Common Law

Under the English common law system that developed during the fourteenth century, two distinct types of courts existed: courts of law, which resolved legal disputes, including those among private citizens, and courts of equity or chancery, which acted on petitions to dispense the "king's justice."[1] These appeals to royal justice were initially heard by the king's Chancellor, often a bishop or other high church official, who was vested with broad and flexible authority to grant remedies to achieve just

---

* The author thanks Jake Sherkow and Norman Siebrasse for valuable comments and discussion of this chapter.
1. Douglas Laycock, *The Death of the Irreparable Injury Rule* (Oxford University Press, 1991), 19; Kirsten Stoll-DeBell, Nancy L. Dempsey & Bradford E. Dempsey, *Injunctive Relief – Temporary Restraining Orders and Preliminary Injunctions* (ABA Publ., 2009), 3.

ends.[2] Eventually, the Chancellor's role became institutionalized in a separate system of equitable "chancery" courts that existed alongside the courts of law. Courts within these parallel systems of law and equity often took jurisdiction over the same cases, sometimes resulting in conflicting and contradictory judgments.[3] These conflicts were addressed, to a degree, by the gradual withdrawal of the chancery courts to a supplemental role in which they regularly declined to take jurisdiction over cases when the plaintiff's harm could adequately be addressed through the courts of law.[4]

In the eighteenth century, the United States inherited this bifurcated system of law and equity from its colonial parent. However, the framers of the US Constitution, particularly Alexander Hamilton and the Anti-Federalists, were suspicious of the broad discretionary powers granted to the Chancellor and the Courts of Chancery.[5] As a result, the jurisdiction of the equity courts in the US was consciously limited to extraordinary matters in which no adequate remedy was available at law. This gap-filling jurisdiction ensured that courts of equity did not displace the more constitutionally prescribed law courts. Specifically, if a substantive right was created at law (e.g., through contract, property or tort), then an equitable court would not grant a remedy unless the legal remedy was inadequate to redress the wrong.

In most cases, the courts of law were authorized to award monetary damages to compensate the aggrieved party for its injury. All other remedies, however, were available to the courts of equity, which had significant latitude to fashion non-compensatory relief to achieve just results. Such remedies can generally be classified as restitutionary (involving the transfer of property (including funds) from one party to another), declaratory (making a definitive legal pronouncement, for example, the proper interpretation of a contractual clause), or, most frequently, coercive (mandating that a party take, or refrain from taking, a specific action).[6] The coercive remedy is what is today commonly known as injunctive relief. An injunction (sometimes referred to as a restraining order) may require the enjoined party to act in any of a number of possible ways: to cease a trespass, to refrain from a business activity, to remove an encroaching structure, to perform a contracted service, to cancel a legal instrument, to abate a nuisance, to reinstate an employee, to join multiple parties in a single legal proceeding (known as "interpleader") or, of most relevance to this chapter, to stop making, using or selling an infringing product or process.

[B] Merger of Law and Equity

Beginning in the mid-nineteenth century, many US states, as well as the federal government, dispensed with the dual law-equity court system and allowed a single set

---

2. Stoll-DeBell et al., *supra* n. 1, at 3.
3. Norman Siebrasse, *Interlocutory Injunctions and Irreparable Harm in the Federal Courts*, 88 Canadian Bar Rev. 515, 519 (2009).
4. *Id.*, n. 14 (citing historical sources).
5. Stoll-DeBell et al., *supra* n. 1, at 4.
6. Dan B. Dobbs, *Dobbs Law of Remedies* Vol. 1 (2nd ed., West Publ. 1993), 56.

of courts to hear claims both in law and equity.[7] In 1938 with the adoption of the Federal Rules of Civil Procedure (FRCP), the federal courts began to utilize the same procedural rules for both legal and equitable actions creating a single "civil action." This unification of claims is generally known as the "merger of law and equity."

Despite the procedural merger of legal and equitable claims, one important procedural distinction remains between law and equity: the jury trial. Recalling the English common law origins of equitable actions, the courts of chancery dispensing the sovereign's justice did not employ a jury, while the courts of law did. And though England has since abolished the right to jury trial in civil matters, this right is enshrined in the Seventh Amendment of the US Constitution, resulting in jury trials today in civil matters, including patent cases.[8] However, as in the English chancery courts, jury trials were never granted in equitable cases in the United States, and questions of equity are still determined by a judge and not by a jury.[9]

[C] Irreparable Harm and the Grant of Equitable Relief

As noted above, US courts sitting in equity jurisdiction historically had the authority to grant a remedy only if available legal remedies were inadequate to redress the wrong. This principle has come to be known as the "irreparable harm" or "irreparable injury" rule: equity will not grant a remedy for the violation of a legal right unless the plaintiff would otherwise suffer irreparable harm.[10] Irreparable harm is often found when the dispute concerns a unique item, such as a parcel of land or an heirloom, when a Constitutional right such as freedom of speech or the right to vote are abridged, when the defendant has engaged in repeated acts requiring multiple suits to resolve, or when monetary relief is either difficult to collect or measure.[11]

While the likelihood of irreparable harm is typically determined by the court based on the facts of a case, in some circumstances a *presumption* of irreparable harm may be imposed by law. Such a presumption has traditionally existed, for example,[12]

---

7. *Id.*, 148–149. The first state to do this was New York, which unified its court system in 1848 (*Id.*, 148). Despite this general unification, some states still retain separate equitable courts. The most notable of these is Delaware, which today still retains a separate Chancery Court of no small importance in corporate law and other matters.
8. Mark A. Lemley, *Why Do Juries Decide if Patents Are Valid?* 99 Virginia L. Rev. 1673, 1678 (2013).
9. Dobbs, *supra* n. 6, at 149; Cotter has proposed that the determination of patent damages be "recast" as a question of equitable restitution in order to remove such questions from the jury (Thomas F. Cotter, *Reining in Remedies in Patent Litigation: Three (Increasingly Immodest) Proposals*, 30 Santa Clara High Tech. L.J. 1, 9, 24–25 [2013]).
10. Dobbs, *supra* n. 6, at 58.
11. *Id.*, 130–131.
12. Mark P. Gergen, John M. Golden and Henry E. Smith, *The Supreme Court's Accidental Revolution? The Test for Permanent Injunctions*, 112 Columbia L. Rev. 203, 220–224 and 231–232 (2012); Stoll-DeBell et al., *supra* n. 1, at 6.

in cases relating to the depletion of a unique resource,[13] an encroachment upon real property,[14] or a violation of civil rights.[15]

The court's inquiry in an equitable matter does not end with a determination of irreparable harm. In addition, the court must balance the equities and hardships associated with the entry of an equitable remedy. In this context, equities generally refer to the fault, ethical position (e.g., good or bad faith) and delay of the respective parties.[16] Hardship refers both to the adverse impact on the plaintiff if relief is *not* granted, as well as the adverse impact on the defendant if relief *is* granted.[17]

In addition to equities and hardships, courts dispensing equitable remedies considered the impact of the requested relief on third parties or the public generally. For example, if a nuisance plaintiff seeks to have the defendant's polluting factory shut down, the court may consider both the positive impact of the closure on the environment as well as its negative impact on the local economy and employment.[18] Other public interest factors considered by the courts in equitable matters include public health and safety, consumer confusion and deception, civil rights and environmental effects.[19]

§1.02 PERMANENT INJUNCTIVE RELIEF IN US PATENT CASES

Under US law, remedies for patent infringement may be legal (involving the award of monetary damages) or equitable (involving the issuance of an injunction to prevent the continuation of the infringing activity).[20] In some cases, both monetary damages and injunctive relief may be awarded. Section 283 of the Patent Act specifically authorizes injunctive relief in patent cases:

> The several courts having jurisdiction of cases under this title may grant injunctions in accordance with the principles of equity to prevent the violation of any right secured by patent, on such terms as the court deems reasonable.[21]

---

13. *See*, e.g., *Pardee v. Camden Lumber Co.*, 73 S.E. 82 (W.Va. 1911) (trespass by cutting of timber should always be enjoined).
14. *See*, e.g., *Vestal v. Young*, 82 P. 381, 382-83 (Cal. 1905) (injunction issued to prevent encroachment that could mature into an easement).
15. *See*, e.g., *Jolly v. Coughlin*, 76 F.3d 468 (2nd Cir. 1996) (presumption of irreparable harm arising from alleged violation of 8th Amendment freedom from cruel and unusual punishment), *Deerfield Med. Ctr. v. Deerfield Beach*, 661 F.2d 328 (5th Cir. 1981) (presumption of irreparable harm arising from alleged violation of 4th Amendment right to privacy), and *Paulsen v. County of Nassau*, 925 F.2d 65 (2nd Cir. 1991) (presumption of irreparable harm arising from alleged violation of 1st Amendment free exercise of religion).
16. Dobbs, *supra* n. 6, at 109.
17. *Id.*, 110.
18. *Id.*, 111.
19. *Id.*, 112.
20. Equity jurisdiction was first conferred on federal courts hearing patent cases under the Patent Act of 1819 (Donald S. Chisum, *Chisum on Patents: A Treatise on the Law of Patentability, Validity and Infringement*, [2015] § 20.02[1]). By the 1870 Patent Act, federal courts were authorized to issue both damages and injunctive relief when a claim was brought in equity (Lemley, *supra* n. 8, 1702-1703).
21. 35 USC § 283.

Thus, when injunctive relief is granted in patent cases, such relief must be "in accordance with the principles of equity." However, the Supreme Court has cautioned that injunctions are "drastic and extraordinary" remedies that "should not be granted as a matter of course."[22] The analysis that a court must undertake before granting injunctive relief is thus a delicate and complex one.

[A]   Before eBay: Presumption of Irreparable Harm

As noted above, the general test for granting equitable relief under the common law requires a finding that the plaintiff would be irreparably harmed if such relief were not granted. However, as also noted above, some forms of harm, such as encroachments on property and violations of civil rights, have traditionally given rise to a presumption of irreparable harm. The same presumption existed in the patent law for many years.

The presumption of irreparable harm in patent cases was largely based on the property-like nature of patents. Under section 154(a)(1) of the Patent Act, a patent gives its owner "the right to exclude others from making, using, offering for sale, or selling the invention." Likewise, section 261 of the Patent Act states that "patents shall have the attributes of personal property." These statutory provisions led courts, particularly the Court of Appeals for the Federal Circuit, to treat patents as unique assets, such as real estate, that should automatically be entitled to protection from unauthorized exploitation through permanent injunctions. As the Federal Circuit explained in 1987:

> In matters involving patent rights, irreparable harm has been presumed when a clear showing has been made of patent validity and infringement. This presumption derives in part from the finite term of the patent grant, for patent expiration is not suspended during litigation, and the passage of time can work irremediable harm... The nature of the patent grant thus weighs against holding that monetary damages will always suffice to make the patentee whole, for the principal value of a patent is its statutory right to exclude.[23]

Accordingly, the Federal Circuit adopted a general rule that a permanent injunction will *automatically* issue once a patent has been adjudged infringed and valid, absent exceptional circumstances.[24] As a result of this rule, injunctions were more likely to issue in patent cases than most other types of litigation.[25] This presumption of irreparable harm for patent cases was recognized in the US until rejected in 2006 by the Supreme Court in *eBay Inc. v. MercExchange, L.L.C* (*see* below).

Though strong, the presumption of irreparable harm in patent cases was not absolute. The presumption could be rebutted under certain circumstances, including

---

22. *Monsanto Co. v. Geertson Seed Farms*, 130 S. Ct. 2743, 2761 (2010).
23. *H.H. Robertson, Co. v. United Steel Deck, Inc.*, 820 F.2d 384 (Fed. Cir. 1987). *See also*, *Richardson v. Suzuki Motor Co.*, 868 F.2d 1226, 1246–47 (Fed. Cir. 1989) ("Infringement having been established, it is contrary to the laws of property, of which the patent law partakes, to deny the patentee's right to exclude others from use of his property.").
24. *See MercExchange LLC v. eBay, Inc.*, 401 F.3d 1323 (Fed. Cir. 2005), rev'd 547 US 388 (2006).
25. Stoll-DeBell et al., *supra* n. 1, at 115–116.

the defendant's showing that future infringement was unlikely (due, for example, to advancement of technology), the patentee was willing to license the patent for monetary consideration, the patentee unduly delayed in bringing suit, or the patentee's market share was large in comparison to the infringer's.[26]

[B] eBay and the Four Factor Test

The availability of injunctive relief in patent cases was definitively addressed by the U.S. Supreme Court in *eBay Inc. v. MercExchange, L.L.C*, 547 US 388 (2006). The *eBay* case involved a patent claiming a business method for operating "an electronic market designed to facilitate the sale of goods between private individuals by establishing a central authority to promote trust among participants" (US Pat. No. 5,845,265). MercExchange, the non-practicing entity that owned the patent, enforced it against online auction site eBay and obtained a jury verdict of validity and infringement. MercExchange also sought a permanent injunction against eBay, which was initially denied by the trial court. On appeal, the Federal Circuit reversed the trial court's denial of the injunction based on its "general rule that courts will issue permanent injunctions against patent infringement" (p. 391). The Supreme Court reversed, rejecting the presumption of irreparable harm that had been recognized by the Federal Circuit and lower federal courts in the US.[27]

Justice Thomas writing for the Court, held that the decision to grant or deny an injunction is an act of judicial discretion that must be exercised in accordance with "well-established principles of equity" (p. 391). He then articulated a four-factor equitable test to be applied by courts considering the grant of injunctive relief.[28] This test requires the plaintiff to demonstrate:

(1) that it has suffered an irreparable injury;
(2) that remedies available at law [i.e., monetary damages] are inadequate to compensate it for that injury;
(3) that considering the balance of hardships between the plaintiff and defendant, a remedy in equity is warranted; and
(4) that the public interest would not be disserved by the award of an injunction.

---

26. *Polymer Technologies Inc. v. Bridwell*, 103 F.3d 970 (Fed. Cir. 1996).
27. *See Robert Bosch v. Pylon Mfg.*, 659 F.3d 1142, 1148–49 (Fed. Cir. 2011) ("*eBay* jettisoned the presumption of irreparable harm as it applies to determining the appropriateness of injunctive relief").
28. Some commentators have observed that the *eBay* four-factor test, which requires that the plaintiff establish each of the four elements of the test in order to obtain an injunction (i.e., in a "conjunctive" fashion), is somewhat inconsistent with traditional equitable principles for assessing injunctive relief, which instead allowed the court to balance the relevant factors (Gergen, Golden & Smith, *supra* n. 12, at 207–211; Thomas F. Cotter, *Comparative Patent Remedies: A Legal and Economic Analysis* (Oxford Univ. Press 2013), 102–103. Nevertheless, the conjunctive nature of the *eBay* factors has now been recognized in subsequent cases. *See*, e.g., *Nichia Corp. v. Everlight Americas, Inc.*, slip op. at 26 (Fed. Cir. Apr. 28, 2017) ("Because Nichia failed to establish one of the four [*eBay*] equitable factors, the court did not abuse its discretion in denying Nichia's request for an injunction").

Applying these factors on remand, the trial court denied MercExchange's motion for injunctive relief.[29]

Though the Court's decision in *eBay* was unanimous, several justices wrote separately to express views that were not addressed by the majority opinion. Chief Justice Roberts, joined by Justices Scalia and Ginsburg, wrote a brief concurring opinion noting the long history of permanent injunctions in patent cases and observing that the Court did not write on "an entirely clean slate" in applying traditional equitable principles to patent injunction cases (p. 395). In other words, these three justices appear to be urging lower courts to continue to favor injunctive relief in patent cases on the basis of long historical practice.

Taking a different approach, Justice Kennedy, joined by Justices Stevens, Souter and Breyer, noted with some concern that in recent years "[a]n industry has developed in which firms use patents not as a basis for producing or selling goods but, instead, primarily for obtaining licensing fees" (p. 396). They feared that such entities could use injunctive relief as "a bargaining tool to charge exorbitant fees to companies that seek to buy licenses to practice the patent" (*ibid.*). Accordingly, these justices appear to recommend that lower courts view requests for injunctive relief by such entities with skepticism.[30]

[C] Determining Irreparable Harm After eBay

The first two prongs of the *eBay* test require that a plaintiff demonstrate that it would suffer irreparable harm absent the issuance of an injunction, and that monetary damages would be inadequate to compensate it for the harm suffered.[31] The requisite showing of irreparable harm has often been made in cases involving competitors, particularly when the patentee stands to lose substantial market share, suffer price erosion and lose customer goodwill if the infringing activity is permitted to continue.[32] Other factors supporting a finding of irreparable harm post-*eBay* include loss of jobs,

---

29. 500 F. Supp. 2d 556 (E.D. Va. 2007).
30. This policy-based approach has been criticized by commentators, who point out that other, more persuasive, rationales for overturning the Federal Circuit's decision existed (Michael W. Carroll, *Patent Injunctions and the Problem of Uniformity Cost*, 13 Mich. Telecomm. Tech. L. Rev. 421, 428–429 [2007]).
31. Some commentators have noted that the first two *eBay* factors are, in fact, one and the same and reflect an imperfect understanding of the traditional equitable consideration of irreparable harm in injunction cases (Gergen, Golden & Smith, *supra* n. 12, at 209). This observation was also made by the district court on remand in eBay itself, which noted that "the irreparable harm inquiry and remedy at law inquiry are essentially two sides of the same coin; however, the court will address them separately in order to conform with the four-factor test as outlined by the Supreme Court" (*MercExchange L.L.C. v. eBay, Inc.*, 500 F. Supp.2d 556, 569 n. 11).
32. Aaron Stiefel and Krista Carter, *10 Years Later – Impact of eBay on Patent Injunctions in the Life Sciences*, Bloomberg BNA Patent, Trademark & Copyright J. – Daily Ed., Jun. 22, 2016; *See*, e.g., *Sanofi-Aventis Deutschland GmbH v. Glenmark Pharms. Inc., USA*, 821 F. Supp. 2d 681, 693–694 (D.N.J. 2011), and *Amgen, Inc. v. F. Hoffman-La Roche, Ltd.*, 581 F. Supp.2d 160, 212 (D. Mass. 2008), *Robert Bosch LLC v. Pylon Mfg. Corp.*, 659 F. 3d 1142, 1150-55 (Fed. Cir. 2011).

the infringer's inability to pay monetary damages, encouragement of other infringers to enter the market, and a patented product with a short market life.[33]

By the same token, a number of factors have been found to rebut a plaintiff's case for irreparable harm after *eBay*. These include the patentee's delay in filing suit, the patentee's demonstrated willingness to accept monetary compensation for licenses of the patent, a lack of direct competition between the patentee and the infringer, the infringer's ability to pay any monetary damages assessed, the availability of non-infringing substitutes, a patentee with a small market share, a market with multiple competitors, and an infringer that is likely to cease infringing activities soon.[34]

Despite the Supreme Court's abolition in *eBay* of the presumption of irreparable harm in patent cases, the Federal Circuit has, at times, continued to espouse a significantly pro-injunction perspective evoking the presumption of irreparable harm. For example, the Federal Circuit explained in *Edwards LifeSciences, AG v. CoreValve, Inc.*, that:

> A patentee's right to exclude is a fundamental tenet of patent law ... Absent adverse equitable considerations, the winner of validity and infringement may normally expect to regain the exclusivity that was lost with the infringement.[35]

It remains to be seen whether the Federal Circuit will continue to tack toward a property-based view of patent rights that favors injunctions, and whether the Supreme Court will speak again on the subject.

[D] Balancing Hardships and Equities

The *eBay* test did not alter a court's need to consider the equities of the parties and the public interest in determining whether to grant an injunction, and in fact has enshrined this balancing as the third prong of the *eBay* test.[36] As noted above, balancing the equities of the parties requires consideration of which party will bear a greater burden if an injunction is issued or not issued. In many cases, this analysis simply favors the smaller party, as the impact of an injunction (or lack thereof) will likely have a greater effect on its business.[37]

The analysis is not always so simple, however. In *Apple v. Samsung*, the Federal Circuit balanced the hardships and equities of two large multinational technology vendors.[38] In that case, Apple sought to enjoin Samsung's sale of smartphones including features that infringed Apple's patents. In seeking to minimize the damages that would be awarded to Apple, Samsung argued that Apple's patented smartphone

---

33. Kimberly A. Moore, Timothy R. Holbrook and John F. Murphy, *Patent Litigation and Strategy* (4th ed., West Publ. 2013), 877.
34. Chisum, *supra* n. 20, at § 20.04[2][c][iv]–[v]; Moore, Holbrook and Murphy, *supra* n. 33, at 877.
35. *Edwards LifeSciences, AG v. CoreValve, Inc.*, 699 F.3d 1305, 1314 (Fed. Cir. 2012).
36. Some commentators have argued, however, that prior to *eBay* these additional factors were simply additional factors to be considered by the court, rather than mandatory elements of a test to be satisfied before injunctive relief could be granted (Gergen, Golden & Smith, *supra* n. 12, at 207).
37. Moore, Holbrook and Murphy, *supra* n. 33, at 883.
38. *Apple v. Samsung*, 809 F.3d 633 (Fed. Cir. 2015).

features could easily be designed around. The Federal Circuit considered these statements in assessing the balance of equities between the parties, reasoning that if Samsung could easily design around Apple's patents, then it would suffer little harm from the entry of an injunction in Apple's favor.[39]

Other factors that may be considered with respect to the hardships and equities of the parties include the relative value of the patented invention to an end product, and whether infringement was intentional or inadvertent.[40]

[E] The Public Interest Factor After eBay

The fourth *eBay* factor expressly requires courts to consider the public interest in determining whether to issue an injunction. The public interest is often implicated by technologies affecting public health and safety. For example, the public interest was found to be affected by the availability of a patented sewage treatment process in *City of Milwaukee v. Activated Sludge*, 69 F.2d 577 (7th Cir. 1934), and by the public availability of cancer and hepatitis testing kits in *Hybritech Inc. v. Abbott Labs.*, 849 F.2d 1446 (Fed. Cir. 1988). The patent holder was denied an injunction in each of these cases.

In addition to health and safety, courts may also consider consumer welfare and choice in assessing the public interest affected by an injunction. Thus, when an injunction could deprive the public of desired products, the public interest may be harmed.

However, mere speculative harm to the public interest is often insufficient to outweigh other factors favoring the issuance of an injunction.[41] Thus, in *Amgen Inc. v. F. Hoffman-La Roche*, 581 F. Supp. 2d 160, 229 (D. Mass. 2008), the court granted an injunction even though doctors and patients might have benefitted from the availability of an additional erythropoiesis stimulating agent. The Court reasoned that an injunction would be warranted absent "solid evidence" that the public would "suffer significant harm if the status quo is maintained."[42]

Moreover, not all public interest factors favor the infringer. Some courts have also identified a public interest in protecting "the rights secured by valid patents."[43] As such, a public interest favoring the continuation of infringement must be weighed against the general public interest in having enforceable patents, and injunctions may

---

39. *Id.*, 645–646; As Long points out, this approach "raises the typical Catch-22 accused infringers encounter when arguing that a patented feature has little value in order to avoid a large damages award, and then that argument being used against them when trying to avoid injunctive relief" (David Long, *Federal Circuit revives injunctive relief against multi-feature products (Apple v. Samsung)*, Essential Patent Blog, Sep. 17, 2015, https://www.essentialpatentblog.com/2015/09/federal-circuit-revives-injunctive-relief-against-multi-feature-products-apple-v-samsung/ (accessed 30 Jul. 2018).
40. Chisum, *supra* n. 20, at § 20.04[2][c][iv]-[v]; Cotter, *supra* n. 28, at 106.
41. Stiefel and Carter, *supra* n. 32.
42. *Amgen Inc. v. F. Hoffman-La Roche*, 581 F. Supp. 2d 160, 210 (D. Mass. 2008).
43. *Polaroid Corp. v. Eastman Kodak Co.*, 228 USP.Q. 305, 343–344 (D. Mass. 1985) (citations omitted).

warrant issuance even if they may "discommode business and the consuming public."[44] The Federal Circuit adopted this reasoning in *Apple v. Samsung*, writing that the enforcement of patent rights "promote[s] the encouragement of investment-based risk" and "may prompt introduction of new alternatives to patented features," thus increasing consumer choice.[45] The court concluded that "the public interest nearly always weighs in favor of protecting property rights in the absence of countervailing factors, especially when the patentee practices his inventions."[46]

[F] Multicomponent Products and Causal Nexus

In his concurring opinion in *eBay*, Justice Kennedy observed that when a patent covers only a small component of a larger product, the threat of an injunction could be "employed simply for undue leverage in negotiations."[47] That is, if the owner of a patent covering any individual component of a multicomponent product has the ability to enjoin sales of the entire product, the patent holder could exert leverage far greater than warranted by the actual value of its patented technology. If this is the case, then a balancing of the equities between the plaintiff and defendant might weigh in favor of not issuing an injunction.[48] Interestingly, however, the analysis of injunctions for multicomponent products has not proceeded down the path of balancing equities and hardships, but irreparable harm.

This issue was recently addressed by the Federal Circuit in *Apple v. Samsung*.[49] As noted above, Apple sought an injunction to prevent Samsung's sales of smartphones that included Apple's patented features. Apple argued that it suffered irreparable harm in the form of lost market share and downstream sales as a result of Samsung's infringement.[50] The district court denied the injunction, holding that Apple failed to show a direct link or "causal nexus" between Samsung's infringement and Apple's alleged losses. The Federal Circuit confirmed that such a causal nexus must exist[51] but rejected the district court's requirement that Apple prove that the infringing features "drive consumer demand" for Samsung's infringing products.[52] In such cases "involving phones with hundreds of thousands of available features, it was legal error for the district court to effectively require Apple to prove that the infringement was the *sole cause* of the lost downstream sales."[53] Instead, the Federal Circuit held that the requisite causal nexus supporting an injunction may be satisfied if the patentee merely

---

44. *Ibid.*
45. *Apple v. Samsung*, 809 F.3d 633, 646 (Fed. Cir. 2015).
46. *Id.*, at 647. In making this argument, the court concedes that "Apple does not seek to enjoin the sale of lifesaving drugs," suggesting that in some cases public health and safety may still outweigh the public's interest in enforcing patent rights.
47. *See MercExchange LLC v. eBay, Inc.*, 401 F.3d 1323 (Fed. Cir. 2005), rev'd 547 US 388, 396 (2006).
48. Carroll, *supra* n. 30, at 436.
49. *Apple v. Samsung*, 809 F.3d 633 (Fed. Cir. 2015).
50. *Id.*, at 639; Apple also claimed irreparable damage to its reputation as an innovator (*Ibid.*).
51. *Id.*, at 640.
52. *Id.*, at 641.
53. *Ibid.* (emphasis added).

shows "some connection" between the patented features and demand for the infringing products.[54]

[G]   Empirical Studies of Injunctive Relief

Despite the tightened requirements for injunctive relief imposed by *eBay*, permanent injunctions issue in large numbers in patent cases in the US. Lex Machina reports that in patent cases that reached the remedy stage from 2012 to 2015, a total of 782 cases resulted in the entry of a permanent injunction (2016, 25).[55] *eBay* has, however, had a significant impact on the availability of injunctive relief to non-practicing entities. Cotter found that through 2011, courts granted permanent injunctions in approximately 75% of patent cases, but that non-practicing entities had a substantially lower success rate, presumably due to the elimination of the presumption of irreparable harm by *eBay*.[56] Seaman found that after *eBay*, permanent injunctions were issued in 72.5% of 218 patent cases in which infringement was found, but in cases in which the patentee was a non-practicing entity, injunctions were issued only 16% of the time.[57] These findings appear to resonate with Justice Kennedy's admonition against the use of injunctions by non-practicing entities.

Gupta and Kesan studied all patent cases filed in U.S. district courts between 2000 and 2012 in which an injunction (permanent or preliminary) was sought (approximately 2,550 cases). They found that the number of cases in which the plaintiff sought an injunction fell substantially after *eBay*, despite an overall increase in the number of patent suits. They also found that while the rate at which injunctions were granted as a percentage of injunctions sought did not change materially after *eBay*, the rate of injunctions granted as a percentage of total patent suits filed did decline significantly after *eBay*. Specifically, they found that in the six years prior to *eBay*, 459 motions for permanent injunctions resulted in the issuance of 381 permanent injunctions (an 83% success rate), while in the 6 years following *eBay*, 384 motions for permanent

---

54. *Ibid.*, at 642. The court went on the elaborate on the contours of "some connection," noting that it "may be shown in a variety of ways, including, for example, evidence that a patented feature is one of several features that cause consumers to make their purchasing decisions, evidence that the inclusion of a patented feature makes a product significantly more desirable, and evidence that the absence of a patented feature would make a product significantly less desirable [A] fourth example [] demonstrate[s] a connection that does not establish a causal nexus—where consumers are only willing to pay a nominal amount for an infringing feature (using example of USD 10 cup holder in USD 20,000 car). There is a lot of ground between the examples that satisfy the causal nexus requirement and the example that does not satisfy this requirement. The required minimum showing lies somewhere in the middle, as reflected by the 'some connection' language" (*Id.*, at 642, n. 1 (internal citations omitted)).
55. Lex Machina, *Patent Litigation Year in Review 2015* (2016), 25. Lex Machina reports that approximately 23,000 patent cases reached termination in the US between 2009 and 2015, approximately 73% of which settled (*Id.*, 26).
56. Cotter, *supra* n. 28, at 103.
57. Christopher B. Seaman, *Permanent Injunctions in Patent Litigation After eBay: An Empirical Study*, 101 Iowa L. Rev. 1949, 1983 and 1988 (2016).

injunctions resulted in the issuance of 308 permanent injunctions (an 80% success rate).[58]

Holte and Seaman studied Federal Circuit review of district court permanent injunction decisions in patent cases.[59] They found (based on 218 district court decisions on injunctive relief between 2006 and 2013) that the Federal Circuit affirmed district court grants of permanent injunctions 88% of the time but affirmed district court denials of permanent injunctions only 53% of the time.[60] This observation supports the hypothesis that the Federal Circuit favors the granting of permanent injunctions in patent cases, in line with its pre-*eBay* property-centric view of patent law.

These and other studies generally support the conclusion that while permanent injunctions continue to be issued in patent cases, *eBay* and the elimination of the presumption of irreparable harm have made it significantly more difficult for non-practicing entities to obtain a permanent injunction.

The impact of the *eBay* case has been felt not only in patent cases but in copyright and other intellectual property cases in which injunctive relief is sought (*see*, e.g., *Salinger v. Colting*, 607 F.3d 68 (2nd Cir. 2010)). More surprisingly, the effect of *eBay* has extended well beyond intellectual property cases. As described by Gergen, Golden and Smith:

> federal courts now commonly accept the *eBay* test as the test for injunctions in virtually all types of cases, from constitutional challenges ... to actions under various federal regulatory or antidiscrimination statutes, to diversity actions centered on state tort, contract, or statutory law.[61]

[H] Scope of Injunctions

In recent years, courts and commentators have considered injunctions that are less than "all or nothing" prohibitions on selling infringing products.[62] In a number of cases, injunctive relief has been shaped so that the effectiveness, duration, scope or effect of prohibitions has been less than absolute, both to mitigate the hardship to the defendant and to serve the public interest.

---

58. Kirti Gupta and Jay P. Kesan, *Studying the Impact of eBay on Injunctive Relief in Patent Cases* (working paper, Jul. 10, 2015), https://papers.ssrn.com/sol3/papers.cfm?abstract_id = 2629399 (accessed 30 Jul. 2018). Compare to Gupta and Kesan's analysis of preliminary injunctions over the same periods in Part C.5, which result in a significantly lower success rates.
59. Ryan T. Holte and Christopher B. Seaman, *Patent Injunctions on Appeal: An Empirical Study of the Federal Circuit's Application of eBay* (working paper, Jul. 29, 2016), https://papers.ssrn.com/sol3/papers.cfm?abstract_id = 2816097 (accessed 30 Jul. 2018).
60. *Id.*, 188, Fig. 6.
61. Gergen, Golden & Smith, *supra* n. 12, at 215 (citations omitted).
62. John M. Golden, *Injunctions as More (or Less) than "Off Switches": Patent-Infringement Injunctions' Scope*, 90 Tex. L. Rev. 1399, 1401 (2012): "injunctions can take any of a number of different shapes having differing degrees of effectiveness"; *Cf.* Colleen V. Chien and Mark A. Lemley, *Patent Holdup, the ITC, and the Public Interest*, 98 Cornell L. Rev. 1 (discussing flexibility in ITC exclusion orders (addressed in §1.05, below)).

Chapter 1: Injunctive Relief in US Patent Cases §1.02[I]

One common means of mitigating the adverse impact of a permanent injunction is to obtain a stay of effectiveness. Courts will grant stays in order to give the infringer time to work around a patent, to clear inventory or to ensure that the public continues to have access to a needed product such as a drug or vaccine.[63] For example, in *Broadcom, Inc. v. Qualcomm Corp.*, the Federal Circuit approved an injunction that allowed the infringer to continue to sell infringing products for a "sunset period" of up to 20 months in order to alleviate hardship on the infringer.[64]

In addition to stays of effectiveness, the scope of an injunction can be limited to cover not an entire infringing product but only the infringing feature or component. For example, in *Apple v. Samsung*, Apple sought an injunction that applied only to the patented features included in Samsung's smartphones, rather than the smartphones themselves.[65] To continue selling smartphones, Samsung needed only to remove the relatively minor features patented by Apple.[66] Courts' flexible approach to injunctive relief in patent cases is both consistent with the traditional exercise of equity jurisdiction and likely to achieve the best balance among the competing interests of patent holders, users of patented technology and the public.

[I] Compulsory Licensing and Ongoing Royalties After the Denial of Injunctive Relief

If a patent is found to be infringed and a court does *not* grant a permanent injunction to prevent ongoing infringement, then the infringer has essentially been granted a license to continue operate under the infringed patent. Because this license is granted against the will of the patent holder through action of the court, it can be construed as a *compulsory* license under the patent.

Several issues present themselves in this context. First, scholars including Paul M. Janicke have questioned whether such compulsory licenses are legitimately available as remedies under US patent law, which only permits damages to be awarded in the form of a lump sum for past infringement and not as an ongoing royalty obligation.[67] Mark Lemley and others dispute this conclusion both on technical and practical grounds.[68]

---

63. Holte and Seaman, *supra* n. 59, 181; Holte and Seaman found (based on 218 district court decisions on injunctive relief between 2006 and 2013) that district courts granted stays of permanent injunctions approximately 23% of the time, and 75% of the time when the patentees were non-practicing entities (*Id.*, 182–183).
64. *Broadcom, Inc. v. Qualcomm Corp.*, 543 F.3d 683, 701, 704 (Fed. Cir. 2008); *See* Golden, *supra* n. 62, at 1461.
65. *Apple v. Samsung*, 809 F.3d 633 (Fed. Cir. 2015).
66. *Apple v. Samsung*, 809 F.3d 633, 638 (Fed. Cir. 2015); Apple's request for relief also allowed Samsung a thirty-day sunset period to phase out infringing products (*Id.*, 638).
67. Paul M. Janicke, *Implementing the "Adequate Remedy at Law" for Ongoing Patent Infringement after eBay v. MercExchange*, 51 IDEA 163 (2011). Janicke argues that following the denial of a permanent injunction, patent holders are *not* entitled to an ongoing royalty for continued infringement, but must periodically bring damages suits to recover for past infringement.
68. Mark A. Lemley, *The Ongoing Confusion over Ongoing Royalties*, 76 Mo. L. Rev. 695 (2011).

Another question is whether the issuance of such compulsory licenses through governmental (judicial) intervention is compliant with US treaty obligations under the World Trade Organization (WTO) Agreement on Trade-Related Aspects of Intellectual Property Rights (TRIPS).[69] Article 31(b) of the TRIPS Agreement authorizes a state to issue a "compulsory" license under one or more patents without the authorization of the patent holder "in the case of national emergency or other circumstances of extreme urgency or in cases of public non-commercial use." While the 2001 Doha Ministerial Declaration on TRIPS and Public Health ("Doha Declaration")[70] clarified the contours of this compulsory licensing regime for pharmaceutical products, there is little WTO guidance regarding the granting of compulsory patent licenses outside this narrow field. It is thus not clear whether routine, non-pharmaceutical cases in which an infringer is permitted to continue to operate under an infringed patent, whether or not a royalty is imposed, would run afoul of US TRIPS obligations.[71]

Another issue arising from permitting ongoing infringement of a patent is what royalty the infringer should pay the patentee. It is generally acknowledged that *some* royalty should be due with respect to the infringer's continuing use, but the means by which that royalty should be calculated are unclear. Cases have suggested a range of possibilities including: the same royalty rate used to calculate damages for past infringement, a multiple of the rate assessed for past infringement (to reflect the infringer's ongoing "willful" infringement of the patent),[72] a negotiated settlement rate, and other measures.[73] Given the significant disarray in the law of "reasonable royalty" patent damages for past infringement,[74] the question of ongoing royalties for continuing infringement after an injunction has been denied will likely continue to vex courts for some time.

---

69. WTO Agreement on Trade-Related Aspects of Intellectual Property Rights (TRIPS), Annex 1C of the Marrakesh Agreement Establishing the World Trade Organization, signed in Marrakesh, Morocco on Apr. 15, 1994.
70. World Trade Organization, Ministerial Declaration of 20 November 2001, WT/MIN(01)IDEC/2 (2001).
71. Christopher A. Cotropia, *Compulsory Licensing under TRIPS and the Supreme Court of the United States' Decision in eBay v. MercExchange* in Toshiko Takenaka and Rainer Moufang (eds), *Comparative Patent Law: A Handbook of Contemporary Research* (Edward Elgar 2008). This argument was advanced in the eBay litigation by the U.S. government, among others, but was not addressed by the Supreme Court (*Ibid.*).
72. A court may award a patentee up to treble damages in its discretion, usually applied in cases of willful infringement. 35 USC § 284; *Halo Electronics, Inc. v. Pulse Electronics, Inc.*, 579 U.S. (2016).
73. William F. Lee and A. Douglas Melamed, *Breaking the Vicious Cycle of Patent Damages*, 101 Cornell L. Rev. 385, 399–401 and 433–434 (2014); Cotter, *supra* n. 28, at 106 and 127–128; Lemley, *supra* n. 68, at 700–707; John M. Golden, *Principles for Patent Remedies*, 88 Tex. L. Rev. 505, 576 (2010).
74. An extensive critical literature regarding reasonable royalty damages exists. *See*, generally, Lee and Melamed, *supra* n. 73; Cotter *supra* n. 28, at 119–139 and Golden, *supra* n. 71, 582–586.

§1.03 PRELIMINARY INJUNCTIONS IN PATENT CASES

[A] Preliminary Injunction Overview

Awards of injunctive relief may be either preliminary or permanent. Preliminary relief (also referred to as interlocutory relief) is typically granted early in a proceeding to prevent the continuation of harm during the pendency of trial.[75] It is not viewed as an ultimate remedy, but a means for preserving the *status quo* during the proceedings, while the factual record is being developed. Federal Rule of Civil Procedure sixty-five authorizes courts to grant preliminary relief but does not specify the grounds on which such relief may be granted, leaving that determination to the discretion of the court. Courts have developed standards for assessing the appropriateness of preliminary relief that are consistent with the standards that have evolved for permanent injunctive relief. Thus, as with permanent injunctions, a plaintiff seeking preliminary injunctive relief must prove irreparable harm, and the court must balance the equities and hardships of the parties, as well as the public interest.[76] However, preliminary relief also requires a demonstration that the plaintiff is reasonably likely to prevail on the merits of its claim.[77] This is the principal difference between the standards for preliminary and permanent injunctive relief in the US.

[B] Likelihood of Success on the Merits

In order to obtain preliminary injunctive relief, a patentee must show that it is reasonably likely to prevail on the merits of its claim. In patent cases, this showing must include both a demonstration that the patentee will prevail on its claim of infringement, and also that the asserted patent(s) will survive any likely validity challenge.[78] If the defendant raises a substantial question regarding either infringement or validity (i.e., asserts an infringement or invalidity defense that the patentee cannot prove lacks substantial merit), the preliminary injunction should not issue.[79]

With respect to invalidity, a defendant opposing a preliminary injunction motion need not meet the "clear and convincing" evidentiary standard for proving invalidity at trial. Rather it must only show that there is a "substantial question" regarding invalidity, a lesser standard of proof.[80] Traditionally, factors tending to support the probable validity of patents in preliminary injunction cases include prior adjudications of validity and acquiescence of the industry to the patentee's rights.[81]

---

75. Chisum, *supra* n. 20, at § 20.04[1].
76. Though these factors are consistent as between permanent and preliminary relief, as Dobbs explains, in the context of preliminary relief "the rules have an entirely different purpose, an entirely different effect, and an entirely different meaning" (Dobbs, *supra* n. 6, at 127).
77. Chisum, *supra* n. 20, at § 20.04[1].
78. *Genentech, Inc. v. Novo Nordisk, A/S*, 108 F.3d 1361, 1364 (Fed. Cir. 1997).
79. *Amazon.com, Inc. v. BarnesAndNoble.com, Inc.*, 239 F.3d 1343 (Fed. Cir. 2001).
80. *Ibid.*
81. Chisum, *supra* n. 20, at § 20.04[1][c][ii]–[iii].

With respect to infringement, the patentee seeking preliminary relief must establish a likelihood of infringement through (1) interpreting the asserted claims, (2) defining the allegedly infringing acts, and (3) applying the claims to those acts.[82] The standard for making these determinations varies among courts, and has been stated as requiring that the patentee show that infringement is likely "beyond question," that it is "clear" or that it is "reasonably clear."[83]

In addition, courts have recently begun to deny preliminary injunctive relief when substantial questions have been raised regarding whether a patent claims patentable subject matter under section 101 of the Patent Act.[84] While these considerations have, in theory, always been part of the analysis under the first prong of the test for preliminary injunctive relief, patentable subject matter has become an increasingly important avenue for challenging patents after cases such as *Mayo Collaborative Services v. Prometheus Laboratories, Inc.*[85] and *Ass'n for Molecular Pathology v. Myriad Genetics, Inc.*[86] in the biotechnology area and *Alice Corp. v. CLS Bank International*[87] in the area of software patents.[88]

[C] eBay and Preliminary Relief

Unlike the traditional equitable test for permanent injunctive relief, which required courts to consider and balance irreparable harm, the hardships and equities of the parties, and the public interest, the traditional test for *preliminary* injunctive relief was a conjunctive four-factor test requiring the existence of every element in order for relief to be granted.[89] That is, if the defendant prevailed on *any* of the four factors in the test for preliminary injunctive relief, relief would not be granted.[90]

The Supreme Court has never ruled explicitly on the standards for the issuance of preliminary injunctions in patent cases.[91] As discussed above, in *eBay*, the Supreme Court, when considering the standard for *permanent* injunctions, developed a four-factor conjunctive test that resembles the traditional test for preliminary relief.[92] Thus, save for the "success on the merits" factor, the tests for permanent and preliminary

---

82. *Id.*, § 20.04[1][d].
83. *Ibid.*
84. Jacob S. Sherkow, *Preliminary Injunctions Post-Mayo and Myriad*, 67 Stanford L. Rev. Online 1, 4 (2014).
85. *Mayo Collaborative Services v. Prometheus Laboratories, Inc.*, 132 S. Ct. 1289 (2012).
86. *Ass'n for Molecular Pathology v. Myriad Genetics, Inc.*, 133 S. Ct. 2107 (2013).
87. *Alice Corp. v. CLS Bank International*, 134 S. Ct. 2347 (2014).
88. Sherkow, *supra* n. 84, 3–4. Sherkow also suggests that questions of patentable subject matter have begun to affect trial courts' analysis under the other three preliminary injunction factors, as well. For example, one court recently reasoned, with respect to the public interest prong of the test, that patents potentially reading on non-patentable subject matter "hindered rather than promoted innovation," "distort[ed] rather than serve[d] the patent system[]," and utilized "a commercial path that turns much of our patent system policy on its head" (*Ibid.*, 7, quoting In re BRCA1- and BRCA2-Based Hereditary Cancer Test Patent Litigation, 2014 WL 931057, at *57).
89. *See* Moore, Holbrook and Murphy, *supra* n. 33, at 883; Gergen, Golden & Smith, *supra* n. 12, at 208–209.
90. Moore, Holbrook and Murphy, *supra* n. 33, at 883.
91. Chisum, *supra* n. 20, at § 20.04[1][a][2].
92. Gergen, Golden & Smith, *supra* n. 12, at 208–209.

injunctive relief today are barely distinguishable. Accordingly, the discussion above of irreparable harm, balancing the hardships and equities and the public interest applies equally to the preliminary injunction analysis. Likewise, the Court's abolition in *eBay* of the presumption of irreparable harm in patent cases appears to be applicable to preliminary, as well as permanent, injunctions.[93]

[D] Posting Bond

Unlike permanent injunctions, which are granted as remedies after a finding of liability, preliminary injunctions do not presuppose the defendant's liability. Thus, notwithstanding the issuance of a preliminary injunction, the plaintiff may fail to prevail on the merits of its case. In such cases, the defendant may be found to have been wrongfully enjoined or restrained and entitled to damages for the period during which its activity was interrupted. To better enable a defendant to recover for such wrongful enjoinment, Rule 65(c) of the Federal Rules of Civil Procedure requires a plaintiff seeking preliminary relief to post bond with the court in an amount deemed adequate to compensate the defendant.[94] The amount of such bond is determined by the court in its discretion, though no uniform standards exist regarding the determination of such amount.[95] The amount of the bond is critical to the defendant, however, as it is generally not entitled to damages for wrongful enjoinment in excess of the bond amount.[96] Likewise, the conditions establishing "wrongful enjoinment" that must be satisfied in order for a defendant to collect on such a bond have historically been somewhat unclear.[97]

[E] Empirical Data: Preliminary Injunctions

Unlike permanent injunctions, preliminary injunctions are comparatively rare in US patent cases. As reported by Lex Machina, for patent cases reaching resolution between 2012 and 2015, only 61 resulted in the award of a preliminary injunction.[98] Gupta and Kesan report that in the six years prior to *eBay*, 1026 motions for preliminary injunctions resulted in the issuance of 236 preliminary injunctions (a 23% success

---

93. Cotter, *supra* n. 28, at 104–105. This being said, courts have considered numerous factors in assessing the irreparability of harm when preliminary injunctive relief is sought, including "price erosion, loss of goodwill, damage to reputation, and loss of business opportunities." *Celsis in Vitro, Inc. v. CellzDirect, Inc.*, 664 F.3d 922, 930 (Fed. Cir. 2012).
94. Chisum, *supra* n. 20, at § 20.04[1][g]; "no restraining order or preliminary injunction shall issue except upon the giving of security by the applicant, in such sum as the court deems proper, for the payment of such costs and damages as may be incurred or suffered by any party who is found to have been wrongfully enjoined or restrained." FRCP 65(c).
95. Harvard Law Review, *Note: Recovery for Wrongful Interlocutory Injunctions under Rule 65(c)*, 99 Harv. L. Rev. 828, 830 (1986).
96. *W.R. Grace & Co. v. Rubber Workers*, 461 US 757, 770 n. 14 (1983).
97. Harvard Law Review, *supra* n. 95, at 838–842.
98. Lex Machina, *supra* n. 55, at 25.

rate), while in the six years following *eBay*, 655 motions for preliminary injunctions resulted in the issuance of 125 preliminary injunctions (a 19% success rate).[99]

There are several reasons that preliminary injunctions may be less common than permanent injunctions in US cases. First, the bonding requirement (*see* §1.03 [D] above) may act as a disincentive for patentees to seek preliminary relief. Second, courts are wary of granting preliminary relief, as it is likely to impose a significant burden on the defendant before the plaintiff has fully proved its case.[100] Finally, the defendant's burden in contesting the validity of asserted patents is lower than it is in a merits trial, making a preliminary injunction motion easier to defeat than the plaintiff's claims at trial. For all of these reasons, preliminary injunctions today do not appear to play a significant role in US patent litigation.

§1.04 INJUNCTIVE RELIEF AND FRAND COMMITMENTS

The formal policies of many standards-development organizations (SDOs) require that participants license any patents that are essential to the SDO's standards (standards essential patents or SEPs) to manufacturers of standardized products on terms that are royalty-free or subject to royalties that are "fair, reasonable and non-discriminatory" (FRAND).[101] Some litigants in the US have argued that a SEP holder, by making a FRAND commitment, concedes that remedies available at law (i.e., monetary damages) *must* be adequate to compensate it for the infringement of its SEPs by parties implementing a standard.[102] They reason that, by committing to grant a license on FRAND terms, the SEP holder should be deemed to acknowledge that it will not seek to exclude others from the market, but will instead collect only a "reasonable" royalty to compensate it for the use of its SEPs.[103] As a result, they argue that the second *eBay* factor can *never* be satisfied by a patent holder that has made a FRAND commitment, and therefore such a patent holder should generally be precluded from seeking injunctive relief to prevent others from operating under its SEPs.[104] The interplay of

---

99. Gupta and Kesan, *supra* n. 58. Compare to Gupta and Kesan's analysis of permanent injunctions over the same periods in Part B.7, above, which result in a significantly higher success rate.
100. Golden, *supra* n. 62, at 1439; Laycock, *supra* n. 1, at 116.
101. Such licensing commitments may also arise in contexts outside formal SDOs, and may be unilateral or coordinated pledges by individual patent holders (Jorge L. Contreras, *Patent Pledges*, 47 Ariz. St. L.J. 533 (2015)).
102. Discussed in Jorge L. Contreras and Richard J. Gilbert, *A Unified Framework for RAND and other Reasonable Royalties*, 30(2) Berkeley Tech. L.J. 1447, 1461–1462 (2015); Cotter, *supra* n. 9, at 6.
103. In addition to being the standard for royalties specified in FRAND commitments, a "reasonable" royalty is also the minimum level of damages that may be awarded in a patent infringement action under 35 USC § 284 ('Upon finding for the claimant the court shall award the claimant damages adequate to compensate for the infringement, but in no event less than a reasonable royalty'). *See also Georgia-Pacific Corp. v. US Plywood Corp.*, 318 F. Supp. 1116, 1120 (S.D.N.Y. 1970), *modified and aff'd*, 446 F.2d 295 (2d Cir. 1971), *cert. denied*, 404 US 870 (1971). In addition to reasonable royalties, US courts may award lost profits and enhanced damages if the circumstances so dictate.
104. *See* Cotter, *supra* n. 9, at 6) (arguing for a general presumption that patent owners who have made FRAND commitments should not be entitled to injunctive relief).

FRAND commitments with the US law of patent injunctions has given rise to several judicial decisions as well as guidance from regulatory and enforcement agencies in the US.[105]

In *Microsoft Corp. v. Motorola, Inc.*,[106] Motorola sought an injunction to prevent Microsoft's continued infringement of Motorola's patents covering two standards (IEEE's 802.11 and ITU's H.264). The court found that Motorola made FRAND commitments with respect to these patents, and that Microsoft agreed to accept a license on reasonable terms. The court evaluated these facts in view of the four *eBay* factors and determined that Motorola did not suffer an irreparable injury or show that monetary damages would be inadequate to compensate it for the infringement. Accordingly, the court denied Motorola's request for an injunction.

In *Realtek Semiconductor Corp. v. LSI Corp.*,[107] the U.S. District Court for the Northern District of California held that a SEP holder breached its FRAND commitment by seeking injunctive relief against an implementer of a standard *before* the patent holder offered a license to the implementer. Again, the injunction was denied.

These district court decisions laid the groundwork for the Federal Circuit to consider the issue of permanent injunctive relief in FRAND-related cases. In *Apple, Inc. v. Motorola, Inc.*, the Federal Circuit analyzed Motorola's request for an injunction seeking to prevent Apple's sale of products allegedly infringing Motorola's FRAND-encumbered SEPs. Judge Posner, the trial judge,[108] denied Motorola's request, reasoning that a patent holder making a FRAND commitment, by definition, has acknowledged that a monetary royalty would be adequate compensation for a license under the patent, thereby eliminating any argument that the infringement would cause the patent holder irreparable harm under *eBay*.[109]

Judge Reyna, writing for the Federal Circuit, upheld Judge Posner's denial of the injunction, but offered different reasoning. Though the Federal Circuit panel was divided on some issues, all three members of the panel concurred that "[t]o the extent that the district court applied a per se rule that injunctions are unavailable for SEPs, it erred."[110] The court reasoned that the *eBay* framework "provides ample strength and flexibility for analysing []RAND committed patents and industry standards in general," and found no reason to create "a separate rule or analytical framework for addressing injunctions for []RAND-committed patents."[111] The court acknowledged that under the *eBay* framework, "a patentee subject to FRAND commitments may have difficulty establishing irreparable harm."[112] However, "an injunction may be justified where an infringer unilaterally refuses a []RAND royalty or unreasonably delays negotiations to

---

105. *See generally* Contreras and Gilbert, *supra* n. 102, pt. I.
106. *Microsoft Corp. v. Motorola, Inc.*, 2012 US Dist. LEXIS 170587 (W.D. Wash. 2012).
107. *Realtek Semiconductor Corp. v. LSI Corp.*, 946 F. Supp.2d 998 (N.D. Cal. 2013).
108. Judge Richard Posner is a well-known member of the United States Court of Appeals for the Seventh Circuit. He sat as the trial judge in this case by designation.
109. *Apple, Inc. v. Motorola, Inc.*, 869 F. Supp. 2d 901, 913–14 (N.D. Ill. 2012), *aff'd in part*, 757 F.3d 1286 (Fed. Cir. 2014).
110. *Id.*, 1331.
111. *Id.*, 1331–1332.
112. *Id.*, 1332.

the same effect."[113] With this in mind, the court goes on to apply the *eBay* "irreparable harm" test and affirms the district court's rejection of Motorola's request for an injunction.

It is here that the members of the panel diverged. Chief Judge Rader, dissenting-in-part, argued that a genuine issue of material fact existed regarding Apple's conduct with respect to the acceptance of a FRAND license from Motorola; he would have remanded the case for further fact finding on this issue.[114] Judge Prost, on the other hand, concurring-in-part and dissenting-in-part, disagreed with the majority's suggestion that an alleged infringer's refusal to negotiate a license could serve as a basis for issuing an injunction on a FRAND-encumbered patent.[115] She reasoned that while a potential licensee's bad faith negotiation might justify an award of enhanced damages, the *eBay* "irreparable harm" test would nevertheless militate against granting an injunction on a FRAND-encumbered patent.[116] However, Judge Prost conceded that an injunction might be appropriate if the patentee is wholly unable to collect the damages to which it is entitled, for example, if the potential licensee refuses to pay an adjudicated damage award or is beyond the reach of the court.[117]

§1.05 EXCLUSION ORDERS AT THE INTERNATIONAL TRADE COMMISSION

[A] The ITC and Patent Exclusion Orders

The US International Trade Commission (ITC) is an independent federal agency responsible for protecting US commerce by barring the importation of infringing goods. In recent years, the ITC has become a popular venue for patent infringement suits. The ITC has no authority to award monetary damages. The principal remedy that the ITC awards is an exclusion order, which prohibits goods that are found to infringe a US

---

113. *Id.* (citing US Dept. Justice (DOJ) and Patent and Trademark Office (PTO), *Policy Statement on Remedies for Standards Essential Patents Subject to Voluntary F/RAND Commitments* (Jan. 8, 2013), https://www.justice.gov/sites/default/files/atr/legacy/2014/09/18/290994.pdf [accessed 30 Jul. 2018]). This phenomenon is known as "hold-out" or "reverse hold-up." It is said to occur when an infringer refuses to accept reasonable license terms offered by a SEP holder, thus making it impossible for the SEP holder to comply with its FRAND commitment and grant the required license. In hold-out situations, many commentators and courts agree that it is reasonable for the SEP holder to seek an injunction against the hold-out infringer, notwithstanding any FRAND commitment that the SEP holder has made. *See* Federal Trade Comm'n (FTC), *Third Party United States Federal Trade Commission's Statement on the Public Interest in the Matter of Certain Gaming and Entertainment Consoles, Related Software, and Components Thereof*, ITC Investigation No. 337-TA-752 (Jun. 6, 2012) (*Microsoft v. Motorola*), https://www.ftc.gov/sites/default/files/documents/advocacy_documents/ftc-comment-united-states-international-trade-commission-concerning-certain-gaming-and-entertaining/1206ftcgamingconsole.pdf (accessed 30 Jul. 2018); Chien and Lemley, *supra* n. 62.
114. *Apple, Inc. v. Motorola, Inc.*, 869 F. Supp. 2d 901, 913–14 (N.D. Ill. 2012), *aff'd in part*, 757 F.3d 1286, 1333–1334 (Fed. Cir. 2014).
115. *Id.*, 1342.
116. *Ibid.*
117. *Id.*, 1343.

intellectual property right from entering the country.[118] In this sense, exclusion orders granted by the ITC are similar to injunctions issued by US courts.

The ITC is not a court and is not bound by Supreme Court precedent. Thus, the ITC is not required to adhere to the *eBay* factors when considering a request for an exclusion order. However, in considering whether to grant an exclusion order, the ITC is required by statute to consider "the effect of such exclusion upon the public health and welfare, competitive conditions in the United States economy, the production of like or directly competitive articles in the United States, and United States consumers."[119] This requirement has generally been referred to as the ITC's "public interest" test.

[B] The ITC's Public Interest Test and FRAND

In several recent cases, the ITC has considered requests for exclusion orders against products infringing one or more FRAND-committed SEPs. In each such case, the ITC considered the potential effect of the exclusion order on the public interest as required by 19 USC § 1337(d)(1).

In the dispute between Apple and Samsung,[120] in 2013 the ITC issued an exclusion order prohibiting Apple from importing devices infringing certain Samsung FRAND-committed SEPs into the US Later that year, the US Trade Representative (USTR), acting in its statutory capacity under 19 USC § 1337(j), disapproved (thereby reversing) the ITC's exclusion order against Apple, reasoning that the ITC did not act on the basis of a sufficient factual record regarding, *inter alia*, "information on the standards essential nature of the patent at issue ... and the presence or absence of patent hold-up or reverse hold-up."[121]

The USTR's disapproval of the ITC's exclusion order against Apple took many by surprise. In subsequent cases, the ITC has more extensively considered factors relating to SEPs when conducting its public interest analysis. Such cases include *In re Certain Wireless Devices with 3G and/or 4G Capabilities and Components Thereof*, ITC Investigation No. 337-TA-868 (Jun. 13, 2014) (relating to InterDigital).

[C] Position of Other US Governmental Agencies

Several other US federal agencies have expressed views regarding the ITC's issuance of exclusion orders for FRAND-encumbered SEPs. In 2013, the US Department of Justice (DOJ) and US Patent and Trademark Office (PTO) issued a joint Policy Statement relating to the consideration of the public interest with respect to ITC exclusion

---

118. 19 USC § 337(a)(1)(A).
119. 19 USC § 1337(d)(1).
120. *In re Certain Electronic Devices, Including Wireless Communication Devices, Portable Music and Data Processing Devices, and Tablet Computers*, ITC Investigation No. 337-TA-794.
121. Letter from Ambassador Michael B.G. Froman, US Trade Representative to Hon. Irving A. Williamson, Aug. 3, 2013.

orders.[122] This Policy Statement, which has been cited by numerous courts and other federal agencies, states that "the remedy of an injunction or exclusion order may be inconsistent with the public interest ... where an exclusion order based on a F/RAND-encumbered patent appears to be incompatible with the terms of a patent holder's existing F/RAND licensing commitment."[123]

In their Policy Statement, the DOJ and PTO acknowledge circumstances in which an injunction or exclusion order *may* be an appropriate remedy. These include cases in which the infringer refuses to accept the FRAND licensing being offered, refuses to pay the required reasonable royalty, refuses to engage in negotiation to determine FRAND terms, or is not subject to the jurisdiction of a court that could award damages.[124]

The US Federal Trade Commission (FTC) has made similar suggestions regarding appropriate circumstances under which the public interest would be served by the issuance of an ITC exclusion order against a product infringing a FRAND-committed SEP. In a written Statement to the ITC,[125] the FTC urged the ITC to adopt the view that the ITC's public interest factors "support denial of an exclusion order unless the holder of the RAND-encumbered SEP has made a reasonable royalty offer."[126] The FTC has also suggested that the ITC consider ways to lessen the impact of exclusion orders in a manner that is supportive of the public interest. Such methods might include delaying the effectiveness of exclusion orders in order to give the infringer time to design around the asserted patent, and carefully circumscribing the scope of orders to cover only infringing articles.[127]

§1.06 ANTITRUST ENFORCEMENT, FRAND AND INJUNCTIVE RELIEF

The DOJ and FTC have each taken an interest in the propriety of parties bound by FRAND commitments seeking injunctive relief. In 2011, the FTC suggested that under *eBay*, injunctive relief might not always be justified in the FRAND context, writing that "[a] prior [F]RAND commitment can provide strong evidence that denial of the injunction and ongoing royalties will not irreparably harm the patentee."[128] And in 2012, the DOJ approved three large patent acquisition transactions only after the involved parties (Apple, Google, and Microsoft) committed not to seek injunctions preventing the use of FRAND-encumbered SEPs.[129]

---

122. DOJ and PTO, *supra* n. 113.
123. *Id.*, at 6.
124. *Id.*, at 7.
125. FTC, *supra* n. 113.
126. *Id.*, at 4.
127. *See also* Chien and Lemley, *supra* n. 62, supporting similar tailoring of exclusion orders. *But see* Cotter, *supra* n. 9 (arguing for a general presumption that patent owners who have made FRAND commitments should not be entitled to ITC exclusion orders).
128. Federal Trade Commission (FTC), *The Evolving IP Marketplace: Aligning Patent Notice and Remedies with Competition* (2011), https://www.ftc.gov/sites/default/files/documents/reports/evolving-ip-marketplace-aligning-patent-notice-and-remedies-competition-report-federal-trade/110307patentreport.pdf (accessed 30 Jul. 2018), 235.
129. Jorge L. Contreras, *The February of FRAND*, Patently-O Blog (Mar. 6, 2012), http://patentlyo.com/patent/2012/03/february-of-frand.html (accessed 30 Jul. 2018).

In late 2012 and 2013, the FTC brought two actions under section 5 of the FTC Act (15 USC § 45(a)(1)) to address suspected violations of FRAND commitments.[130] In the first such action, the FTC investigated Robert Bosch GmbH in connection with its proposed acquisition of a firm called SPX.[131] According to the complaint, SPX participated in an SDO developing standards for automotive cooling systems.[132] Despite having made a FRAND commitment to the SDO, SPX asserted two patents covering the SDO's standards against suspected infringers and then sought injunctive relief to prevent future sales of infringing products.[133] The FTC argued that SPX's attempt to obtain injunctive relief in the face of its FRAND commitment was inherently coercive and oppressive, and thereby constituted an unfair method of competition in violation of section 5. Bosch settled the action by committing that SPX would no longer seek injunctive relief in this context.

The FTC again took action to address a patent holder's attempt to obtain injunctive relief in the face of a prior FRAND commitment in Motorola Mobility LLC and Google, Inc.[134] In that case, Motorola (later acquired by Google) held patents essential to practice standards promulgated by IEEE, ITU, and ETSI. Motorola participated in, and made FRAND commitments to, each of these SDOs. Nevertheless, in separate suits asserting these patents against Apple and Microsoft, Motorola sought exclusion orders at the ITC and injunctions in federal court to prevent future sales of standards-compliant products, even though both defendants were allegedly willing to acquire licenses to Motorola's patents. The FTC asserted that Motorola's attempt to enjoin sales of Apple and Microsoft products using its standards essential patents constituted an unfair method of competition in violation of section 5.[135] The dispute was settled after Google agreed not to seek injunctive relief against an infringer of certain FRAND-committed patents unless the infringer was beyond the jurisdiction of the US courts, stated in writing that it would not accept a license of the patent, refused to enter into a license agreement determined to meet the FRAND requirement by a court or arbitrator, or failed to provide written confirmation of an offer of a FRAND license.[136]

Interestingly, the transition from the Obama of Administration to the Trump Administration in the U.S. has led to changes in the U.S. DOJ's outlook regarding the availability of injunctions in the face of FRAND commitments. In a November 2017 speech, the Assistant Attorney General overseeing the Antitrust Division of the DOJ sharply criticized both the Federal Circuit and District Court decisions in *Apple v. Motorola*.[137]

---

130. Under Section 5 of the FTC Act, the FTC may prosecute "unfair methods of competition" and "unfair or deceptive acts or practices."
131. *Robert Bosch GmbH*, 155 F.T.C. 713 (2013).
132. *Id.*, at 715–719.
133. *Id.*, at 718–719.
134. *In re Motorola Mobility LLC & Google Inc.*, FTC Docket No. C-4410 (Jul. 23, 2013) (decision and order).
135. *Id.*, at 2–3.
136. *Id.*, at 8.
137. Makan Delrahim, Assistant Attorney Gen. Antitrust Div., U.S. Dep't Justice, Take it to the Limit: Respecting Innovation Incentives in the Application of Antitrust Law, Address Before the

§1.07 VOLUNTARY COMMITMENTS REGARDING INJUNCTIVE RELIEF

Injunctive relief in the US is a remedy available to private litigants, and as such may be waived by sophisticated parties acting absent duress and anticompetitive intent. Such waivers occasionally appear in private contracts between commercial parties.[138] More recently, however, such waivers have featured prominently in the standard-setting context.[139] As noted in §1.06 above, Apple, Google and Motorola each voluntarily committed not to seek injunctions under standards essential patents in connection with DOJ approval of their patent-related acquisitions.[140] Likewise, as discussed above, in settling claims brought by the FTC, Google/Motorola agreed to forego injunctive relief with respect to standards-essential patents.[141]

And in 2015, IEEE adopted revisions to its internal policies to require its members to forego seeking injunctive relief against manufacturers of products compliant with IEEE standards except in certain limited circumstances.[142]

§1.08 CONCLUSIONS

The law of patent injunctions in the US experienced a sea change with the Supreme Court's 2006 decision in *eBay v. MercExchange*. Prior to *eBay*, due to the presumption of irreparable harm, permanent injunctions issued almost automatically upon a finding of patent infringement and validity. After *eBay*, the Supreme Court's four-factor test eliminated the presumption of irreparable harm, requiring courts to assess factors weighing both for and against injunctive relief as to the parties, as well as the public interest. The result has been a marked decrease in the number of permanent injunctions issued to non-practicing patent assertion entities.

The availability of an injunction when a patent covering a single component of a multicomponent product has been infringed has until recently been unsettled. The Federal Circuit's 2015 decision in *Apple v. Samsung* brings some clarity to this area, holding that irreparable harm from lost sales may be shown if there is some connection between the patented feature and demand for the infringing product. But the patented feature need not drive consumer demand for the product.

Though *eBay* did not explicitly address preliminary injunctions, the law of preliminary injunctions has also been shaped by the Supreme Court's *eBay* framework. Nevertheless, because a patent holder must show a likelihood of success with respect

---

USC Gould School of Law 12 (Nov. 10, 2017), https://www.justice.gov/opa/speech/file/101 0746/download. See Jorge L. Contreras, *Taking it to the Limit: Shifting U.S. Antitrust Policy Toward Standards Development*, Minn. L. Rev. Headnotes (forthcoming, 2018).

138. For example, Uniform Commercial Code § 2-719(1)(a) permits contracting parties to "provide for remedies in addition to or in substitution for those provided in this Article and may limit or alter the measure of damages recoverable under this Article."
139. Contreras, *supra* n. 101, at 563–564.
140. Contreras, *supra* n. 108.
141. *In re Motorola Mobility LLC & Google Inc.*, FTC Docket No. C-4410 (Jul. 23, 2013) (decision and order).
142. IEEE-SA Standards Board Bylaws § 6 (2015).

to both infringement and validity in order to obtain a preliminary injunction, preliminary relief remains relatively rare in US cases.

One of the most contentious areas of US patent injunction law has emerged in the context of FRAND commitments made by holders of standards essential patents to standards-development organizations. A debate continues regarding whether it is permissible for a patent holder to seek an injunction after it has committed to license its patents on FRAND terms. This debate encompasses both the propriety of injunctive relief in the federal courts, as well as exclusion orders at the International Trade Commission. Numerous federal agencies have weighed in on this question, both through policy statements and antitrust enforcement action. While a consensus may be emerging that seeking such injunctions is disfavored, but not completely prohibited, the Federal Circuit's split 2014 decision in *Apple v. Motorola* remains the only appellate opinion addressing these issues. Given the continuing importance of these issues to technology-driven markets and firms, it is likely that the law of patent injunctions in the US will continue to develop at a rapid pace over the next several years.

Part II EU Law and Law of the Member States

CHAPTER 2
Patent Injunctions in the European Union Law

Rafał Sikorski

§2.01 INTRODUCTION

EU law recognizes the importance of injunctions in the field of intellectual property. Directive 48/2004 requires Member States to ensure that holders of intellectual property rights, including patentees, have recourse to injunctive relief. Most likely injunctions would not have received so much attention if it had not been for the patent litigation in the ICT markets. They would continue to be seen as an obvious remedy, one that should generally be granted in cases of patent infringement.

Patent litigation on ICT markets has clearly shown that injunctive relief can be abused. This abusive potential is particularly visible in the context of standard-setting and access to technologies protected by standard essential patents. Here, injunction threats are frequently used as a tool to obtain excessive royalties from implementers locked-in to technologies which have become technological standards. In such cases, EU competition law, and particularly Article 102 TFEU which sanctions abuse of dominant position, may be used as a defence against SEP holders seeking injunctive relief against standard implementers.

Defences based on Article 102 TFEU are only available when the patentee seeking injunctive relief has dominant position on the market. Patents grant exclusivity, but mere exclusivity may not be equated with market power, let alone market dominance within the meaning of Article 102 TFEU.[1] Market dominance may be assumed with respect to SEPs, but beyond the standardization context, it is much less likely to be the case. Yet, clearly granting injunctive relief may also be highly problematic even outside

---

1. Steven Anderman, Hedvig Schmidt, *EU Competition Law and Intellectual Property Rights* (Oxford University Press 2011), 35.

of standardization context. This is the case when an injunction could cause disproportionate harm to the implementer or when granting injunctive relief would be in conflict with the public interest.

This leads to a question whether injunctive relief could, in light of the EU law and particularly the Directive 48/2004, be applied in a more flexible manner, in order to curb instances of its abuse. Directive 48/2004 seems to allow for some flexibility in applying remedies. In this respect Article 3 and Article 12 are essential. Whereas the latter is not mandatory, the first is and requires that all measures, procedures and remedies – including injunctions – are applied in a proportionate manner and that Member States ensure the existence of safeguards against their abuse. In fact, the question goes further, namely whether Directive 2004/48 requires Member States to equip the courts with competence to apply injunctions in a flexible manner.

§2.02 INJUNCTIVE RELIEF IN DIRECTIVE 2004/48

[A] Introduction

Directive 2004/48 aimed, among others, at harmonizing Member States' laws concerning measures, procedures and remedies necessary to ensure enforcement of IP rights at a high level.[2] It was based on an assumption that providing for effective measures of enforcement of intellectual property rights encourages investment in innovation and creation, which in turn improves competitiveness.[3]

Directive 2004/48 recognized disparities in Member States' laws and explicitly mentioned differences in arrangements for applying injunctions.[4] Indeed, the approach towards injunctive relief varied quite significantly across the EU. There were major differences between civil and common law countries. In common law countries injunctive relief came from equity. There, the courts traditionally enjoy a substantial degree of discretion. In civil law countries on the other hand, injunctions were usually granted automatically when an intellectual property right was infringed.

Since the ability to protect exclusivity is essential for intellectual property rights holders, not surprisingly, Directive 2004/48 deals specifically with injunctive relief. It contains provisions on both interim (interlocutory)[5] and permanent injunctions.[6] The first are a provisional form of relief, whereas the latter may be issued by the court following finding of infringement. It also allows Member States to introduce an exception to the otherwise generally available injunctive relief, by way of an alternative measure which provides that the courts, under certain conditions, may order monetary compensation in lieu of an injunction.[7]

---

2. Recital 10 to Directive 2004/48.
3. Recital 3 to Directive 2004/48.
4. Recital 7 to Directive 2004/48.
5. Article 9 Directive 2004/48.
6. Article 11 Directive 2004/48.
7. Article 12 Directive 2004/48.

Injunctive relief, just like all other remedies provided for by Directive 2004/48, must be applied by the courts in compliance with general principles established in Article 3. This provision expressly states that remedies must be '... fair and equitable and shall not be unnecessarily complicated or costly or entail unreasonable time-limits or unwarranted delays'. It also requires that remedies are '... effective, proportionate and dissuasive and shall be applied in such a manner as to avoid the creation of barriers to legitimate trade and provide for safeguards against their abuse'.

[B] General Framework of the Directive 2004/48

Directive 2004/48 is based on three enforcement principles, namely effectiveness, dissuasiveness and proportionality.[8] The first two principles seem to speak in favour of strong enforcement mechanisms whereas the principle of proportionality favours a certain degree of flexibility and discretion. The first two would certainly welcome an enforcement model where injunctions would be granted automatically once the court establishes that a valid patent was infringed. Proportionality, in contrast, is context-specific and not only allows for but also demands certain degree of discretion, the exercise of which by definition might result in denying injunctive relief. Since the application of those principles might lead in different directions, when deciding whether to grant or deny an injunction, all three principles must be carefully balanced.

Directive 2004/48 sheds some light on the meaning of all three principles. Article 3(1) for example expressly provides that remedies '... shall not be unnecessarily complicated or costly or entail unreasonable time-limits or unwarranted delays'. These requirements may be linked equally to principles of effectiveness and dissuasiveness.[9]

Some light is also shed on the meaning of proportionality. Article 3(1) for example explicitly requires that measures, procedures and remedies be 'fair and equitable'. This in itself does not explain a lot, because the term fair and equitable is generally considered to mean proportional.[10] Additionally, Article 3(1) clarifies that measures, procedures and remedies should be applied in a manner that avoids '... creation of barriers and provides safeguards against their abuse'.[11] Finally, in the preamble to Directive 2004/48 reference is made to specific features of each case, in particular the characteristics of each intellectual property right and fault of the infringer.[12]

---

8. Ansgar Ohly, *Three Principles of European IP Enforcement Law: Effectiveness, Proportionality, Dissuasiveness* in Josef Drexl (ed.), *Technology and Competition: Contributions in Honour of Hanns Ullrich* (Larcier 2009), http://ssrn.com/abstract = 1523277 (accessed 30 Jul. 2018), 1–2; Marcus Norrgård, *The European Principles of IP Enforcement, Harmonization Through Communication*, in: Ansgar Ohly (ed.), *Common Principles of European Intellectual Property Law* (Mohr Siebeck 2010), http://ssrn.com/abstract = 1700584 (accessed 30 Jul. 2018), 6–8.
9. Ohly, *supra* n. 8, at 1.
10. *Ibid.*
11. *Ibid.*
12. Recital 17 to Directive 2004/48. In a document on standardization the Commission, discussing considerations of proportionality, observed that 'Given the broad impact an injunction may have on businesses, consumers and the public interest, particularly in the context of digitalized economy, the proportionality assessment needs to be done carefully on a case-by-case basis'. *See*

[C] Permanent Injunctions and Alternative Measures

[1] Permanent Injunctions

Directive 2004/48 provides in Article 11 that Member States shall ensure that their judicial authorities, upon finding of infringement, may issue an injunction aimed at prohibiting its continuation. Additionally, it also states that, if the Member States so provide, where appropriate the violations of an injunction shall be subject to recurring penalty payments with a view to ensuring compliance. Injunctive relief does not depend on whether the infringement was intentional or merely negligent. An injunction should be available to the patentee also when there was no fault on the part of the infringer.

The wording of Article 11 does not tell us much about how injunctive relief should be applied by the courts. It only requires the Member States to ensure that their judicial authorities have the competence to grant a permanent injunction. It does not require the Member States to ensure that an injunction will be granted in every case of infringement.[13] However, neither does Article 11 make discretion and flexibility mandatory.[14] The obligation to consider whether an injunction should be denied stems from the obligation to abide by the general principles laid down in Article 3 and particularly the requirement of proportionality.

Though injunctions are considered to be a natural remedy for infringement of exclusive IP rights and indeed in majority of patent disputes they will be granted against an infringer of a valid patent, there are cases where the harm that an injunction could inflict upon an infringing implementer of a patent or the harm to the public interest may be far greater than the possible benefits to the patentee resulting from obtaining an injunction. In such cases proportionality would require the court to deny an injunction.[15]

Member States generally did not implement Article 3 into their legislation. This does not mean however that the general principles cannot affect the practice of administering remedies by the Member State courts. Courts of the Member States are

---

European Commission, *Communication from the Commission to the European Parliament, the Council, and the European Economic and Social Committee, Setting out the EU approach to Standard Essential Patents*, COM (2017) 712 final.

13. Ohly, *supra* n. 8, at 6.
14. Reto M. Hilty, *The Role of Enforcement in Delineating the Scope of IP Rights*, Max Planck Institute for Innovation and Competition Research Paper No. 15-03, https://papers.ssrn.com/sol3/papers.cfm?abstract_id=2602221 (accessed 30 Jul. 2018), 15. The author that '... if the European legislation earnestly aimed for such discretion of courts all over Europe, it would be unavoidable to alter Art. 11 into a mandatory provision' (*Id.*, at 17).
15. It is true that Directive 2004/48 was adopted primarily with a purpose of strengthening enforcement mechanisms to combat counterfeiting and piracy rather than to deal with far more complex disputes, particularly those relating to patents. It is therefore not surprising that it did not provide specific guidelines as the meaning of proportionality. *See* Pierre Larouche, Nicolo Zingales, *Injunctive Relief in FRAND Disputes in the EU? Intellectual Property and Competition Law at the Remedies Stage*, 1 Tilburg Law School Legal Studies Research Paper Series No. 01/2017, https://papers.ssrn.com/sol3/papers.cfm?abstract_id=2909708 (accessed 30 Jul. 2018), 5.

always obliged to interpret their national laws in a manner that complies with the goals of EU directives.[16] Although the practical ways to fulfil that obligation are left to the Member States,[17] some solutions appear to be relatively straight forward.

In common law countries, for example, flexibility resulting from Article 3 is not a novelty.[18] Since injunctive relief originates with equity the courts by definition exercise a degree of discretion and in the exercise of that discretion the courts should be influenced by the principles specified in Article 3. This is exactly what happened in *HTC v. Nokia* where Justice Arnold explicitly stated that in deciding whether to grant or deny an injunction, the criteria listed in Article 3(2) should be applied.[19] Also, in civil law countries Article 3 may and indeed should influence the practice of the courts in patent infringement proceedings. In such countries, even when generally injunctions are issued (nearly) automatically when infringement of a valid patent is found, the principle of proportionality could influence courts to apply doctrines such as abuse of rights, to deny an injunction if that injunction would be disproportionate.[20] Thus, the crucial role in delineating the degree of flexibility will be played by the understanding of the proportionality principle.

---

16. Judgment of the Court of 13 November 1990 in case C-106/89 *Marleasing SA v. La Comercial Internacional de Alimentacion SA*, 1990 ECR I-04135.
17. Whether EU Member States' courts consider proportionality when granting injunctive relief seems, with the exception of the UK courts, rather doubtful. The study by the Commission suggests that proportionality does not affect practice of the Member States courts sufficiently. See European Commission, *supra* n. 12, at 39. *See also* Trevor Cook, *Enforcement Directive and Harmonization of Remedies for Intellectual Property Infringement in the EU*, 20(4) Journal of Intellectual Property Rights, 264, 265 (2015).
18. In the UK the leading case on granting injunctive relief in infringement cases was *Shelfer v. City of London Electric Lighting Co* (1895) 1 Ch. 287. In that case LJ Smith specified the circumstances when damages could be granted in lieu of an injunction. One of the conditions was that the injunction would be oppressive to the defendant. Later Justice Pumfrey in *Navitaire Inc v. EasyJet Airline Co Ltd (No 2)* [2004] EWHC 2271 (Ch) stated that the term oppressive should be understood as grossly disproportionate. This understanding was later approved by LJ Jacob in *Virgin Atlantic Airways Ltd v. Premium Aircraft Interiors UK Ltd* [2011] EWCA Civ 163. J Arnold stating in *HTC Corporation v. Nokia Corporation* [2013] EWHC 3778 (Pat) that he recognizes that in IP infringement case he is bound by the criteria laid down in Art. 3(2) Directive 2004/48, seems to have moved away from the traditional approach of the prior cases. It remains unclear how big that shift is. *See also* Lionel Bently, Brad Sherman, *Intellectual Property Law* (Oxford University Press 2014), 1251.
19. *HTC Corporation v. Nokia Corporation* [2013] EWHC 3778 (Pat), Patents Court, England and Wales, 3 Dec. 2013.
20. The purpose of the abuse of rights doctrine is to allow controlling particular instances of exercise of a right, formally is exercised in conformity with rules granting it, on the basis of standards such as good faith, morality, fairness, justice or the (economic) objective of that right. The doctrine serves as a corrective mechanism. *See* Annekatrien Lenaerts, *The General Principle of the Prohibition on Abuse of Rights: A Critical Position on Its role in a Codified European Contract Law*, 18(6) European Review of Private Law 1121, 1122 (2010). *See also* Amandine Léonard, 'Abuse of Rights' in Belgian and French Patent Law: A Case Law Analysis, 7(1) JIPITEC 30 (2016).

[2] Alternative Measure

Drawing from the German Copyright Law,[21] Directive 2004/48 stipulates in Article 12 that Member States may provide in their laws that the courts grant monetary compensation in lieu of an injunction when certain conditions are met. First, the infringer must act unintentionally and without negligence. Second, the execution of the measure would cause the infringer disproportionate harm. Third, pecuniary compensation to the injured party must seem reasonably satisfactory.

The alternative measure as a substitute for injunctive relief has not been a success. Not many Member States introduced Article 12 to its laws.[22] Interestingly, it was also omitted in the UPC Agreement.[23] Additionally, what makes the application of Article 12 more difficult are the quite rigorous conditions for its application.[24]

Article 12 raises a number of important interpretational issues. The first is whether the three conditions referred to in Article 12 are cumulative or non-cumulative. The wording of Article 12 seems to allow for both interpretations. If the conditions are considered to be cumulative than the scope of the application of Article 12 becomes rather narrow. However, when we treat these conditions to be non-cumulative the scope immediately becomes extremely broad.[25] For example, this would allow the infringer who infringes intentionally to be limited to monetary compensation when the injunction would lead to disproportionate harm on part of the infringer. Similarly, in case of infringement without fault the infringer could escape an injunction even though monetary compensation would not be satisfactory to the patentee. The second interpretation would allow for too great an encroachment on exclusive IP rights which would be at the expense of the right holder having recourse to effective judicial protection.[26]

Lack of fault is also a demanding condition for the application of Article 12. When infringement is negligent or unintentional is not exactly clear. Information about granted patents and patent applications is generally available through public registers. Therefore, it generally would be difficult for the infringer to claim that he could not

---

21. The provision on alternative measures was modeled on Art. 100 of the German Copyright Law. Interestingly, when justifying the introduction of the new measure, reference was made to a situation of film producer who incorporated into his film a minor copyrighted work. In such cases, if an injunction was granted, a film producer would be prohibited from distributing his work, denying the public access to it. Such harm to the infringer was seen as disproportionate. See Peter Blok, *A harmonized approach to prohibitory injunctions: reconsidering Article 12 of the Enforcement Directive*, 11(1) Journal of Intellectual Property Law and Practice, 56, 57 (2016).
22. Commission Staff Working Document, *Analysis of the application of Directive 2004/48/EC of the European Parliament and of the Council of 29 April 2004 on the enforcement of intellectual property rights in the Member States*, SEC (2010) 1589 final, 20–21. The Commission's document mentions: Denmark, Estonia, Germany, Lithuania, Malta, Poland, Romania, Sweden.
23. The Agreement on Unified Patent Court discusses only permanent injunctions in Art. 63.
24. The Commission, for example, suggests in its document that particularly the condition of unintentional infringement without negligence is difficult to meet. This is even more so the case when that is coupled with high standard for acting with due care. *See* Commission Staff Working Document, *supra* n. 22, at 21. IP scholars have suggested that the scope of application should be broadened. *See*, for example, Hilty, *supra* n. 14, at 17.
25. Blok, *supra* n. 21, at 59.
26. Ibid.

check the register. This conclusion is not so easily acceptable today, particularly in the ICT market, where there are numerous and often very vague patents. In such markets products are complex and very often incorporate technologies protected by hundreds or even thousands of patented inventions. Manufacturers of such complex products frequently incorporate components delivered by other suppliers. In such circumstances, conducting patent search not only becomes expensive but also not feasible.[27]

[D] The Meaning of the Proportionality Principle

[1] Balancing under the Principle of Proportionality

The text of Directive 2004/48 provides limited assistance in establishing what considerations should be taken into account when assessing proportionality of a remedy. Generally, the question whether a particular remedy in a particular case satisfies the standard of proportionality is in fact a question of adequacy of such a remedy.[28] In the context of injunctive relief in patent law, it requires analysing: (1) whether injunctive relief is adequate to achieve the objectives of patent protection and whether these objectives could be achieved in a less onerous manner; (2) whether granting injunctive relief is adequate to achieve balance between competing fundamental rights, such as right to intellectual property, effective judicial protection and – which is particularly important in the context of patent infringement proceedings – right to conduct business or objectives of general interest recognized by the EU;[29] (3) adequacy of injunctive relief to achieve a balance between protecting the interests of the patentee and concerns over the protection of the public interest.

Injunctions protect patentee's exclusivity to use the patented invention and as such enable the patentee to obtain reward for his innovative efforts either through producing a product that incorporates a patented invention or by licensing the use of that invention to third parties.[30] When the patentee uses the invention himself, an injunction allows him to protect against third parties implementing it in their products, whereas when the patentee licenses third parties, he may conduct the licensing negotiations in the shadow of injunctive relief so as to extract the whole economic value out of the patented technology.

---

27. William F. Lee, Douglas Melamed, *Breaking the Vicious Cycle of Patent Damages*, Stanford Law and Economics Olin Working Paper Series Paper No. 477 (2015), http://ssrn.com/abstract=2577462 (accessed 30 Jul. 2018), 17. Lee and Melamed claim that pre-clearance is still possible in sectors such as pharmaceuticals and biotechnology, where the number of patents still allows conducting a patent search.
28. Commission Staff Working Document, Evaluation accompanying the document: Communication from the Commission to the European Parliament, the Council and the European Economic and Social Committee: *Guidance on certain aspects of Directive 2004/48/EC of the European Parliament and of the Council on the enforcement of intellectual property rights* COM (2017) 708 final, SWD (2017) 432 final, p. 39.
29. *See* Case AT.39985 – *Motorolla – Enforcement of GPRS Standard Essential Patents*, C(2014) 2892 final, 500–534.
30. Federal Trade Commission (FTC), *The Evolving IP Marketplace. Aligning Patent Notice and Remedies with Competition*, 2011, 139.

The scope of the reward will vary depending on the nature of the invention. The greater the improvement which comes with the invention, the more significant the reward.[31] Thus, the reward to the patentee reflects the additional value that comes with the invention in comparison to its next best alternative.[32] Consequently, injunctions by enabling the patentee to obtain financial reward for his innovation, allow the patent system to fulfil its role and provide incentives for innovation.

Generally, injunctions by allowing the patentee to reap benefits of investment in innovation will be an adequate remedy to achieve the goals of patent protection. However, patentees often use the threat of injunctions to obtain higher royalties than the market value of the patented invention.[33] This will be the case when an infringing patent implementer has already sunk costs in designing, manufacturing and marketing his product. The patentee will be able in such cases to obtain royalties in the amount that reflect at least portion of the switching costs that the implementer would have to bear if an injunction would be granted against him.[34] In such cases, a reasonable implementer would be interested not to lose all of the investment costs already incurred, therefore he would generally be ready to pay royalties up to the level of switching costs. This hold-up value exceeds the market value of an invention and can lead to overcompensation of the patentee.[35] In such cases the injunction becomes a burden to the infringer. Additionally, it may hamper innovation as it diverts financial resources from implementers to the patentee in the amount that exceeds the true value of a patented invention.[36]

Granting injunctive relief could also be considered disproportionate when fundamental rights and freedoms that may be involved in a particular case have not been properly balanced.[37] In line with Article 52(1) Charter of Fundamental Rights of the European Union as a result of such balancing the exercise of fundamental rights may be limited either in order to meet objectives of general interest recognized by the European Union or in order to protect the rights or freedoms of others. The Charter also provides that when limiting fundamental rights and freedoms as a result of such balancing, it is necessary that the essence of those rights and freedoms is respected and that such limitations are proportional.

CJEU already balanced competing fundamental rights and objectives of general interest in a number of cases where intellectual property rights were involved. These decisions were primarily issued in the context of litigation relating to copyright law.[38] The decision in *Huawei v. ZTE* case shows that balancing of competing fundamental

---

31. *Id.*, at 139.
32. *Id.*, at 140.
33. Mark A. Lemley & Carl Shapiro, *Patent Hold-up and Royalty Stacking*, 85 Texas Law Review 1990, 1993 (2007).
34. FTC, *supra* n. 30, at 144.
35. *Ibid.*
36. Lemley & Shapiro, *supra* n. 33, at 1993.
37. Article 51 of the Charter of Fundamental Rights of the European Union, EU:C:2012:391, provides i.a. that the provisions of the Charter are addressed to the EU institutions and the Member States when they are implementing Union law. This is recognized in Recital 32 to Directive 2004/48.
38. *See*, for example, C-275/06 *Productores de Música de España (Promusicae) v. Telefónica de España SAU*, EU:C:2008:54. In this case the CJEU had to strike a balance between the rights to

rights is also required in the context of patent litigation. In the latter case the CJEU considered balancing of such fundamental rights as right to property and right to effective judicial protection with the objectives of general interest such as that of establishing internal market, which comprises a market on which competition is not distorted to the detriment of the public interest, individual undertakings and consumers.[39]

[2] Factors Relevant When Applying Proportionality Principle

Studies conducted by EU institutions and relating to Directive 2004/48 show that even though the principle of proportionality gives courts a lot of flexibility in deciding whether to grant or deny an injunction, it would be advisable to have a list of factors that the courts should consider while making use of proportionality in their decision making.[40] Such catalogues of factors relevant for the application of the principle of proportionality were presented by scholars commenting on the Directive 2004/48. Ansgar Ohly, for example, suggested that the court should consider: (1) whether the loss the infringer would suffer by immediately terminating the use of the patented invention would grossly outweigh the benefits that the right holder would obtain from reasonable royalties that the parties to a licensing agreement would have agreed; (2) whether the patentee practices his inventions or is involved in R&D activities or whether that patentee's business model involves merely collecting royalties; (3) whether the technology used by the implementer was developed independently or whether it was copied; (4) whether the infringed patent is a strong or a weak patent; and finally (5) the degree of fault.[41]

Interestingly, the directive on the protection of trade secrets[42] might be of help in determining what factors should be taken into account when deciding on proportionality of injunctive relief. Article 13(1) Directive 2016/943 provides that when the court considers adoption of an injunction and proportionality of such a measure, specific characteristic of each case must be taken into account. It also contains a list of factors

---

property and fundamental judicial protection on the one hand and rights protection of personal data and private life. See also C-324/09 *L'Oreal*, C-70/10 *Scarlet Extended*, C-360/10 *Sabam*, C-314/12 *UPC Telekabel*.
39. C-170/13 *Huawei v. ZTE*, paras 57–60.
40. The Commission, in a document: *Summary of responses to the public consultation on the evaluation and modernisation of the legal framework for the enforcement of intellectual property rights*, admits many respondents admitted that providing criteria for assessing proportionality of an injunction would be helpful and could enhance legal certainty, uniform application of the principle and provide guidance on the application of the principle. Such criteria could also help to achieve the required balance between effectiveness, impact and cost of injunctions and also ensure respect for fundamental rights.
41. Ohly, *supra* n. 8, at 8–9.
42. Directive (EU) 2016/943 of the European Parliament and of the Council of 8 June 2016 on the protection of undisclosed know-how and business information (trade secrets) against their unlawful acquisition, use and disclosure (Text with EEA relevance), OJ L 157, 15.6.2016, pp. 1–18.

which should be considered when deciding whether a remedy would be proportionate.[43] These include: (a) the value or other specific features of the trade secret; (b) the measures taken to protect the trade secret; (c) the conduct of the infringer in acquiring, using or disclosing the trade secret; (d) the impact of the unlawful use or disclosure of the trade secret; (e) the legitimate interests of the parties and the impact which the granting or rejection of the measures could have on the parties; (f) the legitimate interests of third parties; (g) the public interest; and (h) the safeguard of fundamental rights.

Majority of the factors listed in Article 13(1) Directive 2016/943 can also be applied either directly or *mutatis mutandis* in the context of granting or denying injunctions in patent infringement cases.

Article 13(1)(a) mentions the value or other specific characteristics of the trade secret. In the context of patents, the fact that the infringed patent protects only a minor feature of a much more complex product and the protected feature does not drive the demand for that product, would be a factor that could weigh against granting an injunction, particularly if the implementer already invested in the design of his product and if redesigning would result in loss of the costs already incurred.

Article 13(1)(c) points to conduct of the infringer. If the patent implementer acts neither intentionally nor negligently then such behaviour could weigh against granting an injunction. Non-intentional or non-negligent infringement is not unlikely, particularly in industries where products have become extremely complex. Such products are made with components often coming from multiple sources. It is impossible for the producer of the end product to check all of the components. It might be difficult to have to go through all the patent thickets which are common in some industries.[44]

Article 13(1)(e) requires considering the interests of parties and the impact of granting or rejecting a measure. In considering the impact of rejecting injunctive relief and awarding monetary compensation instead, one should among other things take

---

43. The provisions on remedies in Directive 2016/943 are clearly a development of the rules established in Directive 2004/48. Whereas provisions of Arts 6 and 7 Directive 2016/943 have similar wording to that of Art. 3(1) and 3(2) Directive 2004/48, Art. 13 seems to be an important step forward. It states explicitly that Member States shall ensure that in granting injunctions and corrective measures, the courts shall be required to take into account circumstances of the case, including when appropriate the factors listed in Art. 13(1)(a)-(h) Directive 2004/48. Additionally, Art. 13(1) *in fine* seems to be a direct reference to the possibility of tailoring of the relief.
44. The concept of patent thickets describes a situation where a product reads on hundreds or thousands of patented inventions. Patents reading on technologies implemented in a product are often held by multiple patent owners. Patent thickets make entry of new and innovative products more difficult as they often lead to hold-up, increase the likelihood of costly litigation and may result in high transaction costs associated with the need to enter into multiple licensing arrangements. Such a dense web of overlapping patents may have negative impact on incentives to innovate and consequently reduce innovation. See Carl Shapiro, *Navigating the Patent Thicket: Cross Licenses, Patent Pools, and Standard Setting* in Adam B. Jaffe, Josh Lerner & Scott Stern (eds), *Innovation Policy and the Economy* (MIT Press 2001), 119–122; Geertrui Van Overwalle, *Individualism, collectivism and openness in patent law: from exclusion to inclusion through licensing* in Jan Rosen (ed.), *Individualism and Collectiveness in Intellectual Property* (Edward Elgar 2012), 86–89; Bronwyn H. Hall, Christian Helmers, Georg von Graevenitz, Chiara Rosazza-Bondibene, *A Study of Patent Thickets* (Intellectual Property Office 2013), https://www.gov.uk/government/publications/a-study-of-patent-thickets (accessed 31 Jul. 2018), 17–34.

into account the commercialization scheme adopted by the patent holder. If the patentee licenses his patent on non-exclusive basis to unrestricted number of licensees, one may reasonably assume that the patentee is primarily interested in receiving monetary compensation for the use of his invention. In such cases denying injunctive relief would not generally negatively affect the patentee's interests. If, however the patentee licenses on exclusive basis or licenses only a small number of licensees than allowing monetary compensation in lieu of an injunction could have negative impact on the attractiveness of the licenses, as the licensees could lose the technological advantage over their competitors.

Considerations of public interest, referred to in Article 13(1)(g), in the patent context could also strongly favour denying injunctive relief in some cases. For example, it is generally accepted that providing access to SEPs is in the public interest. It allows access to technologies necessary to be present on markets where standard technologies are used. It thus allows for greater competition on product markets and often stimulates follow-on innovation. Holders of SEPs in such cases will usually benefit from wider use of a standard incorporating a SEP, because this will widen their licensing base. However, in case of unwilling licensees, granting rather than denying injunctive relief would be in the public interest. Implementers of patent-protected technologies should not be allowed to free ride on the investment of SEP holders. This would undermine the foundations of the patent system.

The case of SEPs is also interesting when balancing various fundamental rights. Injunctions are certainly important from the perspective of protecting rights to intellectual property, recognized in Article 17(2) Charter of Fundamental Rights. At the same time however, in standards and SEPs context, access to SEPs would be crucial from the perspective of ensuring that others may enter the market and benefit from the freedom to conduct business, protected in Article 16 Charter of Fundamental Rights. Thus, when considering injunctive relief courts will have to strike the appropriate balance between competing fundamental rights and freedoms.

[3]   *Tailoring Injunctions*

Under the principle of proportionality, courts are not left with the choice of either granting or denying injunctive relief. At least in some cases proportionality rather favours tailoring of injunctive relief than denying it entirely. In fact, in light of the principle of proportionality, tailoring should be the preferred option to outright denials of injunctive relief. As a result of tailoring, implementers are protected against excessively onerous effects of injunctions, while the patentee's exclusivity is also limited to a lesser degree. Consequently, tailoring in some cases allows for even better balancing of competing interests.

Tailoring usually takes the form of delaying the entry into force of an injunction, but it could also lead to narrowing the scope of an injunction to some infringing activities while not restraining others.[45] With a tailored injunction, the infringer may be given time necessary for designing around the infringed patent rather than be ousted from the market.[46] Additionally, an injunction with delayed entry into force, may also allow the infringer to sell the remaining inventory of infringing products rather than order their destruction.[47] The time before the injunction enters into force may also be required for training so that the users of a product may shift to a new and non-infringing one.[48]

Tailoring injunctive relief may be beneficial in many respects. First, it addresses both the concern over hold-up as well as hold-out, by reducing the threat of an immediate injunction which allows the patentees to demand excessively high royalties from implementers facing the risk of switching and sunk costs while at the same time alleviating concerns of the patentees that the implementers will delay negotiations over concluding licensing agreements knowing that they will not be confronted with an injunction.[49] Second, it also helps to address public interest concerns and valid concerns of third parties in maintaining access to products incorporating patented inventions.[50]

[4]   Burden of Proof

The principles of effectiveness and dissuasiveness both favour granting injunctive relief when the court finds infringement of a valid patent. It is exactly the severity and inevitability of injunctive relief that makes it an effective remedy capable of deterring infringers. Thus, in case of infringement of a valid patent, there is a presumption that a permanent injunction should be available.

Since all three principles governing granting of remedies were placed on equal footing it seems that the Directive 2004/48 would require some substantial degree of

---

45. John Golden, *Injunctions as More or (Less) than Off-Switches, Patent-Infringement Injunctions' Scope*, 90 Texas Law Review 1399, 1455 (2012).
46. The possibility to grant an injunction allowing time for design around is especially important in case of complex products. When it turns out that a minor feature of the product infringes a patent an injunction would result in prohibiting further sales of that product. Staying an injunction for a period of time on the other hand would allow the manufacturer to continue his presence on the market against payment of royalties for use of the patented invention while at the same time to take steps for designing around the patented invention. *See* Colleen V. Chien & Eric Schulman, *Patent Semi-Comparables*, 25 Texas Intellectual Property Law Journal 215, 248 (2018).
47. P. Andrew Riley, Scott A. Allen, *The Public Interest Inquiry for Permanent Injunctions and Exclusion Orders: Shedding the Myopic Lens*, 17(3) Vanderbilt Journal of Entertainment and Technology Law 751, 778 (2015).
48. *Edwards LifeSciences LLC v. Boston Scientific SCIMED INC*, [2018] EWHC 1256 (Pat).
49. Chien & Schulman, *supra* n. 46, at 250.
50. *See*, for example, *Edwards LifeSciences LLC v. Boston Scientific SCIMED INC*, [2018] EWHC 1256 (Pat). There Justice Arnold decided to stay an injunction for the period of 12 months with the possibility for extension on ground that an injunction without stay would deprive patients access to a lifesaving product transcatheter heart valve (THV) Sapien 3 used in treatment of patients with aortic stenosis. Staying the injunction was necessary for re-training of medical personnel to use another device.

disproportionality to override the two remaining principles.[51] In practice it will be the infringing defendant who will be interested in turning the court's attention to special circumstances weighing against granting an injunction. Thus, burden of proof to refute this presumption on ground of disproportionality of the measure will lie with the infringing defendant.

[E] Preliminary (Interlocutory, Interim, Provisional) Injunctions

Preliminary injunctions offer provisional relief to plaintiffs whose patents were infringed. They are granted before the courts decide on the merits and are aimed at preventing imminent infringement or at prohibiting continuation of infringement. In numerous cases such interim injunctions are granted *inaudita altera parte*. The proceedings leading to granting interim injunctions are usually simplified and the courts decide relatively quickly whether such relief should be granted or denied. In many jurisdictions they become the primary enforcement remedy often leading to a speedy resolution of the dispute through settlement rather than lengthy proceedings.[52]

The need for provisional measures, including interim injunctions, is generally not disputed, indeed most Member States have made such measures available to IP holders prior to adopting Directive 2004/48. Interim injunctions, for example, by allowing to prevent infringement or cease its continuation, prevent injury to the patentee that would frequently be difficult to measure and recover following infringement. However, given the possible adverse consequences that the adoption of such measures may produce for the potential defendants, there is also a compelling need to provide for appropriate safeguards against abuse of these measures by right holders.

Directive 2004/48 requires Member States to provide judicial authorities with the power to grant interim injunctions prohibiting imminent infringement or continuation of infringement.[53] Interim relief is subject to the same principles as granting permanent injunctions, namely proportionality, effectiveness and dissuasiveness.

Directive 2004/48 regulates only selected aspects of provisional relief. Some were regulated with a view to protect the legitimate interests of the right holders, while others aimed to ensure that the rights of defendants were also sufficiently protected. Thus, in order to protect the interests of right holders, it requires that judicial authorities should have the competence to subject non-compliance by the defendant to recurring penalty payments.[54] Member States should also ensure that judicial authorities have authority to grant preliminary injunctions in ex parte proceedings, particularly when delay could cause irreparable harm to the right holder.[55] In turn, to protect the interests of the defendant the directive demands that judicial authorities have the

---

51. See *HTC Corporation v. Nokia Corporation* [2013] EWHC 3778 (Pat). There Justice Arnold stated that the burden on the defendant to justify the disproportionality of injunctive relief would be a heavy one.
52. Commission Staff Working Document, *supra* n. 22, at 13–14.
53. Article 9(1)(a) Directive 2004/48.
54. *Ibid.*
55. Article 9(4) Directive 2004/48.

authority to demand reasonably available evidence substantiating infringement.[56] The defendant should also have, when a preliminary injunction was granted in ex parte proceedings, the right to request review of that measure within reasonable time.[57] Finally, courts should have the authority to subject granting interim relief to the applicant lodging security that could compensate for injury suffered by the defendant if it turns out that there was no infringement, the patent was invalid.[58]

When deciding whether to grant or deny a preliminary injunction Member State courts are bound by the general principles enshrined in Article 3 of the Directive 2004/48. Thus, the fact that Article 9 does not require Member States to expressly provide for flexibility or discretion does not mean that the courts should not apply preliminary injunctions in this manner. Such a flexible, context-specific approach is required by the principle of proportionality. Therefore, when deciding upon interim relief balancing of various competing interests would also be required. Courts should also consider similar factors to those considered when deciding on permanent injunctions. It seems that in the field of preliminary relief considerations of proportionality should play an even more important role since it is granted prior any decision on the merits. In fact, Directive 2004/48 already envisages such a need for proportional approach in interim relief, because it allows making continuation of alleged infringement subject to payment of compensation.[59]

§2.03 STANDARD ESSENTIAL PATENTS, INJUNCTIONS AND EU COMPETITION LAW

[A] Introduction

Generally, it is accepted today that there is no inherent conflict between intellectual property rights and EU competition law. Rather, the dominant view is that these two bodies of law pursue the same goal. Intellectual property law, by providing right holders with exclusive rights, encourages innovation. First, the exclusive character of intellectual property rights incentivizes innovation because it enables the right holders to reap the benefits of their innovation and creativity. Second, the existence of intellectual property rights spurs competition by substitution. It induces other market participants to design around the existing intellectual property rights, thus creating new innovative goods. The EU competition law pursues the same goal of promoting competition and primarily dynamic competition through innovation.

The fact that the goals of these two bodies of law are generally the same, does not mean that intellectual property rights may not be exercised in a way that violates competition rules. There is a substantial jurisprudence by the CJEU dealing with anticompetitive behaviour of the intellectual property holders. In *Magill*,[60] *IMS*

---

56. Article 9(3) Directive 2004/48.
57. Article 9(4) *in fine* Directive 2004/48.
58. Article 9(6) Directive 2004/48.
59. Article 9(1)(a) Directive 2004/48.
60. C-241/91 P and C-242/91 P, *RTE and ITP v. Commission*, EU:C:1995:98.

Health,[61] Microsoft[62] or *Volvo v. Veng*[63] and *Renault v. Mexicar*,[64] the CJEU explained that exercise of IP rights may in exceptional circumstances constitute abuse of dominant position.

In *Huawei v. ZTE*[65] the CJEU had to decide whether SEP holders who seek injunctive relief against SEP implementers may abuse dominant position within the meaning of Article 102 TFEU. It is not disputed that a patentee may assert his standard essential patents against a SEP implementer who is not willing to conclude a licensing agreement and pay royalties.[66] In such cases it is not an abuse of dominant market position for the SEP holder to seek an injunction. The unwillingness of the implementer clearly justifies an injunction. Both the Commission in its *Motorola*[67] and *Samsung*[68] decisions as well as the CJEU in *Huawei v. ZTE* are clear on this point.

The situation changes however once the implementer is willing to conclude a licensing agreement, but the parties disagree over the terms of the licensing agreement. Such disputes are common to negotiations between SEP holders and potential licensees. Parties disagree mostly about the level of royalties, but disagreement as to other terms is also not unusual. In *Huawei v. ZTE*, the CJEU provided a framework that allows for assessment of the parties' willingness to conclude a licensing agreement on FRAND terms, particularly their behaviour during negotiations of the licensing agreement.

[B] The Decision of the CJEU in *Huawei v. ZTE*

[1]   Facts of the Case

The dispute concerned a Huawei patent which was essential for practice of the LTE standard. Anyone who wished to practice the LTE standard had to use the invention protected by Huawei's patent.[69] Huawei, during the standard-setting process before ETSI, notified its patent as a patent that reads on the LTE standard specification and committed to license that patent on FRAND terms.[70] ZTE, a manufacturer of devices implementing the LTE standard, intended to license Huawei's patent. The parties were discussing a licensing agreement for some time; however, they were not able to reach

---

61. C-418/01, *IMS Health*, EU:C:2004:257.
62. T-201/04, *Microsoft*, EU:T:2007:289.
63. Case 238/87, *Volvo*, EU:C:1988:477.
64. C-38/98, *Renault*, EU:C:2000:225.
65. C-170/13, *Huawei v. ZTE*, EU:C:2015:477.
66. *See* Case AT.39985 – *Motorola – Enforcement of GPRS standard essential patents*, C(2014) 2892 final; Case AT.39939 – *Samsung – Enforcement of UMTS standard essential patents*, C(2014) 2891 final.
67. Case AT.39985 – *Motorola – Enforcement of GPRS standard essential patents*, C(2014) 2892 final.
68. Case AT.39939 – *Samsung – Enforcement of UMTS standard essential patents*, C(2014) 2891 final.
69. *Id.*, paras 21, 23.
70. *Id.*, para. 22.

an agreement. Although the negotiations were not finalized, ZTE continued to manufacture products implementing the LTE standard, including the Huawei patent.[71] Huawei sued ZTE and demanded that the *Dusseldorf Landgericht* grants an injunction prohibiting further use of its patented invention by ZTE.[72]

The dispute between the parties concentrated on whether Huawei, by seeking injunctive relief against ZTE, the implementer of a SEP held by Huawei, abused dominant position, held on the technology market, within the meaning of Article 102 TFEU. Essentially, the CJEU was asked by the German court to provide criteria that would allow the national court to establish when a potential licensee is willing to conclude a licensing agreement.

CJEU recognized SEP holders' right to obtain injunctive relief against infringers.[73] At the same time however, it also recognized that access to standard essential patents is necessary for presence on product markets where certain technological standards are implemented. The Court consequently recognized that genuinely willing licensees should not be denied access to SEPs and should not be targeted with injunctions. The Court provided a framework for assessing whether SEP implementers are genuinely willing to conclude licensing agreements. It not perfect, as the discussion below will show, nor is it complete. Generally, however, the framework proposed by the CJEU is a positive development. It guarantees that interests of both standard implementers as well as the SEP holders will be taken into account. It also guarantees that the effectiveness of EU competition law will not be jeopardized.

[2]   *Competitive Harm in SEP Cases*

Refusing access to SEPs on FRAND terms is very likely to have negative impact on competition. First, it may lead to foreclosure of access to downstream product markets where technological standards are implemented. By refusing to enter into licensing agreements on FRAND terms holders of SEPs may capture the downstream product markets for themselves.[74] Second, when access to SEPs is on terms that are not FRAND, for example when royalties charged are excessively high, it is likely to affect the competitiveness of the licensees vis-à-vis other competitors, particularly the vertically integrated SEP holders. Third, standards are the foundation upon which significant follow-on innovation thrives. Denying access to SEPs may affect dynamic competition and further innovation. Ultimately, consumers are likely to be worse off as they will end up with higher prices and products less tailored to their needs.

CJEU recognizes that use of SEPs is indispensable for all manufacturers operating on downstream product markets and is consequently primarily occupied with exclusionary effects that the practice of denying access to SEPs on FRAND terms might have. Indeed, vertically integrated SEP holders which are present on both technology and downstream product markets, may be interested in excluding other competitors from

---

71. *Id.*, paras 24–26.
72. *Id.*, para. 27.
73. C-170/13, *Huawei*, para. 46.
74. C-170/13, *Huawei*, paras 49–52.

that downstream product market.[75] This is often the case when expected profits on the downstream markets are likely to exceed those that might be obtained from licensing on technology markets.

Concerns over reduced price competition are not the only concerns resulting from exclusionary conduct of SEP holders. Restricting access to SEPs may also substantially affect competition on technology markets. Typically, on standard intensive ICT markets there is substantial degree of follow-on innovation that builds on top of the standards. Frequently, such follow-on innovation opens up new markets and allows satisfying new consumers' needs. Consumers benefit from access to standards and innovation that builds upon that access.

[3]   Framework for Negotiating SEP Licenses

The CJEU decision in *Huawei* provides tools that are helpful in assessing whether the licensee and licensor are genuinely willing to enter into a licensing agreement. The fact that both parties are willing to conclude the agreement does not mean that there will be no disputes between the parties over the licensing terms. Having that in mind, the CJEU has also equipped the SEP holders and standards implementers with the basic framework for negotiations.

The way in which the framework for negotiations is structured, particularly the distribution of rights and obligations between the parties during the negotiation process may significantly tilt the balance in favour of either the patent holder or the patent implementer.[76] Once the balance is tilted in favour of the patentee, the patentee would be more likely to extract royalties that exceed the market value of his technology. When opposite is the case, the patentee would likely be undercompensated and the incentives to engage in R&D would be diminished.[77]

---

75. Nicolas Petit, *Huawei v. ZTE: Judicial Conservatism at the Patent-Antitrust Intersection*, CPI Antitrust Chronicle, October 2015 (2), https://www.competitionpolicyinternational.com/assets/Uploads/PetitOct-152.pdf (accessed 31 Jul. 2018), 4.
76. C-170/13, *Huawei*, para. 38. The concerns over creating conditions for hold-up or hold-out were precisely the concerns that led the referring Dusseldorf court to ask the CJEU for a preliminary ruling.
77. German case law preceding the *Huawei* decision shows that particular negotiation framework can strongly favour licensors enabling them to impose licensing terms that could hardly be regarded as FRAND. Indeed, an ill-balanced negotiation framework may also have adverse effects on the overall effectiveness of competition laws, making competition law defense illusory. The German *Bundesgerichtshof* in the *Orange-Book Standard* (case KZR 39/06) provided for a very demanding framework for standard implementers. First, the implementer was required to make an unconditional offer on terms that could not be rejected by the patent holder without infringing competition law. Second, the implementer had to behave as if the license agreement had already been concluded. Thus, the potential licensee had to cover his past obligations as well as his ongoing obligations resulting from practicing an invention. These payments could be made to an escrow account. The Orange-Book framework was problematic. Generally, a FRAND offer should not be discriminatory, otherwise it is not FRAND anymore. This requirement is crucial because it allows the maintenance of a level playing field on product markets. The implementer normally does not have the knowledge necessary to make a non-discriminatory offer, since he is unlikely to know the terms of other licensing agreements concluded by the SEP holder. Second, *Orange-Book* required the implementer to make an offer

Under the *Huawei* framework, the SEP holder, prior to initiating infringement proceedings, is required to notify the implementer of infringement. Such a notice should at least specify the patents and the way in which they were infringed.[78] Properly construed notice allows the standard implementer to assess whether the relevant patent is valid, essential and whether a given patent was actually infringed.[79] This requirement helps to avoid vaguely formulated notices that may be used by patent assertion entities in order to threaten implementers with injunctive relief.

Upon the request of the implementer, patentee is required to present an offer that contains the relevant terms of a licensing contract.[80] CJEU expressly requires that the SEP holder should not only provide the royalty rate but also explain how the royalty rate was calculated.[81] Particular SEPs usually cover only a small portion of the standardized technology used by implementers. The royalty rate should reflect the value of a particular SEP and especially the degree in which it contributes to the value of a particular standard applied by the implementer. CJEU does not however provide guidelines as to how to calculate a FRAND royalty rate. Commentators generally agree that the rate should reflect the *ex ante* value, that is the rate that would be agreed by the parties prior to adoption of a standard, rather than the rate that would be agreed *ex post*, that is after the adoption of a standard, as this would more likely reflect the lock-in effects and switching costs.[82] Again, detailed information on royalty calculation would assist the licensee in the verification of the fairness and reasonableness of the royalty fee offered.

The FRAND offer, apart from being fair and reasonable, should also be non-discriminatory. Some SEP holders make the licensing terms publicly available. Potential licensees may then check whether the terms of the offer match those made available or whether they differ. If that is not the case, potential licensees will usually have no access to other contracts concluded by the licensee. Therefore, it is the SEP holder who is in the best position to offer a license on non-discriminatory terms.[83]

Parties will often differ with respect to what constitutes a FRAND offer. Implementers not only question royalty rates,[84] they also frequently challenge validity,

---

that could not be rejected without violating competitions laws. The potential licensee was supposed to come with contract terms that could not be rejected by the licensor without the licensor breaching competition rules. The *Bundesgerichtshof* in fact asked the licensor to come with worst licensing contract, one that would be just below threshold triggering antitrust liability. Thus, the Bundesgerichtshof made it extremely difficult to raise a competition defence.

78. C-170/13, *Huawei*, para. 61.
79. *Id.*, para. 62.
80. *Id.*, para. 63.
81. *Id.*, para. 64.
82. *See* Mark A. Lemley & Carl Shapiro, *A Simple Approach to Setting Reasonable Royalties for Standard-Essential Patents* (2013), http://ssrn.com/abstract=2243026 (accessed 31 Jul. 2018), 10–12; Norman Siebrasse, Thomas F. Cotter, *A New Framework for Determining Reasonable Royalties in Patent Litigation*, University of Minnesota Law School. Legal Studies Research Paper Series. Research Paper No. 14-45 (2015), http://ssrn.com/abstract=2528616 (accessed 31 Jul. 2018), 10–13.
83. C-170/13, *Huawei*, para. 64.
84. Since SEPs are often licensed in bundles, challenges also relate to the fact that licensors are not willing to change the rate of portfolio royalties during duration of the license, although the value of the portfolio often changes as the assembled patents expire gradually. *See* Korea Fair Trade

essentiality or the infringement[85] as well as other terms.[86] CJEU provides that negotiations should be conducted in good faith[87] giving a number of specific guidelines that help to assess parties' behaviour. First, the CJEU requires that the implementer should act promptly. If he thinks that the offer is not FRAND he should respond with a counter-offer.[88] When the counter-offer is rejected the implementer should provide an appropriate security if he already implements teachings of a SEP.[89] Finally, the CJEU states that when the disputes over terms cannot be resolved amicably then the parties should agree that they shall be determined by an independent third party.[90]

§2.04 CONCLUSIONS

The scope of patent protection is not only defined by the patentable subject matter, scope of rights conferred on the patent owner or the limitations and exceptions. It is also largely affected by enforcement mechanisms available to the patentee. Lack of effective enforcement mechanisms will very likely have negative effect on the ability of patent law to stimulate innovation, whereas overly rigid enforcement mechanisms might lead to excessive litigation, overcompensation of patentees, unjustified restrictions on competition and innovation as well as disregard of the public interest. Injunctions are an excellent example of a remedy that is subject to abuse by patent holders.

Directive 2004/48, by providing that remedies should be proportional, effective and dissuasive, requires that Member State courts are given discretion to deny injunctive relief when granting an injunction would be disproportionate. The concept of proportionality is not elaborated in the text of Directive 2004/48 itself. The directive only demands that circumstances of each case are considered, including specific features of an intellectual property right involved and behaviour of the infringer.

Commission (KFTC), *Press release: KFTC imposes sanctions against Qualcomm's abuse of SEPs of mobile communications* (28 Dec. 2016), 14. KFTC stated: 'Qualcomm has not changed its royalty rate by taking advantage of coercive package licensing for a long or indefinite term even though the contribution of Qualcomm's technologies has lessened substantially as the mobile telecommunications technologies have evolved from 2G to 3G to 4G constantly'.

85. C-170/13, *Huawei*, para. 69.
86. Competition authorities in South Korea, Japan, China and the United States have recently challenged Qualcomm's licensing practices as contrary to FRAND commitments made in the standard setting process and consequently as infringing competition laws. Qualcomm, who held many SEPs reading on various telecommunications standards, was found to violate competition laws by imposing unfair licensing terms in licensing agreements, including bundling SEPs with non-SEPs and imposing royalty-free grant-backs. *See* Joe Zhang, *China's Antitrust Crackdown Hits Qualcomm with US$975 Million Fine: What Can Other Host States Learn from the Story?*, https://www.iisd.org/itn/2015/05/21/chinas-antitrust-crackdown-hits-qualcomm-with-us975-million-fine-what-can-other-host-states-learn-from-the-story/ (accessed 31 Jul. 2018); *FTC v. Qualcomm Inc.*, FTC's Complaint for Equitable Relief in U.S. District Court, Northern District of California, San Jose Division, available at: https://www.ftc.gov/system/files/documents/cases/170117qualcomm_redacted_complaint.pdf (accessed 31 Jul. 2018).
87. C-170/13, *Huawei*, para. 65.
88. *Id.*, para. 66.
89. *Id.*, para. 67.
90. *Id.*, para. 68.

However, when giving more specific meaning to the concept of proportionality in Directive 2004/48, inspiration could be drawn from the text of Article 13 Directive 2016/943. The factors listed there could easily be adopted in patent context. On the whole, the concept of proportionality enshrined in Article 3 Directive 2004/48 is broad enough to cope with majority if not all instances of abusive use of injunctions by patentees.

Denying an injunction, whether because of disproportionality or because demanding an injunction violates EU competition law, cannot take place without considering the interests of the patentee. In infringement cases there is generally a presumption that injunctive relief should be available to the patentee. Both proportionality and EU competition law work as defences. The burden of proof that an injunction would be disproportionate or that it would violate EU competition law, will lie with the implementer. In any case denying an injunction should only be an option when the implementer is willing to conclude a licensing agreement.

CHAPTER 3
Injunctions Against Patent Infringement under English Law

Trevor Cook

§3.01 INTRODUCTION

The main remedies sought by, and available to, a successful patentee in an English[1] patent infringement action are a permanent injunction, delivery up of infringing goods, an order for the recovery of the patentee's legal costs, and an order for the assessment of damages, or as an alternative to the latter if the patentee so elects, an account of the profits made by the infringer. This chapter also discusses the considerations surrounding the grant of interim injunctions, which a patentee may on occasion seek pending a full hearing at first instance on the merits, or when it has succeeded at first instance in establishing that a patent is valid and infringed but such finding is open to appeal; indeed, a patentee that appeals against an adverse finding on the merits on validity and/or infringement may also seek an interim injunction pending the outcome of an appeal.

---

1. The courts of Scotland and of Northern Ireland also have jurisdiction as to proceedings concerning UK or EP (UK) patents, but such proceedings are rarely brought in them, with the result that most patent infringement proceedings in the UK are brought in either the Patents Court, or the Intellectual Property Enterprise Court, both of which are part of the High Court of England and Wales. Although substantive patent law in England & Wales, Scotland and Northern Ireland is identical, and each can grant relief in respect of all the UK, and, subject to the Brussels I Regulation, the rest of the EU, there are considerable differences as between the procedural law in Scotland and that in the other two UK jurisdictions; in particular, it would appear, as discussed at Footnote 15 below, in relation to interim injunctions. Although the Patents Court and the Intellectual Property Enterprise Court are both part of the High Court of England and Wales they have different procedures, and there are financial limits on the jurisdiction of, and costs recoverable in, the latter, their jurisdiction as to, and approach to granting, injunctions, including interim injunctions, in patent infringement proceedings is the same.

Applications for interim injunctions, especially where sought before a full trial on the merits at first instance, must inevitably proceed on a superficial view of the merits of the case, and so the court is primarily concerned with identifying whether the patentee will suffer irreparable harm in the relatively short period though to full trial if no injunction is granted in the meantime. They are in practice rarely granted in English patent infringement actions, although as is discussed in this chapter on those rare occasions on which they are granted this is almost always in pharmaceutical patent cases in which the defendant plans to introduce a generic version of the patentee's product.

A patentee who prevails in an English patent action after a full hearing on the merits will, unless the judgment is the subject of appeal, almost always be able to secure a permanent injunction against a defendant that has been found to infringe a valid patent, despite the court having in theory a discretion as to whether or not to grant a permanent injunction. However, if a judgment on the merits is the subject of appeal the considerations relevant to the question of whether or not to suspend the operation of such permanent injunction pending the outcome of the appeal are similar to those encountered in proceedings seeking an interim injunction. Moreover, for the same reasons an interim injunction that has already been granted may be continued, or a new interim injunction granted, even after the patentee has failed in an action at first instance on the merits, provided that all possibility of appeal has not been exhausted.

For completeness it should also be noted that it is not only as a remedy for patent infringement that injunctions may be sought or granted in the course of English patent infringement proceedings. Thus an injunction can be granted requiring that a party that may not have itself have infringed a patent but, because of some involvement with the allegedly infringing goods, may be able to identify those who can be alleged to infringe, do so.[2] A search order – under English law a type of injunction – can be ordered to secure evidence.[3] An injunction may also be granted requiring that the holder of an intellectual property right publicise a decision of the court in favour of a non-infringer which had been granted a declaration of non-infringement.[4] An injunction can also be sought against unjustified threats of patent infringement,[5] and even against bringing an

---

2. *Norwich Pharmacal Co v. Customs and Excise Commissioners* [1974] AC 133 at 145–146.
3. Where these were granted without notice to the alleged infringer these were formerly called *Anton Piller* orders and although at one time relatively common in some types of intellectual property litigation, notably that concerning trade secrets or copyright, where it was asserted that there was a risk of evidence being destroyed, they were never common in patent actions. There were however instances of their being abused and they are now uncommon, requiring a cogent demonstration of the likelihood of evidence being destroyed if not so secured, as well as the involvement of an independent lawyer to supervise their execution. The ready availability of orders requiring the defendant to a patent action to provide a product or process description, or documentary disclosure as to the alleged infringing product or process, or in extreme cases to permit its inspection, has meant that there has been no need in the English system to provide an inspection remedy analogous to the *saisi* procedure found in some other European jurisdictions.
4. *Samsung Electronics (UK) Ltd v. Apple Inc* [2012] EWCA Civ 1339, [203] FSR 9, a case which concerned registered designs, but the principle could in a suitable case be applied to patents.
5. Patents Act 1977, s. 71. There has over the years been a substantial body of satellite litigation on 'unjustified threats' in respect of patents and other registered intellectual property rights and the law has recently been revised further as a result of the enactment of the Intellectual Property (Unjustified Threats) Act 2017.

action for patent infringement without the leave of the court.[6] Such injunctions are however outside the scope of this Chapter.

As a member – for now[7] – of the EU the UK has also implemented Directive 2004/48/EC on the enforcement of intellectual property rights,[8] and although this has not often been referred to in English judgments concerned with remedies for patent infringement there has been no suggestion that English law is inconsistent with it, but given its rather vague terminology this is hardly surprising. However, more cases seeking interpretations of the Directive are now starting to be referred to the Court of Justice of the EU and as this starts slowly to place flesh on the bones of the Directive[9] its effect on English law may become more significant, at least for so long as the UK remains a member of the EU.

§3.02 INTERIM INJUNCTIONS PENDING TRIAL ON THE MERITS

A patentee may, before the full hearing on the merits and judgement, seek an interim injunction[10] preventing the defendant from infringing the patent pending such judgment. As a condition of this the patentee must give a cross-undertaking in damages, by which it undertakes to the court to reimburse the damage suffered by the defendant – and third parties,[11] should they apply to be joined as beneficiaries of the cross-undertaking – should it transpire that the activity the subject of the interim injunction

---

6. *Fujifilm Kyowa Kirin Biologics Co, Ltd v. AbbVie Biotechnology Ltd & Anor* [2016] EWHC 2204 (Pat), [2017] EWCA Civ 1.
7. On 29 March 2017 the UK Government initiated the two year long process envisaged by Article 50 of the Treaty on European Union by which the UK will leave the EU, after the conclusion of which process, but subject to the transitional provisions of any withdrawal agreement EU legislation such as Directive 2004/48/EC will no longer bind the UK, although by reason of the European Union (Withdrawal) Act Directive 2004/48/EC will continue to form part of UK law, unless and until amended. It is unlikely that there would be any immediate change in UK law in this area, especially because UK law required little revision to take account of Directive 2004/48/EC, and EU law has so far had little if any effect in practice on UK law in the area of injunctions for patent infringement.
8. Directive 2004/48/EC of 29 April 2004 on the enforcement of intellectual property rights (OJ L195 2.6.2004 p. 16) (replacing by way of corrigendum the version published in OJ L 157 30.04.2004) and Statement by the Commission concerning Art. 2 of Directive 2004/48/EC (OJ L94 13.04.2005 p. 37).
9. There is one exception to this, namely injunctions against intermediaries under Art. 11 of Directive 2004/48/EC and the corresponding provision of Article 8(3) of Directive 2001/29/EC, as to which there is now a substantial body of case law in the context of internet intermediaries, as discussed in *Cartier International AG & Ors v. British Sky Broadcasting Ltd & Ors* [2016] EWCA Civ 658; [2018] UKSC 28, but which case law has little or no application to patents.
10. This used formerly to be called an interlocutory injunction, which indeed is what it is called in Art. 9(1)(a) of Directive 2004/48/EC. In Scotland it is referred to as an interim interdict.
11. Such third parties are typically customers, such as healthcare providers, which as a result of the grant of an interim injunction, would have to continue to pay the price set by the patentee for the medicinal product in issue and thus be unable to benefit from the reduction in price caused by generic competition – see *SmithKline Beecham v. Apotex Europe Ltd* [2006] EWCA Civ 658 and *Wake Forest v. Smith & Nephew* [2009] EWHC 45 (Pat).

did not infringe a valid claim of the patent.[12] A decision as to whether or not to grant such an interim injunction is invariably made on the basis of incomplete view of the case, the logical consequence of which proposition the English courts have taken to an extreme degree by relegating consideration of the merits to virtual irrelevance. The authority for this approach is the judgment of the House of Lords – the predecessor to the UK Supreme Court – in *American Cyanamid Co v. Ethicon Ltd:*[13]

> The object of the interlocutory injunction is to protect the plaintiff against injury by violation of his right for which he could not be adequately compensated in damages recoverable in the action if the uncertainty were resolved in his favour at the trial; but the plaintiff's need for such protection must be weighed against the corresponding need of the defendant to be protected against injury resulting from his having been prevented from exercising his own legal rights for which he could not be adequately compensated under the plaintiff's undertaking in damages if the uncertainty were resolved in the defendant's favour at the trial. The court must weigh one need against another and determine where 'the balance of convenience' lies.

This still remains the law to this day, at least in England and Wales, despite cogent criticisms that have been mounted of it.[14] Its consequence is that once it has

---

12. For an example of an assessment of the sum to be awarded on a cross-undertaking in damages see AstraZeneca AB and anr v. KRKA dd Novo Mesto and anr [2014] EWHC 84 Pat, [205] EWCA Civ 484.
13. *American Cyanamid Co v. Ethicon Ltd* [1975] UKHL 1, [1975] AC 396 at 406 per Lord Diplock.
14. *See*, for example, the criticisms set out by Laddie J in *Series 5 Software Ltd v. Clarke and others* [1996] 1 All ER 853, a case that concerned copyright in computer software and concluding with the observation that 'In *NWL Ltd v. Woods* [1979] 3 All ER 614 at 628, [1979] 1 WLR 1294 at 1310 Lord Fraser of Tullybelton commented on the practice in Scotland and compared it with what he understood to be the English practice since *American Cyanamid*, namely that the court is prevented from considering the strength of the parties' cases. He said: "In Scotland the practice is otherwise, and the court is in use to have regard to the relative strength of the cases put forward in averment and argument by each party at the interlocutory stage as one of the many factors that may go to make up the balance of convenience. That is certainly in accordance with my own experience as Lord Ordinary, and I believe the practice of other judges in the Court of Session was the same. Whether the likelihood of success should be regarded as one of the elements of the balance of convenience or as a separate matter seems to me an academic question of no real importance, but my inclination is in favour of the former alternative. It seems to make good sense; if the pursuer or petitioner appears very likely to succeed at the end of the day, it will tend to be convenient to grant interim interdict and thus prevent the defender or respondent from infringing his rights, but if the defender or respondent appears very likely to succeed at the end of the day it will tend to be convenient to refuse interim interdict because an interim interdict would probably only delay the exercise of the defender's legal activities."' Laddie J then went on to observe that 'I can think of no reason in principle why the practice here [in England and Wales] should differ from the practice in Scotland.' *See also National Commercial Bank Jamaica Ltd v. Olint Corp Ltd (Jamaica)* [2009] UKPC 16, noting that 'Among the matters which the court may take into account are the prejudice which the plaintiff may suffer if no injunction is granted or the defendant may suffer if it is; the likelihood of such prejudice actually occurring; the extent to which it may be compensated by an award of damages or enforcement of the cross-undertaking; the likelihood of either party being able to satisfy such an award; *and the likelihood that the injunction will turn out to have been wrongly granted or withheld, that is to say, the court's opinion of the relative strength of the parties' cases.*' (emphasis added).

been established that there is a serious case to be tried – which does not necessarily mean that it must be good case, but essentially that it be one that cannot be struck out as unarguable[15] – an interim injunction will be granted if the patentee can show it will suffer irreparable harm in the period up to judgment on the merits if an injunction is not granted, and that such irreparable harm will outweigh that suffered by the defendant if the injunction is granted. A patentee will not be able to show irreparable harm if it has delayed in any way seeking an interim injunction. However, in practice, given that a patent action will typically get to judgment at first instance in the English courts in a year, and that the courts are prepared in appropriate cases to order a speedy trial, which can result in judgment being given considerably more quickly, interim injunctions are rare in patent actions.

One exception to this is provided by those pharmaceutical patent cases in which the patentee is able to show that generic competition would result in a precipitate drop in price which could never be reversed in the event that the patentee prevails at trial,[16] although even then the court will consider whether a speedy trial would adequately protect the patentee's interests.[17] For this reason it has become common for potential generic competitors to seek to 'clear the way' of potentially problematic patents ahead of intended product launch.[18] Moreover a defendant that has not first 'cleared the way' of potentially problematic patents will commonly not contest the grant of an interim injunction, but will instead undertake to the court through to trial not to infringe the patent asserted against it, provided that the patentee provides a cross-undertaking in damages.[19]

---

15. In *Abbott v. Ranbaxy* [2004] EWHC 2723 (Pat) summary judgment was entered against the patentee, but the judge said that he would otherwise have granted an interim injunction in its favour.
16. The grant or refusal of an interim injunction is a matter for the discretion of the trial judge, and so is only rarely susceptible of challenge on appeal, with the result that there are very few reported decisions on these at an appellate level. For a rare example of such a case *see Smithkline Beecham Plc & Anor v. Apotex Europe Ltd. & Ors* [2002] EWHC 2556 (Patent) [2002] EWCA Civ 137. Interim injunctions are not limited to situations of generic pharmaceutical entry and are on occasion granted in other circumstances. For an example of the grant of one in the field of medical devices *see Wake Forest University Health Sciences & Ors v. Smith & Nephew Plc & Anor* [2009] EWHC 45 (Pat), although one factor favouring such grant was the fact that there was already an action concerning the same patent on foot which meant that a trial on the merits could take place relatively quickly.
17. *See Cephalon, Inc & Ors v. Orchid Europe Ltd & Anor* [2010] EWHC 2945 (Pat), where an interim injunction was sought but instead a speedy trial was ordered. Speedy trials are also sometimes ordered when an interim injunction is granted, or undertakings are given through to trial, as in *NAPP Pharmaceutical Holdings Ltd v. Dr Reddy's Laboratories (UK) Ltd & Anor* [2016] EWHC 1517 (Pat), [2016] EWCA Civ 1053.
18. Indeed, a potential generic entrant is expected so to do – *see Smithkline Beecham Plc & Anor v. Apotex Europe Ltd. & Ors* [2002] EWHC 2556 (Patent) at para. [66], which approach was upheld on appeal in *Smithkline Beecham Plc & Anor v. Apotex Europe Ltd. & Ors* [2002] EWCA Civ 137 at para. [40].
19. As was, for example, the case in *NAPP Pharmaceutical Holdings Ltd v. Dr Reddy's Laboratories (UK) Ltd & Anor* [2016] EWHC 1517 (Pat), [2016] EWCA Civ 1053.

§3.03 INJUNCTIONS AFTER TRIAL ON THE MERITS

A patentee that has succeeded in an action on the merits in establishing that the defendant has infringed a valid claim of its patent will almost always[20] seek a permanent injunction against further infringement. It is important to distinguish between two issues which arise in such cases: first whether it is appropriate that the injunction be stayed pending the outcome of any appeal and second whether, on the assumption that there is no scope for appeal on the merits or that such appeal has been unsuccessful, a permanent injunction should be granted at all.

In each case however the injunction that is granted will be expressed in general terms as not to infringe the patent in suit and will not be expressed more narrowly by reference to a specified type of activity, as is sometimes the practice elsewhere in Europe.[21] The injunction will expire at the same time as the patent, although the English courts have a discretion, which they have been prepared to exercise at least once, as to whether or not to order that an injunction, possibly of more limited scope, extend for a short period beyond patent expiry in order to compensate for the 'springboard' that an infringer might be able to secure if it starts to infringe shortly before patent expiry. [22]

---

20. On occasion patentees have made it clear in advance that they were not seeking a permanent injunction, although this would appear to have been in recognition of the public interest in not keeping potentially beneficial therapies off the market – *see*, for example, *Merck Sharp & Dohme Ltd v. Ono Pharmaceutical Co Ltd & Ors* [2015] EWHC 2973 (Pat) at para. [2]. In *GlaxoSmithKline UK Ltd v. Wyeth Holdings LLC* [2017] EWHC 91 (Pat), the patentee also accepted that there should be no injunction because of the potential impact on public health. In this latter case the patentee sought an order that the defendant should account for its profits from infringing future sales, as to opposed to paying damages on such sales (as provided for by section 50 of the Senior Courts Act 1981 'in substitution for an injunction') but this was refused on procedural grounds and in the exercise of discretion, while leaving open the question of whether the Court had jurisdiction to make such an order.
21. *Coflexip SA & Anor v. Stolt Comex Seaway MS Ltd & Ors* [1999] EWHC Patents 258; [2000] EWCA Civ 242, where the Judge at first instance had granted a more narrowly drawn injunction but the Court of Appeal replaced this with a more generally drawn one. The Court of Appeal observed, at [60] 'It is important that an order, such as an injunction, is drafted so as to set out, with such clarity as the context admits, what may not be done. It is for that reason that the standard form of injunction is in the terms restraining the defendant from infringing the patent. Such an injunction is limited in term and confined to the right given by section 60(1) and (2) of the Patents Act. It also excludes acts, carried out by the defendant and which fall within the ambit of the monopoly, but are excluded from infringement by the Act; for example private use coming within section 60(5)(a) of the Act. Such an injunction is confined to the monopoly as claimed. The claim has been construed by the court with the aid of the parties and in the context of the acts alleged by the plaintiff to infringe and any other potentially infringing acts which the defendant wishes to bring before the court. Of course a dispute can arise as to whether acts, not brought before the court, amount to a breach of the injunction. But such a dispute arises against the background where the ambit of the claim and therefore the injunction has been the subject of consideration by the court and has been construed by it'.
22. See *Dyson Appliances v. Hoover Ltd* [2001] EWHC Patents 30 and the discussion of their legal basis at [16] through [36]. After considering the issues likely to be encountered in assessing post patent expiry damages such an injunction was granted in this case, but limited in scope to a specific device which had been held to infringe.

As to whether it is appropriate that the injunction be stayed pending the outcome of any appeal, the considerations are not dissimilar to those that are encountered on an application for an interim injunction, but the appeal should have a real prospect of success, and matters are to be looked at afresh:[23]

> It is not in dispute that where a plaintiff has at first instance established a right to a perpetual injunction, the court has discretion to stay the operation of the injunction pending an appeal by the defendant against the judgment. On what principles ought such a discretion to be exercised? The object, where it can be fairly achieved, must surely be so to arrange matters that, when the appeal comes to be heard, the appellate court may be able to do justice between the parties, whatever the outcome of the appeal may be. Where an injunction is an appropriate form of remedy for a successful plaintiff, the plaintiff, if he succeeds at first instance in establishing his right to relief, is entitled to that remedy upon the basis of the trial judge's findings of fact and his application of the law. This is, however, subject to the defendant's right of appeal. If the defendant in good faith proposes to appeal, challenging either the trial judge's findings or his law, and has a genuine chance of success on his appeal, the plaintiff's entitlement to his remedy cannot be regarded as certain until the appeal has been disposed of. In some cases the putting of an injunction into effect pending appeal may very severely damage the defendant in such a way that he will have no remedy against the plaintiff if he, the defendant, succeeds on his appeal. On the other hand, the postponement of putting an injunction into effect pending appeal may severely damage the plaintiff. In such a case a plaintiff may be able to recover some remedy against the defendant in the appellate court in respect of his damage in the event of the appeal failing, but the amount of this damage may be difficult to assess and the remedy available in the appellate court may not amount to a complete indemnity. It may be possible to do justice by staying the injunction pending the appeal, the plaintiff's position being suitably safeguarded. On the other hand it may, in some circumstances, be fair to allow the injunction to operate on condition that the plaintiff gives an undertaking in damages or otherwise protects the defendant's rights, should he succeed on his appeal. In some cases it may be impossible to devise any method of ensuring perfect justice in any event, but the court may nevertheless be able to devise an interlocutory remedy pending the decision of the appeal which will achieve the highest available measure of fairness. The appropriate course must depend upon the particular facts of each case.

---

23. *Minnesota Mining & Manufacturing Co v. Johnson & Johnson Ltd (No.3)* [1976] RPC 671 at 676. See also *Novartis AG v. Hospira UK Ltd* [2013] EWHC 1285, EWCA Civ 583, in which the defendant succeeded at trial at first instance and refused to continue after trial the undertakings that it had had given through to trial. The trial judge refused to grant an interim injunction pending the outcome of the patentee's appeal but the Court of Appeal reversed this refusal. See also *HTC Corporation v. Nokia Corporation* [2013] EWHC 3778 (Pat), [2013] EWCA Civ 1759, in which the Court of Appeal also reversed a refusal to stay an injunction after trial at first instance. Similar considerations will apply pending the outcome of applications to appeal to the Supreme Court from an adverse decision of the Court of Appeal, as in *Smith & Nephew Plc v. Convatec Technologies Inc & Ors* [2015] EWCA Civ 803. A patentee that seeks to resist such a stay pending appeal must, in the same way as would have to do were it to apply for an interim injunction, be prepared to give a cross-undertaking in damages.

The English Court has also been prepared to treat a pending central opposition at the EPO as basis for staying an injunction against an unsuccessful defendant to an action under the UK designation of such patent.[24]

But once all possibility of appeal has been exhausted, English courts are almost always prepared to grant a permanent injunction to a successful patentee, as they start from the position that intellectual property being, as its name would suggest, a property right,[25] it is a right which the claimant is prima facie entitled to have protected by injunction. Despite this the English courts have for long accepted that the grant of a permanent injunction, whilst very much the norm, is discretionary, as was explained in *Biogen Inc v. Medeva plc*:[26]

> the court is not bound to grant an injunction because a patent is held valid and infringed and the defendant intends to continue the infringement. However, it would be exceptional if an injunction were refused to prevent continued infringement of an established patent right.

The English Court of Appeal expressed similar views in *Coflexip v. Stolt Comex Seaway*:[27]

> [59.] An injunction is a remedy against further injury and the Court will not make the order if satisfied that no such injury is likely to occur. It is not because a defendant has done a wrong that an injunction will be granted against him. Where a patentee has conclusively established the validity of his patent and that it had been infringed, as a general rule an injunction will be granted. However that will not happen as a matter of course as an injunction is a discretionary remedy. It is for that reason there have been cases where injunctions have been refused, for example, where the defendant satisfied the court that further infringement was not likely.

Despite such observations one is hard pressed to find any English case before the implementation in the UK of the enforcement Directive in which a successful patentee was ever refused a permanent injunction once all appellate routes had been exhausted.[28] Much the same can be said of the period that has passed since the implementation in the UK of the Directive, which it was not considered required any explicit change to UK law in this respect.[29]

Article 11 of the Directive provides, emphasis added, that 'the judicial authorities *may* issue against the infringer an injunction', identifying the existence of a discretion the nature of which is informed by Article 3(2) requiring, emphasis added, that

---

24. *Smith & Nephew Plc v. Convatec Technologies Inc & Ors* [2015] EWCA Civ 803. Although in this case the EPO decision was expected within a reasonable timeframe; it should not be assumed that the simple existence of an EPO opposition would necessarily mandate the stay of an injunction.
25. *Artificial Solutions Germany GmbH v. Creative Virtual Ltd* [2007] EWHC 3185 (Ch) at [50].
26. *Biogen Inc v. Medeva plc* [1993] RPC 475 at p. 483.
27. *Coflexip v. Stolt Comex Seaway* [2000] EWCA Civ 242.
28. In contrast examples of refusals to grant permanent injunctions, whilst rare, have however sometimes been encountered in proceedings for infringement of intellectual property rights other than patents, notably copyright and confidential information, and some examples are discussed in *HTC Corporation v. Nokia Corporation* [2013] EWHC 3778 (Pat) at para. [16].
29. *See* the Intellectual Property (Enforcement, etc.) Regulations 2006 (SI 2006 No. 1028).

"remedies ... be effective, proportionate and dissuasive and shall be applied in such a manner as to avoid the creation of barriers to legitimate trade' and the existence of Article 12, which provides for 'alternative measures' where the defendant 'acted unintentionally and without negligence, if execution of the measures in question would cause him/her disproportionate harm and if pecuniary compensation to the injured party appears reasonably satisfactory'. These provisions of the Directive were considered in *HTC Corporation v. Nokia Corporation*[30] in which it was concluded that:

> [32] Article 3(2) of the Enforcement Directive permits and requires the court to refuse to grant an injunction where it would be disproportionate to grant one even having regard to the requirements of efficacy and dissuasiveness. Where the right sought to be enforced by the injunction is a patent, however, the court must be very cautious before making an order which is tantamount to a compulsory licence in circumstances where no compulsory licence would be available. It follows that, where no other countervailing right is in play, the burden on the party seeking to show that the injunction would be disproportionate is a heavy one.

The reference here to compulsory licences does serve to remind one that despite applications for these being uncommon in the UK these do provide a clear basis, in appropriate circumstances, such as a patent which cannot be practised without infringing another patent,[31] for operating lawfully within the scope of a valid patent, and it is possible to seek one without conceding that one infringes the patent under which it is sought and whilst attacking the validity of such patent.[32]

One case in which the English courts have refused a final injunction in a patent action on the basis that to do so would be disproportionate was one in which the defendant was held to have threatened to do acts which would fall within the claim sufficiently often that they could not be discounted as *de minimis*, but which would nevertheless amount to infringement on a very small scale:[33]

> [170] ... Even if the level of infringement cannot be discounted as *de minimis* in such a case, I consider that an injunction would be both disproportionate and a barrier to legitimate trade. It would be disproportionate because the harm to the patentee from infringement on such a small scale would be indistinguishable from the harm caused by wholly non-infringing acts. It would be a barrier to legitimate trade because the practical effect of such an injunction would be to require the defendant to operate even further outside the boundaries of the claim, and thus

---

30. *HTC Corporation v. Nokia Corporation* [2013] EWHC 3778 (Pat) at [32].
31. *See* ss 48 through 50, Patents Act 1977.
32. *Halcon SD Group's Inc's Patent* [1989] RPC 1 at 7.
33. *NAPP Pharmaceutical Holdings Ltd v. Dr Reddy's Laboratories (UK) Ltd & Anor* [2016] EWHC 1517 at [168] to [170], [2016] EWCA Civ 1053. However, the judge at first instance did not have to decide whether or not to grant a permanent injunction, having found there to be no infringement anyway because the activities complained of did not fall within the claim other than to a *de minimis* extent, having observed at [148], after a review of the authorities at [138] to [147] as to the application of the *de minimis* principle to patent infringement that 'It seems to me that most people, and specifically the skilled person, would be very surprised by the proposition that selling products only 0.01% of which fall within the claim constitutes patent infringement, particularly where the 0.01% are randomly distributed among the remainder. I consider that this is precisely the kind of situation covered by the *de minimis* principle'.

would effectively extend the scope of the patentee's monopoly. In such a case, the appropriate remedy would be a financial one.

The English courts have also shown themselves to be prepared to qualify a final injunction in limited ways, having regard to the public interest. Accordingly in one recent case, after an unsuccessful appeal by the infringer, and the patentee having accepted, in the light of observations by the trial judge at first instance that he would 'certainly be limiting [the final] injunction by reference to the cohort of patients whose lives or health would potentially be put at risk by the grant of an injunction', that the final injunction should be for a certain period, and then be qualified for a further period, with respect to supplies of the specific transcatheter heart valve which had been found to infringe, the court was asked to determine the length of the stay and the scope and duration of the qualification.[34] As to the latter, although it was common ground that the supply of the infringing heart valve to the patients in question should be permitted where there was an appropriate declaration from the responsible clinician, there was a dispute as to the form such declaration should take. The court held that it should certify that, in the clinician's judgment, the patient falls into one of the groups for whom there is no alternative to the specific infringing valve for the reasons which the court had set out in its judgment.

§3.04 INJUNCTIONS AND STANDARDS ESSENTIAL PATENTS

An area in which the English courts might, at first sight, be expected to refuse a final injunction in a patent action is that of a patent which is essential to a technical standard, especially where such standard has been established by a Standard Setting Organisation (SSO), consistent with the rules of which SSO the patentee has declared such patent to be essential to the standard and has also declared that licences under such patent are available on Fair, Reasonable and Non-Discriminatory ('FRAND') terms.

The case law so far has however seen such analysis proceeding not under the enforcement Directive but instead as informed by competition law considerations, as to which the decision of the EU Court of Justice in Case C-170/13 *Huawei v. ZTE* provides guidance.[35] However, despite the substantial amount of patent litigation in the English courts concerning standards essential patents they have only recently, unlike the courts of some other jurisdictions in Europe, had to consider issues of injunctive relief in respect of these. In part this is because the interest of the holder of a standards essential patent is in back damages and future royalty income and it is hard to envisage circumstances in which an English court would ever grant an interim injunction in respect of such a patent, limiting the scope for 'hold-up' to force the user to agree to take a licence at a higher royalty than the courts would assess should the patentee be successful on the merits.

---

34. *Edwards LifeSciences LLC v. Boston Scientific Scimed Inc* [2018] EWHC 1256 (Pat).
35. Case C-170/13 *Huawei Technologies Co. Ltd v. ZTE Corp.* (CJEU 16 July 2015).

Moreover, it is only relatively recently that the English courts have held any such patents to be both valid and essential, and where this has occurred the court has been asked to set a FRAND royalty rate.[36] Even in this case however the English court, having determined a FRAND royalty rate for a global licence of a portfolio of standards essential patents, and being aware of the risk of 'hold-out' by a recalcitrant prospective licensee, has granted an injunction under those UK patents that had been found to be valid and essential in the event that and for as long as the defendant declined to take such a licence.[37]

§3.05 SUMMARY

Although interim injunctions are rare in English patent proceedings, and at first instance are confined almost exclusively to proceedings in the pharmaceuticals sector brought against prospective generic entrants, it has almost invariably been the case that a final injunction will granted to a patentee that succeeds in an action on the merits once all possibility of appeal in the English courts or, in some cases, of centralised revocation of the patent at the EPO, has been exhausted. But the preparedness of the English courts, once they have found a patent to be valid and infringed, to stay the grant of an injunction pending the outcome of an appeal or perhaps of centralised revocation can mean that in practise that it can be some considerable time before a successful patentee ever secures a final injunction.

Final injunctions in English proceedings are expressed in terms of any action which infringes the patent, although the English courts are prepared to qualify these having regard to the public interest, for example to allow for the continued supply of an infringing medical device of specific design. Pharmaceutical companies, in the context of disputes between research based such companies, have held back from seeking an injunction where its effect would be to keep a specific new drug off the market, and so the attitude of the English courts in this respect has not been, and is unlikely to be, tested. Patents that have been declared to be essential to a technical standard might appear to provide an exception to the general rule that a permanent injunction will in practice be granted to a patentee that succeeds in an action on the merits once all

---

36. *Vringo Infrastructure Inc v. ZTE (UK) Ltd* [2014] EWHC 3924 (Pat) (holding the patent in suit to be valid, essential and infringed), *Vringo Infrastructure Inc v. ZTE (UK) Ltd* [2015] EWHC 214 (Pat) (giving directions as to a FRAND trial), *Unwired Planet International Ltd v. Huawei Technologies Co Ltd & Ors* [2015] EWHC 3366 (Pat) and *Unwired Planet International Ltd v. Huawei Technologies Co, Ltd & Ors* [2016] EWHC 576 (Pat) (each holding the respective patents in suit to be valid, essential and infringed), and *Unwired Planet International Ltd v. Huawei Technologies Co Ltd & Ors* [2016] EWHC 958 (Pat) (refusing an application to transfer the competition law aspects of the FRAND trial to the Competition Appeal Tribunal). More recently a patent declared essential to a standard has been held (on appeal) to be valid and infringed in *IPCom GmbH & Co KG v. HTC Europe Co Ltd & Ors* [2017] EWCA Civ 90.
37. *Unwired Planet International Ltd v. Huawei Technologies Co, Ltd & Ors* (Rev 2) [2017] EWHC 2988 [2018] EWCA 2344, determining a FRAND royalty rate for a global licence of a portfolio of standards essential patents, and *Unwired Planet International Ltd v. Huawei Technologies Co, Ltd & Ors* [2017] EWHC 1304 granting an injunction under those UK patents that had been found to be valid and essential in the event that and for as long as the defendant declined to take the licence that the Court had determined to be FRAND.

possibility of appeal has been exhausted, but even in this case the English courts will grant an injunction in the event that and for so long as the infringer fails to take a licence on terms which such courts have determined to be Fair, Reasonable and Non-Discriminatory.

CHAPTER 4
Injunctions in Germany

Arno Riße[*]

§4.01 OVERVIEW

Injunctions are a very efficient and common tool in Germany to stop or even prevent patent infringing activities and can be obtained in both preliminary and main proceedings. Regularly, proof of one infringing action is sufficient. An injunction is granted irrespective of the infringer's fault and, in contrast to many other jurisdictions, generally no balancing of interest or court discretion applies.

In both preliminary and main proceedings basically the same requirements have to be met to obtain an injunction. German Courts interpret acts of infringement quite broadly which is favourable for patentees. Besides questioning infringement, defendants can, as in other jurisdictions, dispute the plaintiff's capacity to sue, especially if he is not the patent owner, and raise various defences, such as exhaustion or, in SEP cases, the FRAND defence which will be addressed as an exemplary defence in more detail. Also a validity defence is possible. However, due to the bifurcated system in Germany, this defence can at most lead to a stay of the infringement proceedings on the merits. Infringement courts in Germany do not have the capacity to invalidate patents. This can only be achieved by way of an opposition or nullity proceedings before the EPO/German Patent and Trademark Office or the Federal Patent Court, respectively.

The procedural requirements differ depending on the procedure. For example, to obtain a preliminary injunction, the applicant has to show that the matter is urgent and, in principle, that the patent in suit is valid.

According to a press release by the Higher Regional Court of Düsseldorf from November 2016, more than half of all patent disputes in Europe are decided by the Regional Court of Düsseldorf in the first instance and the Higher Regional Court of

---

[*] With special thanks to my colleagues Lisa Schneider and Dr Joern Peters for their support.

Düsseldorf in the second instance.[1] Other available data (up until 2011) suggests that more than 60% of all European patent cases are heard by the specialized patent law courts in Germany.[2]

§4.02 SUBSTANTIVE REQUIREMENTS

To obtain an injunction under German law, several substantive requirements have to be met. The burden of proof generally lies with the plaintiff. The defendant can raise several defences which he has to prove in return.

[A] Right to Sue

Several beneficiaries of a patent have a right to sue. First of all, the patent proprietor can apply for an injunction, also if he is only a co-owner.[3] Furthermore an exclusive licensee has an inherent right to sue,[4] if the infringing actions affect his right to use the patented invention.[5] The same applies to the patent proprietor, if he has granted an exclusive license.[6] This is held to be the case, for example, if the proprietor sells the product that is subject to the patent besides the exclusive licensee,[7] or if the royalties are calculated based on the number of units sold by the licensee or based on the licensee's turnover.[8]

A non-exclusive licensee can usually not apply for an injunction in his own right. He can only act on the proprietor's behalf.[9]

[B] Capacity to Be Sued

Turning to potential defendants, first and foremost the 'direct infringer' can be sued, i.e., the person carrying out a patent infringing action himself, such as offering a patented product or putting it on the market. Furthermore persons deliberately supporting an infringement by a third party are liable either as accessory or instigator.[10]

---

1. Oberlandesgericht Düsseldorf, *80 Jahre Patentrechtsstandort Düsseldorf*, http://www.olg-duesseldorf.nrw.de/behoerde/presse/archiv/Pressemitteilungen_aus_2016/20161124_PM_80-Jahre-Patentrechtsstandort-Duesseldorf/index.php (accessed 31 Jul. 2018).
2. Thomas Kühnen & Rolf Claessen, *Die Durchsetzung von Patenten in der EU – Standortbestimmung vor Einführung des europäischen Patentgerichts*, 6 GRUR 592, 594 (2013).
3. Thomas Kühnen, *Handbuch der Patentverletzung* (10th ed., Carl Heymanns Verlag 2018), Ch. D, para. 83, 114; Federal Supreme Court, GRUR 2000, 1028, 1029 – *Ballermann* (trademark case).
4. Federal Supreme Court, GRUR 1996, 109, 111 – *Klinische Versuche I*.
5. Federal Supreme Court, GRUR 1995, 338, 340 – *Kleiderbügel*; Federal Supreme Court, GRUR 2008, 896, para. 27 – *Tintenpatrone I*.
6. Federal Supreme Court, GRUR 2012, 430, para. 15 – *Tintenpatrone II*.
7. Federal Supreme Court, GRUR 2008, 896, para. 24 – *Tintenpatrone I*.
8. *Id.*, para. 27 – *Tintenpatrone I*.
9. Former Imperial Court (Reichsgericht), GRUR 1916, 178, 180.
10. Federal Supreme Court, GRUR 2017, 785 – *Abdichtsystem*, para. 62; Federal Supreme Court, GRUR 2009, 1142, paras 24 et seqq. – *MP3-Player-Import*; Federal Supreme Court, GRUR 2004, 845, 848 – *Drehzahlermittlung*.

Further, also an intermediary who unintentionally supports an infringement by a third party can be held liable. This requires that he promotes or facilitates the infringement of a third party, although he could, with reasonable effort, obtain the knowledge that the act he is supporting infringes the absolute right of the patent proprietor.[11] In addition to the mere (unintentional) contribution to a third party's infringing activities, the breach of a legal obligation is required that also serves to protect the infringed right, such as the obligation to analyse the IP situation.[12] In the cited case 'MP3-Player-Import', the Federal Supreme Court found that the shipping company was ultimately liable for patent infringement. It was recognized by the Court that a shipping company is not per se obliged to check whether the transported goods infringe a patent. However, once it is informed that the products might infringe third party IP rights, such obligation arises and was not met by the shipping company in the case at hand.[13]

Third, also the 'indirect/contributory infringer' can be held liable for supplying or offering to supply means relating to an essential element of the invention, even though an actual, i.e., direct patent infringement might not (yet) have taken place.

The prohibited actions and further requirements of (in)direct infringement will be addressed in more detail in the next section.

[C] Infringement

The substantive requirements to obtain an injunction are defined in section 139 (1) German Patent Act:

> [a]ny person who uses a patented invention contrary to sections 9 to 13 may, in the event of the risk of recurrent infringement, be sued by the aggrieved party for cessation and desistance. This right may also be asserted in the event of the risk of a first-time infringement.

The mentioned sections 9–13 German Patent Act define the patentee's rights to the patented invention.

[1] Direct Infringement

Section 9 German Patent Act stipulates the scope of the patentee's exclusive right and thereby the acts of direct infringement:

> The patent shall have the effect that the proprietor of the patent alone shall be entitled to use the patented invention within the scope of the law in force. In the absence of the consent of the proprietor of the patent, any third party shall be prohibited from

---

11. Federal Supreme Court, GRUR 2009, 1142, para. 29 – *MP3-Player-Import*.
12. Federal Supreme Court, GRUR 2009, 1142, para. 36 – *MP3-Player-Import*.
13. Federal Supreme Court, GRUR 2009, 1142, paras 40 et seqq. – *MP3-Player-Import*.

1. producing, offering, putting on the market or using a product which is the subject matter of the patent, or from either importing or possessing such a product for the purposes referred to;
2. using a process which is the subject matter of the patent or, if the third party knows or if it is obvious from the circumstances that use of the process is prohibited in the absence of the consent of the proprietor of the patent, from offering the process for use within the territorial scope of this Act;
3. offering, placing on the market or using a product which is produced directly by a process which is the subject matter of the patent, or from either importing or possessing such a product for the purposes referred to.

[a]   *Broad Interpretation of Acts of Infringement*

Due to large harmonization efforts worldwide, the list of actions infringing product and process patents will sound rather familiar. However, some German particularities are worth to be mentioned that are based on the traditional patentee-friendly approach of the German courts. Facing an almost unlimited number of cases, in the following only some exemplary cases and general guidelines can be presented with a focus on infringement of product patents and without always specifying the various exceptions that may apply.

(a) Manufacturing in section 9 No. 1 German Patent Act is defined as creating a product that shows all elements of the protected invention.[14] An important example is the reconstruction of an apparatus (opposed to the mere (permissible) repair).[15] Generally, not only the final production step completing the protected product is covered but also all earlier steps that have an objective relationship to the protected teaching.[16] Even the production of essential parts for a patent infringing product that show all essential features of the inventive idea can be sufficient.[17] Usually this will 'only' constitute an indirect infringement though.

(b) The act of an infringing 'offering' is understood, in simplified terms, to cover any act which, according to its objective meaning, presents the product for selling purposes.[18] Also this infringing action is interpreted in a very broad sense. It is irrelevant whether the protected product is offered for sale rent or

---

14. Maximilian W. Haedicke, Henrik Timmann, *Handbuch des Patentrechts* (C.H. Beck 2012), 8, para. 23.
15. Federal Supreme Court, GRUR 1973, 518, 520 – *Spielautomat II*.
16. Federal Supreme Court, GRUR 1951, 452, 454 – *Mülltonne-Fall II*.
17. Federal Supreme Court, GRUR 1995, 338, 341 – *Kleiderbügel*; Federal Supreme Court, GRUR 1982, 165, 167 – *Rigg*.
18. Kühnen, *supra* n. 4, Ch. A, para. 239.

lease,[19] against payment or free of charge.[20] Therefore, also the offer to lend or donate the product can be sufficient.[21]

The infringing offering can in particular extend to the advertisement of a patent infringing product, for example on a trade fair or website. An advertisement (qualifying as an offer) during the term of the patent is prohibited even if it explicitly stipulates that the product will only be available after the patent has expired.[22] Furthermore, it is irrelevant whether the offered product is already existent. Offering a product that yet has to be manufactured and delivered also falls within the scope of this act of infringement.[23]

(c) The patent proprietor further has the exclusive right to put the products on the market that are covered by a patent. 'Putting on the market' is defined as willingly transferring an existing patent infringing product to a third party so that the third party can use the product.[24] The transfer of ownership in a legal sense is not required.[25] In addition, the action has to show a link to commerce, but which can only be questioned in very exceptional cases, for example, if samples are presented and handed out on a trade fair which cannot even theoretically be sold to potential customers as the samples cannot be put in use.[26]

[b]   Infringement on German Territory

Obviously, German patent law only applies to patent infringing actions in Germany. However, according to established case law, already a certain connection to the German territory is sufficient.

It was, for example, held that the following acts qualify as a patent infringing offering in Germany: it is enough if only a part of the offer takes place in Germany.[27] In other words: it is sufficient that either the offering party or the party receiving such offer is situated in Germany.[28] If a patent infringing product is offered somewhere within Germany it does not matter if the sale takes place in a foreign country,[29] unless there is no doubt that the offered products or services are available in foreign countries only.[30] Even presenting a catalogue on a trade fair in a foreign country can, under

---

19. Federal Supreme Court, GRUR 1970, 358, 360 – *Heißläuferdetektor*.
20. Federal Supreme Court, GRUR 1970, 358, 359 – *Heißläuferdetektor*.
21. Rainer Schulte & Ingo Rinken in Rainer Schulte (ed.), *Patentgesetz mit Europäischem Patentübereinkommen. Kommentar* (10th ed., Carl Heymanns Verlag 2017), 9, para. 61.
22. Federal Supreme Court, GRUR 2007, 221 – *Simvastatin*.
23. Federal Supreme Court, GRUR 1960, 423, 425 – *Kreuzbodenventilsäcke*.
24. Federal Supreme Court, GRUR 1957, 231, 234 – *Taeschner* (trademark case).
25. Federal Supreme Court, GRUR 2002, 599, 599 – *Funkuhr*.
26. Kühnen, *supra* n. 4, Ch. A, paras 257 et seq.
27. Regional Court of Düsseldorf, GRUR 1970, 550, 551 – *Diazepam*.
28. Kühnen, *supra* n. 4, Ch. A, para. 257; Higher Regional Court of Düsseldorf, I-2 U 134/10.
29. Regional Court of Braunschweig, GRUR 1971, 28, 29 – *Abkantpresse*.
30. Kühnen, *supra* n. 4, Ch. A, para. 257.

specific circumstances, be an infringing offering in Germany, if the offer is directed to companies and their decision-makers in Germany.[31]

From a forensic perspective, most cases relate to product offers on foreign websites. The mere fact that a website can be accessed from within Germany is not sufficient.[32] Some kind of economic domestic nexus is required but also sufficient.[33] The availability of the website in German is a strong indicator for such link. But also websites in a foreign language can be sufficient, for example if this language (mostly English) is regularly used in the industry at issue[34] and/or if the website includes a reference to a German sales office.[35] To avoid the risk that the offer on a website is mistakenly interpreted to also be meant for the German market, a disclaimer can be used. To be effective, such disclaimer has to be unambiguous, serious (which has to be apparent already from its presentation) and complied with by the offering party.[36]

The same broad interpretation is applied to acts of putting products on the German market: the infringing goods are regularly put on the German market once imported into Germany no matter where the handover to a third party takes place.[37] In principle, it neither matters whether the infringing products stay in Germany or are exported to foreign countries[38] either immediately or after modifications took place.[39] Also exporting a product (manufactured in Germany) to a foreign country often means that it has been put on the German market first.[40] Only the mere transit of patent infringing products from one foreign country to another over German territory does not constitute a putting on the market within Germany.[41] However, if the goods are stored in a German harbour (even in a free port area), an infringing putting on the German market can apply.[42]

Furthermore, also a person in a foreign country who intentionally allows or even promotes an infringing use by a third party on German territory infringes the patent in Germany.[43] The same applies to persons that could have known with reasonable effort that they support a patent infringement in Germany.[44]

[c]   Equivalent Infringement

Devices or methods that do not make literal use of the invention may nevertheless infringe the patent under the doctrine of equivalence. The well-known 'Schneidmesser'

---

31. Higher Regional Court of Düsseldorf, I-2 U 134/10.
32. Kühnen, *supra* n. 4, Ch. A, para. 269.
33. Federal Supreme Court, GRUR 2005, 431, 432 – *Hotel Maritime* (trademark case).
34. Regional Court of Düsseldorf InstGE 10, 193 – *Geogitter*.
35. Kühnen, *supra* n. 4, Ch. A, para. 269.
36. Federal Supreme Court, GRUR 2006, 513 – *Arzneimittelwerbung im Internet*.
37. Federal Supreme Court, GRUR 2002, 599, 599 – *Funkuhr*.
38. Higher Regional Court of Hamburg, GRUR 1985, 923 – *Imidazol*.
39. Higher Regional Court of Karlsruhe, GRUR 1982, 295, 300 – *Rollwagen*.
40. Federal Supreme Court, GRUR 1957, 231, 233 – *Taeschner* (trademark case).
41. Federal Supreme Court, GRUR 2014, 1189 para. 1 – *Transitwaren*.
42. Higher Regional Court of Hamburg, GRUR 1985, 923 – *Imidazol*.
43. Federal Supreme Court, GRUR 2002, 599 – *Funkuhr*.
44. Federal Supreme Court, GRUR 2017, 785 – *Abdichtsystem*; Federal Supreme Court, GRUR 2009, 1142 para. 29 – *MP3-Player-Import*.

decisions[45] provide the basic guidelines to analyse whether a claim is equivalently infringed. They read:

(1) Does the variant solve the problem underlying the invention by means which have objectively the same technical effect?
(2) Was the person skilled in the art on the priority date enabled by his or her expertise to find the modified means as having the same effect?
(3) Are the considerations of the person skilled in the art drawn from the technical teaching of the patent claim?

In the past the most important (and often successful) defence of an alleged equivalent infringer had been to argue that the patent description mentions the variant relied upon by plaintiff but that it was (deliberately) not claimed and that its use can thus not constitute an equivalent infringement.[46] However, recent case law clearly indicates that the Federal Supreme Court does no longer accept the tendencies of the lower courts to apply this defence quite generously.[47] Accordingly, this case law re-establishes Germany as a promising jurisdiction for injunctions also based on equivalent infringement.

[2]   Contributory/Indirect Patent Infringement

German patent law also includes explicit rules on indirect infringement especially in section 10 (1) German Patent Act which states:

> [t]he patent shall further have the effect that any third party shall be prohibited, in the absence of the consent of the proprietor of the patent, from supplying or offering to supply, within the territorial scope of this Act, persons other than those entitled to exploit the patented invention with means relating to an essential element of the invention for use within the territorial scope of this Act if the third party knows or if it is obvious from the circumstances that those means are suitable and intended for using that invention.

As can be inferred already from the wording, section 10 German Patent Act stipulates additional requirements in comparison to direct infringement. Even though the prohibition of indirect infringement aims at preventing direct patent infringing actions, no actual direct infringement is required, i.e., that the offering or supplying of essential means actually resulted in any direct infringement.

The objects of indirect patent infringing actions are 'means relating to an essential element of the invention'. 'Means' are all tangible items capable of being used for direct patent infringement.[48] An element is 'essential' if it is suited to functionally cooperate

---

45. Federal Supreme Court, GRUR 2002, 515 – *Schneidmesser I*; Federal Supreme Court, GRUR 2002, 519 – *Schneidmesser II*.
46. *Cf.* Federal Supreme Court, GRUR 2011, 701 – *Okklusionsvorrichtung*.
47. Federal Supreme Court, GRUR 2016, 1254 – *V-förmige Führungsanordnung*; Federal Supreme Court, GRUR 2016, 921 – *Pemetrexed*.
48. Federal Supreme Court, GRUR 2001, 228, 231 – *Luftheizgerät*.

with one or more features of the patent claim to realize the idea of the patented invention.[49] As a rule of thumb, at least each element mentioned in a patent claim is essential in this sense.[50]

The infringing actions are limited to acts of offering and/or supplying such means. Offering is generally understood as explained above in the section on direct infringement.[51] The act of supplying is similar to putting directly infringing products on the market.[52]

In addition, the stricter nexus to the German territory is worth to be mentioned. The essential means do not only have to be offered or supplied in Germany but also the intended use of these means has to take place here. The German Courts interpret these requirements rather broadly, though. It was, for example, held that supplying means which are related to an essential element to a foreign country can nevertheless be an indirect infringement if these means are used to manufacture a patent infringing product that should ultimately be supplied to Germany.[53]

The means further have to be 'suitable and intended for using that invention'. This is assessed based on objective criteria.[54] Only if the means are objectively useless for the use of the invention, a contributory patent infringement can be excluded. Also, a merely accidental use is not an indirect patent infringement.[55]

Indirect patent infringement additionally requires the presence of subjective elements. It is necessary that the supplier knows or is aware of the suitability of the means and that the means are subjectively designated for the infringing use.[56] As it is difficult to prove such knowledge or awareness, it is sufficient if the suitability of the means is obvious in light of the circumstances of the case at issue. For example it was held that, if a supplier recommends a particular use, the other party would usually follow these instructions and will use the device accordingly.[57]

[D]   Threat of Infringement and Danger of Recurrence

To get an injunction in Germany, generally only one additional condition besides the infringing action has to be met. Either a risk of an additional infringement (danger of recurrence) or an imminent threat of a first infringement has to be present.

---

49. Federal Supreme Court, GRUR 2004, 758, 761 – *Flügelradzähler*; Federal Supreme Court, GRUR 2005, 848, 849 – *Antriebsscheibenaufzug*; Federal Supreme Court, GRUR 2012, 1235, para. 32 – *MPEG-2-Videosignal*.
50. Federal Supreme Court, GRUR 2007, 773, 774 – *Rohrschweißverfahren*.
51. Higher Regional Court of Karlsruhe, GRUR 2014, 59, 62.
52. Schulte & Rinken, *supra* n. 21, sec. 10, para. 9; Peter Mes, *Patentgesetz. Gebrauchsmustergesetz* (4th ed., C.H. Beck 2014), s. 10, para. 9.
53. Federal Supreme Court, GRUR 2007, 313 paras 22 et seq. – *Funkuhr II*.
54. Federal Supreme Court, GRUR 2005, 848, 850 – *Antriebsscheibenaufzug*.
55. Regional Court of Hamburg, GRUR-RR 2001, 257, 258.
56. Federal Supreme Court, GRUR 2001, 228, 231 – *Luftheizgerät*.
57. *Ibid*.

[1] Threat of Infringement

A threat of an infringement can be sufficient to get an injunction in Germany.[58] Accordingly, an injunction is possible in Germany without any infringing action actually being committed (yet).

The threat of an infringement has to be imminent based on tangible indications which have to be proven by plaintiff, if required.[59] This includes that the impended infringing action is specific to an extent that allows the reliable conclusion that all elements of the claim would be met.[60] Depending on the particularities of the individual case, it can be sufficient that the defendant claims to be allowed to perform a patent infringing action, such as the manufacture of a patented product. A serious and immediate or in the near future impending risk of an actual infringing action is required to grant an injunction based on this mere statement.[61]

The threat of infringement, e.g., by a claim as outlined above, can be eliminated through a simple but serious declaration in which this claim is abandoned.[62]

[2] Danger of Recurrence

Alternatively, the risk of further infringements in addition to a past infringing action ('danger of recurrence') is required. There are only very few scenarios in which, in the light of past infringements, a danger of recurrence will be denied. In fact, generally a presumption of danger of reoccurrence applies simply as an infringement has occurred in the past

In contrast to the threat of infringement, the danger of recurrence cannot be eliminated simply by stopping infringing activities or by the mere promise to respect a third party's IP right in the future. To avoid an injunction, the infringer has to provide a cease and desist declaration that includes a penalty clause.[63] Also, the defendant has the burden to prove a 'successful' removal of the danger of recurrence.[64]

[E] Scope

If the above requirements are met, the injunction is granted. In contrast to other jurisdictions, at least in proceedings on the merits, no balancing of interest is required.

An injunction in principle requires the infringer to refrain from the infringing action. Accordingly, he first and foremost has to stop offering, putting on the market, use, possess and import the infringing products or using the process, etc.

---

58. Federal Supreme Court, GRUR 1999, 1097, 1099 – *Preissturz ohne Ende* (Competition case).
59. Federal Supreme Court, GRUR 2014, 883 para. 35 – *Geschäftsführerhaftung*; Kühnen, *supra* n. 4, Ch. D, para. 284.
60. Federal Supreme Court, GRUR 2016, 1187 para. 21 – *Stirnlampen* (Competition case).
61. Federal Supreme Court, GRUR 2011, 1038 para. 44 – *Stiftparfüm* (Trademark case).
62. Haedicke & Timmann, *supra* n. 14, § 10 para. 43.
63. Federal Supreme Court, GRUR 1998, 1045, 1046 – *Brennwertkessel* (Competition case).
64. Federal Supreme Court, GRUR 1998, 1045, 1045 – *Brennwertkessel* (Competition case).

However, the injunction claim can also include the obligation to take action, i.e., by way of deleting the infringing product from a website, as the continuing infringement can only be terminated this way. In addition, there is currently a massive debate in Germany, whether the actions required by defendant to comply with an injunction obligation even extend to 'undoing' (arguably) completed infringing actions such as the delivery of the infringing products to customers by way of issuing a recall.[65]

In competition law, copyright law and trademark law there are quite a number of cases now, stipulating that, if infringing products have been distributed, an injunction can include the obligation to recall those products.[66] The Federal Supreme Court basically argues that the effects of the previous act of infringement continue to last and can only be terminated by recalling them from the customers.[67] Especially if there is a serious expectation of further infringements (by the customers) the defendant is required to exert his actual and legal influence (if any) upon third parties whose actions are economically beneficial for him.[68] It is not required that the defendant actually has any legal means against his customers. Any possible and reasonable attempt is held to be enough, in particular if the customers, in the light of potential claims of the plaintiff, are likely to comply.[69]

It is argued that this case law blurs the distinction between injunctions, claims for abatement or removal and recall. Some authors are of the opinion that, if injunctions were to cover recalls, the 'explicit' recall claim would be redundant and its specific requirements (especially the balancing of interest) would be circumvented.[70] The balancing of interest will potentially be addressed for the first time in the enforcement proceedings. At first glance this may seem to be an academic dispute only. The opposite is true though. The above case law has the potential to significantly affect injunction proceedings on various levels. First of all, an injunction fails to specify any

---

65. *Cf.*, for example, Michael Goldmann, *Pflicht zum Rückruf wettbewerbsrechtlich zu beanstandender Produkte*, 7 GRUR 724 (2016); Clemens Hermanns, *Der Unterlassungsanspruch als verkappter Rückrufanspruch? Eine dogmatische Untersuchung der Ausdehnung tenorierter Unterlassungspflichten auf eine generelle Rückrufpflicht*, 10 GRUR 977 (2017); Richard Dissmann, *Unterlassung und Rückruf – die europäische Perspektive*, 10 GRUR 986 (2017); GRUR-Fachausschuss für Wettbewerbs- und Markenrecht, *„Zwischenruf" des Ausschusses für Wettbewerbs- und Markenrecht der GRUR zum Verhältnis von Unterlassung und Beseitigung im gewerblichen Rechtsschutz und insbesondere im Wettbewerbsrecht*, 9 GRUR 885 (2017); Hans-Jürgen Ahrens, *Beseitigung kraft Unterlassungstitels: berechtigter Aufstand gegen den BGH? Zugleich Besprechung von BGH „Produkte zur Wundversorgung,"* 4 GRUR 374 (2018); Andreas Lubberger, *Zu Risiken und Nebenwirkungen kontaktieren Sie Ihren Anwalt oder Richter. Zugleich Besprechung von BGH „Produkte zur Wundversorgung,"* 4 GRUR 378 (2018).
66. Federal Supreme Court, GRUR 2018, 292, 294 – *Produkte zur Wundversorgung* (Trademark case); Federal Supreme Court, GRUR 2016, 720, 723 – *Hot Sox* (Competition case); Federal Supreme Court, GRUR 2017, 208, 210 – *Rückruf von RESCUE-Produkten* (Competition case).
67. *Cf.*, for example, Federal Supreme Court, GRUR 2015, 258, 263 – *CT-Paradies* (Copyright case); Federal Supreme Court, GRUR 2017, 748, 751 – *Robinson Liste* (Competition case).
68. Federal Supreme Court, NJW 2018, 155, 157 – *Luftentfeuchter*; Federal Supreme Court, GRUR 2017, 208, 211 – *Rückruf von RESCUE-Produkten*; Federal Supreme Court, GRUR 2014, 595, 597 – *Vertragsstrafeklausel*.
69. Federal Supreme Court, NJW 2018, 155, 157 – *Luftentfeuchter*; Federal Supreme Court, GRUR 2017, 208, 211 – *Rückruf von RESCUE-Produkten*.
70. Goldmann, *supra* n. 65, at 724 (for Competition law and trademark law).

recall modalities, in contrast to an 'explicit' recall claim.[71] Also the rules how to enforce an injunction and an obligation to take an action (such as when explicitly obliged to recall a product) differ significantly. Third, enforcing a non-final injunction can lead to damage claims in case the injunction is revoked in appeal. If damages due to a recall shall be avoided, it has to be clear that no recall is requested.

The Federal Supreme Court acknowledges that injunctions and claims for abatement or removal are separate and independent claims. Both claims may exist in parallel and it is for the plaintiff to assert either one of them or both. It ultimately depends on the facts of the case whether complying with the injunction necessarily requires elimination, i.e., whether the injunction (exceptionally) includes a recall obligation.[72] It is further argued that the case law does not grant plaintiff more than he requested. It is, in one opinion, for the plaintiff to precisely define the scope of his injunction request in the statement of claims and if necessary clarify intended restrictions.[73]

It should be noted that it is not entirely clear whether and to what extent the above 'soft IP' case law will be adopted by the competent patent law courts. To date no decision on this topic has been issued by the patent law senate at the Federal Supreme Court. Presiding Judge Kühnen of the Higher Regional Court of Düsseldorf states in his renowned book that cease and desist declarations can include recall obligations.[74] However, a cease and desist declaration aims at avoiding litigation and might thus be construed differently than an injunction order issued in a judgment. There is one patent case in which the Higher Regional Court of Düsseldorf held that an injunction also requires the defendant to undertake reasonable measures to prevent infringements by persons under his authority. In the same decision this Court explicitly stated that the (lower instances) case law understanding an injunction to include an obligation to recall distributed products is not applicable in patent law cases.[75] In light of the recent decisions by the Federal Supreme Court, this case law might change though.

In any event, this broad scope of the injunction obligation is generally only applicable to proceedings on the merits. A recall severely and irreversibly impacts on the customer relationship of the defendant and it may not be possible to sell a recalled product again. Accordingly, it is widely accepted that a recall cannot be granted in preliminary injunction proceedings.[76] This has also been recognized with respect to the 'implicit' recall obligation as part of the injunction claim.[77]

---

71. Nikolai Klute, *Die aktuellen Entwicklungen im Lauterkeitsrecht*, 23 NJW 1648 (2017).
72. Federal Supreme Court, GRUR 2017, 208, 210 – *Rückruf von RESCUE-Produkten*.
73. Wolfgang Büscher, *Aus der Rechtsprechung des EuGH und des BGH zum Lauterkeitsrecht seit Ende 2016*, 2 GRUR 113, 126 (2018).
74. Kühnen, *supra* n. 4, Ch. C, para. 84.
75. Higher Regional Court of Düsseldorf, BeckRS 2013, 21057.
76. Kühnen, *supra* n. 4, Ch. D, para. 657; Dirk Jestaedt, *Die Ansprüche auf Rückruf und Entfernen schutzrechtsverletzender Gegenstände aus den Vertriebswegen*, 2 GRUR 102 (2009).
77. Federal Supreme Court, GRUR 2018, 292, para. 39 – *Produkte zur Wundversorgung*.

[F] Defences

The infringer can raise various defences to prevent the injunction claim from being granted. Amongst others, the infringer can raise a license or exhaustion defence or can rely on various privileges such as the experimental use privilege or the 'Roche-Bolar exemption', covering any studies, experiments and the practical requirements resulting therefrom which are necessary for obtaining a pharmaceutical market authorization. Also a validity defence, or, more precisely, the lack thereof, can be raised. Due to the German concept of bifurcation, some peculiarities apply which are explained in more detail when discussing procedural aspects of injunctions in Germany. Theoretically, also an abuse of rights doctrine and the *venire contra factum proprium* doctrine exist, but they are rarely successful in Germany. The latter can, for example, be raised when the patentee argues in infringement proceedings contrary to his statements during prosecution or in opposition proceedings.[78] However, contradictory statements are not prohibited per se, but additional circumstances are required such as that the defendant also participated in the opposition proceedings and is allowed to trust in the patentee's statements in those proceedings.[79]

One defence, the FRAND defence, is currently vigorously discussed, not only in Germany. As Germany seems to have the highest number of FRAND-related cases (in Europe), this defence will be addressed in more detail below as an exemplary defence against injunction claims in Germany.

[1] FRAND Defence: Background

In the well-known case C-170/13 *Huawei v. ZTE*[80] the ECJ provided a general road map how to handle standard essential patents that were declared essential to a standardization body such as ETSI. The various obligations and counter-obligations of the patentee and the infringer and their dependency on each other can be summarized in Figure 4.1:

---

78. Johann Pitz in Uwe Fitzner, Raimund Lutz & Theo Bodewig (eds), BeckOK Patentrecht. Patentgesetz (7th ed., C.H. Beck 2018), s. 139, para. 205; Haedicke & Timmann, *supra* n. 15, margin no. 422.
79. Federal Supreme Court, NJW 1997, 3377, 3379 et seq. – *Weichvorrichtung II*; Federal Supreme Court, GRUR 2006, 923, 926 – *Luftabscheider für Milchsammelanlage*.
80. Case C-170/13 *Huawei Technologies v. ZTE*, 8 GRUR 764 (2015).

Figure 4.1   FRAND Road Map

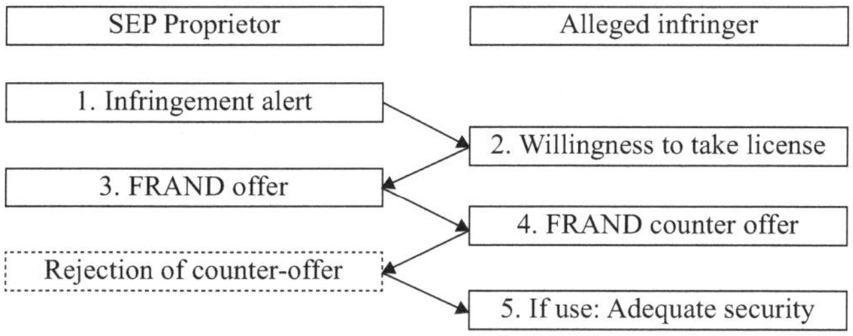

```
┌─────────────────────┐          ┌─────────────────────┐
│   SEP Proprietor    │          │  Alleged infringer  │
└─────────────────────┘          └─────────────────────┘
   ┌──────────────────────┐
   │ 1. Infringement alert│ ──▶
   └──────────────────────┘      ┌──────────────────────────┐
                                 │ 2. Willingness to take license │
   ┌──────────────────────┐      └──────────────────────────┘
   │    3. FRAND offer    │ ◀──
   └──────────────────────┘      ┌──────────────────────────┐
                                 │  4. FRAND counter offer  │
   ┌──────────────────────┐      └──────────────────────────┘
   │ Rejection of counter-offer │ ◀──
   └──────────────────────┘      ┌──────────────────────────────┐
                                 │ 5. If use: Adequate security │
                                 └──────────────────────────────┘
```

German courts already specified many aspects of these rather general rules provided by the ECJ. However, no Federal Supreme Court rulings are available yet. In the following paragraphs we will summarize some exemplary aspects from German case law with respect to these requirements.

[2]   Applicability

The above road map applies, according to the ECJ, to declared standard essential patents (SEPs) that provide the patentee with a dominant position. According to German case law, an SEP is not per se market dominant.[81] While this is generally accepted in telecommunications cases, the Regional Court of Mannheim questioned whether a patent that is essential for the compression standard HE AAC v2 provides the patentee with a market dominant position.[82]

In addition, it is worth noting that the Regional Court of Düsseldorf held that the ECJ road map shown above applies regardless of the identity of the proprietor of the SEP, i.e., whether the proprietor of the SEP is itself active on the product market at issue or a pure patent licensing company (NPE). It is further explained, that there is no reason to treat a patent licensing company any differently per se to a practising entity as the ECJ judgment does not comment on any restrictions for certain SEP proprietors. It was thus concluded that, in principle, each patentee has the same rights and obligations conferred by a patent, independently of its other activities and that it is not apparent that a differentiation is necessary on antitrust grounds.[83]

[3]   Infringement Alert

If the ECJ's road map is applicable, the patentee is required to notify the other party of the alleged infringement. He at least has to provide the publication number of the

---

81. Higher Regional Court of Düsseldorf, BeckRS 2017, 124408; Regional Court of Düsseldorf, 4b O 120/14.
82. Regional Court of Mannheim, 7 O 19/16.
83. Regional Court of Düsseldorf, 4a O 73/14; Regional Court of Düsseldorf, BeckRS 2016, 08040; *Cf. also* Higher Regional Court of Düsseldorf, GRUR-RS 2016, 1679.

patent(s) at issue, the attacked embodiment(s), and the alleged act(s) of infringement.[84] Further the Regional Court of Mannheim requests the designation of the standard.[85] There seems to be a tendency that claim charts can be presented at a later stage during the negotiations. The notification does not have to be sent to the infringing entity and neither to each national distribution subsidiary. It is sufficient for the patentee to send the notification to the parent company to negotiate a worldwide portfolio license.[86]

It is currently discussed whether the notification has to be sent prior to starting court proceedings or whether a notification or an amendment thereto provided after the service of the complaint should also be taken into account.[87] The courts originally disagreed on whether a delayed infringement notification inevitably results in a dismissal of the injunction or whether it may be disregarded if the alleged infringer is not willing to take a license or does not comply with his counter-obligations.[88] The same is discussed with respect to the timing of other obligations of the patentee and the alleged infringer. Very recently, a tendency to harmonize the case law by adopting the less strict approach of the Düsseldorf Courts can be noted.[89]

[4] Willingness

Upon reception of the infringement alert, the alleged infringer has to express his willingness to take a license without any delaying tactics.[90] As this can be a rather simple statement, a reply only after three months[91] or even after five months[92] was held to be delayed. However, the Higher Regional Court of Düsseldorf even accepted a reply one year after the initial infringement alert, as the willingness was expressed before the litigation was initiated.[93]

An infringer can be unwilling, if his willingness is conditional to a final judgment confirming infringement and validity of the SEP at issue.[94] Besides these (exceptional) cases, a lack of willingness has barely ever been accepted by the courts, even though often questioned by the patentee.

---

84. Regional Court of Düsseldorf, 4a O 73/14.
85. Regional Court of Mannheim, GRUR-RS 2016, 18389.
86. Higher Regional Court of Düsseldorf, GRUR-RS 2016, 1679; Regional Court of Mannheim, GRUR-RS 2016, 4228.
87. *Cf.*, for example, Regional Court of Mannheim, GRUR-RS 2016, 06527; Regional Court of Mannheim, GRUR-RS 2015, 20077; Regional Court of Mannheim, 2 O 107/14; Regional Court of Düsseldorf, 4a O 73/14; Regional Court of Düsseldorf, BeckRS 2016, 08040.
88. Regional Court of Mannheim, GRUR-RS 2016, 06527; Regional Court of Mannheim, GRUR-RS 2015, 20077; Regional Court of Düsseldorf, 4a O 73/14.
89. Regional Court of Mannheim, 7 O 43/16; Higher Regional Court of Karlsruhe, GRUR-RS 2016, 10660.
90. Higher Regional Court of Düsseldorf, GRUR-RS 2016, 9323.
91. Regional Court of Mannheim, WuW 2016, 86.
92. Regional Court of Düsseldorf, BeckRS 2016, 08040.
93. Higher Regional Court of Düsseldorf, I-15 U 66/15.
94. Regional Court of Düsseldorf, BeckRS 2016, 08040; Higher Regional Court of Düsseldorf, I-15 U 66/15.

[5] FRAND Offer

If the alleged infringer is willing to take a license, the patentee has to provide a FRAND license offer. The offer can regularly be addressed to the parent company, especially if a worldwide license if offered.[95]

The available case law suggests that worldwide portfolio license offers are possible, if such licenses are customary in the respective industry.[96] In addition, the offer has to specify a royalty rate. Offering determination of the royalty rate by a third party was not accepted.[97] In contrast to other jurisdictions, a range of royalty rates can be FRAND.[98]

The patentee also has to explain the method of calculating the royalty rate and why he thinks the offer is FRAND.[99] According to the Regional Court of Mannheim, these explanations must be 'intersubjectively comprehensible' (*'intersubjektiv nachvollziehbar'*).[100] Further guidance by the court is expected soon to clarify what satisfies this 'intersubjective comprehensibility test'. It is at least not enough for the patentee to present the license programme in general.[101]

These additional explanations to justify that the requested royalty rate is FRAND are the most burdensome for the patentee. As a rule of thumb, the more the patentee presents, the better. This especially applies with respect to the non-discriminatory part of the patentee's FRAND obligations, as the German courts generally request the patentee to disclose comparable existing licenses. These often play a major role in the assessment of the patentee's licensing offer.[102]

The requirement to present existing licenses often raises issues of confidentiality. The German judicial system is based on the concept of transparency, but which is not to be misunderstood that everything will be shared with the public. While oral hearings are generally public (but the public has, for example, been excluded when discussion existing licensing agreements), written submissions are not and can thus not be accessed by third parties. Judgments will be published, but only in an anonymized form. However, all documents presented to the court also have to be shared with the other party. A disclosure to the attorney of the other party only is not possible.[103] A protective order, such as in the USA, does not exist. Therefore, NDAs are the best tool to ensure confidentiality in Germany. As the infringer is obliged to further the licensing negotiations, he is generally required to enter into an NDA and to accept a severe

---

95. Regional Court of Düsseldorf, GRUR-RS 2015, 19564; Regional Court of Mannheim, GRUR-RS 2016, 06527.
96. Regional Court of Mannheim, GRUR-RS 2016, 06527; Regional Court of Düsseldorf, 4a O 73/14.
97. Regional Court of Mannheim, GRUR-RS 2015, 20077; Regional Court of Düsseldorf, 4a O 73/14.
98. Higher Regional Court of Karlsruhe, GRUR-RS 2016, 17467.
99. Regional Court of Mannheim, BeckRS 2016, 108197.
100. Regional Court of Mannheim, 7 O 28/16.
101. Regional Court of Mannheim GRUR-RS 2016, 18389.
102. *Cf.*, for example, Higher Regional Court of Düsseldorf, I-15 U 66/15.
103. Higher Regional Court of Düsseldorf, BeckRS 2016, 114380.

contractual penalty clause[104] amounting to, for example, EUR 1 million for each breach of the confidentiality obligations.[105] However, even if the infringer refuses to sign a (reasonable) NDA, the patentee still has to provide as much evidence as possible to prove that his offer is non-discriminatory.[106]

The German courts (now) fully assess whether an offer is FRAND. The previous ruling of the Regional Court of Mannheim which only wanted to check whether the offer is evidently not FRAND by way of a summary examination[107] was overturned in appeal.[108] The Düsseldorf Courts, in contrast, always understood the ECJ judgment to require the courts to fully examine whether the offer is FRAND or not.[109]

Procedurally, it has been discussed whether a patentee can make up for an insufficient FRAND offer after initiating injunction proceedings. The Regional Court of Mannheim used to be very strict and requested a FRAND offer prior to lodging the complaint. To present an updated offer, the patentee had to withdraw and re-file its complaint (and thereby loosing time and having to bear the costs for the initial proceedings).[110] The Düsseldorf courts have been more generous and considered the interaction between obligations and counter-obligations: it is possible to amend an existing or present a new FRAND offer after filing the complaint, in particular if the infringer originally failed or hesitated to express his willingness to take a license.[111] It seems from later decisions that the Regional Court of Mannheim and the Higher Regional Court of Karlsruhe gradually converge to this case law.[112]

[6] Counter-Offer

If the alleged infringer does not accept the offer by the patentee he has to make a FRAND counter-offer within a reasonable timeframe. In principle, the same rules apply as explained with respect to the patentee's offer.

If both offers are FRAND and still no consent on the royalty rate can be reached, the parties may agree on arbitration.[113] According to one opinion, the FRAND defence continues to prevent an injunction from being issued for the time of the arbitration.[114]

---

104. *Ibid.*
105. Higher Regional Court of Düsseldorf, BeckRS 2016, 114213.
106. Higher Regional Court of Düsseldorf, I-2 U 23/17; Regional Court of Düsseldorf, 4a O 154/15.
107. Regional Court of Mannheim, GRUR-RS 2016, 06527; Regional Court of Mannheim, GRUR-RS 2016, 4228.
108. Higher Regional Court of Karlsruhe, GRUR-RS 2016, 17467.
109. Higher Regional Court of Düsseldorf, GRUR-RS 2016, 1679; Higher Regional Court of Düsseldorf, GRUR 2017, 1219.
110. Regional Court of Mannheim, GRUR-RS 2016, 06527; Regional Court of Mannheim, GRUR-RS 2015, 20077.
111. Regional Court of Düsseldorf, 4a 73/14; Regional Court of Düsseldorf, BeckRS 2016, 08040.
112. Regional Court of Mannheim, 7 O 43/16; Higher Regional Court of Karlsruhe, GRUR-RS 2016, 10660.
113. ECJ, C-170/13 *Huawei v. ZTE*; Regional Court of Mannheim, 2 O 108/14.
114. Thomas Kühnen, *Verspätete Lizenzierungsbemühungen bei standardessentiellen Patenten mit FRAND-Erklärung* in Thomas Kühnen (ed.), *Festschrift 80 Jahre Patentgerichtsbarkeit in Düsseldorf* (Carl Heymanns Verlag 2016), 315.

[7] Security and Rendering of Account

Finally, if the counter-offer is rejected and if the alleged infringer already has products on the market, he has to provide a security payment at least in the amount of the royalty rate for past sales based on his counter-offer.[115] This obligation does not cease to exist, if the alleged infringer terminates the use of the patent.[116] In addition, he is obliged to render account.

§4.03 PROCEDURAL ASPECTS

In this section, exemplary procedural aspects of German patent infringement proceedings are summarized. Generally, proceedings on the merits and preliminary injunction proceedings are to be distinguished. As preliminary injunctions are a powerful tool in Germany to quickly and efficiently enforce patent rights, special emphasis will be placed on these proceedings.

[A] Proceedings on the Merits

[1] Competent Courts and Instances

An injunction can be granted already at first instance by the Regional Court ('*Landgericht*'). Twelve courts in Germany are competent to hear patent cases. Said courts have specialized chambers consisting of three legal judges. The Regional Courts in Düsseldorf, Mannheim, Munich and Hamburg deal with hundreds of patent cases each year.[117] This ensures decisions of extraordinarily high quality.

In general, all decisions of the Regional Court can be appealed to the Higher Regional Court ('*Oberlandesgericht*'). In contrast to other jurisdictions, no special permission to appeal is required. Just like the chambers of the Regional Courts, those of the Higher Regional Court (called 'senates') also consist of three legal judges. Further permission to appeal on questions of law to the Federal Supreme Court ('*Bundesgerichtshof*') might be granted either by the Higher Regional Court or – upon request – by the Federal Supreme Court itself.

[2] Course of Infringement Proceedings

The courts generally invite the parties to submit two briefs each prior to the oral hearing. As the courts are generally very well prepared and summarize their initial views at the beginning of the hearing, a focussed discussion is possible. Oral hearings will thus normally take a couple of hours at most. The court will regularly deliver its

---

115. Regional Court of Mannheim, 2 O 107/14, 2 O 108/14.
116. Regional Court of Mannheim, GRUR-RS 2016, 06527.
117. Kühnen & Claessen, *supra* n. 2 at 592–593.

judgment about four to six weeks after hearing, unless post-trial briefs are allowed. Sometimes the decision will be rendered at the end of the oral hearing.

A first instance decision may, depending on the workload of the court, be handed down within nine to twenty-four months after filing. Similar timelines apply before the Higher Regional Court. Proceedings at the Federal Supreme Court take about another year or more.

[3] Bifurcation

One of the main principles in patent litigation in Germany is the so-called bifurcation ('*Trennungsprinzip*'). Bifurcation basically means that infringement and nullity proceedings are separate from each other.

While infringement cases are heard by Regional Courts, the Higher Regional Courts and the Federal Supreme Court, validity proceedings (opposition and nullity) are heard by the German Patent and Trademark Office, the Federal Patent Court and the Federal Supreme Court.

In practice, bifurcation especially has the following effects: the infringement courts do not have the capacity to invalidate a patent. Neither are they entitled to dismiss a case if the patent in suit is considered to be invalid. The defendant may, however, file a motion to stay the infringement proceedings in order to await the outcome of pending nullity or opposition proceedings (in first instance). The decision to stay the infringement proceedings is in the discretion of the infringement court. In general the courts are reluctant to order a stay as they recognize the impact of lengthy validity proceedings (which regularly take significantly longer than infringement proceedings) on the plaintiff's ability to enforce his time-limited patent. The infringement courts thus request a high likelihood that the patent in suit will be revoked in nullity or opposition proceedings.[118] An additional aspect that can be taken into account is, for example, whether a nullity action was timely filed (i.e., in parallel to the statement of defence) or only with (significant) delay.[119]

However, bifurcation does not mean that the infringement courts are bound by the construction or even the decision of the opposition division/nullity court.[120] If the infringement court is convinced that the ruling on the patent's validity is evidently wrong and will thus be overturned in appeal, it can stay a case even though a patent was upheld in first instance validity proceedings or grant the injunction despite the patent currently being revoked by a non-final decision.[121] It is needless to say, that the infringement courts are very reluctant to issue an injunction based on a currently revoked patent (and vice versa). In fact, the famous 'Olanzapin' decision of the Higher

---

118. Federal Supreme Court, GRUR 2014, 1237, para. 4 – *Kurznachrichten*; Federal Supreme Court, GRUR 1987, 284 – *Transportfahrzeuge*.
119. Federal Supreme Court, GRUR 2012, 93, 94 – *Klimaschrank*.
120. Federal Supreme Court, GRUR 2015, 972 – *Kreuzgestänge*; Regional Court of Düsseldorf BeckRS 2016, 20419.
121. Higher Regional Court of Düsseldorf, GRUR-RR 2008, 329, 331 – *Olanzipin*.

Regional Court of Düsseldorf might have been the only case in the last decade in which the court assessed validity in contrast to the first instance validity decision.[122]

[4] Evidence

In proceedings on the merits evidence may be taken by hearing witnesses, experts or the parties themselves. Also documentary evidence and inspections by the court are possible. In patent law cases, documentary evidence and experts are the most common tools. Under German law only court appointed (and therefore independent) experts are eligible for expert evidence as such. Any expert opinion submitted by a party is only part of the pleadings of the respective party but no evidence in a strict legal sense. A party-appointed expert has nevertheless proven to be effective as it improves the credibility of the factual statements of the respective party, especially in technically complex cases.

Each party has the burden of presentation and proof with respect to the facts that establish their case. In other, simplified words, plaintiff has to show infringement whereas defendant has to present and proof any defences (but exceptions apply, e.g., regarding complex defences such as the FRAND defence).

However, it should be noted that evidence is only taken with respect to facts that are validly disputed by the other party. As the factual basis of a case (e.g., the components of an attacked embodiment such as a drug or the requirements of a standard in a SEP case) are often undisputed, evidence is only taken in exceptional cases, which is one of the reasons why infringement proceedings in Germany are generally rather quick.

[5] Enforcement

First instance decisions, including injunctions, are usually provisionally enforceable. Plaintiff is regularly required to provide a security though (usually by way of a bank guarantee) as the decision is not final and might be overruled in the second instance. The enforcement of an appeal decision does not require such security. The enforcement of a first instance decision under appeal can give rise to a damage claim by the defendant if it is not upheld in appeal.

A defendant has the option to request a stay of the enforcement of the first instance decision. However, the threshold is rather high and the request is thus not successful in most cases. In general it is held that the security provided will adequately protect the defendant's interests,[123] in particular if the patent in suit is about to expire.[124] A stay is ordered only in exceptional cases, if the judgement is evidently

---

122. Ibid.
123. Higher Regional Court of Düsseldorf, I-15 U 132/14; Higher Regional Court of Karlsruhe, GRUR-RR 2015, 326 – Mobiltelefone; Higher Regional Court of Düsseldorf, GRUR-RR 2010, 122.
124. Kühnen, supra n. 4, Ch. H, para. 33.

wrong or if the defendant can show that the enforcement would cause damages exceeding the usual damages caused by the enforcement of an injunction.[125]

[B] Preliminary Injunctions

A preliminary injunction (PI) is a common tool in German patent law. Generally, a PI has the same effect as an injunction granted in proceedings on the merits (the exception as regards the 'implicit' recall claim has already been addressed above) and can thus quickly and efficiently prevent patent infringing activities from taking place or from being continued.

In this section, some peculiarities of PI proceedings in Germany will be summarized. It is by no means meant to be exhaustive.

[1] Competent Courts and Instances

Generally, the courts handling patent infringement proceedings on the merits are also competent to hear PI cases. However, most PI requests are filed with the courts in Düsseldorf, Munich and Hamburg and some also in Braunschweig. In preliminary injunction proceedings, there are only two instead of three instances; a second appeal on questions of law to the Federal Supreme Court is not possible.

[2] Course of PI Infringement Proceedings

A PI can be granted ex parte or *inter partes*. An ex parte PI, i.e., a PI granted without prior notice to the defendant and without oral hearing, has to be requested by the applicant. In very urgent cases, such as trade fairs, such ex parte PI can be obtained within a day or two. Otherwise, the court will issue its decision within about two weeks. If an ex parte PI is granted, the defendant can file an opposition with the first instance court which will then schedule an oral hearing and decide whether or not the ex parte PI is upheld. The losing party can then file an appeal.

The most common tool to avoid an ex parte injunction is to file a protective brief with the central register for protective briefs (*'zentrales Schutzschriftenregister'*). Whenever a PI application is received, the courts check this register for protective briefs and take it into consideration. A protective brief can be understood as an anticipated statement of defence. However, its usual purpose is to prevent the court from issuing an ex parte PI, not to get the PI request dismissed right away.

If no ex parte PI is requested by the applicant or if the court decides to hear the defendant prior to its ruling (especially if it is not fully convinced that the patent is both valid and infringed, e.g., based on the arguments presented by the defendant in a protective brief), *inter partes* PI proceedings will take place. *Inter partes* proceedings also run on a tight schedule. An oral hearing will regularly take place a couple of weeks

---

125. Higher Regional Court of Düsseldorf, GRUR-RS 2016, 1679.

or at most a few months after filing the PI request and a judgment will be issued either at the end of the hearing or shortly thereafter. Also in *inter partes* proceedings, the PI decision can be appealed.

Accordingly, ex parte and *inter partes* PI proceedings are different in that in ex parte PI proceedings an injunction is granted first and the defendant is heard thereafter, whereas in *inter partes* proceedings it is the other way around.

[3]   Urgency

An important difference to proceedings on the merits is that a PI can only be granted in urgent cases. Urgency is not only a matter of time but the particular circumstances of the case must be taken into account.[126]

Most courts consider a matter urgent if an application for a preliminary injunction is filed within four weeks after finding out about the infringing acts, others allow six weeks to pass. This general timeframe can of course vary depending upon the complexity of the case and other individual circumstances. The 'urgency clock' does generally not start before the patentee has actually taken note of the infringement. A negligent lack of knowledge is irrelevant.[127] However, if a patentee does not investigate obvious indications that an infringement might take place, this can allow the conclusion that the patentee has no (urgent) interest in pursuing its rights.[128]

[4]   Validity of the Patent

The validity of the patent is also taken into account in PI proceedings, if an opposition or nullity suit is pending.[129] In contrast to proceedings on the merits, a court will not stay the proceedings if it has doubts as regards the patent's validity as this would be contrary to the concept of PI proceedings to provide a decision on short notice if urgently required (*see* above §4.03 [B] [4]).

The standard to assess validity is different from proceedings on the merits. In PI proceedings, it is upon the patentee to convince the court that the patent in suit is valid.[130] Accordingly, as a general rule (at least according to the Düsseldorf and Mannheim/Karlsruhe courts), only patents can be asserted in PI proceedings that already survived at least first instance opposition or nullity proceedings.[131] This principle sounds much more restrictive than it actually is in practice as the courts established multiple exceptions allowing to assert a patent in PI proceedings that has not yet been confirmed in opposition or nullity proceedings, such as:

---

126. Higher Regional Court of Hamburg, GRUR-RR 2008, 366 – *Simplify your Production*.
127. Kühnen, *supra* n. 4, Ch. G, para. 121.
128. Higher Regional Court of Düsseldorf, BeckRS 2014, 01174; Kühnen, *supra* n. 4, Ch. G, para. 122.
129. Higher Regional Court of Düsseldorf, GRUR-RR 2007, 219 – *Kleinleistungsschalter*.
130. Kühnen, *supra* n. 4, Ch. G, para. 121.
131. Higher Regional Court of Düsseldorf, InstGE 12, 114–125 – *Harnkatheterset*; Higher Regional Court of Karlsruhe, BeckRS 2015, 16515; differing opinion: Higher Regional Court of Braunschweig, GRUR-RR 2012, 97 – *Scharniere auf Hannovermesse*.

- A patent is about to expire and there is no chance to obtain an injunction in proceedings on the merits.[132]
- The defendant was involved in the prosecution and already presented prior art; the decision to grant a patent is thus comparable to a decision in opposition or nullity proceedings.[133]
- The patent's validity has been widely accepted, e.g., if various well-known companies have taken a license.[134]
- The arguments challenging the patent's validity are obviously unfounded.[135]
- Other peculiarities of a case require an exception, which is, for example, assumed in the case of generic drug infringing a patent of the originator as the generics company, on the one hand, takes little to no economic risk in launching a generic version of a well-established drug and a delayed market entrance due to a PI will only cause minor disadvantages for the generics company, whereas the originator, on the other hand, faces an irrevocable drop in the sales price of his product even if the generic drug would only be on the market until a first instance decision on the merits is obtained.[136]

Accordingly, especially if such an exception can be established, the validity discussion in PI proceedings is basically identical to one in proceedings on the merits.

[5] Weighting of Interests

A further peculiarity of PI proceedings is the requirement to consider and weigh the interests of the applicant and the defendant up against one another. Usually the interests of the patent proprietor prevail if there is sufficient evidence showing the infringement of the asserted patent and supporting the patent's validity.[137] This especially applies in pharma cases for the reasons already outlined above.[138]

[6] Prima Facie Evidence

In preliminary injunction proceedings, no 'full' proof of facts is required (or possible) but prima facie evidence is sufficient. According to established case law, to obtain a PI an 'overwhelming likelihood' of infringement is sufficient, which means that after assessment of all means of prima facie evidence the court finds it more likely that the alleged facts are true than vice versa.[139] While the standard in proceedings on the merits is theoretically different (the court has to be convinced to a degree that no

---

132. Higher Regional Court of Düsseldorf, GRUR RS- 2014, 04902 – *Desogestrel*.
133. Higher Regional Court of Düsseldorf, InstGE 12, 114 – Harnkatheterset.
134. *Ibid.*
135. *Ibid.*
136. Higher Regional Court of Düsseldorf, GRUR RS- 2014, 04902 – *Desogestrel*; Higher Regional Court of Düsseldorf, GRUR-RR 2013, 236, 240 – *Flupirtin-Maleat*.
137. Higher Regional Court of Düsseldorf, I-2 U 41/11.
138. *Cf. also* Higher Regional Court of Düsseldorf, GRUR-RR 2013, 236, 240 – *Flupirtin-Maleat*.
139. Federal Supreme Court, NJW-RR 2011, 136, 137.

reasonable doubts remain[140]), this does regularly not play any role in PI proceedings, probably as they are regularly handled just like proceedings on the merits (on an accelerated timeline).

Prima facie evidence can generally be provided in the same way as in proceedings on the merits. However, two important differences apply. First of all, affidavits are allowed as prima facie evidence which is actually the most common way to prove contested facts in PI proceedings. Second, due to the urgent nature of PI proceedings (*see* above §4.03 [B] [3]), only readily available means of evidence will be taken into consideration. The court will thus not take evidence by a court-appointed expert or schedule an additional hearing to hear witnesses that are not present in the first one.

[7]   Enforcement

Both ex parte and *inter partes* first instance PI decisions can be enforced by the applicant but who regularly has to provide a security. While there is no obligation to enforce a PI in a strict sense, an applicant can request the PI to be lifted if it is not enforced within a month. It should further be noted that the enforcement of a PI can give rise to a damage claim by the defendant, if the PI was ultimately unjustified (i.e., if revoked in second instance or if the patent is ultimately revoked in opposition of nullity proceedings).

---

140. Federal Supreme Court, NJW 2004, 777, 778.

CHAPTER 5
Injunctions in French Patent Law

Amandine Léonard

§5.01 INTRODUCTION

[A] Legislative Framework

Patent law provisions are enclosed in the French Intellectual Property Code (IPC). Other relevant provisions are to be found in the Civil Code, the Commercial Code and the Code of Civil Procedure. Provisions of the IPC have gradually been amended to comply with international treaties, such as the Agreement on Trade-Related Aspects of Intellectual Property Rights (TRIPs), as well as to implement European Union Directives. The European Directive 2004/48 on the enforcement of intellectual property rights (Enforcement Directive)[1] was, with a certain delay, implemented into French law by the law n°2007-1544 of 29 October 2007 on Fighting Counterfeiting.[2] Further provisions have been introduced by the law n°2014-315 of 11 March 2014.[3]

[B] Competent Court

It is the ordinary civil court of the *Tribunal de Grande Instance de Paris* (Paris District Court) and on appeal the *Cour d'appel de Paris* (Paris Court of Appeal), which have

---

1. Directive 2004/48/EC of the European Parliament and of the Council of 29 April 2004 on the enforcement of intellectual property rights, OJ L 157/45.
2. Loi n° 2007-1544 du 29 octobre 2007 de lutte contre la contrefaçon (1) (JORF n°252 du 30 octobre 2007 page 17775).
3. LOI n° 2014-315 du 11 mars 2014 renforçant la lutte contre la contrefaçon (1) (JORF n°0060 du 12 mars 2014 page 5112).

exclusive jurisdiction over patent cases.[4] Four Paris District Court chambers and two Paris Court of Appeal chambers[5] are specialized in intellectual property matters. The panels are composed of three judges. Issues of infringement and validity are heard and examined together in the same action. Decisions of the Paris Court of Appeal may be further appealed before the highest civil court in France, i.e., the *Cour de Cassation* (*chambre commerciale*). The Court will only examine issues of law and not issues of fact.

[C] Patent Litigation in France

On the one hand, France is an attractive forum for patent litigation for multiple reasons, e.g., the size of the French market, the fact that litigation involves relatively reasonable costs, and the availability of the *saisie-contrefacon*. On the other hand, and compared to other jurisdictions, the amounts of damages usually granted by French courts in infringement actions are relatively low. They might not seem extremely engaging to patent holders.[6] With an average of 400 new patent matters per year, French courts are one of the most active courts in Europe for patent litigation.[7] They are placed second behind German courts in terms of patent cases.[8] On average and in patent matter, the Paris District Court issues eighty decisions each year, 60% of which are the subject of an appeal. The Paris Court of Appeal issues an average of forty-five decisions each year and an average of twenty decisions are issued by the *Cour de cassation*.[9] Although French Courts are not bound by the rule of precedent, they give consideration to previous decision of other French courts (in particular the *Cour de cassation*). Moreover, they also consider and refer to decisions of the European Patent Office (EPO) Board of Appeal, and to decisions of foreign courts.

---

4. Including all matters involving validity, infringement, entitlement and related unfair competition law claims. Before 2009, the district courts of Paris, Lyon, Marseilles, Bordeaux, Rennes, Strasbourg, Limoges, Nancy and Toulouse shared jurisdiction over patent cases.
5. Two sections of Division 5 of the Court of Appeal are specialized in IP matters and are dealing with appeals from the Paris District Court. Division 1 of the Court of Appeal is not specialized in IP matters but is dealing with appeals of preliminary injunctions decisions when the action on the merits has not yet been initiated and has developed a certain expertise in this matter.
6. According to a study in 2014, on average, damages are below EUR 50.000. (*Étude comparée sur les dommages et intérêts alloués dans le cadre des actions en contrefaçon en France, au Royaume-Uni et en Allemagne*, http://www.entreprises.gouv.fr/files/files/directions_services/etudes-et-statistiques/etudes/dommages-interets-dans-actions-en-contrefacon.pdf accessed 31 Jul. 2018); *See also,* Stuart J.H. Graham & Nicolas van Zeebroeck, *Comparing Patent Litigation Across Europe: A First Look*, 17 Stan. Tech. Law Rev. 655, 655–708 (2014), available at SSRN: http://ssrn.com/abstract=1924124 (accessed 31 Jul. 2018).
7. Thomas Bouvet, *Chapter 17: France* in Michael C. Elmer, C. Gregory Gramemopoulos (eds), *Global Patent Litigation – How and Where to Win* (Bloomberg BNA 2014), 545 and 577.
8. Katrin Cremers, Maximilian Ernicke, Fabian Gaessler, Dietmar Harhoff, Christian Helmers, Luke McDonagh, Paula Schliessler, Nicolas van Zeebroeck, *Patent Litigation in Europe*, ZEW Discussion Paper, No. 13-072 (2013).
9. Pierre Véron, *Le contentieux des brevets d'invention en France. Etude statistique 2000–2009* (2010), https://www.veron.com/veron/publications/Colloques/Stats_contentieux_brevets_France_2000-2009_Veron_et_Associes.pdf (accessed 31 Jul. 2018); For a detailed table on annual patent litigation decisions in France from 2000 to 2011 *see* Bouvet, *supra* n. 7, at 549.

[D] Remark on Recent Developments

Before April 2015, there was no requirement for applicants to contact defendants before initiating an action at the Paris District Court. Since a ministerial decree[10] modifying the French Code of Civil Procedure there is a new obligation for applicants. It is now required that the writ of summons specifies which steps have been undertaken by the parties to reach an amicable solution. This constitutes a mandatory requirement. Few exceptions exist to this new obligation, i.e., if the applicant proves it has legitimate reasons pertaining to urgency not to do so or legitimate reasons related to the matter under consideration, in particular when the *ordre public* is concerned. This provision entered into force on 1 April 2015; therefore its application and the exact meaning of 'legitimate reasons' which could be evoked in patent litigation are still unclear at this point in time. The sanctions for failure to comply with this requirement are also to be tested in court.

§5.02 INJUNCTIVE RELIEF: CONDITIONS AND FLEXIBILITY

Under French law, an injunction (*'injonction'*, *'mesure d'interdiction'*, *'ordre de cessation'*) is an order, delivered by a judicial authority to a patent holder, upon request, to prohibit (or put an end to) the exploitation of an object protected by an intellectual property right. The order can aim at acts considered as direct infringement (Article L613-3 IPC[11]) as well as contributory infringement (Article L613-4 IPC). Two different types of injunctions are available to patent holders, preliminary injunctions and permanent injunctions. When it comes to injunctive relief, French judges do benefit from some, but nonetheless limited, discretionary powers.

[A] Preliminary Injunctions

Preliminary injunctions are governed by Article L615-3 IPC. These measures aim at preventing any imminent infringement or at stopping the continuation of allegedly infringing acts. They consist in a court order essentially requiring a defendant to cease the allegedly infringing activities.[12] It is argued that since the law of 2007 implementing the Enforcement Directive, French courts have granted more easily preliminary

---

10. Décret n° 2015-282 du 11 mars 2015 relatif à la simplification de la procédure civile à la communication électronique et à la résolution amiable des différends (JORF n°0062 du 14 mars 2015 page 4851). New Art. 56 al.3 of the Code of Civil Procédure: 'Sauf justification d'un motif légitime tenant à l'urgence ou à la matière considérée, en particulier lorsqu'elle intéresse l'ordre public, l'assignation précise également les diligences entreprises en vue de parvenir à une résolution amiable du litige'.
11. Article L613-3 IPC has been modified in 2014 to include acts of exportation and transshipment (in French: *transbordement* – i.e., applicable to goods issued from or going to non-EU countries which are in transit in Europe). Art. 6, LOI n° 2014-315 du 11 mars 2014 renforçant la lutte contre la contrefaçon (1) (JORF n°0060 du 12 mars 2014 page 5112).
12. They can also consist in the recall from the channels of commerce or order to disclose particular information.

injunctions than in the past.[13] The implementation led to some modifications of the conditions to obtain preliminary injunctions and these changes have made it easier for patent holders to obtain interim relief.[14] For example, the need for urgency has been eliminated. The text of Article L615-3 IPC now shares the same wording as Article 9.3 of the Enforcement Directive. Preliminary proceedings can be initiated either before or after the introduction of an action on the merits and are decided by one judge. If they are initiated before the introduction of an action on the merits, preliminary injunctions can be requested before the judge in charge of preliminary proceedings (*juge des référés*). In practice, it is the President of one of the panels of the Paris District Court who will handle preliminary proceedings. When an action on the merits has been initiated, the request has to be made to the judge in charge of the case preparation. Preliminary injunctions can be obtained in an *inter partes* or ex parte (rarely)[15] procedure and will be granted until a decision on the merits is reached.

Two main conditions must be met to obtain a preliminary injunction. According to Article L615-3 IPC, applicants for a preliminary injunction must prove they have standing to sue for infringement (first condition) and that evidence, reasonably accessible to them, makes it likely that their rights are infringed or that such infringement is imminent (second condition).[16] Regarding the first condition, applicants must demonstrate that they are the owner of patents still in force. In theory, applicants could also request a preliminary injunction on the basis of patent applications. However, chances to actually obtain the measure on this basis are quite slim. According to Article L615-2 IPC[17] applicants can either be the owners of the patents or exclusive licensees (under certain conditions). Regarding the second condition, since preliminary orders are not decisions on the merits, French judges have to decide in the framework of prima facie validity and likelihood of infringement. Before 2009 and the centralization of patent litigation at the Paris District Court, the presumption of validity led judges to solely base their decisions on whether applicants provided evidence that their rights were likely infringed or that an infringement was imminent. Exceptionally, if patents were manifestly invalid, judges would deny the grant of a preliminary injunction. Since 2009, the situation has changed. French judges not only question

---

13. AIPPI Question Q219 – Groupe français, *Mesures d'interdiction en cas de contrefaçon de droits de propriété intellectuelle* (2011), https://aippi.org/download/commitees/219/GR219france.pdf (accessed 31 Jul. 2018), 21; Bouvet, *supra* n. 7, at 553.
14. Old Art. L615-3 IPC: 'The request for an injunction or for furnishing of a guarantee shall only be granted if the substantive proceedings appear well-founded and are instituted within a short time of the day on which the patentee became aware of the facts on which the proceedings are based' (translation from WIPO).
15. Isabelle Romet, Amandine Métier & Dora Talvard, *Patent Enforcement in France*, in Christopher Heath (ed.), *Patent Enforcement Worldwide: Writings in Honour of Dieter Stauder* (3rd Revised ed., Hart Publishing 2015), 161.
16. Laurence Petit, *The Enforcement of Patent Rights in France*, in Christopher Heath & Laurence Petit (eds), *Patent Enforcement Worldwide: A Survey of 15 Countries: Writings in Honour of Dieter Stauder* (2nd ed., Hart Publishing 2005), 160; Bouvet, *supra* n. 7, at 552; Romet, Métier & Talvard, *supra* n. 15, at 160. AIPPI Question Q219, *supra* n. 13, at 5.
17. Article L615-2 IPC: 'Infringement proceedings shall be instituted by the owner of the patent. However, the beneficiary of an exclusive right of working may, except as otherwise stipulated in the licensing contract, institute infringement proceedings if, after notice, the owner of the patent does not institute such proceedings' (translation from WIPO).

whether there is a potential infringement but also whether the validity of the asserted patents is not seriously contested or if the titles are not obviously invalid. For example, judges may be reluctant to grant a preliminary injunction if an opposition has been filed with the EPO, if revealed prior art is manifestly susceptible to impact the validity of the patents, or if defendants filed a declaration of non-infringement (Article L615-9 IPC). This approach is generally supported by French doctrine[18] and considered to be in line with Article 9 of the Enforcement Directive as well as Article 50 of the TRIPs Agreement.[19] In 2014, the French *Cour de cassation* also strengthened the conditions to obtain ex parte preliminary injunctions.[20] These measures will only be granted ex parte if the applicant can demonstrate the need for the defendant not to be heard and if an injunction is deemed necessary because any delay would cause irreparable harm to the applicant. Ex parte proceedings are therefore highly exceptional.[21] Moreover, in case of injunction granted ex parte, it is still possible for the defendant to institute third party proceedings (*tierce opposition*) before the judge in charge of preliminary proceedings (*procédure en référé*)[22] and to request that interim measures be suspended or withdrawn.[23] In the same vein, it should be noted that, according to Article 524 of the Code of Civil Procedure: 'The first President [of the TGI] may suspend provisional enforcement in the event of a manifest breach of the adversarial principle ... and where execution is likely to have manifestly excessive consequences'.

Upon court order, decisions in preliminary proceedings can be immediately enforceable, notwithstanding an appeal. However, if the decisions are lately reversed, the party enforcing a preliminary injunction may have to compensate the other party.[24] In 2014, the Paris Court of Appeal held that, although an order can be enforced notwithstanding appeal, it is at the risk of the beneficiary of the measure. If a patent is later found invalid or if it is found that the measures were not justified, compensation must take place. The Court considered that such compensation was the counterpart of the exceptional prerogative granted to the applicant to apply for, and to obtain, preliminary injunctions. The Court therefore clarified that a regime of liability without fault could apply in case of enforcement of preliminary injunctions.[25]

---

18. As mentioned in Jean-Christophe Galloux, *Quelques précisions relatives aux mesures provisoires en matière de contrefaçon*', 12(4) Propriété Industrielle, 3 (2013).
19. *Ibid.*; Jean-Pierre Gasnier, 'Quelques observations à propos de la loi de lutte contre la contrefaçon', 6(12) Propriété Industrielle 4 (2007). The Enforcement Directive insists on the right of defence and the proportionality of measures. Parliamentary debates of the law of 2007 implementing the Directive into French law show that it was notably important to protect defendants against predation, since some right holders might use infringement action as a mean to remove a competitor from the market.
20. Cass. Com. 16 Sep. 2014, *Sanofi and Zentiva c. Novartis*, n 13-10.189.
21. Bouvet, *supra* n. 7, at 554; Romet, Métier & Talvard, *supra* n. 15, at 161.
22. An even speedier procedure is also provided for in Art. 485 of the Code of Civil Procedure, called *référé d'heure à heure*. In such exceptional cases, urgency is required and a decision will be made between forty-eight hours and few days.
23. *See also*, Art. 497 of the Code of Civil Procedure.
24. Bouvet, *supra* n. 7, at 553; Romet, Métier & Talvard, *supra* n. 15, at 162.
25. CA Paris (2e ch.) 31 Jan. 2014, *SAS Laboratoires Negma c. SAS Biogaran* (RG 12/05485). The Court of Appeal stated that Art. L111-10 of the Code of Civil Procedure, which establishes a strict and automatic liability regime in case of enforcement of first-instance order, was clear and did not need to be interpreted in light of Art. 9.7 of the Enforcement Directive or the European

In general, it can be contended that French judges are quite cautious in awarding preliminary injunctions. They avert granting measures that would be based on a patent later found invalid or not infringed.[26] The assessment of validity in all cases leads to a quite thorough review of the validity of patents by French judges. The current review process of the conditions to obtain a preliminary injunction is said to be an adequate way for judges to weight the interests of the parties involved. It allows judge to take into consideration, on the one hand, the potential harm suffered by the applicant due to infringement, and, on the other hand, the potential negative and usually irreparable consequences of the grant of such measure on the alleged infringer.[27] Moreover, the text of Article L615-3 IPC clearly stipulates that, if the conditions are met, judges *may* grant the measures. The literal interpretation of the text therefore leads to the conclusion that, even if the conditions are met, judges still benefit from a certain margin of appreciation and may refuse to grant a preliminary injunction if they deem so appropriate.[28]

[B] Permanent Injunctions

The relevant provisions are Articles L611-1, L613-3 and L613-4 IPC read in combination with Article L615-1 IPC. An injunction to cease infringement is granted, upon request by the applicant, following a decision on the merits. In case of urgency, permanent injunctions can also be obtained in accelerated proceedings on the merits (*procédure à heure fixe*). These proceedings are rarely used. It is generally argued that injunctive relief in France is compliant with the Enforcement Directive, in particular Recitals 23 to 28 and Articles 10, 11, and 13 to 15, but also with the TRIPs Agreement, in particular Articles 44–46.[29]

Similarly to preliminary injunctions and upon court order,[30] permanent injunctions can be enforced immediately after a first-instance decision on the merits notwithstanding appeal. Here again, if the decisions are lately reversed on appeal, the party opting for the provisional enforcement of an injunction may have to compensate the other party. They aim at re-establishing the right holder in its position of exclusivity. Under French law, an injunction is a remedy as of right and will *systematically* follow a decision finding infringement, unless exceptional cases justify otherwise (*see infra*). Injunctive relief is considered to be part of the substance of the

---

Convention for the Protection of Human Rights; Privat Vigand, *Exécution de mesures provisions. Responsabilité sans faute*, 13(5) Propriété Industrielle 39 (2014).
26. Romet, Métier & Talvard, *supra* n. 15, at 159–160; Bouvet, *supra* n. 7, at 588.
27. Romet, Métier & Talvard, *supra* n. 15, at 159–160; AIPPI Question Q219, *supra* n. 13, at 7.
28. AIPPI Question Q219, *supra* n. 13, at 14; Reference mentioned for patent and trademark cases: TGI Paris, Ord. Ref., 22 jan. 2008 (RG 08/50559); TGI Paris, Ord. Ref., 16 oct. 2009 (RG 09/58249); TGI Paris, Ord. Ref., 16 oct. 2009 (RG 09/58521); TGI Paris, Ord. Ref., 29 mai 2009 (RG 09/54173).
29. *Id.*, p. 4.
30. Or in the later stage of the procedure upon res judicata.

Chapter 5: Injunctions in French Patent Law §5.02[B]

exclusivity granted by patent law and the 'natural consequence of finding infringement'.[31] It represents the procedural counterpart of the autonomy to individually exploit a patent.[32] As a matter of principle, infringers must be sanctioned for the simple fact that they have infringed. Their actions cannot be excused because of the behaviour of right holders, or for reasons related to the infringers themselves.[33] Aside from the infringement of a valid title, and the fact that a patent holder has to request an injunction, there is no specific requirement to obtain a permanent injunction.

Before going into details concerning the 'exceptional circumstances' under which French judges have some discretionary powers with regard to injunctions, three particular sets of facts should be mentioned, as they may lead to the denial of injunctive relief.

First, if there is no proof that future infringement will take place, or where infringement came to an end during the proceedings, French judges may – and have in some cases – deny injunctive relief. It is argued that the grant of a *preliminary* injunction in this specific set of facts would be denied for lack of object.[34] For example, in *France Telecom et al. v. Electro Depot*, the *Cour de Cassation*[35] confirmed the decision of the Paris Court of Appeal which refused to grant interim relief to patent holders on grounds that the asserted patent had expired at the date of the application. The Court held that, according to Article L615-3 IPC and the principle of proportionality of the Enforcement Directive, patent holders were not admissible to seek a preliminary injunction on the basis of an expired patent. Judges in charge of interim relief can only grant such measures when it is necessary to prevent an imminent infringement or to stop the continuation of an infringement. From the moment of expiration, there can be no infringement justifying an injunction.[36] As for *permanent* injunctions, in rare cases and despite findings of infringement, judges have also refused to grant the measures based on the fact that infringement stopped or that future infringement would be unlikely.[37]

Second, if defendants can prove that patent rights are exhausted (Article L613-6 IPC),[38] French judges will not grant injunctive relief. Although not limited to such exceptional cases, in recent proceedings involving Standard Essential Patents (SEPs)

---

31. Petit, *supra* n. 16, at 165. Ref. to Jean Foyer & Michel Vivant, *Le droit des brevets* (PUF 1991), 349.
32. Hanns Ullrich, *Propriété intellectuelle, concurrence et régulation – limites de protection et limites de contrôle*, XXIII(4) Revue international de droit économique 399, 447 (2009).
33. Christian Le Stanc, *La contrefaçon n'est pas excusable*, 11(7–8) Propriété industrielle 1 (2012).
34. AIPPI Question Q219, *supra* n. 13, at 15.
35. Cass. Com. 21 oct. 2014, *Orange (France Telecom), TDF, Philips, Institut Fur Rundfunktechnik GMBH, Audio MPEG Inc, Societa Italiana Per Lo Sviluppo Dell'Electronica c. Electro Dépôt France* (13-15.435).
36. However, the Court held that, patent holders are entitled to obtain compensation for the harm caused before the expiration of the patent.
37. AIPPI Question Q219, *supra* n. 13, at 15–16. Reference to case law: CA Paris (4e ch.) 6 fév. 2009 (RG 08/03497); TGI Paris, 1 avril 2009 (RG 07/03876).
38. Article L613-6 CPI: 'The rights conferred by a patent shall not extend to deeds concerning a product covered by that patent which are done on French territory after such product has been marketed in France or in the territory of a State party to the Agreement on the European Economic Area by the owner of the patent or with his express consent' (translation from WIPO).

and pledges to licence under Fair, Reasonable and Non-Discriminatory (FRAND) terms, defendants relied on this exhaustion defence to dismiss claims of infringement.[39] In the cases at hand, the defence essentially referred to situations in which alleged infringers already benefited from either (a) a licensing agreement concluded with a previous patent owner who transferred his rights to the applicant or (b) a licensing agreement between the applicant – or a patent owner having transferred his rights – and a manufacturer who was allowed, according to the licence, to supply its customers – i.e., the alleged infringers – with patent-protected products or services. This was notably the case in *Samsung v. Apple*,[40] *Core Wireless v. LG Electronics*[41] and *High Point v. SFR et al.*[42] The exhaustion defence was also raised in *Ericsson v. TCT Mobile*[43] and *France Telecom et al. v. Electro Depot*.[44] However, in the latter cases, the Court found no sufficient proof of a licensing agreement, which would have taken the alleged infringers off the hook of a preliminary injunction.[45] In order to rely on such exception, defendants must therefore provide courts with sufficient evidence demonstrating that a licensing agreement is in place and actually exhausts the rights of the applicant.

Finally, a minor exception to the grant of a final injunction in case of infringement is also to be found in Article L615-10 IPC.[46] According to this provision, even in the

---

39. TGI Paris (ord. réf.) 8 déc. 2011, *Samsung Electronics Co., Ltd. and Samsung Electronics France c. Apple France S.A.R.L.* (RG 11/58301). TGI Paris (3e ch. 2e sct.) 29 nov. 2013, *Telefonaktiebolaget LM Ericsson c. TCT Mobile Europe SAS and TCT Mobile International Ltd.* (RG 12/14922).
40. TGI Paris (ord. réf.) 8 déc. 2011, *Samsung Electronics Co., Ltd. and Samsung Electronics France c. Apple France S.A.R.L.* (RG 11/58301). Samsung had a licensing agreement with Qualcomm and Apple's technology involved in the case was only implementing Qualcomm's chips. In light of the agreement between Samsung and Qualcomm, the District Court of Paris (preliminary proceedings) held that Apple was not infringing Samsung's patent.
41. TGI Paris (3e ch. 2e sct.) 17 avril 2015, *Core Wireless c. LG Electronics* (RG 14/14124). In this case, the exhaustion defence was based on alleged pass-through rights from Nokia to Qualcomm. Core Wireless having acquired patents from Nokia and LG Electronics using Qualcomm's chips.
42. CA Paris (3e ch.) 28 jan. 2014, *SA Societe Française du Radiotelephone – SFR, SAS Huawei Technologies France, SA Bouygues Telecom c. Societe HIGH POINT* (RG 13/08128). In this case, the exhaustion defence was based on alleged pass-through rights from AT&T to Alcatel.
43. TGI Paris (3e ch. 2e sct.) 29 nov. 2013, *Telefonaktiebolaget LM Ericsson c. TCT Mobile Europe SAS and TCT Mobile International Ltd.* (RG 12/14922). TCT Mobile requested that, in order to be able to adequately respond to Ericsson's infringement claims, Ericsson should provide the licensing agreement it concluded with Qualcomm. According to TCT, this agreement would reveal whether its products were covered by the license or not. However, the Court refused to order Ericsson to communicate the licensing agreement. It held that the burden of proof belonged to TCT to demonstrate that there was no infringement and not Ericsson.
44. Cass. Com. 21 oct. 2014, *Orange (France Telecom), TDF, Philips, Institut Fur Rundfunktechnik GMBH, Audio MPEG Inc, Societa Italiana Per Lo Sviluppo Dell'Electronica c. Electro Dépôt France* (13-15.435).
45. Although in *France Telecom et al. v. Electro Dépôt*, no injunction was granted because the asserted patents had expired (*see supra*).
46. Article L615-10 IPC: 'Where an invention which is the subject of a patent application or of a patent is worked, in order to meet the requirements of national defence, by the State or its suppliers, subcontractors and subsidiary suppliers, without a license having been afforded to them, the civil proceedings shall be brought before the First Instance Court sitting in chambers. The Court may order neither the discontinuance nor the interruption of the working nor the confiscation provided for in Articles L. 615-3 and L. 615-7-1' (translation from WIPO).

event of an infringement, there will be no injunction if the infringing acts were made by the State for national defence purposes.

[C] Enforcement Directive and TRIPs Agreement

It is worth mentioning that Article 12 of the Enforcement Directive[47] was not explicitly included in the law of 2007 implementing the directive into French law. French courts have therefore not extensively used the room of manoeuvre offered to judges by Article 12 read in combination with Article 3(1) of the directive. Damages rarely (if not ever) replace an injunction in case of non-wilful infringement.[48] However, it is argued that French judges still have sufficient freedom to decide on appropriate remedies[49] based on the IPC provisions. It appears from the case law that the Enforcement Directive and the TRIPs Agreement[50] do not directly influence injunctive relief. For example, the principle of proportionality enshrined in Article 3.2 of the Enforcement Directive does not systematically – but only sporadically – come into play when courts assess the grant of a permanent injunction. The principles and objectives behind the Directive as well as the TRIPs Agreement do however play a certain role regarding measures for preserving evidence or other interim measures (e.g., communication order, publication order) that are not banning commercialization.[51] Litigants frequently argue that the grant of such measures is – or could be if ultimately granted – disproportionate. French judges pay particular attention to the argument of proportionality. It is nonetheless worth mentioning that judges also recognize that although French patent law has to comply with the Enforcement Directive, it does not prevent the legislator from providing a regime more favourable to right holders. This is notably justified by the fact that it is compliant with the objective of the Directive to ensure a high level of protection in the enforcement of intellectual property rights.[52]

---

47. 'Art. 12 – Alternative measures: Member States may provide that, in appropriate cases and at the request of the person liable to be subject to the measures provided for in this section, the competent judicial authorities may order pecuniary compensation to be paid to the injured party instead of applying the measures provided for in this section if that person acted unintentionally and without negligence, if execution of the measures in question would cause him/her disproportionate harm and if pecuniary compensation to the injured party appears reasonably satisfactory'. For an interesting piece on the (under-exploited) potential of Art. 12 and injunctive relief see Peter Blok, *A harmonised approach to prohibitory injunctions: reconsidering Article 12 of the Enforcement Directive*, 11(1) Journal of Intellectual Property Law & Practice 56, 56–60 (2016).
48. Alice Pezard, *Pouvoir d'injonction et interdiction 'Patent troll'*, Présentation at ASPI (11 Dec. 2013), https://www.aspi-asso.fr/attachment/467438/ (accessed 31 Jul. 2018), 8.
49. Christian Le Stanc, *L'abus dans l'exercice du droit de brevet: les 'patent trolls'*, 9(10) Propriété Industrielle 3 (2010).
50. In French literature, the TRIPs Agreement is essentially discussed with regard to compulsory licenses and not so much regarding injunctive relief.
51. In particular, reference to Art. 7 of the Enforcement Directive and Art. 50 of TRIPs Agreement.
52. For exmaple, TGI Paris (ord. réf.) (3e ch. 3e sct.) 15 fév. 2013, *Boulanger et Sourcing & Création c. France Telecom et al.* (RG 12/15552).

§5.03 EXCEPTIONAL CIRCUMSTANCES

There are essentially two types of exceptional circumstances arising from outside the realm of patent law which have been taken into consideration by French judges to deny injunctive relief. *First*, defendants can rely on a 'competition law defence'. *Second*, they can rely on an 'abuse of rights defence'. In the particular context of patent litigation involving patent holders who have committed to license their SEPs on FRAND terms, defendants can also rely on a 'FRAND-defence' which relies essentially on competition law arguments. Additionally, in this setting, arguments based on 'abuse of rights' or 'good faith' are more or less systematically raised by defendants.

[A] Competition Law

Competition law defences based on arguments of anticompetitive agreement (Article 101 TFEU and Article L420-1 French Commercial Code) or abuse of dominant position (Article 102 TFEU and Article L420-2 French Commercial Code) may be relied upon in patent litigation. A defence based on competition law can be raised irrespective of the status of the patent e.g., whether the patent has been approved during the standardization process, is implemented in a de facto standard, or has no connection at all with a standard. While, French judges will allow the enforcement of patents as long as it does not conflict with the rules of competition law,[53] the increasing role of competition law in patent litigation raises some concerns. It is feared that competition law acts as a 'spare wheel' in the realm of IP[54] and might not always be the most appropriate remedy to issues of enforcement of IP.[55] However, as mentioned by Larouche and Zingales (2017) without more harmonized rules regarding injunctive relief and enforcement in general, 'competition law acts as a white knight for IP law'.[56]

Competition law defences have regularly been relied upon to deny injunctive relief. For example, in 2013, the Paris Court of Appeal,[57] following a decision of the French competition authority,[58] refused to grant interim relief due to an abuse of dominant position by a patent holder. The patent holder engaged in disparagement in the press and contacted customers of the alleged infringer in order to discourage them from buying competitive products. Although the anticompetitive behaviour was not

---

53. Sabine Agé, *La contrefaçon de brevets essentiels à une norme technique*, Présentation Grapi, https://www.veron.com/veron/publications/Colloques/2011-01-18_GRAPI_contrefacon_brevets_essentiels.pdf (accessed 31 Jul. 2018); E.g., TGI Paris (3ᵉ ch. 3ᵉ sct.) 26 jan. 2005, *Luk Lamellen c. Valeo* (RG 2000/16758).
54. Nicolas Petit, *Le droit européen de l'abus de position dominante en 2014*, 5 Contrats Concurrence Consommation, dossier 3, 6 (2015).
55. David Bosco, '*Patent war*': *les conditions de la qualification d'abus de position dominante sont précisées*, Contracts Concurrence Consommation, no. 1, comm. 13 (2015): 2. Questioning whether competition law was the appropriate remedy for the questions involved in *Huawei v. ZTE*.
56. Pierre Larouche & Nicolo Zingales, *Injunctive relief in FRAND dispute in the EU? Intellectual Property and Competition Law at the Remedies Stage*, TILEC Discussion Paper (2017), https://papers.ssrn.com/sol3/papers.cfm?abstract_id=2909708 (accessed 31 Jul. 2018).
57. CA Paris (5e ch.) 18 déc. 2014, *Sanofi SA & Sanofi-Aventis France* (RG 2013/12370).
58. Aut. Conc., 14 mai 2013, *Sanofi SA & Sanofi-Aventis France* (n. 13-D-11).

materialized in the fact that the patent holder requested an injunction, the outcome of the case was that the anticompetitive behaviour of the patent holder led to the denial of such relief.

It is argued that defendants particularly invoke Article L420-2 of the French Commercial Code in order to have the court deny the grant of a permanent injunction. This provision and the relevant case law is said to be in line with Article 102 TFUE and its interpretation by the CJEU.[59] Since its decision in *Huawei v. ZTE*,[60] the Court of Justice provided an additional framework to assess if patent holders abuse their dominant position when requesting an injunction. To date, the framework of negotiation developed in this case has only been applied in a small number of French cases. The first French FRAND-case is *Wiko v. SISVEL*.[61] In this case, the Commercial Court of Marseille held that demand letters sent to customers of *Wiko* (which markets mobile phones, products and telecommunication services) by *SISVEL* to notably warn them against possible infringement, did not amount to acts of unfair competition by disparagement (based on ex-Article 1382 of the French Civil Code) and could constitute an offer to license FRAND. *Wiko* sued *SISVEL* for disparagement because *SISVEL* sent letters to several of its retailers to inform them that the products they sold (and which were supplied by *Wiko*) incorporated the LTE technology (4G) and were covered by LTE patents. In its assessment, the court took into account the fact that *SISVEL* communicated a list of patents at stake, a table compiling information on such patents, a description of the LTE standards and a basic form sheet for a potential license. Moreover, the court considered that it was possible for the receivers of the letters to challenge the information received and it was still open for them to challenge the validity of the patents. In light of these elements, it was concluded that *SISVEL* did not demand that the distributors put an end to the sales of allegedly infringing products but rather offered to license its technology under FRAND terms, which was in conformity with the decision of the CJEU in *Huawei v. ZTE* (in particular with paragraph 61 of the decision which states that a SEP holder cannot initiate an action without prior notice or consultation).

This first case does not provide much information on the proposed licensing terms or the meaning of FRAND. However, it shows that a demand letter which includes certain information on patents accompanied by an offer to license following a basic scheme is conform to the first step of the negotiation framework developed by the CJEU. More generally, the approach adopted by the Court still has to be tested by French courts. It remains to be seen how courts will, in practice, adopt a different analysis under the exceptional circumstances of SEPs and promises to licence FRAND compared to more traditional settings.

---

59. Romet, Métier & Talvard, *supra* n. 15, at 173.
60. C-170/13, *Huawei Technologies Co. Ltd. v. ZTE Corp. and ZTE Deutschland GmbH*, 16 Jul. 2015.
61. T. Comm Marseille, 20 Sep. 2016, *Wiko SAS c. Sisvel UK Ltd.* (RG 2016F01637). *See* Stanislas Roux-Valliard, *France: Disparagement or FRAND offer?* LimeGreen IP News (9 Dec. 2016), http://www.limegreenipnews.com/2016/12/france-disparagement-or-frand-offer/ (accessed 31 Jul. 2018).

[B] Abuse of Rights

The prohibition of abuse of rights constitutes a jurisprudential construction essentially built upon Article 1240 of the French Civil Code (ex- Article 1382 of the Civil Code).[62] This provision provides for a regime of extra-contractual liability with fault. It requires the fulfilment of three conditions in order for an individual to be held liable for his actions, i.e., a fault, harm and a causal link. According to French courts, an abuse will be sanctioned if it is *caractérisé*, i.e., when a right holder does not act as a normally prudent and reasonable person would in the same circumstances.[63] In French doctrine, much ink has been spilled on the fact that rights must be exercised in a manner, which respect their 'functions'[64] or legal purposes. Pursuant to this standard, the legislator has conferred rights upon individuals with specific social aims in mind and right holders should respect these aims.[65] If rights are exercised for other objectives or if the exercise is diverted from its legitimate purpose, the rights can no longer be protected and/or enforced.[66] As any other right, the right to sue for infringement and the right to seek injunctive relief are not absolute and can be the object of legitimate limitations.[67] Therefore, it is generally contended that when litigants institute legal procedures – or persevere in a legal action – with the sole purpose of harming the defendant, in a disproportionate manner or with a particular objective not intended by the legislator, they may be sanctioned based on an 'abuse of rights'. The threshold for defendants to win a case on the argument of abuse is nonetheless fairly high. Even confronted with patent holder's actions which are somewhat frivolous or irritating, French courts may still consider these behaviours insufficient to fully substantiate a claim of abuse.[68] It is necessary to demonstrate that a particular action can be considered *malicious*, conducted in *bad faith* or the result of a *gross mistake* which can amount to *fraud*.[69] If counterclaims for abusive proceedings have long constituted a defence to a *preliminary*

---

62. Article 1240 Civil Code: 'Tout fait quelconque de l'homme, qui cause à autrui un dommage, oblige celui par la faute duquel il est arrivé, à le réparer'. Ordonnance n° 2016-131 du 10 février 2016 portant réforme du droit des contrats, du régime général et de la preuve des obligations.
63. Jacques Flour, Jean-Luc Aubert & Eric Savaux, *Les obligations – 2. Le fait juridique* (Dalloz 2007), 123. Jacques Ghestin & Gilles Goubeau, *Traité de droit civil – Introduction générale* (Librairie Générale de Droit et de Jurisprudence, 1994), 736.
64. Carine Jallamion, *La fortune de Josserand – Fonction(s) des droits de propriété intellectuelle*, 10 Propriété Industrielle dossier 2 (2010). Louis Josserand, *De l'esprit des droits et de leur relativité* (2nd ed., Dalloz 1939). Louis Josserand, *De l'abus des droits* (Rousseau 1905).
65. Shael Herman, *Classical Social Theories and the Doctrine of 'Abuse of Rights'*, 37 La. L. Rev. 747 (1977).
66. Julio Cuerto-Rua, *Abuse of Rights*, 35 La. L. Rev. 965 (1977).
67. Gaëlle Eloy, *La procédure téméraire et vexatoire*, in *Droit judiciaire. Commentaire pratique* (1.5-1-1.5-34, 2015): 9.
68. Amandine Leonard, *'Abuse of Rights' in Belgian and French Patent Law – A Case Law Analysis*, 7 JIPITEC 30 para. 1 (2016).
69. The classic formula is the following: 'L'exercice d'une action en justice constitue, en principe, un droit et ne dégénère en abus pouvant donner naissance à une dette de dommages-intérêts fondée sur l'article 1382 du code civil que dans le cas de malice, de mauvaise foi, ou d'erreur grossière équipollente au dol'.

injunction in French case law,[70] the impact of such a defence on *permanent* injunction is however, less clear.

In the particular context of standardization, questions may arise as to the role the prohibition of 'abuse or rights'. To date, French courts have not extensively accepted this defence in patent litigation although the argument has been frequently relied upon. Interestingly, in 2006, the Paris District Court[71] held that it was abusive to initiate an infringement action based on patents obtained in striking violation of the principle of *mutual trust* that needs to reign within the standardization process. The case concerned the aircraft manufacturer *AIRBUS* who solicited a common reflection amongst various developers in order to create a new electronic connector, which would become a global standard in the aeronautic. The companies *Souriau* and *Deutsch Distribution* were part of the process. The participants to this common effort shared their results concerning the potential new connector, but soon after the discussions, *Souriau* decided to apply for a patent on the newly developed technology. Once the patent granted, it pursued its action by initiating an infringement action against *Deutsch Distribution*. The latter counterclaimed that the action was, in light of the circumstances of the case, abusive. The Paris District Court held that, in light of the 'standardization' process established by *AIRBUS* and the trust developed amongst the parties to the process, the attitude of *Souriau* in obtaining a patent and then asserting it against a competitor was abusive. To initiate an infringement claim, in an attempt to neutralize a competitor by relying on a patent which was not only insufficiently disclosed, but and for which the different claims actually came from various partners within the consortium, amounted to an 'abuse of rights'.

[C] Somewhere Between Competition Law and Abuse of Rights?

Regarding the right to sue for infringement, it is said that French case law generally follows the decision of the CJEU in *ITT Promedia*[72] in order to assess the exceptional circumstances under which, to initiate an action could amount to an abuse of dominant position.[73]

In *Technofirst v. Alfacoustic*,[74] the TGI Paris did not explicitly referred to *ITT Promedia* but mentioned that the CJEU case law clarified that, under exceptional circumstances, an owner of property rights – here, the patent holder – may exercise abusively its right to institute legal proceedings. Such exceptional circumstances notably cover the case in which proceedings are initiated as part of a plan to eliminate

---

70. Petit, *supra* n. 16, at 160; AIPPI Question Q219, *supra* n. 13, at 22.
71. TGI Paris (3e ch. 3e sct.) 22 fév. 2006, *SAS Souriau c. SAS Compagnie Deutsch Distribution, SAS Connecteurs Electriques Deutsch et SAS Compagnie Deutsch France* (RG 06/05796).
72. T-111/96, *ITT Promedia NV c. Commission*, 17 Jul. 1998.
73. For example, Cons. Conc., 7 déc. 1999, *Télésélection c. M6, M6 Interactions et Téléshopping* (N. 99-D-77). Cons. Conc., 13 juin 2002, *Ste Spinevision* (N.02-D-35). Cons. Conc., 23 juin 2004 (N.04-D-23).
74. TGI Paris (3e ch. 1e sct.) 05 nov. 2015, *SA Technofirst c. Alfacoustic et al.* (RG 10/10178).

a competitor.[75] In this case, the Court held that although the patent holder (*Techno-First*) has the right to have its patent monopoly respected, it cannot however, via the use of infringement procedure, eliminate new competitors entering the market. In this case, *TechnoFirst* multiplied seizure measures and requested many minutes and reports from bailiffs, to then initiate an infringement action which it voluntarily discontinued[76] as soon as it heard that its competitor was undergoing a legal liquidation. According to the Court, this behaviour could only be explained by the fact that the patent holder had no further need of the proceedings since its competitor was eliminated from the market. *TechnoFirst* actually diverted the infringement action from its initial purpose (i.e., to actually safeguard its rights) by acting frivolously and with an intention to harm a competitor. Based on other factual elements of the case, the Court held that the patent holder was liable for abuse (under ex-Article 1382 of the Civil Code) and caused commercial harm to the defendants that needed to be compensated.

Interestingly, although the court seems to rely on the test of abuse developed in *ITT Promedia*, it does not develop much on the question of abuse of dominant position from a competition law perspective (claim which was actually not raised by the defendant). It seems to incorporate the conditions of abuse under the case law of the CJEU into a more traditional approach based on 'abuse of rights' from a civil law perspective. The legal ground for sanctioning the patent holder in this case being Article 1382 of the Civil Code and the general principle of abusive proceedings and not Article 102 TFEU or Article L420-2 of the French Commercial Code.

§5.04 STANDARDIZATION AND FRAND

France is in a particular position regarding enforcement of SEPs and issues of FRAND litigations. The European Telecommunications Standards Institute (ETSI) is located in France and its rules (including undertakings to license under FRAND terms) are subject to French law.[77] Further, some high-stakes international arbitrations are held in Paris, including arbitration on FRAND licenses.[78] In recent years, French courts were confronted with a number of cases related to FRAND issues.[79] On average, defendants

---

75. This seems to clearly refer to the analysis made by the Commission and mentioned to in *ITT Promedia*, pt. 30: 'The Commission considers that 'in principle the bringing of an action, which is the expression of the fundamental right of access to a judge, cannot be characterised as an abuse' unless 'an undertaking in a dominant position brings an action (i) which cannot reasonably be considered as an attempt to establish its rights and can therefore only serve to harass the opposite party, and (ii) which is conceived in the framework of a plan whose goal is to eliminate competition'.
76. After some seizures, goods had been kept at the premises of the bailiff. TechnoFirst did not pay the extra consignment costs of such evidence, although the products under custody were the only elements of the case which could have supported its infringement claim.
77. ETSI IPR Policy (point 12).
78. Cyrille Amar, *Are French Court Patent-FRANDly?*, Iam Magazine (2016), http://www.iam-media.com/Magazine/Issue/78/Management-report/Are-French-courts-patent-FRANDly (accessed 31 Jul. 2018).
79. Romet, Métier & Talvard, *supra* n. 15, at 171–173.

involved in such cases have been more successful than patent holders[80] as applications for preliminary injunctions were more often dismissed than granted. Unfortunately, no cases related to permanent injunctions can be reported to date.

[A] Case Law

As mentioned *supra*, in *Samsung v. Apple*, the Paris District Court dismissed the application for interim relief in view of the likelihood of the exhaustion of *Samsung's* rights. *Samsung* sought to obtain interim relief against *Apple* in accelerated proceedings. The measures requested were not only aimed at imposing a ban on *Apple* but also to call back allegedly infringing products from the market. According to the Court the interim relief sought by *Samsung* was blatantly disproportionate.[81] *Apple* also tried to rely on an abuse of rights defence. The Court held that *Samsung* somewhat acted frivolously by failing to provide the relevant information concerning its contractual relationship with *Qualcomm Inc*. However, *Apple* failed to demonstrate a distinct harm resulting from the alleged abuse, the Court therefore dismissed the claim. This case expresses the general difficulty of the 'abuse of rights' defence. If misconducts can easily be identified by courts, to prove that a distinct harm actually stems from this behavior is a hurdle for defendants.

In a second instance, opposing *Ericsson* to *TCT Mobile*, the Paris District Court[82] dismissed the application for interim relief on grounds of ongoing negotiations between the parties for the renewal of a license.[83] Despite the fact that the parties agreed on a geographical and technological scope for the licensing agreement, they could not reach an agreement on the level of royalty rate. The Court held that, as a matter of principle, the patent holder of SEPs has to license its patents on FRAND terms. Therefore, in this particular context, interim relief should be proportionate to the interests involved. The contractual relationship between the parties, i.e., the fact that negotiations regarding SEPs were ongoing, was taken into consideration. Since the parties were still negotiating, their power relationship had to be balanced and could not unduly advantage the party who would obtain an interim injunction. To do so would be contradictory to the

---

80. For example, TGI Paris (ord. réf.) 8 déc. 2011, *Samsung Electronics Co., Ltd. and Samsung Electronics France c. Apple France S.A.R.L.* (RG.11/58301). TGI Paris (3e ch. 2e sct.) 29 nov. 2013, *Telefonaktiebolaget LM Ericsson c. TCT Mobile Europe SAS and TCT Mobile International Ltd.* (RG12/14922).
81. TGI Paris (ord. ref.) 8 déc. 2011, *Samsung Electronics Co., Ltd. and Samsung Electronics France c. Apple France S.A.R.L.* (RG 11/58301): 21: 'Il convient de constater de surcroit le caractère disproportionné de la mesure d'interdiction formée par les sociétés SAMSUNG à l'encontre des sociétés APPLE est patent'.
82. TGI Paris (3e ch. 2e sct.) 29 nov. 2013, *Telefonaktiebolaget LM Ericsson c. TCT Mobile Europe SAS and TCT Mobile International Ltd.* (RG 12/14922): 9.
83. Amandine Métier, *Antitrust and IP*, Véron & Associés Seminar on Lessons learnt from patent case law in Europe in 2013 and 2014 (6 Feb. 2015); AIPPI Special Committee on Patents and Standards Q222 – *Report: Availability of injunctive relief for standard essential patents, incl. FRAND-defence in patent infringement proceedings* (March 2014), 16, http://aippi.org/wp-content/uploads/committees/222/Report222AIPPI + report + on + the + availability + of + injun ctive + relief + for + FRAND-committed + standard + essential + patentsEnglish.pdf (accessed 31 Jul. 2018).

principle according to which licenses have to be granted on FRAND terms, and would put unjustified pressure on the future licensee.[84] In January 2016, The Court stayed the proceeding on the merits to await the decision of the District Court for the Central District of California having to decide on the terms of a global license.[85]

The two cases are in line with the traditional assessment conducted by the Court before granting a preliminary injunction.[86] In *Samsung v. Apple* the Court took into consideration the fact that the defendant *seriously contested* determinant factors for the grant of the injunction to dismiss the application. In *Ericsson v. TCT Mobile*, the Court considered the application for a preliminary injunction to be *disproportionate*. Therefore, it could be argued that, due to the room of manoeuvre given to judges by the rules governing the grant of interim relief (i.e., the balance of interests and the question of proportionality), there is a lesser need for 'abuse of rights' to come into play. However, it is possible that after the grant, and on the level of enforcement of the injunction, the prohibition of abuse of rights kicks in again as the enforcement could be abusive in itself.

A FRAND-defence in infringement proceedings on the merits has also been raised in two recent cases.[87] In *Vringo v. ZTE France*, the Paris District Court held that when asserting alleged SEPs, and before being able to request an injunction, a patent holder first has to show that the process claimed in the asserted patent is identical to the process disclosed in the underlying standard.[88] ZTE alleged that, under the ETSI IPR policy, *Vringo* was bound by its commitment to license FRAND[89] and would be abusing its dominant position by breaching its FRAND commitment. ZTE also claimed that *Vringo*'s practices were anticompetitive as they were equivalent to tied selling and privateering.[90] On infringement, the Court notably held that[91] *Vringo* limited itself to assertions and did not prove its claim. It essentially relied on the fact that *ZTE's* network complied with the UMTS standard and by extension was infringing *Vringo's* SEPs.[92] The Court observed that the different steps included in the process claim of the patent were not identical to the process exposed by the norm, even though they lead to

---

84. TGI Paris (3e ch. 2e sct.) 29 nov. 2013, *Telefonaktiebolaget LM Ericsson c. TCT Mobile Europe SAS and TCT Mobile International Ltd.* (RG 12/14922): 9, 10.
85. TGI Paris (3e ch. 2e sct.) 29 jan. 2016, *Telefonaktiebolaget LM Ericsson c. TCT Mobile Europe SAS, TCT Mobile International Ltd. and TCT Mobile Ltd.* (RG 12/14922).
86. *See supra* on the conditions to obtain a preliminary injunction.
87. TGI Paris (3e ch. 2e sct.) 17 avril 2015, *Core Wireless c. LG Electronics* (RG 14/14124). TGI Paris (3e ch. 3e sct.) 30 oct. 2015, *Vringo Infrastructure Inc. c. ZTE Corporation and ZTE France SASU* (RG 13/06691).
88. Stanislas Roux-Valliard, *France – Uneven Standards: SEP infringement requires claimed process identical to the standard*, LimeGreem IP News, Hogan Lovell (2 Dec. 2015), http://www.limegreenipnews.com/2015/12/france-uneven-standards-sep-infringement-requires-claimed-process-identical-to-the-standard/ (accessed 31 Jul. 2018).
89. Vringo was enforcing two patents that had been declared essential to ETSI by Nokia. EP 1 221 212 (declared in 2002 for the standard TS 124 022) and EP 1 186 119 (declared in 2001 for the standard TS 125 211). The latter patent has been opposed by Qualcomm in 2007 but maintained in an amended form.
90. TGI Paris (3e ch. 3e sct.) 30 oct. 2015, *Vringo Infrastructure Inc. c. ZTE Corporation and ZTE France SASU* (RG 13/06691): 8.
91. *Id.*, p. 17.
92. *Id.*, p. 22.

the same result. The process claim of the patented invention was not included in the standard, therefore, the patent (in its process claim) could not be considered essential.[93] Since the patent was not essential and that *Vringo* relied solely on the fact that ZTE was implementing the norm to support the infringement claim, the Court held that there could be no infringement. The court did not address the ancillary competition law defence.

In an accelerated proceeding on the merits opposing *Core Wireless*[94] to *LG Electronics*, the Paris District Court held that when asserting alleged SEPs in litigation, a patent holder could not just presume the essentiality of its patents, this characteristic must be proven by reliable evidence. The Court rejected the infringement claims of *Core Wireless* because it failed to demonstrate the essentiality of the asserted patents. It was not clear, from the evidence provided,[95] that by implementing the UMTS and LTE standards in its cell phones, *LG Electronics* was also implementing the patented processes. Additionally, both parties requested the Court to set a FRAND royalty rate. However, *Core Wireless* (who did not seek injunctive relief) sought the determination of a rate applicable to a portfolio of over 1,200 patents by invoking five of these patents as 'non-exhaustive examples'. *LG Electronics* argued that the rate should only apply to patents that were valid, essential, not expired, not exhausted and implemented in its products. However, since the Court held that the patent holder failed to demonstrate the essentiality of its patent, and because a FRAND rate is mandatory for SEPs only, the Court found no reason to set a FRAND royalty rate.

This case also saw two other defences being raised by the alleged infringer, i.e., competition law defence and 'abuse of rights' defence. With regard to competition law, *LG Electronics* argued that, in this particular context, the introduction of accelerated proceedings on the merits was an act of abusive dominance (Article L420-2 French Commercial Code). *Core Wireless* responded that since it did not aim at obtaining an injunction, but only at obtaining the determination of a royalty rate, it did not abuse a dominant position.[96] The Court held that to initiate an action to determine the level of royalties which could not have been agreed upon during negotiations, cannot, absent other circumstances revealing a manifest intention to prevent *LG Electronics* from exploiting the patented technology in return for an appropriate and proportionate level of royalties, constitute an abuse of dominant position.[97] With regard to the 'abuse of

---

93. *Id.*, p. 28: 'Ainsi, les étapes du procédé mis en œuvre par la caractéristique 'd' de la revendication 1 du brevet ne sont pas identiques au procédé exposé par la norme, quand bien même ils parviennent à un résultat identique. Aussi la caractéristique 'd' de la revendication n. 1 du brevet n'est pas mise en œuvre dans la spécification technique Etsi T 125 2011 v.3.12.0 de la norme UMTS. Il s'ensuit que la revendication 1 ne saurait être retenue comme étant essentielle à la norme en cause'.
94. Core Wireless is a monetizing entity holding a portfolio of more than 2,000 patents acquired from Nokia, 1,261 of these patents have been declared essential to ETSI (incorporation in the GSM standard [2G], UMTS [3G] and LTE [4G]).
95. Core Wireless limited itself to file an analysis drafted by a chosen expert, without proceeding to a meticulous, precise and understandable expertise, which would have demonstrated that the patents were necessarily reproduced by all cell phones implementing the standards.
96. TGI Paris (3e ch. 2e sct.) 17 avril 2015, *Core Wireless c. LG Electronics* (RG 14/14124): 28.
97. *Id.*, p. 29: 'Comme elle le fait valoir à bon droit, le seul fait d'introduire une action en justice pour voir fixer judiciairement des redevances qui n'ont pu l'être de façon amiable ne saurait

rights' defence, *LG Electronics* claimed that *Core Wireless* only introduced accelerated proceedings on the merits to artificially pressure the defendant into a licensing agreement. The Court held that it was not abusive per se for an applicant to choose such a procedure as long as the legal requirements were met and assessed by a judge. It reiterated that the action could only be held abusive if initiated with a malicious intent, bad faith or gross negligence.

These two proceedings on the merits show that the Paris District Court has established stringent requirements that must be met by owners of SEPs.[98] Notwithstanding the declaration of essentiality to a standards organization, there is a high threshold to prove the essentiality of the patent.[99] Evidence that the technical teachings of the patent are integrated in the standard, that no technical alternative is available and that there is a compliance with the technical specifications of the standard, is mandatory and not merely optional.[100] In theory, the burden of proof of infringement might be easier for patent holders. They can rely on the fact that their SEPs have been implemented in a standard used by the alleged infringer.[101] However, the decisions of the Paris District Court show that this might not always be the case. Owners of SEPs have to demonstrate that, on the one hand, their patents are not only essential but also implemented in a standard and, on the other hand, that the defendant's products are actually infringing the said-essential patents. In addition to this burden, SEPs holders are not immune against competition law or abuse of rights defences.

With regard to injunctive relief, since no prohibitory injunction was granted in *Vringo* due to lack of validity and essentiality of the asserted patents, and since there was no request for injunction in *Core Wireless*, the Paris District Court had no opportunity to rule on this issue. The decision in *Huawei v. ZTE* was given after the *Core Wireless v. LG Electronics* decision and after the *Vringo v. ZTE France* pleadings. Thus, neither claimants nor defendants could rely on the ECJ's ruling in their submissions and pleadings; nor could the Paris District Court apply it.

[B]   FRAND Pledges and Requirement to Act in Good Faith

French doctrine has not provided for one legal characterization of the obligations stemming from FRAND pledges. Some argue that the tripartite scenario between standards organizations, SEPs holders and potential licensees, should be analysed

---

constituer, en l'absence d'autres circonstances montrant notamment une volonté manifeste de priver la société LG de sa possibilité d'utiliser lesdits brevets en contrepartie d'une redevance honnête et proportionnée, un abuse de position dominante'.
98. Amar, *supra* n. 78.
99. In the cases mentioned *supra* the Court highlighted the fact that the declaration of essentiality to the ETSI was not a guarantee of true essentiality since the ETSI does not verify whether the patents are actually valid and essential.
100. Amar, *supra* n. 78.
101. Sabine Agé & Amandine Métier, Litigating standard-essential patents – FRAND and antitrust implications, Managing IP (2009), http://www.managingip.com/Article/2251025/Litigating-standard-essential-patents-FRAND-and-antitrust-implications.html (accessed 31 Jul. 2018).

under the *'stipulation pour autrui'*[102] regime (i.e., third party beneficiary contract). This regime is a derogation to the traditional principle of privity of contracts and creates a right for the beneficiary directly enforceable against the promisor. By offering to negotiate a licence and committing to grant a licence FRAND to a standard setting organization (the *stipulant*, e.g., ETSI), it is argued that, patent holders (promisors) create a direct right between themselves and beneficiaries (e.g., implementers). The conditions of the said FRAND licence are left to be discussed with the potential licensee. This situation is understood by some as preventing patent holders from obtaining injunctive relief against the users of the standard implementing their patents.[103] According to others, the pledge to license FRAND could be analysed as a simple promise to enter into negotiations to conclude a licence FRAND. In this case, patent holders are not prevented from injunctive relief if parties cannot reach an agreement. To *see* FRAND undertaking as a *stipulation pour autrui* is actually the approach which has been followed by Justice Birss in the *Unwired Planet v. Huawei* (UK) case[104] in his interpretation of French law governing the ETSI rules. By doing so, Justice Birss follows one strand of French literature on the topic.

It should nonetheless be mentioned that, it is clear from the case and from general doctrine that French experts have very different views on the meaning and effects of a FRAND undertaking under French law and that this question is not solved yet. French courts will have to comply with the decision in *Huawei v. ZTE*, which does not support the hypothesis according to which SEPs holders having pledged to license FRAND have waived their rights to injunctive relief per se. Other questions remain unanswered so far. For example, it remains to be seen how French courts will interpret the 'legitimate expectations' referred to in *Huawei v. ZTE*, and how they will articulate the refusal to grant a FRAND licence, with the provisions on abuse of dominant position and the 'legitimate expectations' of the potential users/licensees.[105]

---

102. Christophe Caron, *L'efficacité des licences dites 'FRAND' ou l'indispensable conciliation entre la normalisation et le droit des brevets d'invention grâce à la stipulation pour autrui*, 7-8 Communication Commerce électronique étude 12 (2013); Christophe Caron, *Un cocktail explosif: abus de position dominante, action en contrefaçon, brevet essentiel à une norme et licence FRAND*, 9 Communication Commerce électronique, comm. 65 (2015). See also, Art. 1205 of the Civil Code: 'On peut stipuler pour autrui. L'un des contractants, le stipulant, peut faire promettre à l'autre, le promettant, d'accomplir une prestation au profit d'un tiers, le bénéficiaire. Ce dernier peut être une personne future mais doit être précisément désigné ou pouvoir être déterminé lors de l'exécution de la promesse'.
103. Sabine Agé, *Brevet essentiel et licences Frand – La problématique juridique*, Présentation – Groupe français de l'AIPPI (12 Juin 2014); Agé & Métier *supra* n. 101; Ullrich, *supra* n. 32, at 448.
104. *See Unwired Planet v. Huawei*, [2017] EWHC 711 (Pat) 806: 'In summary, my conclusions on the law are: (1) As a matter of French law the FRAND undertaking to ETSI is a legally enforceable obligation which any implementer can rely on against the patentee. FRAND is justiciable in an English court and enforceable in that court'. Recognizing however that (pt. 146) 'the enforceability of the FRAND undertaking in French law is not a clear cut question. Prof. Libchaber stated that there remains widespread uncertainty about the issue of whether the doctrine of *"stipulation pour autrui"* can be applied to ETSI. In my judgment it can be applied in that way and should be' (Emphasis added).
105. Jérôme Passa, *Action en contrefaçon concomitante à la négociation d'une licence FRAND sur un brevet essentiel à une norme : conditions de l'abus de position dominante*, 11 Propriété industrielle, étude 20, 3 (2015).

If, according to case law, SEPs holders have to meet stringent requirements, French judges also expect that alleged infringers adopt an acceptable behaviour. FRAND pledges are not interpreted as imposing one-sided obligations.[106] Some commentators argue that potential licensees, who do exploit a technology covered by a standard, should come forward with their intention to obtain a licence FRAND and that patent holders do not lose their right to obtain an injunction if the user of the norm clearly indicated he was not willing to pay FRAND royalties for the use of the patented technology.[107] To our knowledge, the Paris District Court has not rule on the question of 'willingness' of alleged infringer so far. However, in some cases, the court paid specific attention to the 'good faith' of both parties during negotiation processes. For example, in *Core Wireless v. LG Electronics*,[108] the negotiations lasted for more than two years. The Paris District Court held that, in light of the length and depth of the negotiations, neither party acted in bad faith since none felt like putting a formal end to the negotiations. Moreover, since each company offloaded the burden of 'bad faith' onto the other and that elements from the negotiations were not available to the Court, it could not conclude that one of the parties conducted the said negotiations in bad faith. [109] Potential licensees will be considered 'willing licensees' as long as they are acting in good faith. For example, it has been considered a sign of 'willingness' to deposit fair and reasonable royalties on a blocked account while awaiting a decision on licensing terms and conditions (which would be in line with the framework of negotiation clarified by the CJEU). 'Good faith' may also include cases where potential licensees try to obtain amicably or via judicial redress the execution of the FRAND-pledged patent holder to contract into a licensing agreement. On the contrary, dragging negotiations unnecessarily in order to freely benefit from the patented technology for a certain period of time will be considered a sign of bad faith. The same will apply if it is clear that the alleged infringer has no interest in concluding a licensing agreement or to pay fair and reasonable royalties.[110]

[C] **Royalty Rate and FRAND Terms**

As a matter of principle, patent holders should be free to determine the terms and conditions of a license. However, some argue that, in case of SEPs, the organization in charge of the norm may have to fix and publicize the conditions of SEPs included in the

---

106. Caron (2013), *supra* n. 102.
107. Agé, *supra* n. 53.
108. TGI Paris (3e ch. 2e sct.) 17 avril 2015, *Core Wireless c. LG Electronics* (RG 14/14124).
109. In a non-FRAND related litigation, the Paris District Court held that a patent holder acts with sufficient loyalty when, in light of existing commercial relations, he offers an alleged infringer to regularize amicably the situation by subscribing to a licensing program sufficiently disclosed (i.e., including a royalty rate and a base). *See* TGI Paris (3e ch. 1e sct.) (ord. ref.) 09 juillet 2015, *Société Commerce Spectacle Industrie, SCV Hi Tech & SCV Audio c. Philips Lighting North America Corp* (RG 15/08803).
110. Caron (2013), *supra* n. 102; Caron (2015), *supra* n. 102.

norm.¹¹¹ French doctrine supports an increased 'transparency' in standard organizations in charge of establishing a FRAND level of royalties.¹¹² In case of non-agreement between the parties, courts may have to decide on the terms and conditions of licensing agreements. They can rely on experts in order to establish the appropriate level of royalties (which is increasingly encouraged by courts) but they can also resort to mediation or conciliation.¹¹³ To date, there is no case in which a French court had to decide on the rate of royalties related to a license FRAND. Some guidance can nevertheless be found in *Ericsson v. TCT Mobile*¹¹⁴ and *Samsung v. Apple*.¹¹⁵ Arguably, in the specific context of standardization, FRAND royalties may be influenced by a series of factors.¹¹⁶ These factors include e.g., the economic value of the patents, the total number of patents concerned by the norm, the total amount of royalties which can be applied on one product, the fact that a licence covers a patent portfolio and/or is granted worldwide, etc. Judges need to compare *ex ante* royalties and *ex post* royalties in order to determine if patent holders are not exploiting the fact that their patents are essential to obtain excessive rates. Moreover, royalties must be determined on a basis, which would have emerged from a binding system between alternative technologies before the adoption of the norm. Judges can also take into account the risk of royalty stacking and the frequency of cross licensing agreements. It is also contended that competition law may be useful to determine the level of royalties.¹¹⁷

Absent fixed guidance for FRAND terms, French Courts can also rely on traditional ways to determine *compensatory royalties* (Article L 615-7 CPI).¹¹⁸ When available and relevant, comparables among license agreements are also relied upon by French court to determine the adequate level of royalties.¹¹⁹ In the absence of such comparables, courts set a hypothetical rate based on evidence submitted by the injured

---

111. AIPPI Question Q157 – Groupe français. *Relations entre les normes techniques et les droits de brevet* (2008), 17 http://www.aippi.fr/upload/Melbourne%202001%20Q155%20156%20157%20158%20159/gr157france_fr.pdf (accessed 31 Jul. 2018).
112. Dominique Guellec, Thierry Madiès & Jean-Claude Prager, *Les marchés de brevets dans l'économie de la connaissance: Rapport* (Direction de l'information légale et administrative 2010), http://www.cae-eco.fr/IMG/pdf/094.pdf (accessed 31 Jul. 2018), 96. Benoit Galopin, *Comment concilier propriété intellectuelle et normalisation?*, 11(7-8) Propriété Industrielle 2 (2012), alerte 12; Caron (2013), *supra* n. 102, at 4.
113. Caron (2015), *supra* n. 102, at 374.
114. Agé, *supra* n. 53; TGI Paris (3e ch. 2e sct.) 29 nov. 2013, *Telefonaktiebolaget LM Ericsson c. TCT Mobile Europe SAS and TCT Mobile International Ltd.* (RG 12/14922).
115. TGI Paris (ord. réf.) 8 déc. 2011, *Samsung Electronics Co., Ltd. and Samsung Electronics France c. Apple France S.A.R.L.* (RG 11/58301).
116. Agé, *supra* n. 53; Caron (2013), *supra* n. 102.
117. Isabelle Liotard, *Persistance et intensité des conflits entre normalisation et propriété intellectuelle: les enseignements de la 3ᵉ génération de téléphonie mobile*, XXII(1) Revue internationale de droit économique 47, 47-65 (2008).
118. As mentioned in the AIPPI study report for France on quantification of monetary relief: 'French law does not recognize the concept of a "reasonable" royalty. However, the CPI expressly authorizes the use of a calculation based on royalties, referred to as "compensatory," to set the amount of damages due to an injured party ...'. AIPPI 2017 – study report (France) – quantification of monetary relief (May 5, 2017), http://aippi.org/committee/quantification-of-monetary-relief/ (accessed 31 Jul. 2018), 5.
119. *Id.*, at 6.

party.[120] For example, in a recent case, the Paris District Court[121] took into account the number of sold-products incorporating the patent as a base for the determination of royalties. It also relied on the fact that the asserted patents covered only an accessory part of the end products. The Court found its decision on an expert report to estimate the conventional and traditional rate applied in license agreement of the asserted patents and increased the said-rate because of the acts of infringement.

§5.05 EXPLORING NEW TERRITORIES

[A] On Acquiescence (Tolerance), Legitimate Expectations and Estoppel 'à la française'

An element which may be of interest with regards to flexibility in injunctive relief is the question of acquiescence, i.e., when a right holder does not act for a certain period of time although a third party is exploiting a patented technology. The question is whether such tolerance from patent holders could notably raise some legitimate expectations with third parties to the point where patent holders would be estopped from obtaining injunctive relief. The question of legitimate expectations can also be connected to the promise to license FRAND. In this context, it could be argued that a FRAND undertaking creates legitimate expectations in the sense that a patent holder will not enforce its rights or at least will not request an injunction.

In French IP law, limitation or extinction of rights due to acquiescence only exists in trademark law (Articles L. 716-5 al.4 and L. 714-3 al.3 CPI). There is therefore no legal basis for such argument in patent law and is generally strongly opposed by doctrine. As for legitimate expectations and the common law concept of estoppel, there is a general sentiment of distrust from French academics and practitioners vis-à-vis this foreign concept.[122] The more conventional and traditional general principles of good faith or abuse of rights are generally preferred as corrective mechanisms to a specific doctrine of estoppel or legitimate expectations.[123] The maxim of *venire contra factum proprium* or the *Verwirkung* doctrine known under German law, as well as the concept of *rechtsverwerking* known under Belgian and Dutch law, do not find exact equivalents in French law. However, they all present ramifications with the general principle of good faith, and to some extent, the principle of abuse of rights which are well-known in French law. Moreover, even if French judges do not rely on these specific principles,

---

120. Without evidence from the injured party, courts may simply refuse any compensation for material prejudice. *Id.*, at 7.
121. TGI Paris (3e ch. 4e sct) 02 juillet 2015, *Vorwerk & Co. Interholding GmbH c. SAS Guy Demarle et al.* (RG 12/11488).
122. Denis Mazeaud, *La confiance légitime et l'estoppel*, 58(2) Revue internationale de droit comparé 363 (2006); Bénédicte Fauvarque-Cosson, *La confiance légitime et l'estoppel*, 11(3) Electronic Journal of Comparative Law 30 (2007).
123. Fauvarque-Cosson, *supra* n. 122.

general considerations of equity (in the broad sense of the term) fairness or proportionality, may lead to similar outcomes in terms of sanctions.[124]

Despite this resistance from French doctrine, there is a certain evolution[125] in the case law, and it is argued that French courts have adopted and developed a certain type of estoppel 'à la française', i.e., a principle according to which a person may not contradict itself to the detriment of another person (*principe d'interdiction de se contredire au détriment d'autrui*). It is essentially in the field of (international) contract law, that a more welcoming approach from French judges is witnessed. In this context, and depending on the circumstances of a case, the sanction of a breach of legitimate expectations stemming from an already formed and accepted contract can lead to e.g., the liability of the person who created those legitimate expectations, a limitation in the exercise of his right or even the forfeiture of the right or exercise of a right. The *Cour de Cassation* also held that if, due to the length of negotiations, advancement or costs involved, negotiation between parties raised some legitimate expectations, but that an abrupt or unforeseen breakdown in negotiation appears, it can trigger the liability of the negotiator. In this case, the victim will be entitled to damages to repair the harm caused by the breakdown. Under the traditional principle of freedom to contract, it is difficult to support the idea that the sanction should be to impose a contract between the parties.

Beside contract law, the principle according to which one cannot contradict itself to the detriment of others, has also been recognized in the field of procedural law. In 2010, the French Supreme Court[126] recognized that a litigant could (only) be estopped if there was a change of legal position of a nature to mislead an opponent. In such a case, the claims of the litigant would be inadmissible in court. In 2015, it was added as a condition that the change of legal position had to take place in the same proceedings. In 2017, the Court[127] confined the use of legitimate expectations and estoppel in procedural law to even more limited circumstances. Estoppel can only refer to submissions (i.e., claims in the proceedings but not allegations of facts) filed with a court in the same judicial debate. It is only if there is a change of claims between e.g., first instance and appeal, that a litigant could be sanctioned based on legitimate expectations or estoppel. The room of manoeuvre of an estoppel 'à la française', is therefore very limited.

---

124. *See,* e.g., Filippo Ranieri, *Bonne foi et exercice du droit dans la tradition du civil law,* 50(4) Revue internationale de droit compare 1055, 1055–1092 (1998). According to Ranieri, the forfeiture or limitation of the exercise of a right as a sanction for the unfair use of such right or a use which would contradict the legitimate expectations that others have built on the behaviour of the right holder, is shared among many legal systems in continental Europe. (*Id.,* at 1089).
125. For the first case in which the Cour de Cassation explicitly referred to the principle of estoppel in the field of international arbitration *see,* Cass. Civ. 1er, 6 juillet 2005, *Golshani c. Gouvernement de la Republique islamique d'Iran.* Bull Civ. I, n°302.
126. Cass. Civ. 1er, 3 fév. 2010, *Merial c. Klocke Verspackung* (08-21.288). For an application of the principle in a patent case *see also,* Cass. Com., 20 sept. 2011, *Negerco c. Mavil & Maviflex* (10-22.888).
127. Cass. Civ. 2e, 22 juin 2017, *F+P+B* (15-29.202).

With regards to patent law, there is to this date no case law that would give us any indication on the reception of a principle based on legitimate expectations. For the time being it seems that patent courts would rather rely on principles and legal rules which have their roots in civil law (including competition law) and in the tradition of French law. However, it could be argued that with the current trends in enforcement of SEPs and promises to license FRAND, if courts take into account considerations of good faith from both parties in the framework of FRAND negotiations, it could be worth exploring further the potential for an estoppel under French patent law. This would also be the case if a pledge to license FRAND is understood as a *stipulation pour autrui* generating rights and obligations presenting similarities with more traditional contracts. In this case, the sanction for the breach of the promise to license FRAND could potentially either be the allocation of damages (if we believe we are still in a pre-contractual or negotiation phase) or a limitation on the exercise of rights of the promisor (if we understand the pledge as creating clear contractual obligations between the parties).

Nevertheless, many uncertainties remain. First, it is unclear to what extent a FRAND undertaking is equivalent to a *stipulation pour autrui* and the legal effects that this qualification may have on injunctive relief. Second, the legal basis, the regime or scope of application of the concept of legitimate expectations to French law[128] in general, and more specifically to patent law, is far from being set in stone. It presents connection with other fundamental principles such as good faith, abuse, fraud, procedural loyalty or the theory of appearance, but it currently lacks its own standing. Finally, judges do have – to some extent – discretionary powers and a room to manoeuvre when it comes to relief. Therefore, it is questionable whether the adoption of a specific principle regarding legitimate expectations is either necessary or desirable.

[B] The Complex Product Issue

It is here questioned whether French judges could limit or deny injunctive relief in cases where the enforced patent covers only small aspects or a small part of a more complex device. Traditionally, this aspect has been taken into account for the determination of damages. French courts have assessed whether to include in the calculation of damages the more complex device or if such remedy should only relate to the smaller patented part. Some computation therefore takes place leading to a tailoring of damages.[129]

---

128. Mazeaud, *supra* n. 122, at 381.
129. For a detailed explanation on the quantification of damages *see*, AIPPI 2017 – study report (France) – quantification of monetary relief (5 May 2017). Available at: http://aippi.org/committee/quantification-of-monetary-relief/ (accessed 31 Jul. 2018). 'Where the product reproducing the intellectual property right constitutes a part of a product: (i) the court seeks to ascertain whether said part is merely an accessory to a whole or (ii) whether it constitutes a decisive factor in the mind of the consumer for the purchase of the product' (*Id.*, at 6).

With regards to the impact on injunctive relief, it is argued[130] that such a factual situation could result in decisions in which injunctive relief would not automatically be granted. It could notably be considered disproportionate to grant an injunction in such a case as it would cause tremendous harm to the infringer compared to the advantages of the injunction for the patent holder. Depending on the circumstances of a case, it could also be argued that, damages for past infringement could be sufficient in order to repair the infringement and that an injunction would therefore be unjustified. Once again, such interpretation would fall within the scope of Article 3 of the Enforcement Directive. Case law embracing this approach is however lacking so far and a clear determination from French courts on when such factual situations could play a role vis-à-vis injunction is uncertain.

§5.06 US CONCERNS

[A] The Impact of eBay on Injunctive Relief in France

Although discussed at the doctrinal level, the decision in *eBay v. MercExchange*[131] and the four-factor test developed by the Supreme Court of the United States of America, did not impact patent law or the practice of French courts with regard to the grant or denial of injunctive relief.[132] French literature is not particularly favourable to a test such as the one elaborated in *eBay v. MercExchange* for different reasons.[133] First, French law is based on written rules that can be completed, when necessary, by the interpretation of judges. Second, some authors claim that injunctive relief should be automatic because the patent system should be strong in order to support R&D initiatives and should not be a 'reward to infringement'.[134] Third, the possibility to sanction patent holders should be circumscribed to a specific and justified set of circumstances since they benefit from an exclusive right.[135] In that respect, it is argued that the system of exclusivity and protection granted by patent law should be sustained, even in the event where judges have the impression that the protection is too easy to obtain, too wide, too long or if the exceptions to exclusivity seem to be missing or are too narrow.[136]

---

130. Stephen Bennett, Stanislas Roux-Vaillard & Christian Mammen, *Shifting attitudes to injunctions in patent cases*, managingip.com (Feb. 2015), http://www.managingip.com/Article/3420480/Shifting-attitudes-to-injunctions-in-patent-cases.html (accessed 31 Jul. 2018).
131. *eBay Inc. v. MercExchange, L.L.C.*, 547 U.S. 388 (2006).
132. AIPPI Question Q219, *supra* n. 13, at 25.
133. *Ibid.*
134. Cyra Nargolwalla, *Les injonctions permanentes devant la Juridiction Unifiée du Brevet: Les arguments en faveur du maintien du principe de la cessation de la contrefaçon*, Presentation at the Journée ouverte du Groupe Français de l'AIPPI, Cabinet Plasseraud (12 Juin 2014), http://www.aippi.fr/upload/juin%202014%20licences%20frand/6.-12062014-aippi-injonctions-permanentes-jub-cyra-nargolwalla.pdf (accessed 31 Jul. 2018).
135. AIPPI Question Q157 – Groupe français. *Relations entre les normes techniques et les droits de brevet* (2008), http://www.aippi.fr/upload/Melbourne%202001%20Q155%20156%20157%20208%20159/gr157france_fr.pdf (accessed 31 Jul. 2018), 19.
136. Ullrich, *supra* n. 32, at 441.

With regard to *preliminary* injunction, in each case, judges have the possibility to assess the appropriateness of the measures. The discretion in the hands of French judges makes the typical Anglo-Saxon reliance on a 'test' superfluous.[137] French requirements to obtain a preliminary injunction combined with some degree of judicial discretion (including the fact that judges have the opportunity to balance the interests of the parties involved in patent litigation before granting a preliminary injunction)[138] appear to provide sufficient flexibility to French judges. Regarding *permanent* injunctions, French literature supports the system currently applied by the Paris District Court. If a patent is valid and infringed, the rule must be that a permanent injunction will be granted, unless justified otherwise by exceptional circumstances.[139] Injunctive relief is considered to be the natural sanction in case of violation of property, and should only be denied in case of 'abuse of rights' or anticompetitive behaviour.[140] It is nonetheless argued that, with some audacity from judges, it is not inconceivable that French judges would take into account the attitude of patent holders, especially when they are acting for speculative purposes or without industrial considerations, to only grant damages as a sanction for infringement.[141] In the context of FRAND-pledge and SEPs, it is contended that French judges should be able to decide on an appropriate sanction and may repair infringement by equivalent instead of granting injunctive relief.[142] On a more general and European level, this solution would notably fall in line with an interpretation of Articles 11 and 12, read in combination with Article 3.2 of the Enforcement Directive, and the principle according to which remedies should be 'effective, proportionate and dissuasive and shall be applied in such a manner as to avoid the creation of barriers to legitimate trade and to provide for safeguards against their abuse'.

[B] Patent Trolling Scenarios under French Patent Law

French patent law does not make any distinction between patent holders. The grant of injunctions is not subordinated to the effective exploitation of patents.[143] Therefore 'aggressive' patent holders (such as some non-practicing entities, patent assertion entities or so-called patent trolls) can sue alleged infringers with the prospect of obtaining injunctive relief.[144] Similarly to other patent holders, the denial of injunctive relief requires the proof that these entities have adopted a reprehensible behaviour[145] such as engaging in anticompetitive behaviour or abusing their rights. There is also no legal provision regarding the consequences of the fact that a patent holder may wish to

---

137. AIPPI Question Q219, *supra* n. 13, at 24.
138. Galloux, *supra* n. 18, at 3; AIPPI Question Q219, *supra* n. 13, at 24.
139. AIPPI Question Q219, *supra* n. 13, at 25.
140. Pezard, *supra* n. 48.
141. Christian Le Stanc, *Les malfaisants lutins de la forêt des brevets : à propos des patent trolls*, 7(2) Propriété Industrielle 5, étude 3 (2008).
142. Caron (2013), *supra* n. 102.
143. AIPPI Question Q219, *supra* n. 13, at 12; Bouvet, *supra* n. 7, at 573. Pezard, *supra* n. 48.
144. Bouvet, *supra* n. 7, at 589.
145. Pezard, *supra* n. 48.

take advantage of the compulsory situation of the patent user when bringing an infringement action or an injunction claim. It is worth mentioning however that, under French law, to warn an alleged infringer before initiating proceedings, or to warn customers of the alleged infringer, should be conducted with caution. The notice should not turn into acts of disparagement, which are characteristic of unfair commercial practices.

In practice, the situation is more nuanced. In proceedings on the merits, the lack of exploitation or the sporadic commercialization of a product covered by the patent, can impact the amount of damages granted to repair past infringement. For example, in a recent case, the Paris Court of Appeal[146] overturned a decision of the TGI which awarded damages to a NPE because the damages had solely been based on the actual profits made by the infringer. The court considered that this was contrary to the principle according to which victims of infringement must justify their actual losses in order to be fully compensated. In light of the circumstances of the case and the fact that the patent holder was not exploiting the patent at stake, it could not obtain the profits made by the infringer without actual proof of negative economic consequences for the patent holder. According to AIPPI study report for France on quantification of monetary relief: 'In this case, the Court appears to have been mindful of the particular circumstances of the case and of the risk that taking into account only the profit made by the infringer would encourage patent trolls'.[147] This case aligns with other decisions in which it was decided that, in the event of patent holders who do not exploit the patents at stake, they will obtain damages equivalent to royalties which should have been paid if the infringer had obtained the authorization to exploit the patent from its holder.[148] The level of royalties will nonetheless be higher than for a contractual licensee since acts of infringement must be taken into consideration (Article L.615-7 IPC).

The absence of exploitation or commercialization can also, but under exceptional circumstances only, impact injunctive relief (preliminary or permanent).[149] According to French literature, courts may have the opportunity to deny the grant of a permanent injunction where the applicant uses his patents to hamper the market or in a purely financial manner, but also where the applicant uses his patents in a manner considered to be a diversion of the object or the function of patent law.[150] This would notably include cases where the applicant does not exploit his patents, where he did not

---

146. CA Paris (2e ch.) 09 déc. 2016, *SARL Carrera c. SA Muller et cie.* (RG 16/02891).
147. AIPPI 2017 – study report (France) – quantification of monetary relief (5 May 2017), 8. Available at: http://aippi.org/committee/quantification-of-monetary-relief/.
148. By opposition to the actual prejudice suffered and evaluated on the basis of loss of earnings incurred by the right holder, or unfair profits made by the infringer. For example, TGI Paris (3e ch. 4e sct.) 22 nov. 2012, *SA France Telecom et al. c. TCT Mobile Europe et al.* (RG 10/18196): 33: 'En effet, leurs activités économiques relatives à l'exploitation du brevet, avant qu'il n'expire, ne consistant qu'à percevoir des redevances, elles ne peuvent prétendre avoir subi un préjudice économique lié à la baisse des ventes de leurs produits du fait de la commercialisation des produits contrefaisants'. See also, TGI Paris (3e ch. 4e sct) 02 juillet 2015, *Vorwerk & Co. Interholding GmbH c. G. Demarle Grand Public et al.* (RG 12/11488): 26.
149. AIPPI Question Q219, *supra* n. 13, at 12.
150. Le Stanc, *supra* n. 49. AIPPI Question Q219, *supra* n. 13, at 25.

develop the invention himself or where the applicant uses his patents for the sole purpose of enforcement.[151] A permanent injunction may also be denied where there is a striking disproportion between the measure and the damages resulting from the injunction on the user.[152] These exceptional circumstances can be subsumed to either a 'competition law' defence (Articles L420-1, L420-2 or even L442-6[153] of the French Commercial Code) or an 'abuse of rights' defence as explained *supra*.

To circumvent injunctive relief, defendant could also rely on Articles L613-11 IPC to L613-14 IPC. Although not yet allowed by courts, Article L613-11 IPC mentions 'non-exploitation' as a cause to obtain a licence. It is said that this provision could represent a useful mechanism against so-called patent trolls that do not exploit patents.[154] However, legal requirements must be met in order to benefit from such a compulsory license. There must be evidence of a lack of exploitation and the patent holder (or its licensees) had no legitimate reasons for the non-exploitation for more than three years from the date of the grant of the patent, or that the exploitation has been interrupted for more than three years. It is not important that the infringer already infringed the patent, as long as it can be showed that that the infringer was refused an amicable license (L.613-12 CPI). It is suggested that to propose excessive rates could be considered as a refuse to license. If these conditions are met, the infringer who has the capacity to seriously and effectively exploit the patent could obtain a license.[155]

To date, French courts do not have a long history of cases involving 'patent trolls'. However, as stated by some commentators, the Luxemburg-based company *High Point SARL* (a subsidiary of *Inpro Licensing*[156]) qualifies as a Patent Assertion Entity, and was recently involved in two patent cases in France. The Italian undertaking *SISVEL*[157] took part in multiple litigations in France in recent years.[158] Although *SISVEL* is essentially a licensing company engaged in monetization of SEPs, it has also been called a Patent Assertion Entity by some in the media and in literature. In 2014, the Paris Court of Appeal[159] overturned a first-instance decision granting interim relief to *High Point* on the basis that it limited itself to asserting claims without providing any proof of infringement.[160] The Court held that, since interim measures such as the ones

---

151. Julien Pénin, *Le problème des 'patent trolls': comment limiter la spéculation sur la propriété intellectuelle dans une économie fondée sur les connaissances?* 32(2) Innovations 35, 35–53 (2010). AIPPI Question Q219, *supra* n. 13, at 25.
152. Le Stanc, *supra* n. 141, at 4; AIPPI Question Q219, *supra* n. 13, at 25.
153. Article L442-6 of the French Commercial Code deal with discriminatory practices. It is argued that if a patent troll threatens to raise its royalty rate in case a first-proposed potential licensee only takes a license after another alleged infringer, the first-proposed could raise an argument based on discriminatory practices. See Le Stanc, *supra* n. 49, at 1.
154. Le Stanc, *supra* n. 49.
155. Le Stanc, *supra* n. 141, at 4.
156. Inpro Licensing owns, acquires and manages portfolios of Intellectual Property worldwide, and realises its commercial value by licensing it to others, http://www.inprolicensing.com.
157. Societa Italiana Per Lo Sviluppo Dell'Electronica, http://www.sisvel.com.
158. For example, CA Paris (4e ch.) 06 déc. 2006, *SISVEL SPA c. Safran SA* (RG 05/15570).
159. CA Paris (3e ch.) 28 jan. 2014, *SA Société Française du Radiotéléphone – SFR, SAS Huawei Technologies France, SA Bouygues Telecom c. HIGH POINT* (RG 13/08128).
160. And therefore, did not comply with the requirements to obtain interim relief as mentioned *supra*. See also, TGI Paris (3e ch. 3e sct.) 30 oct. 2015, *Vringo Infrastructure Inc. c. ZTE Corporation and ZTE France SASU* (RG 13/06691). CA Paris (3e ch.) 28 jan. 2014, *SA Société*

obtained in first instance (i.e., seizure measures and access to documents of the defendants) are of an exceptional severity, in particular when they are non-adversarial, patent holders cannot simply rely on assertions and allegations. In light of the circumstances of the case, to grant such interim relief would have been excessive. The Court also held that a patent holder must act with fairness and loyalty when asserting its claim, and notably provide the court with essential information vis-à-vis all the circumstances surrounding the case (e.g., licensing agreements, opposition at the EPO...).[161] *SISVEL* has been involved in various patent cases in France. It was notably part of dispute between *France Telecom* and *Electro Depot* where the *Cour de Cassation*[162] affirmed previous decisions which held admissible the claims to obtain interim relief, but which have been dismissed for lack of object since the asserted patent had expired.

Another concern related to the 'patent troll' debate is the creation of state funds. In 2011, the investment fund 'France Brevets' was created. The fund is jointly owned by the French government and the *Caisse des Depots et Consignations*. It is said to be dedicated to international patent licensing, to the growing and monetizing of innovation and to the development of strategic patent positions and monetization through effective and focused licensing efforts in favour of French SMEs.[163] According to France Brevets, it 'does not adopt a "sue first" posture' contrary to patent trolls.[164] However, its role and the appropriateness of its actions are questioned. Some qualify France Brevet as a 'state-owned patent troll' created by the French government with taxpayer money, which is detrimental not only to innovation but also to the Internal Market.[165] With regard to the latter, it is argued that France Brevets' actions might constitute illegal state aids (Article 107 TFUE) and may be representative of a strategy of national protectionism since it only supports actions of French companies.[166] In May 2016,[167]

Française du Radiotéléphone – SFR, SAS Huawei Technologies France, SA Bouygues Telecom c. Société HIGH POINT (RG 13/08128): 7: 'La cour ne peut que constater que la société HIGH POINT procède par affirmation; qu'il n'est fourni aucune pièce au soutien de ces assertions'. In 2016, High Point decided to discontinue the proceeding. TGI Paris (3e ch. 1e sct.) 17 mars 2016, *HIGH POINT c. SA Société Française du Radiotéléphone et al.* (RG 12/12354).

161. See also, TGI Paris (3e ch. 3e sct.) (ord. ref.) 08 juillet 2009, *Zhejiand Huakang Pharmaceutical C. Ltd c. Roquette Freres* (RG 09/08704).
162. Cass. Com. 21 oct. 2014, *Orange (France Telecom), TDF, Philips, Institut Fur Rundfunktechnik GMBH, Audio MPEG Inc, Societa Italiana Per Lo Sviluppo Dell'Electronica c. Electro Depot France* (13-15.435). See also, TGI Paris (ord. ref.) 28 juin 2011, *S.A. France Telecom, S.A.S. TDF, societe de droit neerlandais Koninklijke Philips Electronics N.V., societe de droit allemand Institut Fur Rundfunktechnik GMBH, societe Audio MPEG Inc, Societa Italiana Per Lo Sviluppo Dell'Electronica c. Electro Depot France* (RG 11/55030). TGI Paris (3e ch. 4e sct) 20 oct. 2011, *SA France Telecom, Societe TDF, Societe Koninklijke Philips Electronics N.V., Institut fur Rundfunktechnik GMBH, Audio MPEG Inc., cieta Italiana Per Lo Sviluppo Dell'Electronica c. Leroy Merlin France, Texas de France (Worldsat)* (RG 10/05787).
163. France Brevets: The Patent Generation. http://www.francebrevets.com/.
164. France Brevets: The Patent Generation. 'What we do'. http://www.francebrevets.com/.
165. Thibault Schrepel, *France Brevets: a state-owned patent troll, harmful...and illegal?* New Direction Discussion Paper (February 2014), http://europeanreform.org/files/New_Direction_-_France_Brevets_%284%29.pdf (accessed 31 Jul. 2018).
166. *Id.*, p. 9.
167. TGI Paris (3e ch. 1e sct.) 26 mai 2016, *Mme N. Walthert & SAS France Brevets c. SARL Nintendo France & Nintendo Europe* (RG 14/05090).

the Paris District Court in *N. Walthert & France Brevets v. Nintendo* denied injunctive relief to France Brevets because of the invalidity of the asserted patent. The defendant attempted to rely on a competition law defence. It argued that the agreement between the original patent holder and France Brevets was equivalent to an illegal state aid (Article 107 TFEU). However, the Court rejected the argument since the defendant did not sufficiently substantiate its claim. The Court also found admissible arguments of unfair commercial practices and 'abuse of rights' but ultimately considered them ill founded.

In 2015, the French Government and the *Caisse des depots et consignations* have created a second fund, the 'Fonds souverain de la propriete intellectuelle' (FSPI). The fund is to be active in the acquisition of patents in order to encourage the development of French and European industry in the dissemination of innovation. The FSPI also wishes to include patents stemming from French R&D in international standards. The new structure raises similar concerns to those identified for France Brevets.[168]

§5.07 CONCLUSIVE REMARKS

French courts have a long history of cases in which the conditions and requirements to obtain injunctive relief have been tested. It can be concluded that judges do beneficiate from a certain room to manoeuvre before granting or denying an injunction (preliminary or permanent). Even though the grant of a permanent injunction is considered to be systematic in case of infringement, French judges have taken advantage of their discretionary powers where the circumstances of the case required them to do so. French courts have taken into consideration the behaviour of both parties involved in litigation before deciding on injunction. Judges can rely on their judicial discretion, the room of interpretation left open by the relevant provisions – including an interpretation in compliance with the rules of the Enforcement Directive and the TRIPs Agreement – competition law defences or 'abuse of rights' defence to deny injunctive relief and deliver justice in a proportionate and fair manner.

---

168. Nicolas Binctin, *Le Fonds souverain de la propriété intellectuelle*, 6 La Semaine Juridique Entreprise et Affaires 1077 (2015).

CHAPTER 6
Patent Injunctions in Dutch Law

Matt Heckman

§6.01 INTRODUCTION TO DUTCH PATENT LAW

A Dutch patent can be obtained under the Dutch Patent Act of 1995[1] (Patent Act), the European Patent Convention and the Patent Cooperation Treaty. Article 2(1) of the Patent Act complies with Article 52(1) of the European Patent Convention, stating that a patent can only be granted to those inventions which are: new, involve an inventive step and are capable of industrial application. The Patent Act came into force on 1 April 1995, replacing the earlier Patent Act of 1910. Initially, the Patent Act distinguished between a six and a twenty-year patent. In June 2008, the Patent Act was revised. The six-year patent ceased to exist and as a new element, the novelty search for all new patents was introduced. The duration of a Dutch patent is twenty years from the date of application (*Article 36(5) Patent Act*).

  A Dutch patent can be revoked by a court decision. The District Court of the Hague has exclusive jurisdiction in the first instance for the invalidation of a patent (*Article 80(1)(a) Patent Act*). Court cases on the infringement or nullity will always be decided in the Hague, initially by the District Court, then possibly by the Court of Appeal and ultimately by the Supreme Court of the Netherlands. The purpose of the system is to guarantee that by centralizing the relevant court system, the judges will become more knowledgeable and specialized in patent cases.

---

1. https://www.ivir.nl/syscontent/pdfs/163.pdf.

§6.02 GENERAL OVERVIEW OF REMEDIES AND PROCEDURE IN PATENT INFRINGEMENT DISPUTES

The Hague District Court has exclusive jurisdiction in patent infringement cases. Proceedings are initiated by summoning the opposing party with a writ. There are three forms of infringement proceedings. First, there are preliminary proceedings leading to granting of provisional measures. In such proceedings a preliminary injunction may be obtained within months, or in urgent cases within days. A preliminary injunction (*Kort Geding*) can be obtained in proceedings between the parties or ex parte. Preliminary proceedings must be followed by accelerated proceedings on the merits. Second, there are accelerated proceeding on the merits. In accelerated proceedings, the claimant must petition the court for permission. The court then sets a strict schedule, including pre-set dates for serving the writ, the statement of defence and pleadings. The proceedings last between eleven and fifteen months. Third, there are proceedings on the merits. These generally last from one year up to two and a half years, excluding appeal proceedings.

Generally, the following final remedies are available to a patent owner in case of patent infringement: damages, including lost profits; infringer's profits resulting from the infringement; compensation for legal costs incurred; surrender or destruction of infringing products; information about the infringing trade; corrective measures (e.g., in a public newspaper). Seizure of infringing products and of evidence is also possible. These remedies are based on Directive 2004/48.

The Dutch Civil Code provides for the procedure known as *Kort Geding,* which is – as the name suggests – a shortened version of court proceedings. These are preliminary relief proceedings, that can be used in urgent cases. The infringement of a patent is by definition an urgent case; hence patentees may obtain an injunction as a provisional measure. Such a preliminary injunction comes with a penalty sum (*astreinte*). If the defendant continues to infringe the patent, he will face a financial penalty per day which can be very substantial. The penalty must be paid to the patent owner. A preliminary injunction will restore patentee's exclusive market position rather quickly, and therefore is often preferred to claim for damages. When a cross-border injunction is granted in the Netherlands it will stop effectively infringements in other Member States at relatively low cost. The fees of Dutch attorneys are considerably lower than the fees of German or British colleagues and the patent owner only needs to litigate in one Member State.

In very urgent matters, especially if delay would cause irreparable harm to the patentee, the patentee can request the Provisions Judge to issue a so-called ex parte injunction (Article 1019e Dutch Code of Civil Procedure), i.e., an injunction without hearing the alleged infringer. Such an ex parte injunction decision can usually be obtained within two or three days.

Generally, however preliminary injunction proceedings are *inter partes*. The same applies to provisional injunction claims pending proceedings on the merits. In case of an ex parte injunction request, the alleged infringer will find out about it when the ex parte injunction decision is served on it. Whether or not a negative decision on an ex parte injunction request is published, is at the discretion of the Judge. The Hague

District Court has the policy not to publish negative decisions on ex parte injunction requests, unless the Judge would be of the opinion that the decision contains a new development which is relevant for the IP law practice. In that case, the decision to be published would be anonymized as much as possible. The Court could also decide not to grant the ex parte injunction request immediately, but to schedule an *inter partes* hearing first. If that is the case and the request is not withdrawn, the claimant and defendant will find out about the decision at the same time.

The preliminary injunction decision can be appealed before a Court of Appeal. Appeal proceedings in the Netherlands are *de novo*, which means that the parties can raise additional facts and arguments in support of their positions. No permission for appeal is required. The appeal term for decisions in preliminary relief proceedings is four weeks. Decisions of the Court of Appeal can be appealed before the Supreme Court.

Protective letters aim to prevent a Court from issuing an ex parte injunction or evidentiary seizure on an ex parte basis. Protective letters contain arguments explaining why no such measure should be ordered. Protective letters are not a guarantee that no ex parte measure will be issued. The Provisions Judge will simply consider the arguments in the request and the protective letter when rendering a decision on whether to grant the requested measure.

Dutch court will award a final injunction if it finds the patent valid and infringed. An injunction will only be refused in case of exceptional circumstances. These exceptional circumstances include abuse of rights or a conflict with pre-contractual good faith. Although there are no specific requirements that can be deducted from Dutch case-law obviously the willingness to negotiate in good faith is very relevant. Competition law concerns like the abuse of rights will be discussed below.

§6.03 PRELIMINARY (INTERIM) INJUNCTIONS

Dutch commercial civil procedure law provides for provisional remedies in preliminary proceedings. These proceedings give an immediate provisional relief, however in urgent cases only. Given the urgency of the case, the timeframe in preliminary proceedings is relatively short.

In preliminary proceedings, the normal rules regarding burden of proof are not applicable. The court makes a provisional assessment of the case (which may include balancing of interests) and will only grant the relief if urgency requirement is present. The court will evaluate whether there is a serious chance that the patent will be held invalid in opposition proceedings (if applicable) or proceedings on the merits. The court examines whether it is sufficiently evident that there is a (threat of) infringement. Preliminary injunctions are normally immediately enforceable notwithstanding appeal. They must be followed-up by proceedings on the merit.

Preliminary injunctions can be obtained within four to six weeks after commencement of the proceedings. If the court is of the opinion that the patent is infringed and that there is not a significant chance that the patent will be revoked in opposition or nullity proceedings, it is likely to grant a preliminary injunction. However, it is not uncommon that the subject matter will be considered too complex to be dealt with in preliminary proceedings. Therefore, preliminary injunctions are usually not granted in complex patent infringement cases.

Dutch courts, before granting preliminary injunctions, consider a number of factors. These include patent validity, urgency, likelihood of infringement, complexity of the case and balance of interest between parties. Each if the above-mentioned factors will be dealt with briefly below.

[A] Patent Validity

Dutch courts do not evaluate patent validity in the preliminary injunction proceedings directly. Nevertheless, courts anticipate possible outcome of the decision on the merits and the opposition or nullity proceedings. The decision on the preliminary injunction can be heavily influenced (and possibly an injunction may be denied) if the court has strong indications that the patent will be revoked in opposition or nullity proceedings. If the patent is revoked preliminary injunction most likely will not be granted, unless the patentee is able to show that obvious mistakes were made during such proceedings. Thus, the outcome of the opposition or nullity proceedings plays a major role. If the patent has been upheld, the court will assume validity and grant a preliminary injunction. However, if there is a reasonable chance that the patent will be revoked in the appeal proceedings, the court will refrain from granting preliminary relief.

[B] Urgency

The patentee must show that he has an urgent interest in getting a preliminary injunction. Dutch courts require that the patentee does not wait before starting the preliminary injunction case. The Dutch Supreme Court held in *Impag v. Hasbro* that when there is an ongoing infringement of IP rights, the patentee still has to show urgency.[2] This is a change from the past practice in patent cases where urgency was automatically assumed on the basis of a continuing infringement. If significant amount of time elapses between sending of an infringement letter and the serving a writ of an injunction, urgency is lost.[3]

[C] Likelihood of Infringement

Dutch courts, in preliminary proceedings, evaluate infringement claims on a prima facie basis. If the court thinks that the patent is valid and that there is an infringement,

---

2. Decision of 29 June 2001, NJ; 2001, 602 https://www.ivir.nl/publicaties/download/noot-impag-hasbro.pdf.
3. In a recent decision (case C/09/508927/ KG ZA 16-454 of June 17, 2016) even a final decision of the EPO Board of Appeal on the validity of the patent could not prevent the urgency criterion being lost. See for more background, Managing Intellectual Property of 24 August 2016: M. Klok in Urgency defined in patent case. Also, Presentation Gertjan Kuipers: Nederlandse jurisprudentie 2015/2016 Wolters Kluwer.

preliminary injunction will be granted. In case the infringement is heavily disputed between parties, Dutch courts will be more reluctant to grant a preliminary injunction.

[D]   Complexity of the Case

Dutch courts may conclude that the complexity of the patent infringement case, makes it impossible to render a preliminary injunction. The difficulty of establishing patent infringement on a prima facie basis, would be another reason for declining a preliminary injunction.

The threshold regarding complexity is very high. Complexity defence can only be raised in relation to facts, not in relation to the law. Given the provisional nature of the preliminary injunction and the inherent right of the plaintiff to obtain an injunction, this defence is rarely raised. There is a possibility off course that the defendant will try to use the complexity argument for strategic reasons. However, it is not necessarily prudent to claim that the court cannot understand the complexity of the case.

[E]   Balance of Interests

The most important factor in preliminary injunction proceedings is the balance of interests. The courts when deciding whether to grant a preliminary injunction are bound to consider interests of all parties involved. Save in exceptional circumstances, the right to enforce IP rights will prevail. When balancing interests, the following circumstances are taken into account: provisional nature of the injunction, severity of the consequences arising out of the injunction, extent of damages incurred, fear for repetition of patent infringement, availability of possible alternative ways to meet the interests of claimant (e.g. a security deposit).

Dutch courts acknowledge that during the preliminary relief proceedings there is much more room for balancing of interests.[4] The balancing act consists of weighing consequences of the injunction for the defendant and the actual or potential damages that can be incurred by the plaintiff. Courts, recognizing the interim character of a preliminary injunction may decide not to grant an injunction, if the interests of the plaintiff could be served in a different way, less burdensome for the defendant.[5]

[F]   Standard of Proof and Other Procedural Requirements

The plaintiff is required to prove that he owns the patent or has rights as a licensee to enforce the patent, that the patent is in force and that the patent has been infringed. Often the patentee will use a claim chart that demonstrates both the claims of the patent and the characteristics of the infringing product.

Parties may resort to various means of evidence in the court proceedings. Expert reports, documents and witness reports can all be used. On average the proceedings on

---

4. Supreme Court 15 Dec. 1995, NJ 1996, 509; *Pampers/Huggies*.
5. For example, President of the District Court of Roermond 3 Apr. 1986, BIE 1993, 2 (*Berkers/GEM*).

the preliminary relief will start two weeks after the writ of summons is received. Three weeks after the hearing the decision is given. Pending the proceedings, temporary injunctions cannot be granted, but parties may request the permission to seize infringing products.

In the preliminary proceedings, courts will indicate the relevant time-period in which the claimant has to start proceeding on the merits. If the claimant does not start proceedings on the merits within a reasonable time-period, the preliminary relief order will lapse. No undertaking or bond is required to obtain a preliminary injunction. Preliminary injunctions are usually subject to penalty payments. If the injunction decision is violated, the claimant can claim payment of the penalties. In addition, the claimant can claim damages in relation to the violation.

[G] Judicial Discretion

Courts exercise a large degree of discretion regarding the burden and standard of proof. They also exercise a certain degree of discretion in determining the scope and duration of the injunction and conditions to be met before the injunction takes effect.

In most cases Dutch courts favour patentee's legitimate interests to enforce his patent against infringers. The fact that the defendant suffers severe damage does not justify denial of an injunction, especially when the patentee offers security.

In principle Dutch courts may grant preliminary injunctions in ex parte proceedings but in practice ex parte grants of injunctions are limited. This takes place when the plaintiff can successfully rely on previous decisions or when patent infringement is obvious.

§6.04 PERMANENT INJUNCTIONS

Permanent injunctions are based on Article 3:296 of the Dutch Civil Code which provides that *'Unless it otherwise follows from the law, the nature of the obligation or a juridical act, the person obliged to give, to do or not to do something as regards another will be ordered to do so by the court upon the demand of the person to whom the obligation is owed.'*

Therefore, if the validity of an IP right and the (real threat of) infringement is established, the court will order an injunction, unless the law, the nature of the obligation or a juridical act, provides otherwise. Examples of these exceptions are, for example: lack of interest (Article 3:303 DCC); reasons of compelling social interests (6:168 DCC); criteria of reasonableness and fairness (6:2 DCC) and abuse of law.[6]

Additionally, Dutch courts may also exercise a certain degree of discretion in determining the scope of a final injunction as well as the duration and conditions to be met before the injunction takes effect. Article 233 of the Dutch Code of Civil Procedure enables the court to grant an injunction which is not immediately enforceable or is enforceable only under specific conditions. The court may, for example, require that

---

6. *See also* http://www.aippi.nl/nl/documents/AIPPIReportQ219TheNetherlands.pdf.

the patent holder provides security for possible damage that may result from the enforcement of an injunction and which must be remunerated in case the injunction is overturned on appeal.[7]

In one of the cases the Court held that the interests of patients could outweigh the financial interest of a patentee trying to obtain an injunction.[8] Article 6:168 of the Dutch Civil Code allows to deny an injunction on the basis of significant public interest. The case-law in this field is however limited and very ambiguous.[9]

§6.05 CROSS-BORDER INJUNCTIONS

Cross-border injunctions became popular in the Netherlands in the 1990s. There are generally two types of cross-border patent disputes. First, the patentee can request an injunction before a national court regarding a patent valid in another EU Member State, or for several national parts of one European patent. Second, the potential infringer may request a negative judgement declaring that several national parts of one European patent are not infringed.

Dutch courts assessed jurisdiction in cases where multiple defendants infringed parallel IP rights in the Netherlands and other EC Member States.[10] Pan-European injunctions were issued in preliminary proceedings and in proceedings on the merits. This was made possible due to a broad interpretation of Article 6(1) of the Brussels Convention.[11]

[A] *Roche v. Primus*

In 1998 The Hague Court of Appeals introduced the so-called spider in the web concept. The Court held that it could assume jurisdiction over co-defendants domiciled outside of the Netherlands and in relation to infringements committed outside of the Netherlands. It required however that the defendant domiciled in the Netherlands coordinated the infringing acts of the co-defendants.[12]

The question whether Dutch courts have jurisdiction to rule in cases against multiple defendants domiciled in various Member States was the subject of a preliminary ruling by the CJEU as a result of the request by the Dutch Supreme Court in *Roche v. Primus*.[13] The CJEU concluded that Article 6(1) of the Brussels Convention was not applicable in European patent proceedings involving various firms domiciled in different Member States in relation to acts committed in one or more of those Member States, even when companies were part of the same group and acted in a common way. This put an end to the 'spider in the web' doctrine in the Netherlands.

---

7. Supreme Court 29 Nov. 1996, NJ 1997, 684 (*Gommers/Evers*).
8. *Ibid.*, note 9.
9. *See also* https://aippi.org/download/commitees/202/GR202the_netherlands.pdf.
10. *Interlas v. Lincoln*, Supreme Court, 24 Nov. 1989, BIE 1991, 23, p86; NJ 1992, 404.
11. Now Art. 6 para.1 of Regulation 44/2001.
12. *EGP/Boston Scientific*, 23 Apr. 1998, BIE 2002, 8, p. 25 and *Boston Scientific/Cordis*, 26 Nov. 1998, BIE 2002, 10, p. 46.
13. *Roche v. Primus* (C-539, 13 Jul. 2006).

[B]   GAT-LuK

In *GAT v. LuK* case the CJEU was asked to interpret Article 16(4) of the Brussels Convention (now Article 24(4) Regulation 1215/2012 (Brussels I Regulation Recast), which provides that the court where the patent right is registered has exclusive jurisdiction in all proceedings relating to registration and invalidity of the patent.

The request for a preliminary ruling came from a German court in a patent dispute between two German companies GAT and LuK operating in the motor industry. LuK owned two French patents on mechanical dumper springs. LuK alleged that these patents were infringed by GAT when it offered these patents protected springs to a German vehicle manufacturer. GAT brought an action for declaratory judgement claiming that it did not infringe the French patents and that additionally the French patents were invalid.

The Dusseldorf Regional Court held that it had jurisdiction both with respect to the infringement claim as well as with respect to the plea alleging nullity of the two French patents. The Regional Court dismissed the action by GAT and ruled that the two French patents were valid. On appeal the Higher Regional Court decided to stay the proceedings and refer questions on the interpretation of Article 16(4) of the Brussels Convention.

The Higher Regional Court asked the CJEU to give ruling on the scope of the exclusive jurisdiction within the meaning of Article 16(4) of the Brussels Convention. The Court in particular asked whether exclusive jurisdiction covered all proceedings where the question of invalidity is raised, irrespective of whether invalidity is raised by way of an action or plea in objection or whether the exclusive jurisdiction is limited to proceedings where it is raised by way of an action.

In *GAT v. LuK* the invalidity was raised in proceedings for the declaration of non-infringement by way of a plea alleging invalidity. In infringement proceedings where the right holder seeks an injunction, the issue of invalidity is also raised as a defence and by way of a plea.

The CJEU ruled that exclusive jurisdiction within the meaning of Article 16(4) covered all proceedings where the issue of invalidity is raised whether by way of an action or as a result of a plea alleging invalidity. The reasoning of the CJEU was based on the following three arguments:

(1) the rules on exclusive jurisdiction would be seriously undermined, if a court of a Member State other than the Member State where the patent had been registered, when seized of an action for infringement or an action for declaration of non-infringement could also indirectly establish invalidity of a patent. This would allow the parties to circumvent the rules on exclusive jurisdiction by formulating their claims in a particular way.

(2) limiting the application of Article 16(4) to cases where there is an action for invalidity would result in multiplying heads of jurisdiction. This would hinder the predictability of the jurisdiction rules of the Convention and would lead to lack of legal certainty, which is one of the main objectives of the Convention.

(3) allowing courts other than the court in the country where the patent is registered to decide indirectly on validity would multiply the risk of conflicting decisions limiting the effectiveness of the Convention.

[C]   *Solvay v. Honeywell*

In March 2009 Solvay brought in the Dutch court an action against a number of Honeywell companies for infringement of the national parts of its European patent in Denmark, Ireland, Greece, Luxembourg, Austria, Portugal, Finland, Sweden, Liechtenstein and Switzerland. Solvay alleged that Honeywell companies marketed a product covered by Solvay patent. Later, in the course of the infringement proceedings, Solvay also sought provisional relief in the form of a cross-border prohibition against infringement for the period of proceedings on the merits.

In the proceedings for provisional relief, Honeywell companies raised the defence of invalidity of the national parts of the European patent concerned. They have not however brought nor declared their intention of bringing proceedings for the annulment of the national parts of the Solvay patent. Neither did they contest the competence of the Dutch court to hear both the main and the interim proceedings.

Here, the CJEU was *inter alia* asked to give a preliminary ruling on the relationship between Article. 22(4) Brussels I Regulation (formerly Article 16(4) of the Brussels Convention) and Article 31 Brussels I Regulation. Specifically, the CJEU was asked to rule whether Article 22(4) Brussels I Regulation in the circumstances of this case precluded the application Article 31 of the same Regulation.

The first of the provisions provides that in proceedings concerned with validity of the patents courts of the Member State where that patent was registered shall have exclusive jurisdiction. In turn, Article 31 provides that with respect to provisional measures the application for such measures may be made to a court of a Member State even though that court would not have jurisdiction to hear the substance of the matter.

CJEU came to the conclusions that Article 22 (4) of the Brussels I Regulation must be interpreted as not precluding the application Article 31. The Court explained that the two provisions regulate different situations and have distinct scope of application. Neither of them refers to the other. The decision on the interim measures, also when invalidity defence was raised, does not affect in any way the decision of the court deciding on the merits. The court deciding on interim measures only makes its own an assessment as to patent validity. The final decision on validity will be made by the court having jurisdiction to hear the substance.

Dutch Courts have continued to grant cross-border interim injunctions.[14]

---

14. *PTC v. APE Holland*, Preliminary Relief Judge of The Hague, 4 Oct. 2011, www.iept.nl (IEPT20111004); and *YPM v. Yell*, The Hague Court of Appeal, 12 Jul. 2011, www.iept.nl (IEPT20110712).

§6.06 INJUNCTIVE RELIEF FOR STANDARD ESSENTIAL PATENTS: ANALYSIS OF THE RELEVANT CASE LAW

In the Netherlands, SEP holders are not generally precluded from claiming injunctive relief. The existence of FRAND commitments does not deprive them of the right to demand injunctive relief. FRAND commitments are seen however as showing the intention of the patentee to enter into constructive and meaningful negotiations with potential licensees. Thus, when a FRAND commitment is made, enforcement of SEPs can in certain circumstances be qualified as an abuse of rights.

Consequently, SEP holders may enforce their patents, also through an injunction, in case of an obvious and blatant unwillingness of the infringer to conclude a licensing agreement. When assessing unwillingness of the potential licensee prior negotiations of the parties, the actual offers that were made and the respective IPR-rules of the SDOs, are taken into account.

[A] Philips v. SK Kassetten

In *Philips v. SK Kassetten*,[15] the Hague District Court found that SK Kassetten infringed several standard essential patents owned by Philips. SK Kassetten argued that it was entitled to a FRAND licence. According to SK Kassetten Philips should not be allowed to enforce its patents.

SK Kassetten raised a *compulsory license under cartel law* defence. The Dutch court did not accept this defence. According to the Court SK Kassetten should have sought a licence before entering the market. Because SK Kassetten did not seek a licence before entering the market, Philips was entitled to enforce its SEPs.

The Court rejected the Orange-Book defence. It stated that the German Orange-Book decision '*(i) flies in the face of patent law [...] (ii) brings about legal uncertainty [...] and (ii) is unnecessary for the protection of the legitimate interests of the defendant [...].*' It stated that the interests of SK Kassetten were sufficiently guaranteed by the fact that the firm could ask for a compulsory licence.

Interestingly, the Court observed that even in light of the Orange-Book criteria, SK Kassetten could not be considered a 'willing licensee.' SK Kassetten admitted that they did not reserve money to pay royalties and actually never made any royalty payments to Philips. In paragraph 6.24 of the judgment, the Court stated: '*It cannot be excluded that this would under certain circumstances be different, but such circumstances have not been argued nor have appeared in this case.*'

Unfortunately, the Court did not elaborate or explain these 'special circumstances' that would allow to deny injunctive relief. The position of the Hague District Court was perceived as much more patentee-friendly than the German *Bundesgerichtshof* Orange-Book standard decision.

---

15. *Koninklijke Philips Electronics N.V. v. SK Kassetten GmbH & Co.* KG, Infringement, FRAND, The Hague District Court, The Netherlands, 17 Mar. 2010, Joint Cases No. 316533/HA ZA 08-2522 and 316535/HA ZA 08-2524.

[B] *LG Electronics v. Sony*

The Hague District Court again dealt with special circumstances that could justify denial of injunctive relief in case *LG Electronics v. Sony*.[16] LG Electronics asked for a preliminary injunction and border seizure measures (based on Regulation 1383/2003) against Sony. LG owned standard essential patents with respect to the Blu-ray standard. These LG SEPs were used by Sony in its PlayStation 3 devices. LG applied for the preliminary injunction during the contract negotiations with Sony. LG made an offer to Sony that the latter could either accept or reject. Both firms were part of the Blu-ray Disc Association. In their bylaws, the Blu-ray Disc Association has an arbitration clause, requiring members to refer FRAND-disputes to an arbitration panel. Consequently, the arbitration panel can take a binding decision regarding the FRAND terms and conditions.

The Court stated: '*A member is obliged to offer a license relating to its essential patents on FRAND terms. If negotiations between the members do not lead to an agreement regarding the terms, the bylaws prescribe the appointment of an arbitrator to decide the matter. For now, the judge in interlocutory proceedings concludes that the [Blu-ray Disc Association] bylaws necessarily lead to the grant of a license by a member to other members.*'

Evaluating the conditions for preliminary relief, the Court decided that given the arbitration clause, it was 'inevitable' that both parties would seek dispute settlement through arbitration. As long as the parties were still negotiating, or during the arbitration proceedings, LG may not assume that there is an infringement of its patents. The Hague District Court relied heavily on the history of the negotiations between LG and Sony. An important point would be the willingness of Sony to keep negotiating and trying to find a solution for the dispute at hand. The Court also stressed that under the bylaws of the Blu-ray Disc Association the parties were under an obligation to refer disputes to arbitration if they were not able to reach an agreement within 120 days.

The Court concluded that under 'special circumstances' of the case LG could not seek a preliminary injunction in order to enforce its standard essential patents.

The Court further explained: '*The parties agree that the [Blu-ray Disc Association] Bylaws (...) are decisive for the legal position of the parties. (...) The parties did however recognize that the terms "fair and reasonable" should be decisive for interpreting the Bylaws and that this interpretation is in close approximation with an interpretation based upon the rules of good faith, as in the Dutch jurisprudence. (...) The judge in interlocutory proceedings understands that the purpose of the Bylaws is to commercialize the Blu-ray Standard in a manner which is advantageous to the members (see also Clause 3 and also Clause 16, par. 4). In principle it is incompatible with this that members bombard each other with infringement actions.*'

---

16. *LG Electronics Inc v. Sony supply Chain Solutions (Europe) B.V.*, Provisional Relief Judge, District Court The Hague, 10 Mar. 2011.

[C] *Samsung v. Apple*

Preliminary Injunction Proceedings

In the *Samsung v. Apple* Dutch courts had a chance to give decisions in preliminary proceedings as well as in proceedings on the merits.

In 2012, in the preliminary injunction proceedings, the Hague District Court again looked at 'special circumstances' in relation to a FRAND defence.[17] Samsung accused Apple of infringing four patents related to the 3G/UMTS standard. Samsung filed a motion for preliminary injunctive relief against Apple. Samsung filed for four separate preliminary injunctions and later started three separate proceedings on the merits. In all these cases Samsung relied on FRAND and exhaustion defences.

The Court stated that Samsung could not ask for a preliminary injunction, while Apple was still willing to negotiate a licence on FRAND terms. The Court shed some light on the negotiation process itself. First, the licence-seeking party should open negotiations with a request for a FRAND licence. Second, the patent holder should react with a FRAND offer. Third, the attitude and behaviour of the parties during the licensing negotiations is important. The licensee must show willingness to enter into the agreement. He must react to an offer and to demonstrate its good faith attitude during the negotiations. Counter-offers must be rejected with detailed reasoning, relating *inter alia* to the royalty rates.

The Court also expressed its position on the legal character of the FRAND commitments. It started from the premise that FRAND commitments were part of ETSI's IPR policy and that automatically French law should be applicable. The Court added that FRAND declarations must be evaluated in detail. It reached a conclusion that the FRAND declaration made by Samsung did not amount to a general offer to enter into a licence agreement. The Court also observed that by making a FRAND pledge Samsung had not forfeited its right to enforce its FRAND-encumbered patents. In the opinion of the Court, FRAND promises do not create legitimate expectation that the party making a FRAND pledge would no longer invoke its patents and seek an injunction.

The Court very carefully analysed the history of negotiations between the parties. It is here that the Court looked for the special circumstances that could justify denying preliminary injunction. The Court was not convinced that Samsung genuinely intended to conclude a licensing agreement whereas in the opinion of the Court Apple acted as a willing licensee. Unfortunately, many details of Samsung's attitude during the negotiations were not published, on confidentiality grounds.

---

17. *Samsung Electronics Co. Ltd v. Apple Inc. et al*, joined cases, The Hague District Court, The Netherlands, 14 Mar. 2012, Case numbers 400367 / HA ZA 11-2212, 400376 / HA ZA 11-2213 and 400385 / HA ZA 11-2215. The special circumstance was that this case was not directly linked to a competition law defence but to the fact that Samsung was not willing to negotiate in good faith on a FRAND licence.

The Court concluded that Samsung moved for preliminary injunctive relief, while it still had an obligation to negotiate FRAND terms and conditions of the licence. This justified denial of interim injunctive relief.

During preliminary relief proceedings, Apple also raised patent exhaustion defence. Apple claimed that since Samsung had already concluded licensing agreements with its (non-EU based) suppliers, Samsung's patent rights had been exhausted. The Court concluded that Apple did not give sufficient evidence of these licensing agreements. It also added that these licences did not imply that Samsung gave permission to its non-EU suppliers to bring their chipsets to the EU market. This proves that it may be very difficult to provide convincing evidence for the purposes of establishing exhaustion of patent rights in the EU Member States.

Proceedings on the Merits

In the main proceedings, the Hague District Court again had to deal with both the exhaustion and FRAND defences.

Apple gave evidence of contracts concluded by Samsung with Qualcomm, one of the companies that supplied Apple with Samsung chips. The Samsung-Qualcomm contract had a non-assert clause in relation to Qualcomm customers and their affiliates. This clause guaranteed that Samsung would not start proceedings against customers of Qualcomm.[18]

Apple's FRAND defence was based on three different elements. First, Apple claimed that the FRAND declaration by Samsung and the implementation of the relevant standard by Apple led to conclusion of a licensing agreement. Second, Apple claimed that Samsung by demanding an injunction abused its rights, abused its dominant position and violated principle of good faith during the pre-contractual negotiations. Third, Apple claimed that Samsung either did not disclose its patents or disclosed its patents too late during the standardization process.

Regarding the first point, the Court followed the reasoning of the preliminary relief judge. The FRAND-declaration is an invitation to start negotiations on the terms and conditions of the licence. Obtaining an injunction for SEPs is not an abuse of rights. The Dutch court followed in its reasoning the Google-Motorola decision of the EU Commission which had just been published a week before.[19] The main reasoning of the Dutch Court and the EU Commission was that SEP-holders are legally entitled to seek and enforce an injunction and that this does not conflict with competition law.

It is therefore the responsibility of the licence-seeking party (the defendant) to obtain a licence prior to entering the market. If the defendant fails to do this, the patentee may enforce his rights by seeking an injunction. In an earlier-mentioned case (*LG Electronics v. Sony*), the Dutch Court did qualify LG's behaviour as an abuse of

---

18. Under the ETSI declaration Samsung was bound to give irrevocable licences. The court case against Apple would lead to the revocation of a licence.
19. Case COMP/M.6381, para. 126: '*Furthermore, the seeking or enforcement of injunctions on the basis of SEPs is also not, of itself, anti-competitive. In particular, and depending on the circumstances, it may be legitimate for the holder of SEPs to seek an injunction against a potential licensee which is not willing to negotiate in good faith on FRAND terms.*'

rights. LG sought an injunction against Sony, despite the fact that both parties were still in constructive negotiations and that the bylaws of the DVD-association referred disputes to arbitration.

On the second point, the Court held that seeking an injunction is not generally an abuse of a dominant position. As the Hague District Court earlier stated in the *Philips v. SK Kassetten*, the patentee may enforce his patent rights unless 'special circumstances' exist. In this case, such special circumstances were indeed present because Samsung was unwilling to negotiate a licensing agreement in 'good faith.' The Court concluded that '(...) the filing [by Samsung] for an injunction during the FRAND licence negotiations should be considered abusive and contrary to the principles of pre-contractual good faith, as the threat of the requested injunction puts Apple under improper pressure in these negotiations to agree to licence terms that are not FRAND.'

Samsung's threat of preliminary relief was evidence of the fact that Samsung was not willing to negotiate in good faith. Thus, the behaviour of the patentee is crucial. If a patentee is willing to negotiate a FRAND licence in good faith he may obtain an injunction against an unwilling licensee. Whereas if a patentee is not acting in good faith, the injunction will most likely be denied.

The Hague District Court demonstrated that Samsung did not enter the negotiating process in good faith.[20] It came to the conclusion that Samsung had taken an uncompromising and inflexible stand during the negotiations with Apple. The following elements were important for the Court:

(a) Apple properly indicated that it was willing to take out a licence for all relevant Samsung patents. Apple was informed about the relevant terms and conditions.
(b) Samsung only responded with one 'opening offer' to Apple.
(c) Apple's second counteroffer was limited to the disputed patents and geographically limited to the territory of the Netherlands.[21]
(d) Apple rejected the request made by Samsung to cross-license some non-essential patents in the United States. The District Court found that this rejection was unrelated to the case at hand and did not prove the 'unwillingness of Apple' to obtain a FRAND licence for the patents in the Netherlands.
(e) Apple made reasonable and well-motivated offers and thereby had conducted the negotiations in good faith.
(f) Apple's offer was mainly based on the cumulative royalty ceiling. The Court did consider this first offer as 'not unreasonable' as a starting bid and noted that the offer was well-documented. Apple made the assumption that the cumulative royalty ceiling had to be divided equally over all 1889 patent

---

20. Apple indicated at an early stage, its willingness to take a licence. Samsung started proceedings against Apple, but only made one offer and one counteroffer after the court proceedings in the Netherlands had already started.
21. In the *Philips v. Archos* case (*see* note 22) the Dutch court declared that the patentee has a wide discretion. The patentee can define the legal framework as long as it is not abusive. A worldwide licence can be FRAND, but the patentee may also limit the geographical scope.

families. Samsung owned 103 patent families thereof. The Court accepted Apple's reasoning that all patents have equal value.
(g) The Court considered Samsung's argument that the offer of Apple was geographically limited to the Netherlands. Since Samsung started proceedings in the Netherlands, the court found it not unreasonable that Apple's offer was just limited to the Netherlands.

[D] Archos v. Philips

In *Archos v. Philips* the Hague District Court dealt with access to standard-essential patents and FRAND licensing terms.[22] Proceedings were launched by Archos in reaction to infringement claims brought in the same court by Philips against Archos. Philips' claims concerned Dutch parts of its three European SEPs. Philips patents were registered as standard essential patents with the European Telecommunications Standards Institute (ETSI). Archos raised a FRAND defence to infringement on the ground that Philips had not complied with its obligations under the *Huawei* decision to offer a licence on FRAND terms. During the negotiations Philips started with an offer of EUR 0.70 per product sold and while Archos presented a counter-offer of EUR 0.07 per product sold. As a result, Philips sought an injunction against Archos. Archos claimed that since the initial offer was not FRAND applying for an injunction constituted abuse of dominant position on the part of Philips. Archos argued that the EUR 0.7 was too high for their low cost smart phones and that Philips was inflexible during negotiations.

The Hague District Court rejected claims brought by Archos. The Court said that the Philips' offer was FRAND. According to the Court FRAND is a range, a band width. Archos failed to negotiate actively a FRAND rate. The negotiations actually took place before the *Huawei* judgement. At that time the burden of making a first FRAND offer was with the SEP user. The patentee (Philips) can define the legal framework as long as it is not abusive. Since Archos never made a FRAND offer, Philips could apply for an injunction. Philips did enter into effective negotiations and hence applying for the injunction was not an abuse of dominance on the part of Philips.

§6.07 FLEXIBILITY AND EQUITABLE CONCERNS IN GRANTING INJUNCTIVE RELIEF

[A] FRAND Licensing

The early case law started in 2002 with the case *Philips v. EMI*[23] followed by *Philips/Princo*[24] in 2005. Initially, injunctive relief cases did not involve discussions about FRAND commitments.

---

22. *Archos v. Philips* 8 Feb. 2017, http://eplaw.org/nl-archos-v-koninklijke-philips-frand/.
23. District Court of The Hague, 26 Juni 2002, Koninklijke Philips Electronics/EMI Compact Disc (Holland).
24. District Court of The Hague, 13 Jul. 2005, 02/2947, *Philips v. Furness*.

The first case on FRAND commitments was the previously discussed *Philips v. SK Kassetten*. In the early case law, the Hague District Court identified the main obligation of the defendant stating that the defendant is obliged to ask for a licence prior to entering the market and before using the patented technology.

In case the patent owner refuses to give a FRAND licence, the defendant should ask for a temporary compulsory licence or negotiate in good faith. In general Dutch courts find the Orange-Book decision of the German Supreme Court unsuitable in the Netherlands. The main reason is that this decision is inconsistent with the Dutch law on compulsory licensing or contrary to the requirement of legal certainty.[25]

The LG/Sony case showed that suing a member of the same SSO (Blu-ray) is contrary to the intention to license.

The *Samsung v. Apple* case demonstrated that the patent owner should resort to threats of enforcement, applying unjustified pressure to force the defendant to accept licensing terms and conditions that are not FRAND. The patent owner, by seeking an injunction, abused his rights violating the pre-contractual obligation to negotiate in good faith.[26]

Below are the important factors resulting from the decisions of Dutch courts:

(a) Dutch courts will consider whether the patent owner explicitly tolerated the defendant's use of his SEPs.
(b) Dutch courts will consider whether the defendant applied immediately for a FRAND licence.
(c) The main rule is: ask for a FRAND licence prior to using the patented technology unless 'special circumstances' entitle the patent owner to obtain injunctive relief.
(d) If the SEP holder does not act continuously in good faith an injunction will be denied.
(e) If the party seeking a license does not act continuously in good faith an injunction will be granted.
(f) Enforcement of SEPs is abusive if the FRAND negotiations, conducted in good faith, are still pending.
(g) Dutch courts have not determined FRAND terms so far, but undoubtedly have the power to do so. Complicated and costly exercise, Dutch court seems to favour the use of court-appointed experts in combination with 'educated guess.' This lack of certainty should be a strong incentive for conflicting parties to reach a bilateral agreement on FRAND terms and conditions.

---

25. Dutch courts have not directly referred to the IP enforcement directive. The IP Enforcement Directive might have had an indirect influence on ex parte injunctions at the time of implementation. Some case-law hints at a higher threshold for the assumption of infringement. Ex parte injunctions are exceptional but possible in case of repeated infringement.
26. The doctrine of abuse of right and the principle of proportionality in Dutch civil law require parties in a legal relationship to act in accordance with the requirements of reasonableness and equity. This means that parties cannot act solely in their own interests but also have to consider the interests of the other party at hand.

(h) The Samsung proposed royalty fee of 2.4% of the chipset fee for each of its asserted patents did not constitute a FRAND offer according to the Dutch District Court.

During infringement proceedings Dutch courts are unlikely to accept a defence raised by a party that refused a FRAND licence unless the patentee's behaviour was abusive or not in good faith. Dutch courts find it difficult to deviate from other national IP decisions outside the Netherlands but sometimes still do.

In a recently decided case *Archos v. Philips*[27] the Hague Court again stated that FRAND is a range and refused to set a FRAND royalty rate. The Court stated that abusive behaviour of the patentee could consist in not negotiating actively. The Court is willing to rule on substantive arguments with regard to the calculation of a FRAND offer. An objection by the SEP implementer regarding the FRAND calculation methods, may backfire. The Court holds that such objections could have been raised during the negotiations, hence the SEP user can be seen as unwilling during the negotiations. Regarding the defendants' obligations, the Dutch courts mainly ruled on 'willingness' and seem to take a more patentee-friendly approach.

In general, Dutch court will hold a pre-hearing on SEPs and then continue to discuss the technical part of the cases. First, the courts discuss FRAND and then consequently start the case. Patentee must show that the offer is FRAND. The Dutch court will accept the advice of an economist on the FRAND rate. It is likely to ask the following questions: Is the patentee's offer a portfolio offer? Is there a relevant industrial standard?

[B] Patent Trolls

Dutch courts have not yet dealt with cases regarding patent trolls. Patent trolls have a negative impact on innovation and competition. The business model of patent trolls is based upon creating a positive expectation for investors (FRAND licensing terms, favourable licensing terms, non-disclosure of patents, etc.) and consequently waiting until the defendant has sunk investments into the technology. After the lock-in of the defendant into the technology, patent trolls will then hold-up the defendant with an injunction. Patent trolls have large patent portfolios and the financial means to threaten the defendant with costly litigation.

Another aspect is the charging of 'hold-up royalties,' consisting of the switching costs, the costs of the patent and the opportunity costs of not taking a license. Obviously, most of the just mentioned tactics are not part of negotiating or acting in good faith. Hence depending on the behaviour of patent trolls, Dutch courts would see this as an abuse of rights. The exact differences between patent assertion entities, patent aggregators and patent trolls are not easy to make and should be defined not by the official classification but by the conduct of the participating firms. Since the patent

---

27. *Archos v. Philips*, 8 Feb. 2017, http://eplaw.org/nl-archos-v-koninklijke-philips-frand/.

trolls are Non-Practicing Entities, the forces of 'nuclear deterrence' cannot be used.[28] The invulnerability of the trolls is based upon the absence of downstream markets that might be affected by a counterattack by competitors, which is a relevant factor in the discussion of injunctions.

---

28. In a conflict of practicing entities both parties have patent portfolio's and the possibilities to start a court case.

CHAPTER 7
Injunctive Relief in Polish Patent Law

Rafał Sikorski, Piotr Andrzejewski & Piotr Ruchała

§7.01 INTRODUCTION

The origins of modern Polish patent law go back to post-World War I period when Poland regained its independence in 1918. From the very beginning Polish patent law made injunctive relief available to patentees.[1] This has not changed after World War II during the period of the communist rule.[2] Injunctive relief is also available under the currently in force Law on Industrial Property (IPL).[3]

Under IPL, in case of infringement the patentee has a wide variety of remedies to choose from. Article 287 section 1 IPL provides explicitly that the patentee may seek a permanent injunction.

IP scholars in Poland have traditionally perceived injunctive relief as one of the most important, if not the most important, remedy in intellectual property law.[4] On the one hand, from a more formal perspective, injunctions are perceived as a necessary corollary to intellectual property rights. IP rights are exclusive rights and injunctions enable right holders to protect that exclusivity. On the other hand, injunctions are seen as a tool that enables the patentee to protect himself from sometimes irreversible

---

1. Article 24 Dekret z dnia 4 lutego 1919 r. o patentach na wynalazki, o ochronie wzorów rysunkowych i modeli, o ochronie znaków towarowych, Dz.P.P.P. 1919 poz. 137; Art. 23 Ustawa z dnia 5 lutego 1924 r. o ochronie wynalazków, wzorów i znaków towarowych, Dz.U. 1924 nr 31, poz. 306; Art. 25 s. 1 Rozporządzenie Prezydenta Rzeczypospolitej Polskiej z dnia 22 marca 1928 r. o ochronie wynalazków, wzorów i znaków towarowych, Dz.U. 1928 nr 39, poz. 384.
2. Article 56 s. 1 Ustawa z dnia 31 maja 1962 r. – Prawo wynalazcze, Dz.U. 1962 nr 33, poz. 156; Art. 57 s. 1 Ustawa z dnia 19 października 1972 r. o wynalazczości, Dz.U. 1972 nr 43, poz. 72.
3. Dz.U. 2017, poz. 776.
4. Bogusław Gawlik, *Cywilnoprawna ochrona praw majątkowych* in Stefan Grzybowski & Andrzej Kopff (eds), *Prawo wynalazcze: Zagadnienia wybrane* (Państwowe Wydawnictwo Naukowe 1978), 351; Michał du Vall, Elżbieta Traple, Piotr Kostański, Justyna Ożegalska-Trybalska & Paweł Podrecki, *Prawo patentowe* (2nd ed., Wolters Kluwer 2017), 618.

consequences of patent infringement.[5] Therefore, when – during the course of patent infringement proceedings – the court finds that the patent has been infringed, it will issue a permanent injunction (nearly) automatically.

In 2007 Polish law was amended in order to implement provisions of Directive 2004/48/EC on the enforcement of intellectual property rights (Directive 2004/48).[6] This has resulted in a number of changes in the area of remedies available to holders of intellectual property rights. These amendments also affected patentees.

With respect to permanent injunctions, the most important change was the introduction of the so-called alternative measure.[7] The relevant provision was modeled on Article 12 of Directive 2004/48. Poland decided to introduce the alternative measure even though its introduction was not mandatory under the Directive 2004/48.[8]

The purpose of the alternative measure was to allow courts to deny a permanent injunction and order monetary compensation in lieu of an injunction. It can be applied in case of patents and other industrial property rights, such as trademarks, registered designs and utility models. The alternative measure was also introduced to Law on copyright and neighboring rights,[9] Law on the protection of databases[10] and Law on legal protection of plant variety rights.[11]

The alternative measure allows the court to deny a permanent injunction if granting such an injunction would be disproportionate. Not surprisingly, the new provision attracted some attention from IP scholars in the EU, including Poland. It certainly holds the potential to bring more flexibility to injunctive relief in the countries where injunctions are not rooted in equity. So far however it has not been applied by the Polish courts neither in patent infringement proceedings, nor in proceedings relating to infringement of other intellectual property rights.[12] It also seems that the Directive 2004/48 has not affected the practice of granting injunctive relief in patent infringement proceedings in the EU.[13]

Since injunctive relief is granted in the course of patent infringement proceedings, it is important to note that Polish patent system is a bifurcated one. Invalidity proceedings are separate from infringement proceedings. A patent – once it has been granted – benefits from the presumption of validity. It is deemed valid until it is invalidated in the course of the requisite proceedings before the Patent Office. The

---

5. *Ibid.*
6. Corrigendum to Directive 2004/48/EC of the European Parliament and of the Council of 29 April 2004 on the enforcement of intellectual property rights, OJ L 157, 30.04.2004.
7. Article 287 s. 3 IPL.
8. Article 12 Directive 2004/48 provides explicitly that Member States may implement the so-called alternative measure.
9. Article 79 s. 3 Ustawa z dnia 4 lutego 1994 r. o prawie autorskim i prawach pokrewnych, Dz.U. 2016, poz. 666.
10. Article 11 s. 3 Ustawa z dnia 27 lipca 2001 r. o ochronie baz danych, Dz.U. 2001 nr 128, poz. 1402.
11. Article 36a s. 3 Ustawa z dnia 26 czerwca 2003 r. o ochronie prawnej odmian roślin, Dz.U. 2018, poz. 432.
12. Database searches of leading law databases on Polish law, namely LEX and Legalis report no case law on the application of the alternative measure by the Polish courts.
13. Trevor Cook, *Enforcement Directive and Harmonization of Remedies for Intellectual Property Infringement in the EU*, 20(4) Journal of Intellectual Property Rights, 264, 265 (2015).

courts seem to be attached to the patent validity presumption to the extent that they are generally unwilling to take into account potential invalidity to stay infringement proceedings. The Code of Civil Procedure (CCP) however allows to stay infringement proceedings, though staying such proceedings is optional.[14]

Bifurcation makes the Polish patent system susceptible to the phenomena of the so-called injunctions gap. Indeed, infringement proceedings might be concluded earlier than administrative proceedings related to patent validity. The system as it is – one might conclude – creates a favorable environment for patentees. In such a bifurcated system, injunctions provide the patentee with even more bargaining power.

Patentees whose patents have been infringed may also seek a preliminary (temporary) injunction. Preliminary injunctions may be issued prior to the decision on the merits. Interestingly, Polish law generally provides for the grant of preliminary injunctions in ex parte proceedings. The defendant gets a chance to be heard at the second instance once the decision to grant preliminary relief is appealed. The defendant is not deprived of various protective mechanisms; however, the model of preliminary injunctive relief applied in Polish law is generally very favorable towards the patentee.

One of the aims of this chapter would be to analyze possible grounds for greater flexibility in granting injunctive relief. Particular emphasis will be paid to the discussion of the conditions for the application of the alternative measure as well as availability of other defenses that infringers might resort to when faced with threat of an injunction.

EU Competition law defense will largely be skipped for two reasons. First, it is discussed in the EU law chapter. Second, the FRAND negotiation framework resulting from the *ZTE v. Huawei*[15] decision by the CJEU, has not been applied by Polish courts. The experience of German and UK courts cannot be matched.

§7.02 PERMANENT INJUNCTIONS AND ALTERNATIVE MEASURES

[A] Permanent Injunctions

Article 287 section 1 IPL provides that a patentee whose patent has been infringed may demand that the court issues a permanent injunction against the infringer.

First and foremost, it is the patentee who may seek injunctive relief in case of patent infringement. Additionally, Article 76 section 6 IPL states that also exclusive licensees, whose licenses were entered in the register, may claim the grant of an injunction, unless the exclusive license provides otherwise. However, the exclusive

---

14. Article 177§1 (3) Code of Civil Procedure. *See* Andrzej Jakubecki, *Dochodzenie roszczeń z zakresu prawa własności przemysłowej w postępowaniu cywilnym* in Ryszard Skubisz (ed.), *System Prawa Prywatnego. Tom 14B. Prawo własności przemysłowej* (1st ed., C.H. Beck 2012), 1642.
15. C-170/13 *Huawei Technologies Co. Ltd v. ZTE Corp. and ZTE Deutschland GmbH*.

licensee's right to demand injunctive relief only is limited to infringements falling within the scope of the exclusive license.[16]

The patentee may demand that a permanent injunction is issued irrespective of the fault of the patent infringer. The encroachment on exclusivity of the patentee is sufficient to trigger an injunction.

In order to seek permanent injunctions, the plaintiff has to precisely specify in the lawsuit which actions of the defendant constitute patent infringement and thus have to be ceased. This is a general requirement of Polish civil procedure. Its importance results from the fact, that the court is bound by the plaintiff's claim and may not rule beyond claims specified in the lawsuit. The wording of the court's decision will in most cases closely reflect the wording used by the plaintiff. Proper specification of plaintiff's claims is important for ensuring the enforceability of the final judgment.[17]

An injunction is a court order directed to the infringer demanding that the infringer ceases activities that constitute patent infringement. The purpose of granting a permanent injunction is to stop the ongoing infringement and to prevent such infringement in the future. Therefore, generally the patentee may demand an injunction when the infringement is still continuing.[18] The patentee may also seek injunctive relief when the infringement stopped but when there is serious threat that the infringer would likely infringe in the future.[19] Consequently, the fact that the infringer ceased his infringing activities in the course of proceedings does not automatically lead to denying injunctive relief.[20] In many cases the risk of future infringements would be beyond doubt and therefore the court should grant an injunction. This approach fully corresponds with the purpose of permanent injunction, which is not only to stop current infringements, but also to prevent future infringements.

One of the typical defenses raised by defendants in patent infringement proceedings is the patent invalidity defense. As already mentioned, Polish patent system is a bifurcated one. While patent infringement cases are heard before civil courts, patent invalidity proceedings take place before the Patent Office. A patent – once it has been granted – benefits from the presumption of validity.

Nevertheless, the court, if faced with claim of patent invalidity, has the option of staying infringement proceedings for the duration of invalidity proceedings before the Patent Office.[21] The analysis of case law suggests that Polish courts are rather reluctant

---

16. Maciej Kubiak, Commentary to Art. 287 in: Arkadiusz Michalak (ed.), *Prawo własności przemysłowej. Komentarz* (1st ed., C.H. Beck 2016), para. 1.
17. Paweł Podrecki, *Środki ochrony praw własności intelektualnej* (LexisNexis 2010), Chapter II, pt. 1.1; Gawlik, *supra* n. 4, at 352.
18. Paweł Podrecki & Elżbieta Traple, *Roszczenia z tytułu naruszenia praw własności przemysłowej* in Ryszard Skubisz (ed.), *System Prawa Prywatnego. Tom 14C. Prawo własności przemysłowej* (1st ed., C.H. Beck 2017), 389.
19. *Ibid.*; Gawlik, *supra* n. 4, at 352.
20. Krystyna Szczepanowska-Kozłowska, in Ewa Nowińska, Urszula Promińska & Krystyna Szczepanowska-Kozłowska, *Własność przemysłowa i jej ochrona* (1st ed., LexisNexis 2014), Chapter IX, pt. 3; *Same* Michał du Vall, Ewa Nowińska & Urszula Promińska, *Prawo własności przemysłowej* (5th ed., LexisNexis 2011), pt. 4.4.2.
21. *See* Stanisław Włodyka, *Tryby postępowania w sprawach wynalazczości* in Stefan Grzybowski & Andrzej Kopff (eds), *Prawo wynalazcze: Zagadnienia wybrane* (Państwowe Wydawnictwo Naukowe 1978), 478–479.

to stay infringement proceedings on this ground. Traditionally, the motion to stay proceeding has been perceived by courts as a way to unnecessarily prolong infringement proceedings, though it is worth noting that there has been a slight shift in this respect recently.[22] Polish Supreme Court stated that even though staying infringement proceedings in case of a claim for invalidity is discretionary, it should be carefully considered in each case. That is because the court is theoretically bound by a decision granting a patent, but if faced with reasonable arguments of the defendant contesting validity, the court should stay proceedings and let the Patent Office examine validity of a patent. These conclusions apply as well in case of European patents.[23]

The decision of Patent Office on validity of patent is final. It may be later contested before administrative courts and if such proceedings are initiated, the civil court which is hearing patent infringement dispute may find it reasonable to stay the infringement proceedings, as the administrative court may set aside the decision of Patent Office. This would be justified in particular when the administrative court stays the execution of a decision.[24]

Additionally, infringement proceedings may also be stayed in the event of initiating proceedings before the Patent Office on granting compulsory license; however, no such license has been granted in Poland since 1990.[25]

The decision of the Court of First Instance to grant a permanent injunction cannot be enforced immediately. A patentee will be able to enforce the permanent injunction only after the decision of the first instance court has become final. That would be the case if the defendant does not appeal the decision of the first instance court. When the decision is appealed, the judgment of the second instance would be final and therefore enforceable.

Though granting injunctive relief has been traditionally perceived as a natural and practically an automatic consequence of patent infringement, developments in foreign jurisdictions, particularly the U.S. Supreme Court decision in *eBay v. Mercexchange*,[26] have not passed unnoticed in Polish jurisprudence.[27] There was a growing awareness that in some jurisdictions injunctions are not automatically granted even though the court hearing the case finds patent infringement. It has become apparent that injunctive relief may be abused by patentees.

---

22. Judgment of the Supreme Court, 18.02.2016 r., II CSK 282/15.
23. Article 138 of European Patent Convention, Art. 255 s. 1 pt. 1^1 IPL.
24. Judgment of the Supreme Court, 7.10.2010 r., IV CSK 206/10. This would require, however, an application of Art. 177 para. 1 pt. 3 CCP by analogy. See further Paweł Grzegorczyk, Commentary to Art. 180–181 in Tadeusz Ereciński (ed.), *Kodeks postępowania cywilnego. Komentarz. Tom I. Postępowanie rozpoznawcze* (5th ed., Wolters Kluwer 2016), para. 12; Katarzyna Celińska-Grzegorczyk, Roman Hauser, *Sądy administracyjne a system sądownictwa powszechnego* in Roman Hauser, Zygmunt Niewiadomski, Andrzej Wróbel (eds), *System Prawa Administracyjnego. Tom 10. Sądowa kontrola administracji publicznej* (2nd ed., C.H. Beck 2016), 121–123.
25. Anna Miszczak, *Licencjonowanie przymusowe w prawie unijnym oraz umowach międzynarodowych wiążących Rzeczpospolitą Polską*, 78(4) Ruch Prawniczy, Ekonomiczny i Socjologiczny 123 (2016).
26. eBay v. Mercexchange, 547 US 388 (2006).
27. See Michał du Vall, *Prawo patentowe* (1st ed., Wolters Kluwer 2008), 410.

[B] Compensation in Lieu of Injunction (Alternative Measure)

Though injunctions were hardly a major topic of scholarly debates among Polish academics, generally the alternative measure introduced in Article 12 of Directive 2004/48 once implemented to Polish law, was seen as a positive development, though various authors were also of the opinion that the application of the measure would be problematic.[28] It is perceived as providing flexibility to the court when granting an injunction would be unduly burdensome for the patent implementer. Unfortunately, there is no reported case-law on its application neither with respect to patents nor other intellectual property rights, therefore the discussion below will mostly be a recollection of scholarly debates. These debates concentrate on the conditions for application of the alternative measure and the degree of discretion awarded to the courts.

Commentators disagree on the consequences of granting monetary compensation to the patentee. As a result of denying an injunction and ordering compensation the infringer is allowed to practice the patented invention. Some commentators conclude that the patent is still infringed, however the order of the court to grant monetary compensation excludes for the period specified by the court the right to injunctive relief.[29] Others however conclude that the patent implementer will no longer infringe the rights of the patentee. Thus, consequently the use of a patented invention as a result of the court order becomes lawful.[30]

Article 287 section 3 IPL clearly specifies the requirements for the application of the alternative measure. It mirrors the wording of Article 12 Directive 2004/48. *First*, the infringer must act unintentionally and without negligence. *Second*, the execution of a permanent injunction must be capable of causing disproportionate harm to the infringer. *Third*, pecuniary compensation must be reasonably satisfactory to the injured party. *Fourth*, the infringer must file a motion for the court to apply the alternative measure in lieu of an injunction. Finally, even when these requirements are met the court has discretion to adopt the alternative measure in lieu of an injunction. The court also has discretion upon the conditions for the use of the invention which it will impose on the infringing implementer, such as time, field of use, conditions of payment of the compensation, etc.

As stated earlier, the alternative measure was also introduced in other areas of Polish intellectual property law, namely in copyright, sui generis database and plant variety rights. Interestingly, Polish implementation in those fields of IP added yet another requirement for the application of the alternative measure, namely consent of the right holder. One of the commentators claims that the consent requirement is also required in patent infringement cases.[31] This does not seem to be the correct approach. First, this additional requirement of consent is missing in Article 12 Directive 2004/48. Second, the consent would in fact undermine the whole idea behind the alternative

---

28. Podrecki & Traple, *supra* n. 18, at 415.
29. Du Vall, *supra* n. 26, at 411.
30. Elżbieta Traple & Paweł Podrecki, *Roszczenia w przypadku naruszenia patentu*, 1 Studia Prawa Prywatnego 163, 180 (2011).
31. Anna Tischner, Commentary to Art. 287 in Piotr Kostański (ed.), *Prawo własności przemysłowej. Komentarz* (2nd ed., C.H. Beck 2014), para. 14.

Chapter 7: Injunctive Relief in Polish Patent Law   §7.02[B]

measure, namely ensuring the court the discretion to deny an injunction in certain circumstances. The probable source of the above-mentioned incorrect implementation of Article 12 Directive 2004/48 is its faulty translation into Polish.[32]

Lack of Fault

Only when infringement is neither intentional nor negligent the court may consider substituting injunctive relief with monetary compensation. The burden of proof with respect to lack of fault, as with respect to the remaining requirements for the application of the alternative measure, is on the patent implementer.[33]

The discussion of the fault requirement should begin with two primary observations. First, IPL explicitly provides that the patent register is public,[34] that entries to the patent register are presumed to be correct and that everyone knows the content of those entries.[35] These presumptions – of correctness and knowledge of the entries to the register – are rebuttable. The question that arises in the context of these presumptions is whether the existence of presumption of knowledge always implies fault, or at least negligence.[36] Certainly, if that was the case, the scope of application of the alternative measure would be extremely narrow. Second, generally in Polish civil law negligence may be assumed when a person does not exercise the degree of care that can be expected from that person in the given circumstances.[37] This is assessed objectively, taking into account *inter alia* provisions of law, rules of good faith and practices in particular areas of commerce, etc.[38]

Generally, commentators seem to agree that the degree of care required from various categories of operators at various levels of the manufacturing and distribution chain will not be the same.[39] Most of those who deal with the issue of fault subscribe to the view that manufacturers will normally be required to check whether they infringe a product or process patent.[40] One of the commentators provides an example of a well-established manufacturer operating on the pharmaceutical market, arguing that in such a case the required degree of care in conducting patent searches would be rather high.[41] Importers, wholesalers and retailers would be on the opposite side. Commentators assume in such cases that those businesses that are involved in the distribution of products should not be required to conduct extensive patent searches.

---

32. English version of Art. 12 Directive 2004/48 *in fine*: *if pecuniary compensation to the injured party appears reasonably satisfactory*. Polish version translates to: *if pecuniary compensation appears reasonably satisfactory to the injured party*.
33. Du Vall et al., *supra* n. 4, at 620.
34. Article 228 s. 3 IPL.
35. Article 228 s. 4 IPL.
36. Paweł Podrecki & Elżbieta Traple, *Roszczenia z tytułu naruszenia praw własności przemysłowej* in Ryszard Skubisz (ed.), *System Prawa Prywatnego. Tom 14B. Prawo własności przemysłowej* (1st ed., C.H. Beck 2012), 1407.
37. Article 355 Civil Code.
38. *See* Maciej Gutowski, Commentary to Art. 355 in Maciej Gutowski (ed.), *Kodeks Cywilny. Tom I. Komentarz* (1st ed., C.H. Beck 2016), 1254–1260.
39. Podrecki & Traple, *supra* n. 35, at 1407.
40. *Ibid.*
41. Du Vall et al., *supra* n. 4, at 620–621.

After all they are not involved in designing and manufacturing the product and the obligation to conduct such searches would lead to additional substantial costs.[42]

Additionally, it is also assumed that when a manufacturer seeks advice from professional and independent counsel who conducts patent search and assesses likelihood of infringement, and if the independent counsel comes to the conclusion that patents will not be infringed, a manufacturer who obtained such advise may not be regarded as acting negligently, even when such advise proves to be wrong.[43]

These are of course only general guidelines. One may also claim that manufacturers of highly complex products who rely on supply of various components by third parties should probably be treated differently than manufacturers operating in fields where conducting a patent search would be significantly less complicated and as a result less costly. On the other hand, however it is common in various markets for the patentees to seek royalties from the manufacturers of end products rather than producers of various components, so a manufacturer of an end product should not assume that such components were placed on the market with patent holder's consent and thus are subject to the principle of exhaustion.

It is important to add that the issue of fault will generally not play a role when patent implementers seek protection against injunctions sought by holders of standard essential patents who committed during the course of standard setting to license these patents on FRAND terms. Of course, SEP implementers could in such cases ask the court to order monetary compensation in lieu of an injunction, but this would not be the only route for the implementer to ensure access to such patents. In such cases EU competition law defense or national competition law defense and the general doctrine of abuse of rights would also be available to the implementer offering a more certain route to legalize patent use.

Balancing Interests of the Patentee and the Infringer

Article 287 section 3 IPL requires that the court looks at how the injunction would affect the interests of the patent infringer. Monetary compensation may be ordered only if the execution of the injunction could cause disproportionate harm.

One of the examples of such disproportionate harm resulting from granting injunctive relief could be the loss of substantial investment made by the infringer as a result of granting an injunction.[44] This would be the case when the infringer incurred substantial costs to implement a patent-protected technology and as a result of an injunction he would neither be able to benefit from the investment made nor would he be able to recover the costs incurred. If at the same time it turns out that the patentee does not practice the patent and is only interested in monetizing the patented invention through granting non-exclusive licenses, then monetary compensation would seem to be a reasonably satisfactory for the patentee. The same would be the case if the

---

42. Podrecki & Traple, *supra* n. 35, at 1408.
43. Du Vall, *supra* n. 26, at 410.
44. Kubiak, *supra* n. 16, para. 6.

patentee practices the patented invention, however operates on different markets than the infringer.

Commentators also suggest that an injunction could be denied, and monetary compensation could be ordered when the patent protects a minor feature of a complex product.[45] If that feature does not drive the demand for the products or when the value of the invention depends on the ability to use it together with other complementary inventions, then ordering monetary compensation would normally be satisfactory for the injured patentee and at the same time it would not lead to sunk costs as well as potentially significant design around costs.

Generally, monetary compensation would likely be satisfactory to the patentee if the injunction would not put the patentee in a better position than mere monetary compensation. Thus, an injunction would not be satisfactory if the patentee intends to monetize his patent by granting exclusive licenses. It could also not be ordered in lieu of an injunction if the patentee practices the patents and the patented feature gives him advantage over his competitors.

Infringer's Motion

The court may not order monetary compensation without a motion by the infringer. Burden of proof related to all circumstances necessary for application of alternative measure lies with the infringer. Therefore, he will be obliged to prove i.a. that the infringement was not culpable.

Such motion will usually indicate the amount of the monetary compensation that the infringer is willing to pay in lieu of an injunction. It seems that infringer should also define the period of intended use. If the court intends to change the conditions of use of the patented invention, e.g., because the court believes that the conditions are not reasonably satisfactory for the patentee, then the implementer should have the right to give consent or reject the terms proposed by the court, if he finds these conditions unsatisfactory.

Discretion of the Court in Granting Monetary Compensation in Lieu of Injunction

Though the court must ensure that conditions for the application of monetary compensation are met, and particularly that the monetary compensation awarded to the patentee is reasonably satisfactory, still it retains a significant degree of discretion.[46]

Commentators point to the fact that the court will have to decide on a number of issues when granting monetary compensation. First, the court has to set the amount of the monetary compensation. Commentators express the view that the pecuniary compensation should be set at least at the rate of reasonable royalty.[47] Some also add

---

45. *Ibid.*
46. Podrecki & Traple, *supra* n. 18, at 415.
47. Du Vall, *supra* n. 26, at 411.

that the level of reasonable royalty should rather be the floor for setting the compensation.[48] Second, the court has to decide on the possible fields of use of the patented invention. One of the commentators adds that the scope of use in the future should not differ from the scope established by the court while setting the monetary compensation.[49] Third, the court should also decide on the period of time when the implementer may use the invention. Some commentators underline that the court may decide that the implementer will be allowed to use the patented invention as long as the patent is in force.[50] Others suggest that the period when the implementer is entitled to use the patented invention should be rather short, as licensing conditions and particularly the royalty rates may change over time.[51] Some still suggest that the time should be such as to allow to sell the products already manufactured by the infringer.[52]

Since the court has a significant degree of discretion it seems that Article 287 section 3 IPL allows for tailoring. The particular result of that tailoring will depend on the circumstances of the case. In some cases, the court will likely allow the implementer to use the patented invention possibly until the patent expires. In other cases, the time might be significantly shorter so as to give the implementer reasonable time required to design around the patented invention.

§7.03   ABUSE OF RIGHT DOCTRINES

Generally, abuse of rights doctrine provides a defense when rights are exercised within the limits defined by law, however they are exercised in an abusive manner. The doctrines serve as a corrective mechanism which resorts to such standards as: morality, good faith, fairness, proportionality as well as reasonableness and social functions of rights. Typically, abuse doctrines operate to limit the exercise of rights.

Polish law provides for abuse of rights defense in general provisions of the Civil Code. Article 5 Civil Code states that: "A right may not be exercised contrary to its socio-economic purpose or rules of good faith. Such behavior by the right holder shall not be regarded as exercise of that right and shall not be protected." The provision applies horizontally to the exercise of all private rights, including intellectual property rights.

The application of the abuse doctrine in the context of exercise of patent rights is slightly more complicated, because Polish Industrial Property Law has its own provisions on abuse of industrial property rights, namely Article 68 sections 1 and 2. Article 68 section 1 states that:

> A patent holder or a licensee may not abuse his right, in particular by preventing the use of a patented invention by a third party, if such use is necessary to satisfy the demand on the national market, especially when it is in the public interest, and

---

48. Kubiak, *supra* n. 16, para. 8.
49. *Id.*, para. 7.
50. *Ibid.*
51. Podrecki & Traple, *supra* n. 18, at 417.
52. Du Vall et al., *supra* n. 4, at 622.

the product is not available to the public in proper quantity or quality or is available but at excessively high price.

Section 2 provides however that: "Preventing third parties from using a patented invention within the period of 3 years following patent grant, shall not be deemed an abuse of right."

The fact that abuse of rights is regulated both in the Civil Code and in the Industrial Property Law raises questions relating to the relationship between these two regulations. Generally, two approaches are taken by the commentators. Some commentators believe that Article 68 IPL is *lex specialis* which preempts the application of the general abuse doctrine of the Civil Code. These authors claim that the exercise of a patent may only be abusive in the circumstances specified in Article 68 section 1 IPL.[53] Others claim that Article 68 IPL does not preclude the application of the general abuse of rights defense in circumstances other than those specified in Article 68 IPL.[54]

The author is of the opinion that the fact that abuse of patents is specifically regulated in Article 68 IPL does not preclude the application of Article 5 Civil Code, both in cases that fall within the scope of application of Article 68 IPL as well as in cases that are outside the application of that provision. First, Article 68 IPL regulates a special case of patent abuse when due to the exercise of a patent by the right holder or the licensee, the demand of the national market is not met. When conditions specified in Article 68 IPL are satisfied, the Polish Patent Office – according to Article 82 IPL – may grant a compulsory license. Thus, the purpose of Article 68 is to define the circumstances that allow a third party to request a compulsory license. The general abuse doctrine, as regulated in Article 5 Civil Code, provides a defense against the patentee who exercises his patent. Thus, for example, when a patentee demands an injunction in circumstances described in Article 5 Civil Code, such an exercise of the right shall not receive protection from the court and consequently an injunction will be denied. Second, Article 68 IPL applies when general (public) interest is at stake. This is implied by the requirement that the use of patented invention is necessary to meet the demand of the national market. The patentee, particularly by preventing others from using the invention, leads to a situation when that demand is not satisfied.

Thus, it seems that the Article 5 Civil Code general abuse doctrine concentrates more on the private interests, rather than general (public) interests.

In light of Article 5 Civil Code the exercise of rights is abusive when its either contrary with its socio-economic purpose or with rules of social conduct. The "socio-economic purpose" clause is widely criticized by the Polish scholars as being anachronic and contrary to the basis of the economic system of the Republic of Poland –

---

53. Du Vall, *supra* n. 26, at 290; Helena Żakowska-Henzler, *Nadużycie patentu* in Ryszard Skubisz (ed.), *System Prawa Prywatnego. Tom 14A. Prawo własności przemysłowej* (1st ed., C.H. Beck 2012), 712–713 and 730.
54. Andrzej Szewc, Gabriela Jyż, *Prawo własności przemysłowej* (2nd ed., C.H. Beck 2013), 171; Rafał Sikorski, *Nadużycie prawa* in Ewa Nowińska, Krystyna Szczepanowska-Kozłowska (eds), *System Prawa Handlowego. Tom 3. Prawo własności przemysłowej* (1st ed., C.H. Beck 2015), 455–461.

namely, market economy, private ownership and freedom of economic activity.[55] This stance, however, seems to be superficial.[56] The clause refers to the social and economic function of the right (or a claim based on a right) as intended by the lawmaker. Patents are usually legitimized by the purpose they serve – to encourage innovation. If this objective is rather jeopardized than promoted by the way the patent is exercised,[57] the defendant should be able to raise the abuse of right defense. Therefore, the "socio-economic purpose" clause could be used as a defense against some non-practicing entities, e.g., if they seek a permanent injunction while not practicing a patent themselves.

The "rules of social conduct" clause is seen as referring to moral values such as goodness, fairness, equity, loyalty, good faith, human dignity, etc.[58] Exercising the rights contrary to social and moral norms is therefore abusive. One of the cases where the exercise of a patent would be abusive because of the rules of social conduct, is when the patentee acts contrary to his promises, for example commitments to license on FRAND terms. In this case, though the exercise of a patent could also be contrary to the public interest, this would not be decisive. Acting contrary to one's promise, in breach of the reliance induced would be crucial for the application of Article 5 doctrine of abuse (according to *venire contra factum proprium nemini licet* rule).

Polish authors point to a number of circumstances when the general abuse of right defense found in Article 5 of the Civil Code, could be applied successfully.

First, it is the case of the patentee tolerating the use of patented invention by the infringer over a longer period of time. If, after having knowingly tolerated infringement over a substantial period of time, the patentee demands an injunction, the implementer could successfully raise an abuse of rights defense. The assumption is that the rules of good faith, to which Article 5 Civil Code refers, dictate that the right holder proceeds against the infringer without unnecessary delay.[59] However, various authors also suggest that when the patentee demands an injunction after having tolerated it over a longer period of time yet allows the infringer to sell the stock of infringing products, then the exercise of the rights by the right holder would not be found abusive.

Second, the implementer may resort to abuse of right defense when the parties negotiate a licensing agreement and the potential licensee, relying on the statements made by the patent holder, implements the patented invention[60] and later the patentee without any serious grounds, withdraws from the negotiations and demands that the implementer ceases to use the invention.

---

55. *See*, for example, Marek Safjan, *Klauzule generalne w prawie cywilnym (przyczynek do dyskusji)*, 11 Państwo i Prawo 48, 57–59 (1990); Maciej Gutowski, Commentary to Art. 5 in Maciej Gutowski (ed.), *Kodeks cywilny. Tom I. Komentarz* (1st ed., C.H. Beck 2016), 42–43; Piotr Machnikowski, Commentary to Art. 5 in Edward Gniewek, Piotr Machnikowski (eds), *Kodeks cywilny. Komentarz* (7th ed., C.H. Beck 2016), 18.
56. *See* Małgorzata Pyziak-Szafnicka, *Prawo podmiotowe* in Marek Safjan (ed.), *System Praw Prywatnego. Tom 1. Prawo cywilne – część ogólna* (2nd ed., C.H. Beck 2012), 899–903.
57. Fritz Machlup, *An Economic Review of the Patent System* (US Government Printing Office 1958), 10.
58. Pyziak-Szafnicka, *supra* n. 56, at 906–908; Machnikowski, *supra* n. 55, at 15–16.
59. Żakowska-Henzler, *supra* n. 53, at 728–729.
60. *Id.*, 729.

In both cases, breach of reliance is the trigger for the general abuse of right defense. Breach of reliance may also occur in other circumstances. One of the possibilities would be to raise the defense when a patentee demands that the patent implementer ceases the use a of patented invention contrary to its prior commitment (a patent pledge), especially when that commitment is made in public, to license on (F)RAND terms to any willing licensee. Such pledges, whether made within the standard-setting context or outside of such context, may induce reliance on part of the potential implementers.[61]

The abuse of rights doctrine is also subject to limitations. First, it is widely accepted that the abuse of rights defense should be applied carefully only in special cases.[62] This is especially emphasized in B2B situations,[63] which is the case in most patent disputes, and in relation to *actio negatoria*,[64] which strongly resembles permanent injunction in patent law. Second, the abuse of right defense can only be raised by a party that is genuinely willing to enter into a licensing agreement. Though this factor has not been given much attention in the literature it seems self-evident that when one of the parties raises the defense, that party should also come with "clean hands."[65] Third, the rights are presumed to be exercised in good faith and therefore the party which raises the abuse of rights defense should be able to prove the circumstances indicating that the patentee acted contrary to the socio-economic purpose of a patent or to the rules of social conduct.

§7.04 EU COMPETITION LAW/NATIONAL COMPETITION LAW DEFENSE

The CJEU in *ZTE v. Huawei* specified the conditions when seeking an injunction would constitute abuse of dominant position in light of Article 102 TFEU. It specifically described a set of procedural steps that need to be taken by the SEP holder prior to seeking an injunction. Polish courts as community courts, if faced with EU competition law defense raised by the patent implementer acting as a willing licensee would have no choice but to deny injunctive relief. Competition law defense could also be based on the national competition law.[66] That would be required if due to lack of effect on trade between Member States Article 102 TFEU could not be applied. Unfortunately, there is no case law of Polish courts applying the *ZTE v. Huawei* framework.

---

61. On various types of patent pledges *see* Jorge L. Contreras, *A patent pledge taxonomy* in Jorge L. Contreras, Meredith Jacob (eds), *Patent Pledges: Global Perspectives on Patent Law's Private Ordering Frontier* (Edward Elgar 2017), 7–37.
62. Pyziak-Szafnicka, *supra* n. 56, at 924.
63. Judgment of the Supreme Court of 6.07.1999, III CKN 310/98.
64. Judgment of the Supreme Court of 10.03.2011, V CSK 287/10.
65. *See*, e.g., Judgment of the Court of Appeal in Wrocław of 17.01.2013, I ACa 1192/12; Pyziak-Szafnicka, *supra* n. 56, at 925.
66. Article 9 Ustawa o ochronie konkurencji i konsumentów z dnia 16 lutego 2007 r., Dz.U. 2018 poz. 798.

§7.05 ENFORCEMENT OF PERMANENT INJUNCTIONS

A final decision of the court granting permanent injunction obliges the defendant to refrain from specified activities that constitute patent infringement. If the infringer does not comply with the permanent injunction the patentee may initiate enforcement proceedings. However, the specificity of injunctive relief affects the way this claim can be enforced. In this case the goal of the enforcement proceedings would be to force the infringer to obey the injunctive order.

Polish civil procedure provides for two ways to enforce an obligation of non-performance. The patentee may either ask the court to impose a fine on the infringer[67] or to order the infringer to pay to the patentee a specified amount of money for each case of breach.[68]

If the patentee chooses to demand to fine the infringer, the court will proceed to hear both parties in the first place. If the court finds that the infringer has not complied with permanent injunctive order, the fine will be imposed. Such fine may be imposed repeatedly. A single fine may not exceed ten thousand Polish zloty (ca. EUR 2,300.00) unless the fine imposed twice has proved ineffective. The total sum of imposed fines may not exceed one million Polish zlotys[69] (ca. EUR 230,000.00). When imposing a fine, the court should at the same time rule that a failure to pay such a fine will result in the fine being replaced with detention.[70] The court should also provide clear rules settling the number of days of detention, corresponding with the amount of fine. The total detention period in the same case may not exceed six months. If the infringer is a legal person, the person detained will be its employee who is responsible for non-compliance with a permanent injunction order, and if it is difficult to identify such an employee, the representatives of such legal person will be detained. Most commentators agree that if the fine is not paid in time it should not be executed, but the infringer should each time face a detention.[71]

Alternatively, the patentee may demand that the court orders the infringer to pay to the patentee a specified amount of money instead of imposing a fine. At the same time the court may warn the infringer that he will be ordered to pay a specific amount of money for each further breach of his obligations. There is no specific limit as to the amount of money which may be ordered from the infringer, either as a single payment or in total, for all cases of infringement. The amount of money which will be ordered is limited in the first place by the demand of the patentee, and in the second place by the court's discretion. The court should set the amount at the level which would deter the infringer, but at the same time at the level that would not be unnecessarily

---

67. Article 1051 § 1 CCP.
68. Article 1051¹ § 1 CCP.
69. Article 1052 CCP.
70. Article 1053 § 1 CCP.
71. Michał Krakowiak, Commentary to Art. 1053 in Janusz Jankowski (ed.), *Kodeks postępowania cywilnego. Tom II. Komentarz* (2nd ed., C.H. Beck 2015), para. 2, *Same* Tadeusz Ereciński, Henryk Pietrzkowski, Commentary to Art. 1053 in: Tadeusz Ereciński (ed.), *Kodeks postępowania cywilnego. Komentarz. Tom V. Postępowanie egzekucyjne* (5th ed., Wolters Kluwer 2016).

burdensome but still would provide adequate satisfaction to the patentee.[72] A ruling of the court, ordering the infringer to pay specific amount of money to the patentee, can be later executed.

The above-mentioned means of enforcement provided by Polish law lead to the result mentioned in Article 11 of Directive 2004/48, which provides that non-compliance with an injunction shall, where appropriate, be subject to a recurring penalty payment, with a view to ensuring compliance.

§7.06 INTERIM (PRELIMINARY, INTERLOCUTORY) INJUNCTIONS

Regardless of the possibility to demand a permanent injunction, Polish legal system provides patentees with the possibility to file a motion for an interim injunction. The aim of an interim injunction is to offer immediate protection to the right holder and to ensure the effectiveness of future ruling granting a permanent injunction. Therefore, interim injunctions in patent law can be perceived as an effective way to prevent imminent infringement of a patent or continuation of infringement.

Interim relief is granted according to provisions of Polish Code of Civil Procedure.[73] Patentees are not restricted as to the moment in which they may demand that the court grants provisional protection. Motion for interim injunction may be filed prior to initiating proceedings on the merits, at the time when initiating proceedings on the merits as well as during such proceedings.[74]

In order to obtain an interim injunction, the patentee has to prove two conditions.[75] First, the patentee has to provide sufficient prima facie evidence of his claim for injunctive relief. Second, the patentee will also be required to substantiate that he has the so-called legal interest in obtaining interim relief. The standard of proof in interim proceedings is lower than in the proceedings on the merits; the patentee is not required to provide such evidence that removes any doubts, but only has to convince the court that the grounds for interim relief potentially exist, even though there may be still some degree of uncertainty.[76]

As for the prima facie evidence relating to a claim for an injunction, the patentee has to provide evidence as to: (1) the existence of the patent; (2) the fact that he is a patent holder or exclusive licensee whose license was entered into the register; (3) patent infringement, which is the most demanding task.[77] Commentators point to the fact that establishing potential infringement for the purposes of interim proceedings is

---

72. Andrzej Adamczuk, Commentary to Art. 1051^1 in Małgorzata Manowska (ed.), *Kodeks postępowania cywilnego. Komentarz. Tom II* (3rd ed., Wolters Kluwer 2015).
73. Article 730 CCP and further.
74. Jakubecki, *supra* n. 14, at 1650.
75. Article 730^1§1 CCP.
76. Maciej Muliński, Commentary to Art. 730^1 in: Janusz Jankowski (ed.), *Kodeks postępowania cywilnego. Tom II. Komentarz* (2nd ed., C.H. Beck 2015).
77. Aleksandra Kuźnicka, *Zabezpieczenie roszczeń z zakresu prawa własności intelektualnej na czas trwania procesu* in Krystyna Szczepanowska-Kozłowska, Adam Andrzejewski, Aleksandra Kuźnicka, Agnieszka Laskowska, Justyna Ostrowska, Marta Ślusarska-Gajek, Justyna Wilczyńska-Baraniak, *Własność intelektualna: Wybrane zagadnienia praktyczne*, 2013, Chapter III, pt. 2.2.1.

especially difficult if both parties provide the court with reliable means of evidence, e.g., private expert opinions but leading to contradictory conclusions on likelihood of infringement. In such cases courts are more likely to refuse granting an interim injunction.[78]

The patentee will also be required to show that he has the so-called legal interest in obtaining interim relief. The claimant has a legal interest in obtaining interim relief if without such relief achieving the goals of the proceedings on merits will either not be possible or will be significantly more difficult.[79] It is generally recognized that the purpose of seeking an injunction in proceedings on the merits is to stop continuation of infringement because this may result in irreversible consequences for the patent holder resulting from implementation of the invention. This may be the case, for example, when the demand for the product would be satisfied by the infringer. Thus, without an interim injunction the purposes of the proceedings on the merits would not be attained.

The claimant should specify the type of interim relief it claims from the court. The claimant may demand an order for interim relief which is equal in its effects with a permanent injunction, ie. he may demand that the court orders the patent infringer to cease infringement, for the time of proceeding on the merits. Such interim relief would be only possible if it is necessary to eliminate the risk of damage or other adverse effects for the claimant. If the claimant proposes few alternative types of reliefs the court is able to pick the one which is the most suitable.[80]

General rules of Polish civil procedure require that the interim measures are proportional, and that interests of both parties are taken into account.[81] The court should each time consider if the specific type of interim relief which claimant is seeking is necessary to provide legal protection without being excessively burdensome for the other party. This assessment takes place in the final stage of proceedings on interim relief, when the court decides if proposed type of interim relief is adequate.[82] To ensure that interim relief is granted, the claimant may propose several types of interim relief so that the court may one that it considers both effective but the least onerous for the defendant.[83]

Generally, proceedings on interim relief are ex parte. In most cases, the defendant will learn about such proceedings only after a decision to grant interim relief has been taken.[84] The potential defendant may monitor what motions are filed against him in the courts that may be competent to decide on interim relief, but he will not be formally notified that the motion has been filed. Polish law does not provide the defendant with the right to file a protective letter with the court, which – as in German law – leads to the court holding a hearing on the motion for preliminary relief. This means that the

---

78. Ibid.
79. Article 730¹§2 *in fine* CCP.
80. Article 755 § 1 CCP.
81. Article 730¹§3 CCP.
82. Dariusz Zawistowski, Commentary to Art. 730¹ in: Henryk Dolecki, Tadeusz Wiśniewski (eds), *Kodeks postępowania cywilnego. Komentarz. Tom IV. Artykuły 730–1088* (2nd ed., Wolters Kluwer 2013).
83. Ewa Stefańska, Commentary to Art. 730¹ in Małgorzata Manowska (ed.), *Kodeks postępowania cywilnego. Komentarz. Tom II* (3rd ed., Wolters Kluwer 2015).
84. Article 740 CCP.

defendant in most cases only has a chance to present his case in the appeals proceedings when challenging the decision of the first instance court which grants interim relief. In some cases, the defendant may even have no chance to contest interim relief – that would be the case if first instance court refuses to grant a relief, but after the claimant's appeal the second instance court issues an appropriate order.[85]

The court which grants interim relief will also set the time for initiating proceedings on the merits. The time to initiate such proceedings should not be longer than 2 weeks.[86] If the proceedings on the merits are not initiated the interim relief will cease to have effect. The court may also make provisional relief subject to lodging by the applicant of an adequate security to ensure that the defendant may compensate his claims for damages in the event the plaintiff loses the case or decides to withdraw his case.[87] If the plaintiff does not provide the security required, the interim relief may not be enforced. The defendant is entitled to damages if the plaintiff does not initiate proceedings or if the plaintiff loses.[88]

Interim relief may also include a warning addressed to the infringer that if he breaches his obligations under the interim relief order, he may be ordered to pay a specified sum of money to the patentee.[89] Such warning will be included only if the claimant files appropriate motion. There is no limit or guidelines as to the amount of money which can be awarded for breach of obligations specified in an interim relief order. It appears that in this regard the court should follow the general rules and should balance the interests of both parties, to provide legal protection to the patentee without excessively burdening the infringer. If interim relief includes such a warning and the infringer breaches obligations specified in the interim relief order, the court will issue a decision obliging him to pay specified amount. Patentee will be able to enforce such a decision and receive that amount of money from infringer. Having such warning included in interim relief orders provides the patentee with fast and convenient way to enforce compliance with interim relief orders. This is yet another indication that interim relief proceedings are favorable towards the claimants (patentees).

§7.07 CONCLUSIONS

The position of the patentee is relatively strong in the Polish patent system. This is particularly the case because of the unusually – when compared to other legal systems – strong position of the patentee in preliminary injunction proceedings. The ex parte proceedings favor the patentee. The patent holder gets the chance to put to the court just his part of the patent infringement story, whereas the court has a chance to hear the defendant's part of the story only at the appeals level. Consequently, the potential infringer effectively loses at least one instance. Usually, getting an interim injunction

---

85. Andrzej Jakubecki, Commentary to Art. 741 in Andrzej Jakubecki (ed.), *Kodeks postępowania cywilnego. Komentarz aktualizowany. Tom II* (Wolters Kluwer 2018).
86. Article 733 CCP.
87. Article 739§1 CCP.
88. Article 746 CCP.
89. Article 756^2 § 1 CCP.

gives the patentee an immense leverage in negotiations with the potential infringer, allowing him to settle the case on more favorable terms.

With respect to permanent injunctions, Polish law seems to be properly equipped with legal tools that ensure enough flexibility, so as to allow the courts to consider interests of patentees, implementers as well as the public interest. These stem both from EU competition law, the alternative measure allowing the courts to grant compensation in lieu of an injunction and the general abuse of rights doctrine, which should be interpreted and applied in light of the proportionality principle enshrined in Article 3 of the Directive 2004/48. Even though the conditions for the application of the alternative measure are rather strict, the general abuse of right doctrine allows the courts to address the most typical cases when the patentee intends to abuse injunctive relief. In reality, however these flexibilities have not yet been tested, so it remains to be seen how they would work in practice.

Part III Asia

CHAPTER 8
Injunctive Relief in China's Patent Law

Liguo Zhang

§8.01 INTRODUCTION

This chapter aims to investigate the legislation and judicial decisions concerning injunctive relief in China's patent law. It plans to answer the question: when a patent holder seeks an injunction to prevent infringement of its patent from a competent authority in China, in what circumstances an injunctive relief may or may not be awarded while infringement of a valid patent is established. It, in particular, analyses several cases that relate to the injunctive relief regarding standard-essential patents (SEP).

The provision of injunctive relief in patent law is an international obligation. A variety of international treaties has resulted in the harmonization of many features of the national patent system. Of particular significance to the enforcement of patents is the World Trade Organization (WTO) Agreement on Trade-Related Aspects of Intellectual Property Rights (TRIPS). Regarding the enforcement of intellectual property (IP), Article 41 of the TRIPS Agreement requires:

> [m]embers shall ensure that enforcement procedures as specified in this Part are available under their law so as to permit effective action against any act of infringement of intellectual property rights covered by this Agreement, including expeditious remedies to prevent infringements and remedies which constitute a deterrent to further infringements. These procedures shall be applied in such a manner as to avoid the creation of barriers to legitimate trade and to provide for safeguards against their abuse.[1]

In addition, Article 44 of the TRIPS Agreement provides for the obligation for the parties of the provision of injunctions in their domestic laws, which states that "[t]he

---
1. Article 41 of the WTO TRIPS Agreement.

judicial authorities shall have the authority to order a party to desist from an infringement..."[2]

China joined the WTO in 2001, and its Patent Law has been updated to be in line with the requirements laid down in the TRIPS Agreement. Nonetheless, some special instances may arise where the grant of an injunction may be inappropriate. Therefore, injunction may be declined, though there may not be an explicit statutory authorization. This chapter examines such special instances by analysis of the currently applicable legislation, examination of relevant judicial decisions, and scholarly works. Specifically, this chapter finds three defenses that may be used against injunctions in patent infringement cases: good faith, public and national interests and illegal monopoly practices. However, how to define the concepts and scopes of these defenses in judicial practice is unclear. The first section of this chapter gives a brief introduction to the available remedies and the competent institutions that grant remedies for the infringement of patents in Chinese law. The second section describes the conditions and procedures to apply for a preliminary injunction and permanent injunction against infringement of patents in China. The third section deals with the defenses that may be used to decline injunction in patent infringement proceedings. The fourth section examines in particular the injunctive relief in enforcing standard-essential patents (SEPs) while keeping in line with the fair, reasonable and non-discriminatory (FRAND) principles and the competition rules.

[A] Remedies for Patent Infringement in Chinese Law

In China, the remedies for infringement of patents are covered by not only the Patent Law but also the General Principle of Civil Law, the Tort Law, and the Civil Procedure Law. The basic principles stipulated in civil law such as good faith may apply as well. China enacted its first Patent Law in 1984. China's Patent Law grants patents for inventions, utility models, and designs. The 1984 Patent Law has been further amended three times in 1992, 2000 and 2008. Since China joined the WTO in 2001, China's patent law has been improved to comply with the standards established in the TRIPS Agreement. Concerning enforcement of patents, Articles 65, 66 of the Patent Law provide for damage and preliminary injunction but do not stipulate permanent injunction in judicial proceedings at all. Consequently, seeking an injunction in patent infringement cases must rely on the relevant provisions in other legislation. The remedies for the infringement of any civil rights are defined in the General Principle of Civil Law (1986), and these remedies are further clarified in the Tort Law (2009). As a result, seeking remedies for infringement of patents needs to refer to the General Principle of Civil Law and the Tort Law. Article 2 of the Tort Law provides that the infringement of civil rights and interests, shall bear tort liability in accordance with this Law. Moreover, Article 2 further defines patent be one of such civil rights and interests.

Article 15 of the Tort Law defines 8 principal remedies when infringement occurs, which includes stopping the violation or infringement; removing obstacles; eliminating

---

2. Article 44 of the WTO TRIPS Agreement.

the danger; returning the property; restoring to original condition; repairing, reworking, replacing; compensating for loss; eliminating ill effects and rehabilitating reputation; making a full apology. These remedies may be applied singly or in combination. In theory, all these forms of remedies may apply in patent infringement cases. Nonetheless, in practice, usually stop of the violation or infringement—injunctive relief, and compensation for loss—damage apply in patent infringement cases.

[B] Who Awards an Injunction in China: A Court or Administrative Entity

In China, not only the courts but also administrative entities are entitled to award injunctions in patent infringement cases. When infringing a patent occurs, a patent holder and other interested parties may seek an injunction from either a competent court or an administrative entity against the infringer.

[1] Judicial Institutions

When infringing a patent occurs, a patent holder or other interested party may seek an injunction from a competent court. Not every court is qualified to hear patent infringement cases in China. According to the Constitution (1982) and the Organic Law of the People's Courts (1980), the Chinese courts are divided into four levels: at the highest level is the Supreme People's Court (SPC) in Beijing, which supervises the administration of all subordinate "local" and "special" people's courts. Local people's courts, which make up the remaining three levels of the court system, consist of "high people's courts" at the level of the provinces, autonomous regions, and special municipalities, "intermediate people's courts" at the level of prefectures, and municipalities, and "basic people's courts" at the level of counties, cities, and municipal districts. In China, the decision of the second instance is the final except where the SPC hears the first instance in exceptional circumstances. With respect to the cases of infringement of a patent, a local court at the venue where the infringement occurs or the defendant resides has jurisdiction to hear the first instance; then the parties can appeal to the higher level court for the second instance. Only intermediate people's courts that locate in the provincial capital city and the above level, and the local courts designated by the SPC are competent to hear patent infringement cases. One latest move is that China established three special IP courts: Beijing IP court, Shanghai IP court and Guangzhou IP court in 2014. These three IP courts exclusively hear the first instance IP disputes occurred in their local territory respectively. The decision made by these three IP courts may be appealed to the Beijing High People's Court, Shanghai High People's Court or Guangdong High People's Court respectively. At the end of 2016, the SPC decided to establish 4 IP tribunals in Nanjing, Suzhou, Wuhan and Chengdu 4 cities that have cross-region jurisdictions over technology related IP disputes in its territory respectively.

[2] Administrative Authority

In China, as an alternative, a patent holder or other interested party may seek an injunction from a competent administrative authority instead of going to a court. The State Intellectual Property Office (SIPO) is in charge of the patent administration throughout the country. In addition to accepting and examining patent applications and granting patents for inventions, utility models, and designs in accordance with the law, the SIPO's subordinate bodies at the local level are entitled to grant an injunction to stop the infringement of a patent.[3] When infringing a patent occurs, a patent holder or interested party may choose either to sue the infringer before a court or to petition an administrative entity to handle the infringement.

A competent local IP administrative entity has the power to collect evidence and investigate the infringing activities and based on such evidence it decides whether to award injunction against and impose a fine on the infringer.[4] However, an administrative entity is not entitled to award preliminary injunction and damage. Therefore, an administrative entity may be an effective way to prevent infringement without litigation cost. Nonetheless, if a patent holder would like to claim for damage in addition to an injunction, it has to go to a court. When an administrative entity makes a decision in a patent infringement case, if a party is dissatisfied with the decision, it may sue the administrative entity in a court.[5] Because such administrative decisions are subject to judicial review, this chapter focuses the judicial decisions regarding injunctions in patent infringement cases.

§8.02 PRELIMINARY INJUNCTIONS AND PERMANENT INJUNCTIONS: PROCEDURE AND CONDITIONS

Injunctive reliefs in Chinese law have two forms: preliminary injunctions and permanent injunctions.

[A] Preliminary Injunctions

A preliminary injunction may be sought before taking legal action or during a pending infringement proceeding. Article 66 of Patent Law provides for a pre-trial provisional remedy, according to which a patentee and other interested parties may file a petition to a court for ordering another to cease specific activities before filing a lawsuit or arbitration. Article 100 of the Civil Procedure Law provides for the procedures and conditions regarding an attachment of property and preliminary injunction during a pending proceeding. A petition for preliminary injunction must fulfill the following conditions: first, the claimant proves that it has the legitimate right to the patents in question; second, the infringer is conducting or is about to conduct infringement

---

3. Article 79 of the Implementing Regulations of the Patent Law (2010 Revision).
4. Article 64 of Patent Law.
5. Article 60 of Patent Law.

activities; third, the infringement activity has already resulted in or is about to result in an irreparable injury to the claimant; fourth, the claimant furnishes a bond.

After receiving a party's petition for an order of preliminary injunction, the competent court will make a ruling within forty-eight hours. If a ruling grants a preliminary injunction, the injunction will be enforced immediately. The party that is dissatisfied with the ruling may file once for review, but the injunction is not suspended during the period of review. If the claimant fails to file a lawsuit or arbitration within fifteen days after the court has ordered a preliminary injunction, the court will cancel the order. If the petition is wrong, the claimant has to compensate the losses suffered by the respondent due to the ceasing of relevant activities.[6]

There have been very few cases demonstrating how a court decides on issuing a preliminary injunction until 2016. In June 2016, the Guangzhou IP court made a decision over a preliminary injunction concerning infringing design patents.[7] This decision may shed some light on what factors that a court would consider to issue a preliminary injunction. In this case, the claimant Christian Louboutin was a Frenchman, who owned three design patents in China. The claimant alleged three respondents of making, selling and offering to sell the infringing goods without the claimant's permission, and claimed for preliminary injunctions. And the claimant deposited one million yuan as bond for the preliminary injunction. In order to decide whether a preliminary injunction should be issued in this case, the court specifically figured out six factors to evaluate. The first factor was whether the patents in question were valid and stable. Because a design patent in China is granted without substantial examination, it may not be stable. In order to prove the stability of a design patent, the court requested to provide an evaluation report of the design patents, the maintenance decision in the patent review proceedings made by the patent re-examination committee, any court decisions that have found the patent infringed, etc. The second factor was whether there was the likelihood of infringement of the patents in question by the respondents' ongoing conduct. The third factor was whether the claimant's legitimate interest would be subject to irreparable injury in case of taking no actions. As to the third factor, the court indicated that if the reputation of right holder was not injured, or the damage could be precisely calculated, and the respondents had sufficient capacity to pay the damage, then the damage could be paid after the final decision was made, therefore it was not necessary to issue a preliminary injunction. The court clarified further that in a patent infringement case, one of the following circumstances should be regarded as an irreparable injury to the right holder's interest: the right holder's reputation was injured; the infringer had no sufficient capacity to pay the damage; and the damage was difficult to calculate. With respect to the meaning of the damage is difficult to calculate, the court held in any one of the circumstances this condition would be considered satisfied, such as where the joint damage resulted from the declined price and the loss of market shares; where there were several infringers and it was unlikely to calculate the shares assumed by each infringer; where it was unlikely

---

6. Article 66 of the Patent Law.
7. See 广州知识产权法院民事裁定书, 2016粤73行保1、2、3号。(Guangzhou Intellectual Property Court Civil Ruling (2016) Yue 73 Xing Bao No. 1, 2, 3.).

for the right holder to recover the market price, which had been declined due to the competition from the infringers, to the former original level. In this case, the court specifically held that the alleged infringing products had been put on the market at the half of the claimant's price, so that it seized the market share and the claimant lost its market share, and it was difficult for the claimant to recover the price to the original level, as a result, the damage was difficult to calculate. The fourth factor was whether the damage caused to the respondents by issuing an injunction was less than or equivalent to the damage caused to the claimant by not issuing an injunction. The fifth factor was whether granting an injunction would harm the social and public interests. The sixth was whether the claimant had provided a valid and appropriate bond. After reviewing these six factors, the court found all conditions satisfied and granted the preliminary injunctions against two respondents.[8]

It seems that the preliminary injunction procedure can provide an expeditious remedy for patent infringement. However, it also raises concerns that the procedure provides less protection for the alleged infringer because it is hard to determine whether there is an actual infringement of the patent in question before the court hears and examine the evidence, especially considering the complex technical issues involved in a patent infringement case. Practically, the court may grant a preliminary injunction without hearing the opinion of the alleged infringer.[9] Judges may also feel difficulty in making a decision. The time for a court to determine a claim for a preliminary injunction is limited, and it is tough for the judges to evaluate every factor in granting a preliminary injunction correctly. The likelihood of infringement is a factor to be considered to grant a preliminary injunction. However, the likelihood of infringement in patent cases is very difficult to decide without an examination of relevant evidence, though such examination is not required in a preliminary injunction proceeding. Moreover, whether the claimant's legitimate interest will be subject to irreparable injury is a precondition to granting a preliminary injunction. However, because a patent is a property right, in most cases, infringement of a patent can be compensated by monetary damages. Namely, the injury is rarely irreparable.[10]

In considering these concerns, commentators proposed to adopt a hearing procedure in which both parties' arguments and evidence regarding the preliminary injunction may be heard, and it should allow the respondent to furnish a bond to avoid granting a preliminary injunction.[11] Indeed the current rules on the preliminary injunction seem cause inconvenience for both the judges and the respondents because the judges have to decide without the examination of evidences, and the alleged

---

8. Another respondent is exempted from injunction because the court found no evidence proving it had conducted any infringing activities.
9. 张晓薇, "知识产权诉讼诉前禁令探析," 知识产权, no. 03 (2008): 66. (Xiaowei Zhang, *An Investigation and Analysis of Intellectual Property Injunction before a Litigation*, 3 Zhishi Chanquan, 66 (2008)).
10. 刘晓军, "知识产权诉前禁令制度的变革与重构," 知识产权, no. 12 (2016): 22. (Xiaojun Liiu, *Reform and Reconstruction of Intellectual Property Injunction before a Litigation*, 12 Zhishi Chanquan 22 (2016)).
11. *Id.*, 24–25.

infringers cannot stop an preliminary injunction while it may be wrong and significantly affect their interest. However, adoption of a hearing procedure in preliminary injunction could give the alleged infringers time to destroy evidence and to hide infringing goods and tools. Nonetheless, it is fair to allow alleged infringers to furnish a bond to avoid granting a preliminary injunction. Hopefully, in the next amendment, these concerns may be taken into account.

[B] **Permanent Injunction**

China's patent law does not provide for a permanent injunction in judicial proceedings at all. However, Article 11 of the Patent Law provides that once a patent for invention or utility model issues, no one may use the patent without the permission of the patentee. And the Tort Law provides for a remedy of stopping infringement. They are the actual legal basis for courts to issue a permanent injunction to stop a patent infringement. Usually, where a court finds infringement of a valid patent in a civil proceeding, naturally it will grant an injunction if a plaintiff has claimed for it. The alleged infringer may raise a defense and provide sufficient evidence in case it considers an injunction should not be granted.

In practice, courts tend to award injunction even when the infringer has given up the infringing activities. In *Shanghai Henghao Glass Technology Co Ltd. v. Chunguang Glass Co Ltd.* for patent infringement, the plaintiff Henghao owned three design patents for glass products, the defendant Chunguang purchased molds and other devices to imitate Henghao's patented designs. The plaintiff brought three lawsuits against Chunguang for infringing three its patents and sought injunction and damage. The court found that when the defendant was informed of the allegations, it had stopped the production and operation, as well as disclosed the origin of the infringing devices. However, the court still granted injunctions besides the damage.[12] Furthermore, the research found that in fifty patent infringement cases heard by an intermediate people's court, forty-three cases were granted injunctions in forty-four cases in which the court found the infringement of patents. The only exception was that both the plaintiff and defendant confirmed that the infringing activity had been ceased since the lawsuit was filed, then the court did not grant an injunction.[13]

---

12. 上海恒昊玻璃技术有限公司与岳阳经济技术开发区春光玻璃有限公司专利侵权纠纷上诉案，湖南省高级人民法院民事判决书(2005)湘高法民三终字第58、60、61号。(*Shanghai Henghao Glass Technology Co., Ltd. v. Yueyang Economic and Technological Development Zone Chunguang Glass Co., Ltd.* for patent infringement appeal, the Hunan Provincial Higher People's Court Civil Judgment (2005) Xiang Gao Fa Min San Zhong Zi No. 58, 60, 61.).
13. 李玉香，孙浩源．"专利侵权诉讼不判决停止侵权的法律探讨．"*湖南大学学报:社会科学版* 28.2(2014):150-154, p. 151. (Li Yuxiang & Sun Haiyuan. *Legal discussion on verdicts not to stop the infringement in patent infringement lawsuit*, 28(2) Journal of Hunan University: The social sciences edition 150, 151 (2014)).

§8.03 DEFENSES AGAINST AN INJUNCTION

Some recent cases have demonstrated that in some exceptional circumstances, courts may not award injunction automatically even though the infringement of the patent in question is established. In March 2016, the SPC issued a judicial interpretation that clarifies several instances where a permanent injunction may not be granted even though the patent in question is infringed already. Moreover, the Patent Law also enumerates five particular instances where a compulsory licensing, which indeed deprive a patent holder's right to seek an injunction, may be granted.

[A] Public Interest Defense

A public interest argument may decline to award a permanent injunction in patent infringement cases. The public interest defense first was developed in some individual cases, later has been adopted by the SPC into the judicial interpretations, which have the legally binding effect to all the courts in China. In *Zhuhai Jingyi Glass Engineering Co Ltd. v. Guangzhou Baiyun Airport Co Ltd., Guangdong Airport Management Group* and *Shenzhen Sanxin Special Glass Technology Co Ltd.* for patent infringement, the plaintiff owned a utility model patent ZL97240594.1, "a moving connection device for curtain wall."[14] When the defendant Baiyun Airport authorized another defendant Sanxin to build and install glass curtain walls in its airport terminal buildings, Sanxin used the plaintiff's patented devices without the permission to complete the construction works. The court found the plaintiff's patent infringed by the two defendants Baiyun Airport and Sanxin. However, the court awarded an injunction ordering only one defendant Sanxin to stop the infringement, and it did not grant an injunction against Baiyun Airport, on the ground that even though Baiyun Airport should have stopped using the infringed technology any longer, considering the special circumstances of the airport, ordering an injunction to prohibit Baiyun Airport from using the infringing products would have violated the public interest, therefore Baiyun Airport could continually use the infringing products, but reasonable royalty should be paid.[15] Moreover, the court ruled Baiyun Airport to pay the plaintiff CNY 150,000 as a patent license fee, and ordered Guangdong airport management group and Sanxin to pay CNY 300,000 as damage. However, the court did not clarify what the public interest in this case was.

Nonetheless, there has been inconsistency in the similar cases in different courts. Another typical case is *Fischerwerke Artur Fischer GmbH & Co.KG v. Shanghai Luming Construction Material Co. Ltd, Shenyang Kaixing Decoration Engineering Co. Ltd. and Shanxi Museum* for patent infringement. In this case, the plaintiff was a German

---

14. 珠海市晶艺玻璃工程有限公司诉广州白云国际机场股份有限公司等专利权侵权纠纷案，广东省广州市中级人民法院民事判决书，（2004）穗中法民三知初字第581号。(*Zhuhai Jingyi Glass Engineering Co. v. Guangzhou Baiyun International Airport Co., Ltd.* and other for patent infringement, Guangzhou Municipal Intermediate People's Court Civil Judgment (2004 Sui Zhong Fa Min San Zhi Chu Zi No. 581.).
15. Ibid.

company that owned a patent ZL91100552.8 "fastener" in China; the plaintiff alleged the three defendants of infringing the patent and claimed for injunction and damage. The court found that the first defendant Luming had already sold 5,000 units of the infringing goods, which it had obtained from a legitimate source, to the second defendant Kaixing. However, the evidence showed that Kaixing owned 48,112 units of the infringing goods that it failed to indicate the legitimate origin, and it had installed most of the infringing goods in the glass curtain walls for the third defendant Shanxi Museum. The court found Kaixing had infringed the patent in question and granted an injunction ordering Kaixin to stop using and selling the infringing goods. However, the court declined to grant an injunction against Shanxi Museum on the ground that the use of the building that incorporated the infringing goods was not for the purpose of making a profit and therefore not infringing the plaintiff's patent.[16]

These two cases share some similarities. For example, the patented technologies were used in the construction business; the infringing goods had been installed in the construction of buildings, so that it is impossible to be separated without destroying the buildings; the defendants included the unauthorized manufacturer of the infringing goods, the construction contractors that installed the infringing goods in their construction or installation works without the patent holder's permission and the owner or operator of the buildings in which the infringing parts had been installed. In all these cases, the injunctions were not granted against all defendants. In these decisions, although the courts refused to grant injunctions against the building owners and operators, the rationales were diverted. In Baiyuan Airport case, the court held that the building owner had infringed the patent in question as well and ordered the building owner to pay the damage. The reason to decline an injunction in such a case was that it was not practicable to stop infringement and would have been in conflict with public interest. While in Shanxi Museum case, the court held that the building owner did not infringe the patent because its use of the patented goods was not for business purpose. Therefore, neither an injunction nor damage was awarded.

The SPC also held that public interest could be a defense to refuse an injunction in *Wuhan Jingyuan Environmental Engineering Co Ltd. v. Kubota Kasui Corp. and Huayang Electric Power Co Ltd.* In this case, the plaintiff Jingyuan owned a patent 95119389.9, "a method for desulfurizing gas flues," which was granted by the SIPO on September 25, 1999. The second defendant Huayang Electric purchased the equipment from the first defendant Kubota Kasui to install and use in its electricity plant. The equipment fell within the scope of patent 95119389.9. Jingyuan alleged the two defendants of infringing its patent and claimed for injunction and damage in Fujian Provincial High People's Court. The court found the infringement of the patent in question by the defendants and awarded an injunction ordering Kubota Kasui to stop the infringement. The court also ruled Kubota Kasui to pay damage to the plaintiff.

---

16. 阿图尔－菲舍尔工厂有限两合公司诉上海绿明建筑材料有限公司等专利侵权纠纷案，上海市第二中级人民法院民事判决书，（2006）沪二民五（知）初字第186号. (*Artur – Fischer Factory GmbH & Co. KG v. Shanghai Luming Building Materials Co., Ltd.* and other for patent infringement, the Shanghai Municipal Second Intermediate People's Court Civil Judgment (2006) Hu Er Zhong Min Wu Zhi Chu Zi No.186.).

However, the court refused to issue an injunction against Huayang Electric. Instead, it ruled Huayang Electric to pay a royalty to the plaintiff until the patent expires. The plaintiff appealed to the SPC. With respect to the injunction claim against Huayang, the SPC held that while the relevant parties had the obligations of not infringing the patentee's right, considering that the installation of the infringing equipment had fitted into the principal policy of environment protection and the state industrial policy, and the supply of electricity would have an impact on local economy and people's well-being, in order to balance the individual interest and the public interest, the court would not issue an injunction against Huayang Electric, but it had to pay Jingyuan licensing fee until the end of the term of patent protection. Moreover, the SPC held that since the equipment had already been installed in the electricity plant, and the plant had already been in operation, ordering an injunction would have imposed a significant impact on the public interest.[17] The SPC sustained the decision on the part of the injunction. However, the decision is not completely convinced; the first question is what if the infringing equipment did not involve the function of desulfurizing gas flues, which is fitted into the principal policy of environment protection as noted by the SPC. The second question is what if the building was not an electricity plant. These cases show when being conflict to the public interests are used as a defense to prevent an injunction, the circumstance in terms of the public interest usually is decided by court discretion.

    The SPC has been expressing the opinion that the public interests should be taken into account when a court decides whether an injunction should be awarded in a patent infringement case. In 2008, Judge Cao Jianming, the vice president of the SPC pointed out in an official presentation that "where infringement is still going on by the time when the first instance court makes its decision, the court should usually award an injunction to stop infringement. A reasonable balance should be maintained between the interests of the relevant parties and those of the general public according to the specific circumstances of a case. If an injunction is likely to cause significant imbalance between the parties' interests, or is not in line with the public interest, or practically difficult to enforce, the court may evaluate the interests according to the specific circumstances of the case, and may not award an injunction on condition that sufficient and feasible damage or monetary compensation is awarded."[18] On April 21, 2009, the SPC released "Opinions of the Supreme People's Court on trials of IPRs shall serve the overall interests under the current economic situation." Section 15 of the Opinions specifically pointed out that "according to the claims of the parties, the specific circumstances of a case and the actual necessity to enjoin infringement, courts may

---

17. 武汉晶源环境工程有限公司诉日本富士化水工业株式会社、华阳电业有限公司侵犯发明专利权纠纷案，中华人民共和国最高人民法院民事判决书，（2008民三终字第8号. (*Wuhan Jingyuan Environmental Engineering Co., Ltd. v. Kubota Kasui Corp. and Huayang Electric Power Co., Ltd.* for patent infringement, People's Republic of China Supreme People's Court Civil Judgment (2008 Min San Zhong Zi No. 8).
18. 最高人民法院副院长曹建明在第二次全国法院知识产权审判工作会议上的讲话，"求真务实，锐意进取，努力建设公正高效权威的知识产权审判制度"（2008年2月19日）。(Cao Jianming, the speech at the Second National Conference on IPR Trial, *Pragmatic, forge ahead, and strive to build a fair, efficient and authoritative IPR Judicial System*, Feb. 19, 2008).

explicitly order the parties to destruct materials, tools for making infringing products. Destruction measures should be taken only when it is necessary and in proportion to the severity of infringing activities, and should not cause unnecessary losses. In the event that stopping certain activities may cause great imbalance between parties' interests, or be in conflict with public interests, or be unlikely to enforce, courts may evaluate the interests according to the concrete circumstances of a case, and may not award injunction, instead may adopt alternative measures, such as more sufficient damage or monetary compensation, etc. to settle disputes."[19]

In the end, these policies have been incorporated into a judicial interpretation, which has the legally binding effect on all the courts throughout China. In March 2016, the SPC issued a judicial interpretation "Interpretations on several issues in the application of the law in hearing disputes over the infringement of patents, part II." (hereinafter "the 2016 Interpretation") Article 26 of the 2016 Interpretations provides that where a defendant infringes a patent, and the patent holder claims for an injunction to enjoin infringing activities, the courts shall sustain the claim. Nonetheless, while considering the state interest or public interest, the courts may not award an injunction. Instead, the courts may order the defendant to pay a reasonable royalty. However, this article does not clarify how to define the scope of the state interest and the public interest.

It may raise concern the public interest may be interpreted very broadly to cover a scope that is not necessary to be covered in the name of public interests. It seems that the courts fail to make a distinction between the harm to public interest and the abuse of right. The principle of public interest aims to protect the societal public interest, while the abuse of right doctrine aims to protect the individual interest. The principle of public interest aims to reconcile the individual interest and the public interest, and to prevent the exercise of individual rights from harming the public interest. The abuse of right doctrine aims to reconcile the conflict between the individual's rights and to make the exercise of right and performance of obligation more harmonious. Although in some occasions, the public interest may be overlapped with individual rights, in most cases the distinction between them is clear.[20] Therefore, distinguishing them in judicial decisions is necessary to secure the legal certainty and the correct application of the law. In these cases, enforcing an injunction namely to demolish the building that embodies the infringing parts would cause a loss to the infringer which is significantly higher than the interest of patent holders.[21] Obviously, it falls into the scope of the doctrine of abuse of right.

Nonetheless, in the General Principle of Civil Law, there is no such clause on the abuse of right. Instead, it provides for the principle of public interest and good faith.

---

19. "最高人民法院关于当前经济形势下知识产权审判服务大局若干问题的意见," （2009 年 4 月 21 日印发, 法发〔2009〕23 号）。(*Opinions of the Supreme People's Court on Several Issues of intellectual property right Trials under the current economic situation in serving the overall situation*, Apr. 21, 2009, Fa Fa (2009) No.23).
20. 梁上上, "公共利益与利益衡量," 政法论坛, no. 06 (2016): 8. (Shangshang Liang, *Public Interest and the Evaluation of Interest*, 6 Zhengfa Luntan 8 (2016)).
21. 汪渊智, "论禁止权利滥用原则," 法学研究, no. 05 (1995): 21. (Yunzhi Wang, *The Principle of Prohibition of Abuse of Right*, 5 Faxue Yanjiu 21 (1995)).

That might be why the SPC and judges to interpret such cases under the principle of public interest or good faith rather than abuse of rights. In the newly enacted General Provisions of the Civil Law (enacted in March 2017 and came into effect on 1 October 2017), Article 132 provides the legal basis for developing the doctrine of abuse of right. However, it may take a long time for the courts to switch to the doctrine of abuse of right in those patent infringement cases because the public interest principle has generally been applied in this type of cases.

[B] Good Faith

[1] Patentee Violating the Principle of Good Faith

As in many other civil law countries, the principle of good faith has a predominant position in Chinese private law. In theory, the violation of the principle of good faith may be used as a defense in a patent infringement case. In a recent decision made by Beijing Intellectual Property Court, the Court defines that a malicious action usually refers to a party to obtain illegal or improper interests deliberately files a lawsuit without a factual or legal basis, therefore causing a loss to the other parties in the proceeding. In this case, a party filed a lawsuit based on the patent claims some of which had been abandoned in an early patent invalidation proceeding. The court found such a lawsuit violated the principle of good faith and amounted to a malicious action.[22] The party that files a malicious action in a patent infringement case may bear the liability of damage. A malicious action can be a defense against the injunction claim in a patent infringement cases based on the principle of good faith as long as the defendant can prove the existence of a malicious action.

[2] Infringer Using a Patent in Good Faith

When an end user of an infringing embodiment can prove it has paid a reasonable price for the infringing goods and had no knowledge of that the goods have infringed another's patent, it may be exempted from an injunction. This may also be found in Article 44 of the TRIPS Agreement, which provides that "Members are not obliged to accord such authority in respect of protected subject matter acquired or ordered by a person prior to knowing or having reasonable grounds to know that dealing in such subject matter would entail the infringement of an intellectual property right."

Article 70 of the Patent Law provides that a person, for a business purpose to use, to sell and to offer for sale patented products without knowing that the products are made without the permission of patentee, does not bear the liability of damage. It implies that the infringer in good faith may still bear the liability of stopping the infringement while the liability of damage is exempted.

---

22. 北京远东水泥制品有限公司诉北京四方如钢混凝土制品有限公司因恶意提起知识产权诉讼损害责任纠纷案 (Beijing Intellectual Property Court Civil Decision (2015) Jing zhi min chu zi No. 1446).

Nonetheless, in practice, as to whether the end user of the infringing goods without knowing the infringement should bear the liability of injunction and damage, the courts in different regions have made discorded decisions, as showed in Baiyuan Airport case and Shanxi Museum case. In order to clarify the situation, Article 25 of the 2016 Interpretation provides that for business purpose, where a party uses, offers to sell and sell an infringing product without knowledge of the goods have been made and sold without permission of the patentee, and proves the legitimate source of the goods, court shall sustain the claim of injunction, unless the user of the infringing goods has proved that it has paid reasonable price for the goods. The legitimate origin is defined as the infringing product is obtained through a legitimate distribution channel, the usual sales contract, and other reasonable commercial manners.[23]

Obviously, this article in the 2016 Interpretation is based on Article 70 of Patent law. The 2016 Interpretation further adds one more condition that the infringer has paid a reasonable price for obtaining the goods, then the liability of injunction may be exempted as well if all the conditions are satisfied.

[C] Compulsory License

Article 48 of the Patent Law provides for several instances where a compulsory license for a patent may be granted: not yet exploit patents sufficiently,[24] monopoly,[25] dependent patents,[26] state emergency,[27] and public health.[28] When a compulsory license is granted, certainly the patent holder cannot seek an injunction against the patent users. However, it seems that an infringer cannot directly invoke any of these instances as a defense in a patent infringement proceeding. Instead, any would-be licensees have to file an application to the SIPO for granting a compulsory license of

---

23. Article 25 of the 2016 Interpretation.
24. According to Art. 48 (1) of Patent Law, a party that has capacity to implement the patent at issue is entitled to file a petition for granting a compulsory license of using the patent where the patent holder has not exploited its patent at all or not exploited its patent sufficiently without any legitimate justifications within three years from the date of granting the patent and within 4 years from the patent filing date.
25. According to Art. 48 (2) of Patent Law, where the enforcement of a patent is held as a monopoly practice, to eliminate or reduce the negative effect on competition caused by the monopoly practice, any parties that are capable of implementing the patent are entitled to file a petition for granting compulsory license of the patent.
26. According to Art. 51 of Patent Law, where a patented invention or utility model is a significant technological advancement over an early granted patent and has prominent economic significance, where exploitation of the patent depends on the implementation of the earlier granted patent, the patent holder can request a compulsory license for using the previous patent. If a compulsory license is granted, the holder of the early patent is entitled to ask for a compulsory license for using the advanced patent.
27. According to Art. 49 of Patent Law, in the event of an emergency or other extreme urgency of the state, or for the purposes of public interests, a competent department under the State Council may request the SIPO to grant a compulsory license for implementing a patented technology to a designated qualified party.
28. According to Art. 50 of Patent Law, for the purpose of public health, any parties that are capable of implementing the patent are entitled to file a petition for granting a compulsory license for manufacturing and exporting a patented medicine to a least developed country in accordance with international treaties that China has joined.

using the patent concerned. Only once is a compulsory license granted, the applicant may legally use the patent in the prescribed scope. Therefore, to avoid an injunction, any would-be licensees may invoke the procedure to seek a compulsory license beforehand.

[1] Procedure to Apply for a Compulsory License in China

To petition for granting a compulsory license, a would-be licensee must file a petition to the SIPO affiliated with the required documents or evidence. If all the formality requirements are fulfilled, the SIPO will accept the petition. Then the SIPO forwards a copy of the petition to the relevant patent holder. Then the patent holder has a chance to comment on the petition within fifteen days. The SIPO will review the reasoning, information and relevant evidence submitted by the petitioner, and review the opinion of the patent holder. If necessary, the SIPO may dispatch two staffs to have an onsite check. If a party requests a hearing proceeding, the SIPO shall organize and conduct an oral hearing. In the hearing proceeding, the petitioner and patent holder and other relevant parties may defend themselves and cross-examine the evidence. Unless it involves state secrets, business secrets or personal privacy, the hearing proceeding is open to the public. After examining all the relevant information, the SIPO delivers a preliminary decision to both parties for comments. After considering these comments, it will make the final decision to grant or not to grant a compulsory license. Each party that does not satisfy with a decision is entitled to petition for administrative reconsideration or to appeal to a court. The rules also include a procedure for determining a royalty rate for a compulsory license, and a procedure for terminating a compulsory license, which is similar to the procedure for granting compulsory license highlighted above. However, to date, none of such a compulsory license has been issued.

[2] Compulsory License Procedure and Injunction

In patent infringement proceedings, it is common that the alleged infringer files a patent invalid proceeding. However, what if an alleged infringer files a petition for a compulsory license? Does it pause the infringement proceeding? Also, it is possible that an alleged infringer files a petition for a compulsory license, meanwhile file a patent invalidation application with the SIPO. In such a case, there will be a parallel administrative proceeding for a compulsory license and another parallel proceeding for patent invalidation along with the patent infringement proceeding. As a result, a court may grant an injunction, while the administration may grant a compulsory license to use the infringed patent. To avoid such conflict, it is necessary to coordinate these procedures. In such a case, an injunction may not be granted. A commentator proposes that in such a case, the court may continue to hear the claims other than the injunctive claim.[29]

---

29. 康添雄, "专利强制许可的公共政策研究," 科技进步与对策, no. 06 (2013): 107. (Tianxiong Kang, *Public Policy on Patent Compulsory License*, 6 Keji Jinbu yu Duice 107 (2013)).

§8.04 INJUNCTIONS FOR SEPs and FRAND Commitments

Industrial standards define design or performance characteristics that products or services must have, they inevitably cover some claims of patents. When a patent is essential to a standard, it is unlikely that one will be able to bypass the patent in implementing a standard. In the process of making technical standards, some patent holders may voluntarily make commitment according to the standard-setting organization (SSO)'s IPR policies declaring to grant irrevocable licenses on FRAND terms and conditions. However, the negotiation of licenses is left to parties concerned and is performed outside SSOs. In the last decades, many SEP holders have involved in endless patent wars seeking injunctions against another's business. The injunction relief for SEPs is especially complicated. It is controversial to what extent a FRAND commitment may be used as a defense against a SEP holder's injunction claim.

The recent practice in China regarding enforcement of SEPs shows that seeking an injunction by a SEP holder may amount to an abuse of dominant position in the meaning of the Anti-Monopoly Law (AML). Since 2013, the Chinese standardization authority and the SIPO have requested a declaration of SEPs and of licensing SEPs on FRAND term in making national standards.[30] Recent several cases concerning licensing SEPs have been decided according to the newly enacted the AML. The main provision of the AML concerning abuse of dominant position is contained in Article 6, which provides that undertakings holding a dominant position on the market shall not abuse that dominant position to eliminate or restrict competition. The application and interpretation of this article have been directly linked to the availability of injunctive relief with respect to the enforcement of SEPs.

[A] In re Qualcomm by the NDRC

The National Development and Reform Commission (NDRC) is one of the AML enforcement agencies. In November 2013, the NDRC initiated an investigation against Qualcomm accused of its abusing dominant position in the market of licensing SEPs relating to the CDMA, WCDMA and LTE wireless standards and the baseband chip market. In February 2015, the NDRC made its decision which found that Qualcomm held dominant positions in the wireless SEPs licensing market and the baseband chip market, and Qualcomm had violated the AML by abusing its dominant positions.[31] In re Qualcomm was the first significant case that the AML enforcement agency had taken measures to handle IPR issues. Though this case does not directly deal with the injunction, the method of determining several critical factors in Article 6 of the AML may deliver some valuable information on how seeking an injunction for SEPs may violate this article.

---

30. See国家标准委、国家知识产权局发布《国家标准涉及专利的管理规定(暂行)》。Article 9 of the Regulations on National Standards Involving Patents (Interim)) Dec. 19, 2013.
31. 国家发展和改革委员会行政处罚决定书发改办价监处罚〔2015〕1号. (National Development and Reform Commission, the administrative penalty decision Fa Gai Jia Ban Jia Jian Chufa [2015] No. 1.) http://www.sdpc.gov.cn/zwfwzx/xzcf/201503/t20150302_754177.html/.

[1] Qualcomm's Dominant Position in the Relevant Markets

The NDRC found that Qualcomm held dominant positions in two relevant markets: the wireless SEP licensing market and the baseband chip market. And it ruled that Qualcomm had the ability to control the relevant market.

Though it is not dominant position per se for a firm to hold a patent, the method of determining the relevant market in this case makes a patent holder vulnerable to be held as holding a dominant position in the patent licensing market. Although a patent confers the power to exclude with respect to a specific product, process, there are often actual or potential close substitutes to prevent the exercise of market power. In re Qualcomm shows whether there exists substitute to the patented technology in question is a crucial factor for determining the existence of market power.

When the NDRC defined the relevant market in Qualcomm, it tried to establish that there was no viable substitute for a wireless standard that has been extensively implemented because of technological, regulatory and cost reasons. Given the definition of SEPs, when a patent claim is incorporated into a standard, thereof being essential to the standard, each essential patent will become unique and unsubstitutable. With respect to the substitutability of the SEPs, the NDRC conducted a demand-side substitute analysis and found that missing any of these essential patents would make the handsets incompatible with the networks, therefore being excluded from the market. From the perspective of demand-side, consumers could go for an alternative technology when the price for the license of a patented technology became too high. However, when a patent was incorporated into a standard, and due to the lock-in effect, namely it was not practically possible to switch to other standards because all the original investment for using the current standard would have become sink costs. Therefore, even though there was an alternative technology available, it was unlikely for the consumers to switch to it. From the perspective of supply-side, it found that each essential patent was unique, once a standard was adopted and implemented, it was impossible to find an alternative to the essential patent while implementing the standard. Hence, the NDRC concluded that the market for licensing each SEP constituted an independent relevant market. When Qualcomm put all its SEPs into a portfolio to license out, the relevant market was the collection of each single relevant market in licensing each SEP. Consequently, Qualcomm held 100% market share in the relevant market. When licensing a patent is defined as a relevant market for assessing the market power, it is natural that holding a SEP would give rise to a per se dominant position.

This decision clearly demonstrates that a SEP holder usually will be considered holding a market power in the licensing SEP market unless it can prove that there exists alternative technology to its essential patent, and the user may switch to such an alternative. Seeking for an injunction by a SEP holder against a SEP user may imply to exclude it from the market. Nonetheless, market definition is only the first step which is followed by to determine whether the dominant position in the market exists. Indeed, it is not an offense in itself for a firm to have a dominant position. Even when a patented technology does enjoy market power, that fact alone does not give rise to a violation of the AML unless it has engaged in some abusive conducts that are prohibited by law.

[2] Licensing Offers Violating the ALM

The NDRC found Qualcomm's licensing offer had involved two categories of abusive conducts: excessive pricing and attaching unreasonable conditions on the license contracts.

The NDRC investigated Qualcomm's conducts involving bundling non-SEPs with the SEPs and the expired patents, the free licensing back provisions. However, the NDRC linked all these conducts to unfair pricing. Qualcomm's patent portfolio includes both essential patents and non-essential patents. The NDRC found this practice could stifle the technologies that were alternative to those non-essential patents, consequently stifling innovation and detrimental to consumer's interest. Therefore, the NDRC concludes that these practices have violated Article 17.1.1 of the AML, which prohibits dominant undertakings from selling products at an unfairly high price. Qualcomm argued that although the patent portfolio included some expired patents, every year some new patents had been added to the portfolio. Nonetheless, the NDRC held that Qualcomm failed to prove the added patents had the value equal to those expired patents. The NDRC found that the amount of the patents in the portfolio had changed, but the royalty remained unchanged. Moreover, the NDRC found that some licensees were required to license back their relevant SEPs to Qualcomm free of charge, and were required not to enforce their patent against Qualcomm's customers. Based on these findings, the NDRC concluded that these practices had deprived licensee's opportunity of fair negotiation.

It is common that a license agreement contains no-challenge clauses that expressly prohibit the licensees from challenging the licensors' patents or other IPRs. Article 17.5 of the AML prohibits tying goods or attaching unreasonable transaction conditions without legitimate justification. The NDRC found that the conclusion of a non-challenging agreement was a condition for a licensee to obtain Qualcomm's baseband chips, and if a potential licensee did not sign a license agreement that includes such unreasonable clauses, Qualcomm would refuse to supply baseband chips. Moreover, where a licensee that had to sign a non-challenging agreement had a dispute with Qualcomm regarding the license agreement and filed a lawsuit, Qualcomm would stop supplying baseband chips to the licensee. The NDRC held that it was a licensee's right to raise a dispute regarding its license contract and to file a lawsuit, and Qualcomm's conducts restricted a licensee's legitimate right by leveraging its dominant position. As a result, those that would not accept the unreasonable contract conditions would be excluded from the market, thereof eliminating or restricting competition in the market. The conduct had violated the paragraph 1.5 of Article 17 of the AML.

[3] Licensing Offers Violating the AML as a Defense Against an Injunction

Though this is an administrative case which does not directly involve granting an injunction, it raises a question whether the patent holder can apply for an injunction when a patent holder offers to license its patents under conditions that violate the AML and a would-be licensee rejects such an offer. In good faith negotiations between willing licensees and licensors, the licensees should not be presented with licensing terms that violate AML. A licensee remains a willing licensee even though the licensee rejects such terms. In such a case, an injunction should not be granted against a willing licensee based on the good faith principle.

In this case, the NDRC mandated that (1) Qualcomm should provide a detailed list of the patents included in its patent portfolio to be licensed, and remove all expired patents from its patent portfolio; (2) Qualcomm was forbidden to force its licensees to grant reciprocal patent license for free or at unreasonable low price; (3) Qualcomm was forbidden to calculate its licensing fee based on the price of the entire handset while charging high licensing rate; (4) Qualcomm was forbidden to tie-up its non-SEPs with the SEPs in licensing its patent portfolio; (5) Qualcomm was forbidden to sell baseband chips on the condition that the chip customers sign a license agreement including the terms that the NDRC found to be unreasonable, such as non-challenging the patents, licensing expired patents, free licensing back patents. For licenses of Qualcomm's 3G and 4G essential Chinese patents for branded devices sold for use in China, Qualcomm agreed that it would charge royalties rate of 5% for 3G devices (including multimode 3G/4G devices), and 3.5% for 4G devices (including 3-mode LTE-TDD devices) that did not implement CDMA or WCDMA standards, in each case royalty base would be 65% of the net selling price of the device. Qualcomm would give its existing licensees an opportunity to elect to take the new terms for sales of branded devices for use in China as of January 1, 2015. The NDRC imposed a fine of CNY 6.088 billion on Qualcomm, which was 8% of its turnover in the Chinese market in 2013.

[B] Huawei v. InterDigital

As early as in 2008, the SPC has delivered a point of view on the exercise of patents covered in a standard,

> ... [w]here a patent holder has participated in standard making, or with its permission, its patent has been included into a national, industrial or regional standard, it is deemed that the patent holder agrees to license others to use the patent while others are implementing the standard. The activity of using the patent does not amount to the infringement defined in the Article 11, 60 of the Patent Law. The patent holder may claim for certain royalty, but the amount of royalty should be lower than the normal royalty rate.[32]

---

32. 最高人民法院关于朝阳兴诺公司按照建设部颁发的行业标准《复合载体夯扩桩设计规程》设计、施工而实施标准中专利的行为是否构成侵犯专利权问题的函，（[2008]民三他字第4号）。(The Supreme People's Court's letter on whether Chaoyang Xingnuo Company that

However, there have not been any significant cases regarding licensing SEPs to test what is the legal effect of seeking an injunction in relation to enforcing a SEP until *Huawei v. InterDigital* at Shenzhen Intermediate People's Court in 2011. In *Huawei v. InterDigital*, the court found InterDigital had abused its dominant position in the 3G SEP licensing market by seeking an injunction in the U.S. against Huawei. This decision suggests that a SEP holder may lose the right to seek an injunction against infringers where it violates the law or good faith principle in the process of licensing negotiation.[33]

Huawei and InterDigital had negotiated on the terms for Huawei to use InterDigital's wireless communication patents both through emails and in-person meetings in Shenzhen, China, but could not reach an agreement. Subsequently, InterDigital filed lawsuits on July 26, 2011 at both the U.S. International Trade Commission (ITC) and a U.S. District Court against Huawei, for allegedly infringing seven of its US patents related to the 3G technologies. Faced with InterDigital's litigation pressure in the US, Huawei sued InterDigital on December 6, 2011 at the Shenzhen Intermediate People's Court in China for allegedly violating its obligation to license certain patents on the FRAND terms. Huawei filed two complaints. In one complaint, Huawei claimed that InterDigital had abused its dominant position in licensing the SEPs in the 3G wireless communications standard by imposing tying, discriminatory conditions, and other unreasonable conditions, as well as by initiating sudden lawsuits against Huawei in the U.S. Huawei alleged that, in essence, such abusive conducts were equivalent to a refusal to deal, and had harmed Huawei's operations and reduced competition in the market. Huawei sought injunctions against the alleged abusive conducts and damages of CNY 20 million. Separately, in another complaint, Huawei alleged that InterDigital violated its FRAND commitments and asked the court to determine the appropriate FRAND licensing rate.[34]

The Shenzhen Intermediate People's Court found that the licensing rate that InterDigital had offered to Huawei was about 100 times higher than it had offered to Apple and ten times higher than to Samsung. Then the court held that InterDigital's licensing offer to Huawei failed to satisfy the requirements of the FRAND terms because first, the licensing offer combined the SEPs and non-essential patents in the global scope, while Huawei only would accept license of the SEPs in Chinese territory; second, InterDigital requested Huawei to license back its patents to InterDigital free of charge; third, the licensing offer was not negotiable; and InterDigital sued Huawei for the infringement of its patents and sought injunctions while the negotiation was going

---

designs, constructs in accordance with an industrial standard made by the Ministry of Construction thereof implementing patents in the standards constitutes patent infringement ([2008] Min San Ta Zi No. 4).).

33. 华为技术有限公司与IDC公司滥用市场支配地位纠纷上诉案〔广东省高级人民法院(2013)粤高法民三终字第306号民事判决书〕。(*Huawei Technologies Co., Ltd. v. IDC* for abuse of market dominance position appeal [the Guangdong Provincial Higher People's Court civil judgments (2013) Yue Gao Fa Min San Zhong Zi No. 306]).

34. 华为技术有限公司与IDC公司标准必要专利使用费纠纷上诉案,广东省高级人民法院(2013)粤高法民三终字第305号民事判决书。(*Huawei Technologies Co., Ltd. v. IDC* for the royalty of standards essential patents appeal, the Guangdong Provincial Higher People's Court civil judgments (2013) Yue Gao Fa Min San Zhong Zi No. 305).

on. Based on these findings, the court held that InterDigital had violated its FRAND commitments and abused its market power in its licensing practices. The court ordered InterDigital to cease the alleged excessive pricing and improper bundling of InterDigital's essential and non-essential Chinese patents and to pay Huawei CNY 20 million in damages. The court also ruled that the royalties to be paid by Huawei for InterDigital's 2G, 3G, and 4G essential Chinese patents should not exceed 0.019% of the actual sales price of each Huawei's product, which was decided according to the royalty rate that InterDigital offered to Apple. Soon after the Shenzhen court's decision, InterDigital appealed, but the Guangdong Provincial High People's Court affirmed the Shenzhen court's decision on October 28, 2013. On January 2, 2014, InterDigital and Huawei reached a settlement agreement, ending their global patent litigation and pledging to resolve their disputes through arbitration.

This decision shed some light on how a willing licensor and licensee should or should not behave. First, good faith is the top guiding principle for both parties in the negotiation of a licensing agreement. The court held that Article 4 of the General Principles of the Civil Law, which stipulates that "the civil activities shall follow the principles of voluntary, fairness, compensation for equal value and good faith," and Article 5 of the Contract Law which stipulates that "the parties shall abide by the principle of fairness in prescribing their respective rights and obligations," and Article 6 of the Contract Law, which provides that "the parties shall abide by the principle of good faith in exercising their rights and performing their obligations," should be used to interpret the meaning of the FRAND terms.

Second, sufficient negotiation prior to any legal action is necessary. The Guandong Provincial Higher People's Court upheld the opinion of the court of the first instance that the patentee should not refuse straightway to grant a license to a standard implementer who is willing to pay a fair royalty. The court's approach interpreting the FRAND commitments is similar to that of Court of Justice of European Union in *Huawei v. ZTE* on this point.

Third, the court also noted that when calculating royalty rate, any factors other than the patents as such should be excluded. It should ensure on one hand that a patentee gets sufficient returns from its technological innovation, on the other hand, should avoid a SEP holder from leveraging its strong position created by a standard to obtain a high license rate or to impose unreasonable conditions. As to royalty rate, the court highlighted several factors to be considered in determining royalty rate. The Court held that, first of all, where the parties could not reach an agreement on the royalty rate, they could ask the people's court to determine. Second, when determining royalty rate, the following factors should be taken into account: the profit resulting from the implementation of the patent or a similar patent, and the profit's proportion in the sales profit or sales revenue of the licensee's related products. Moreover, the court held that technology, capital, licensee's operation and labors, and other factors together contributed to the final profit of a product, the license fee could only be part of the profits and should not be the whole. And a single patentee did not provide all the technology, so a patentee only had the right to receive the proportion corresponding to its profit part. Furthermore, because the contribution of a patentee was its innovative technology, the patentee could only be entitled to obtain the profit from its patent rather than the standard. Third, the royalty rate should take into account the number of essential patents in the technical standards, a demand for standard implementers to pay royalties for non-essential patents was unreasonable. Forth, the royalties of a patent should not exceed the percentage of its profits in a product, and a reasonable distribution of royalties between all the patentees should be taken into account.

With respect to the "non-discriminatory" conditions, the court held that where the transaction conditions were roughly identical, a roughly same royalty rate should apply. Where a SEP holder charged a licensee a lower royalty rate but charged another a higher rate regardless of the same conditions, the latter had reason to believe that it was subject to discriminatory treatment. In this way, the SEP holder violated the non-discriminatory commitment.

The latest judicial interpretation issued by the SPC seems having adopted the approach in this case largely. Article 24 of the 2016 Interpretation clarifies that the court may not grant an injunction against a SEP infringer where a SEP holder does not honor the obligation of FRAND licensing term in the process of negotiation. When the parties cannot reach a licensing contract, they may request a court to decide the licensing term according to the Interpretation. It provides that

> [w]here recommended national, industrial or regional standards have disclosed essential patent information, when a patentee and an alleged infringer are negotiating patent licensing terms, the patentee intentionally breaches its licensing obligations of FRAND commitments made in standard-making process, resulting in no patent licensing contracts concluded, and the alleged infringer has no obvious fault in the negotiation, courts generally shall not support the claim to stop the implementation of standards concerned.

[C] *Huawei v. Samsung*

In *Huawei v. Samsung*, Shenzhen Intermediate People's Court has developed an approach to evaluate the fault of both parties in the SEP licensing negotiation to decide whether an injunction should be granted.

In May 2016, Huawei filed two patent infringement lawsuits against Samsung and its affiliations in China in Shenzhen Intermediate People's Court. Huawei alleged that Samsung infringed its patents No. 201010137731.2 and 201110269715.3, and requested the defendants immediately to cease infringement of its patents. The court made decisions in January 2018 and granted injunctions against Samsung.[35]

Huawei asserted that these patents were essential to the 3GPP LTE standards, and Samsung infringed the patents. The plaintiff also emphasized that it had always followed the principle of FRAND throughout the licensing negotiation process, providing a large number of examples of claim chart and a list of SEPs in the negotiations,

---

35. 华为技术有限公诉诉三星（中国）投资有限公司等专利侵权案，广东省深圳市中级人民法院民事判决书，（2016）粤03民初816号，（2016）粤03民初840号。*Huawei Technology Co Ltd. v. Samsung (China) Investment Co Ltd.* etc. for patent infringement, Guangdong Province Shenzhen Intermediate People's Court Civil Judgments (2016) Yue 03 Min Chu No.816, and No. 840.).

making the FRAND licensing offer several times. When there was no progress in the negotiations, the plaintiff proposed to establish a FRAND licensing conditions through a third party arbitration. It accused that Samsung had refused to negotiate in good faith during the last five years of licensing negotiations, adopting delaying tactics and violating the principle of good faith, therefore causing unlikely to reach a patent licensing agreement and refusing to pay the license fee while it was continuing to implement the patents involved.

The defendants jointly defended that they had not infringed the plaintiff's patent rights, and even if the defendant had committed an infringement of the plaintiff's patent, the defendant should not be liable for the cessation of infringement on the basis of the defense of the patent interference, the exhaustion of the patents, the public interest and the balance of interests. Moreover, the defendants argued that Samsung had no obvious fault in the licensing negotiations, and Huawei had violated its FRAND licensing obligation in the negotiations, therefore the plaintiff's claim for the injunctions should not be supported.

The court held that the case involved two major issues, one is the FRAND issue, the other is the technical facts. On the issue of FRAND, it involved that which party in the negotiation of the SEP cross licensing, had fault for the failure of reaching a license agreement. The issue of technical facts included whether the patent concerned was essential to the 4G standard, whether the defendant had infringed the patents, and whether the defendants' defense could be established.

The court found that in the process of negotiation of SEP cross licensing, Samsung had a clear fault, violating the FRAND principle, and the plaintiff Huawei had no obvious fault and did not violate the FRAND principle. The court's finding was based on these facts. First, Samsung in the negotiation of the scope of and the prerequisite for cross licensing insisted on covering both the SEP and non-SEP patents, and refused to negotiate only on the SEPs for cross licensing, therefore leading to the SEP cross licensing negotiations between the two parties seriously delayed. Second, Samsung had not responded positively to the claim charts of the SEPS submitted by Huawei, which led to a serious delay in the negotiation of SEP cross licensing between the two parties. Third, Samsung did not either positively make a licensing offer to Huawei, or actively respond to Huawei's offer. This indicated that Samsung had intentional fault for the delay of the negotiations. Fourth, when Huawei proposed to pass the matter to a neutral third party arbitration to facilitate the SEP cross licensing, Samsung unjustified refused, which meant that Samsung had the subjective fault for the delay of the negotiations. Fifth, in the process of the court's mediation proceeding, Samsung did not propose a substantive conciliation plan, maliciously delaying the negotiation and having the subjective fault. The court then held that Huawei had no obvious fault in the process of the negotiation of the SEP cross licensing with Samsung and did not violate the FRAND principle.

Because both Huawei and Samsung own patents that are essential to the 3GPP standards, each party has to use the other's SEPs, and each party may request royalty from the other. However, the other party may assert to countervail the royalty. In this case, the court evaluated several factors to decide whether one party's licensing offer and the counter-offer was in line with the FRAND principle. The court held that it was necessary to analyze both parties' strength in the SEPs according to the evidence submitted by them. Then based on the strength of SEPs owned by each part to determine whether the licensing offer given to the other party conform to the FRAND principle, the court established three measurements to determine the strength of SEPS of each party in the LTE standards: the number of the approved proposal submitted by each party that are adopted by the 3GPP SSO; the numbers of declared SEPs in the ETSI and the number of the evaluated SEPs in the ETSI in terms of the 3G/UMTS and 4G/LTE standard; the cases of that the patents involved is declared invalid. Based on these criteria, the court found that Huawei and Samsung had comparable strength in the SEPs globally, but Huawei has much strength than Samsung in the SEPs in China. Therefore, the court held that the licensing offer made by Huawei according to its strength in SEPs was in line with the FRAND principle, while the offer made by Samsung in accordance with its strength in the SEPs was not in line with the FRAND principle.

Finally, the court concluded that in the negotiation between Huawei and Samsung in terms of cross licensing SEPs, the plaintiff Huawei in the negotiation process had no obvious fault, and was in line with the FRAND principle, while Samsung was found obvious fault, and did not conform to the FRAND principle from both the procedural and the substantial perspectives. The plaintiff Huawei sought injunctive relief from the court after the effort to seek negotiations and the attempt to resolve the issue of cross licensing between the two parties through arbitration did not succeed. Moreover, Samsung in the mediation process still intentionally delayed the negotiations. Given this, the court ruled the defendants to stop infringing the plaintiff's patents, that was, to stop the implementation of the SEPs in the 4G standards.

Nonetheless, Huawei and Samsung sued each other in the US., and Samsung requested the U.S. court to issue an antisuit injunction. The court ordered in April 2018 that Huawei should not enforce the injunction awarded by the Shenzhen Intermediate People's court.[36] It seems that now there is an injunction deadlock which also happened in the SEPs disputes between Microsoft and Motorola in Germany and the US years ago.[37]

§8.05 CONCLUSIONS

The availability of injunctive relief in patent law is an important indicant of the strength of patent protection in a country. In China, injunctive relief is generally available according to the Patent Law, the Tort Law, and the Civil Procedure Law. When infringing a patent occurs, the right holder or other relevant parties may seek an injunction in a court or administrative authority. Compared to many countries, Chinese Patent Law also empowers the IP administrative authority to grant an injunction against infringers. So, when a patent is infringed, the patent holder may choose to go to a court or administrative authority.

---

36. *Huawei Technologies, Co, Ltd et al v. Samsung Electronics Co, Ltd. et al*, No. 3:2016cv02787 – Document 130 (N.D. Cal. 2017).
37. *Microsoft Corp. v. Motorola Inc.*, 696 F.3d 872 (9th Cir. 2012).

The courts have developed some rules according to which an injunction may be denied even though the court finds the infringement of a patent. These defenses largely include good faith defense, public and national interest defense, and FRAND commitments in SEPs. In China, both patent law and the AML may play a role in dealing with licensing SEPs. The court may not grant an injunction against a SEP infringer where a SEP holder does not honor the obligation of FRAND terms in the process of licensing negotiation. In recent *Huawei v. Samsung* decisions, the court further developed means to evaluate the fault of each party in the negotiation of licensing SEPs in deciding whether to grant an injunction for SEPs.

Many decisions and the SPC's opinions on injunctive relief show the deficiency with respect to public interest defense. The deficiency of current approach regarding the defense against an injunction is that the public interest defense has been adopted to cover too broad scope. Under the current scheme, patentees whose patents involve a dependent patent or patent trolls can be denied an injunction in the name of public interest. In many cases, it does not directly link to the public interest. Abuse of right as a defense may be more reasonable in some cases that do not directly link to public interest and only involve the balance between individual's interests. In the current system, there lack clear rules, explicit standards and procedure to define the scope of public interest in patent infringement cases. It is necessary to develop methods to define the public interest defense to avoid the unreasonable limitation on injunctive relief in patent infringement cases.

CHAPTER 9
Patent Injunction Heuristics in India
Yogesh Pai[*]

§9.01 INTRODUCTION

India's independence from the colonial rule led to enactment of the Patents Act, 1970, which has been amended thrice to comply with obligations laid out in the TRIPS Agreement and Paris Convention.[1] A review of the working of the then prevailing patent system was found not to be working in national interest since it stifled domestic industrial growth, self-sufficiency in drug production and created barriers to access lifesaving medicines.[2] Hence the 1970 Act placed substantial restrictions on patentability in pharmaceuticals and agrochemicals, included a regime for license of rights along with limitations on remedies.[3] Although these have been substantially diluted or withdrawn in the post-TRIPS context, an overly deep suspicion of the patent system still informs and dominates the intellectual discourse in India.[4]

At the heart of this discourse is the critical question of availability of injunctive relief. Patent injunctions in India are extremely controversial due to its immediate and potential impact on local businesses, local production and consumer access, especially

---
[*] The author would like to thank Arpit Agarwal, student fellow at CIIPC for providing research assistance and Ms Shrinkhala Jaiswal, Research Fellow, CIIPC for editorial inputs.
[1]. For a general overview of historical evolution of the Indian patent system, *see* Prashant Reddy T. & Sumathi Chadrashekaran, Create, Copy, Disrupt: India's Intellectual Property Dilemmas (Oxford University Press 2017).
[2]. Although the patent system in India dates back to the British era (Patents Act, 1911), its need and role were re-discovered only in the post-colonial period. *See* Justice N. Rajagopal Ayyangar, Report on the Revision of the Patent Laws (September 1959).
[3]. *See* text accompany *infra* n. 66–70 for a discussion on how the Patents Act, 1970 was amended to remove the limitations on remedies.
[4]. *See* Reddy and Chandrashekaran (2017), *supra* n. 1 at p. 30 and pp. 55–78 [noting that very few voices have been in favour of the patent system while legislating the 1970 Act. The amendments in the post-TRIPS context have also been highly controversial]. *See* Basheer on end of exclusivity.

in the context of pharmaceuticals.[5] India has been at the centre-stage of the remedies debate typically because of the grant of ex parte and *ad-interim* injunctions before addressing the critical question of patent validity.[6] An explosion in patent litigation in India during the last decade provides a testimony on the role and importance of availability of injunctive relief in a situation where a large number of cases are yet to conclude trial.[7] As a common law jurisdiction, Indian courts have conclusively resolved in favour of evaluating the grant or denial of injunctions based on equitable principles.[8] However, two fundamental criticisms can be briefly raised: absence of any reasoning in granting ex parte/interim injunctions, and/or erroneous application of equitable principles in specific cases leading to disproportionate outcomes.

India is also a unique jurisdiction in many different ways since courts have often shied away from concluding infringement trials (which demands deeper technical analysis based on scientific evidence), but have been keen to provide interim remedies, often immediately after the institution of the suit.[9] This is compounded by the inability of courts to evolve any useful framework for granting patent damages.[10] In fact, the first trial involving a FRAND-encumbered SEP where damages were awarded concluded only in July, 2018.[11] There is a trend to extend the interim stage and grant injunctions, which in effect could lead to de facto settlement of a dispute in a money suit (where patentee plaintiffs demand monetary damages).[12] Some other courts have

---

5. *See* Shamnad Basheer, *Affordable Drugs Need a Compensatory Patent Commons*, https://thewire.in/health/affordable-drugs-need-a-compensatory-patent-commons (accessed 10 Jul. 2018).
6. *See* Shamnad Basheer, Jay Sanklecha & Prakruthi Gowda, *Pharmaceutical Patent Enforcement: A Developmental Perspective,* in *Patent Law in a Global Perspective* 603–635 (eds Ruth L. Okediji and Margo Bagley, Oxford University Press 2014).
7. *See* Prashant Reddy, *143 patent infringement lawsuits between 2005 and 2015: Only 5 judgments*, https://spicyip.com/2017/06/143-patent-infringement-lawsuits-between-2005-and-2015-only-5-judgments.html (accessed 10 Jul. 2018).
8. *Gujarat Bottling Co. Ltd. v. Coca Cola Co.* – AIR 1995 SC 2372.
9. *See* Basheer et al., *supra* n. 6. While there are many reasons that may be attributed to trial pendency, the most glaring reason is the lack of expertise among generalist judges to deal with complex patent trials. Moreover, the specialized Intellectual Property Appellate Board (IPAB) does not have jurisdiction to determine infringement. It can only take appeals from the patent controller and revoke patents. It is expected that the constitution of the commercial courts under Commercial Courts Act (2015), where specialized benches could help in tackling pendency due to its time bound adjudication process. Whether or not commercial courts will tackle the expertise issues is doubtful. *See* Jacques de Werra, Denis Borges Barbosa, Pedro Marcos Nunes Barbosa, Hong Xue, Shamnad Basheer & Susan Isiko Štrba, *Specialised Intellectual Property Court-Issues and Challenges, Second Issue, Global Perspectives for the Intellectual Property System*, CEIPI-ICTSD, Issue Number 2, 2016.
10. J. Sai Deepak, Evolving a Culture of Damages, https://thedemandingmistress.blogspot.com/2016/04/evolving-culture-of-damages.html (accessed 31 Jul. 2017); J. Sai Deepak, *Towards Evolving a Culture of Damages: Analysing the Christian Louboutin Verdict of the Delhi High Court,* http://thedemandingmistress.blogspot.com/2018/02/towards-evolving-culture-of-damages.html (accessed 31 Jul. 2017).
11. *See Phillips Electronics v. Rajesh Bansal,* https://spicyip.com/wp-content/uploads/2018/07/Phillips-Judgment.pdf (Delhi High Court 12 Jul. 2018).
12. (Where the non-practising patentee plaintiff claims injunctive relief with a demand for monetary damages for past infringement and is willing to provide a licence based on negotiated royalties.).

Chapter 9: Patent Injunction Heuristics in India §9.02

picked a certain notion of requirement of 'working' and 'public interest' to deny injunctive relief.[13]

This chapter makes an attempt not only to provide a general commentary but also a deeper analysis of issues that are routinely argued and debated in Indian courts. Section I of this chapter follows debate on patent injunctions in India by contextualizing it within the global scholarly debate on controversies surrounding patent injunctions. It aims to provide a bird's eye view of some similarities and contrasts between the global and Indian debate. Section II discusses the statutory foundations for patent injunctions in India. It locates the statutory basis in the Patents Act, 1970 and the Code of Civil Procedure, 1908 (CPC), which is the general remedies law in order to assess the evolution of the equitable factors. Section III examines the application of equitable principles by Indian courts for granting patent injunctions. Although the focus is on how Indian courts have evaluated the equitable factors in granting *ad-interim* injunctions, the specific standard applied by the courts in granting ex parte, *quia-timet* and permanent injunctions are critically evaluated in the context of the specific fact situations involved in those cases. An attempt is also made to provide insights into how courts have fashioned remedies due to sector specific needs since it is often argued that patent law is technology specific.[14]

So when optimal solutions are not in the horizon, it is not difficult to imagine why courts would often fall back on a 'trial and error' method, or in short, 'injunction heuristics'. This perhaps explains the grand narrative of patent injunctions in India. But the deficiency of analysis in the most 'celebrated' judgments remind us of how often courts skip through or pick and choose which factors to lay emphasis on.[15] The chapter finally concludes by stating that very limited observations can be made in the context of a general narrative on the law of patent injunctions in India. While the Indian courts have not followed a cautious approach in granting ex parte and interim injunctions, courts must develop injunction heuristics to delineate the cases where they may be rightly due.

§9.02 SITUATING PATENT INJUNCTIONS IN INDIA IN THE CURRENT DEBATE

The global debate on patent injunctions provides clarity on why they have turned controversial over the recent years. There is a wider consensus that patent notice must align with remedies because of its impact on third parties and competition.[16] Since patent validity is often critical to the question availability of remedies, ex parte and

---

13. See Ashish Bharadwaj, *Patent Injunction and the Public Interest in India* 40 EIPR 1, 55 (2018).
14. Dan L. Burk & Mark A. Lemley, *Is Patent Law Technology-Specific*, 17 Berkeley Tech. L.J. 1155 (2002) (available at http://scholarship.law.berkeley.edu/btlj/vol17/iss4/1).
15. *See Ericsson v. Intex*, 2015 SCC Online Del 8229 (Del. High Ct. 2015) (where a single judge bench of the Delhi High Court overlooked the factor of balance of convenience); *But see Vringo Infrastructure v. India Mart*, 2014 SCC OnLine Del 3970 (Del. High Ct 2014), the single judge glossed over the criteria of irreparable harm.
16. *See* Federal Trade Commission, *The Evolving IP Marketplace: Aligning Patent Notice and Remedies with Competition*, https://www.ftc.gov/sites/default/files/documents/reports/

temporary injunctions have been generally denied in many jurisdictions. Furthermore, even when patents are shown to be conclusively valid after trial, there is a strong argument in favour of denial of injunctive relief due to exclusionary effects in markets which are beyond the scope of rights of the patent holder. It has been argued by various scholars that a powerful exclusionary remedy[17] is unwarranted in most cases of patent infringement since patents are routinely invalidated when challenged (due to their probabilistic character) or if a defendant's act is non-infringing.[18] Patent injunctions in the context of the rise of NPEs and PAEs are generally viewed as anticompetitive.[19] Thus tailored injunctive relief is now the norm for granting remedies in the post-eBay environment to tackle the scourge of NPEs and PAEs.[20]

While there is an ongoing debate on what empirical evidence must inform whether or not the crises is systemic or anecdotal,[21] it is not difficult to see how these debates have deeply influenced the scholarship on the question of remedies for patent infringement. It is observed that 'if patents fail to increase the rate and range of innovation or only do so marginally, then one can safely institute compensatory liability schemes without unduly worrying about the allegedly reduced incentives to innovate'.[22] In fact, some others observe that patent enforcement is generally inefficient since there is no active technology transfer.[23] However, it is doubtful if the value of NPEs to the innovation ecosystem can be simplistically concluded when innovation

---

evolving-ip-marketplace-aligning-patent-notice-and-remedies-competition-report-federal-trade/110307patentreport.pdf (accessed 31 Jul. 2017).

17. The term exclusionary remedy is used synonymously with patent injunction although the term exclusionary remedy could represent grant of patent injunctions for a suit of patent infringement in domestic court or invoking a temporary administrative remedy such as border measures to stop goods from entering the domestic or regional borders. Border measures as applied to patents also have exclusionary effects, but are limited in nature. However, border measures can also be abused when coupled with the willingness of the Indian courts to grant ex parte injunctions. See Ramkumar patent controversy, *infra*.
18. See Mark Lemley, *Ignoring Patents*, 19 Mich. St. L. Rev., 1 (2008). Also see, Sichelman, Ted M., *Purging Patent Law of 'Private Law' Remedies* 92, Tex. L. Rev. 516, 571 (2014), https://ssrn.com/abstract = 1932834 [rejecting the private law premise of patent law and instead arguing for a public law regulatory regime designed for optimizing innovation incentives].
19. See Hovenkamp Erik & Cotter Thomas F., *Anticompetitive Patent Injunctions*, 100, No. 3 Minnesota Law Review (2016), https://ssrn.com/abstract = 2477965 [for an argument that when there are no dynamic gains and static welfare losses, injunctions must not be granted]; *Also see*, Carl Shapiro, *Patent Remedies*, 106(5) American Economic Review: Papers & Proceedings 198, 202 (2016). [Arguing that the US 'Supreme Court's decision in eBay v. MercExchange, the patent remedy system in the United States is now a hybrid system: a mixture of property rules and liability rules'.].
20. John M. Golden, *Injunctions as More (or Less) Than Off Switches: Patent-Infringement Injunctions' Scope*, 90 Tex. L. Rev. 1399 (2012).
21. Jonathan Barnett, *Has the Academy Led Patent Law Astray?* 32:4 Berk.Tech. LJ. (2017) (available at https://ssrn.com/abstract = 2897728).
22. See Shamnad Basheer, *The End Of Exclusivity: Towards A Compensatory (Patent) Commons*, 58 IDEA 229 (2018).
23. See Mark Lemley & Robin Feldman, *Is Patent Enforcement Efficient?* 98 Bost. Uni. L. Rev. (2018), https://ssrn.com/abstract = 3135945 [arguing that NPEs do not engage in technology transfer and hence most NPE law suits and licensing demands cannot be justified]. For a contrary perspective on the importance of injunctions for NPEs, see Miranda Jones, *Permanent Injunction, a Remedy by any other Name is Patently Not the Same: How eBay v. MercExchange Affects the Patent Right of Non-Practicing Entities*, 14:14 Geo Mason L. Rev. 1035 (2007).

is highly divergent (where incentives are aligned with 'less IP' business models) [24] and where the role of patents is often seen as a regulation rather than an instrument for preserving the competitive process in the market.[25] Notwithstanding the bias against patent injunctions for various reasons discussed above, the evolution in normative goals of the patent system could perhaps reverse the trend and save patent injunctions from fading into irrelevance.

The working of remedies in the Indian context, however, is not disconnected from these global debates in the post eBay world that has occupied courts, scholars and agencies.[26] The grant of interim injunctions can be seen as an outcome of structural challenges in litigation process,[27] and less of an outcome on the normative debates surrounding the patent system. Some peculiar differences in the Indian context could have implications on the normative bias against granting injunctive relief: first, provisions introduced to prevent the 'ever-greening' phenomenon were an attempt to weed out questionable patents.[28] Second, there is no presumption of validity in the Patent Act, 1970.[29] Third, there is an opportunity presented for early opposition at the Indian patent office through the pre-grant and post-grant opposition. This could have some impact on availability of injunctive relief since an unsuccessfully opposed patent at an early stage would likely be valid.[30] This is complemented with overly broad provisions on revocation of patents in a large variety of cases that move beyond patentability and patent-eligibility grounds.[31] There are a few instances where the Government has used its powers to revoke patents in public interest, particularly in cases where they did not qualify for the grant in the first place.

While there are no systematic empirical studies which track the time taken for concluding patent trials, it is generally observed that Indian courts are unable to conclude trials in a large number of patent cases. A commentator has noted that in 143

---

24. Johnathan Barnett, *The Host's Dilemma: Strategic Forfeiture in Platform Markets for Informational Goods* 124 Har. L. Rev. 1861 (2011).
25. Mark Lemley, *The Regulatory Turn in IP*, 36 Har. J. of L. & Pub. Pol. 109 (2012). For a contrary view, see Daniel Spulber, *How Patents provide the Foundation of the Market for Inventions* (available at https://papers.ssrn.com/sol3/papers.cfm?abstract_id=2487564) (accessed 31 Jul. 2018).
26. In the post-eBay world, patent injunctions have been extensively debated across several jurisdictions. Although many countries, including the courts in India, clearly followed the requirement to apply equitable test in the grant of injunctions, the U.S. Supreme Court's decision in *eBay Inc. v. MercExchange*, L.L.C., 547 U.S. 388 (2006) can be easily seen as the turning point in the global scholarly discourse on patent remedies.
27. Aditya Swarup, *The Prima Facie Standard for Interim Injunctions in India*, 4 NLUD Student L. Journal 22 (2017).
28. A recent study shows that the anti-evergreening provision like section 3(d) has not been successful since secondary patents in pharmaceuticals were granted as combinations by showing synergistic effects. 7 out of 10 patents were likely grant in error. See Feroz Ali, Sudarsan Rajagopal, Venkata S. Raman & Roshan Josh, *Pharmaceutical Patent Grants in India: How our safeguards against evergreening have failed, and why the system must be reformed*, https://www.accessibsa.org/media/2018/04/Pharmaceutical-Patent-Grants-in-India.pdf (accessed 31 Jul. 2018).
29. Eashan Ghosh, *Whither the 'Six-Year Rule'? Reconstructing India's Law on the Presumption of Patent Validity*, 10(2) JIPLP 109 (2015).
30. See Basheer et al., *supra* n. 6.
31. See The Patents Act 1970, s. 64–66.

patent suits initiated between 2005 and 2015, only five judgments have seen the light of the day.[32] This is reflection of a legal regime in India with overall pendency in different areas of litigation.[33] It has led to an overly acute emphasis on availability of interim relief.[34] Although there is no comprehensive data available on injunctions granted in India,[35] a recent study based on limited data does reflect the fact that interim injunctions are widely granted in India.[36] The Indian Supreme Court has in a recent decision expressed serious concern over granting interim relief by conducting a mini-trial. Calling this a 'disturbing trend', the court has ordered speedy disposal of IPR cases that are pending at different stages.[37] Notwithstanding, interim injunctions have been historically granted during pendency of proceedings to prevent prejudice to the plaintiff and has statutory basis in Indian law.[38]

Often in a situation where infringement is difficult to locate (patent infringement is a strict liability without independent innovation defence),[39] or where pre-clearance is not possible in multicomponent devices,[40] or where the patentee does not 'work' her

---

32. See Prashant Reddy, *143 Patent Infringement Lawsuits Between 2005 and 2015: Only 5 Judgments*, https://spicyip.com/2017/06/143-patent-infringement-lawsuits-between-2005-and-2015-only-5-judgments.html (accessed 31 Jul. 2018).
33. See Aditya Swarup, *supra* n. 27.
34. *Ibid.*
35. It is practically impossible to exhaust the universe of patent injunctions in India due to a lack of judgment reporting by district courts who have original jurisdiction in patent infringement matters.
36. In a study which analysed all patent disputes decided between 2000 and 2016 in India where an injunction was claimed, it found that in more than 60% of the cases interlocutory injunction was granted. The study noted that while in 60% of the cases while interim injunctions had been granted in only 30% of the cases was a permanent injunction granted after conclusion of the suit. All the while a considerable number of injunctions granted were also ex parte. See Ramakrishna Thammaiah, *An Indian Perspective on Establishing Prima-Facie Case in Patent Suits* 8, https://ssrn.com/abstract=3047057 (accessed 31 Jul. 2018).
37. *Ms. Az Tech v. Ms. Intex Technologies*, https://indiankanoon.org/doc/143862514/ 'Having read the order of the High Court of Delhi dated 10 Mar. 2017 passed in FAO(OS) No.1/2017 we find that it is virtually a decision on merits of the suit. We wonder if the High Court has thought it proper to write such an exhaustive judgment only because of acceptance of the fact that the interim orders in Intellectual Property Rights (IPR) matters in the Delhi High Court would govern the parties for a long duration of time and disposal of the main suit is a far cry. This is a disturbing trend which we need to address in the first instance before delving into the respective rights of the parties raised in the present case'.
38. See Gujarat Bottling, *supra* n. 8.
39. Mark A. Lemley, *Should Patent Infringement Require Proof of Copying?*, 105 Mich. L. Rev. 1525 (2007) (available at https://ssrn.com/abstract=954988) [arguing that an independent innovation defence will be helpful in dealing with 'patent trolls']. Or a slightly contrary argument on the utility of absolute liability for patent infringement, see Robert Merges, *A Few Kind Words for Absolute Infringement Liability in Patent Law*, 31 Berkeley Tech. LJ. 1 (2016) (available at https://ssrn.com/abstract=2464756 or http://dx.doi.org/10.2139/ssrn.2464756) [arguing that patent system encourages scientific communication for diffusion by making proof of copying irrelevant].
40. Lee & Melamed, *Breaking the Vicious Cycle of Patent Damages*, 101 Cornell L. Rev. 385 (2016) [Arguing that 'a profusion of overlapping and unclear patent rights in these fields make full patent preclearance—i.e., avoiding infringement by obtaining in advance licenses to all relevant patents—literally impossible in many situations and, in others, so costly that it is not feasible as a practical matter and that the current flaws in patent damages lead to overcompensating the patent holders'].

patents (typically NPEs or PAEs),[41] or where grant of damages (money) can compensate all harms,[42] or when patents are encumbered by FRAND obligations,[43] the new found wisdom among courts across jurisdictions is to deny injunctions.[44] Again, the Indian patent law is extraordinary in this regard. Local working of the patent in India is in addition to the quid pro quo of the disclosure requirement in the patent system.[45] India is among the unique jurisdictions which requires of its patentees to provide annual statements of 'working'.[46] Such statements of working have been used in the context of application for compulsory licensing and in the context of evaluating equitable tests for denying an injunction due to lack of working by the patentee. However, the effect of NPEs in the context of the requirement of working of complex products, particularly in the ICT sector, remains unclear.[47]

Similarly, the existence of specific grounds for compulsory licences to remedy certain situations such as unmet demand, high prices and lack of territorial working have been specifically provided in the Patent Act.[48] It is simplistic to assume that a denial of an injunction is effectively a judge made compulsory license, although in effect it is a liability rule.[49] The equitable nature of remedies requires of the court to conceptually distinguish between a compulsory license and an injunction by not double counting the objectives in the later. It may otherwise led to redundancy of the mechanisms such as a compulsory licence if price, working or unmet demand were to

---

41. David L. Schwartz & Jay P. Kesan, *Analyzing the Role of Non-Practicing Entities in the Patent System*, 99(2) Cornell L. Rev. 425 (2014) (available at https://papers.ssrn.com/sol3/papers.cfm?abstract_id=2117421).
42. Steven M. Amundson, *Federal Circuit Decisions Concerning Smartphones Have Created Uncertainty Regarding the Evidence Needed to Prove Irreparable Harm and Establish Entitlement to Injunctive Relief*, 42 Rutgers Computer & Tech. L.J. 231 (2016) [for an argument that without guidance from courts, 'parties and judges may have difficulty determining what evidence demonstrates a sufficiently strong connection between the infringement and the alleged irreparable harm'.].
43. Joseph Farrell, John Hayes, Carl Shapiro & Theresa Sullivan, *Standard Setting, Patents and Holdup*, 74(3) Antitrust Law Journal 603 (2007) [For a view that argues for preserving the FRAND bargain through voluntary licensing], *see* Epstein, Richard and Noroozi, Kayvan B., *Why Incentives for 'Patent Holdout' Threaten to Dismantle FRAND, and Why It Matters*, Berkeley Technology Law Journal, Forthcoming (available at https://ssrn.com/abstract=2913105).
44. *See* Epstein & Kayyan, *supra* n. 43.
45. *See* Ayyangar Report, *supra* n. 2.
46. The Patents Act 1970, s. 146.
47. Jorge Contreras, Rohini Lakshané & Lewis, Paxton, *Patent Working Requirements and Complex Products*, 7 NYU J. Intell. Prop. & Entertainment L. 1 (2017) (available at https://ssrn.com/abstract=3004283).
48. The Patents Act 1970, s. 84.
49. *See* Asish Bharadwaj, *supra* n. 13. [For example, denying injunctions by factoring in higher prices, unmet demand or working of a patent may create a judge made compulsory licence in terms of its effect but not in terms of its intent. Hence the courts must bear in mind the general scheme of the Act to distinguish between assessments of equitable factors in the context of injunctions with other broader public policy goals to remedy 'abuse of patents' for which compulsory licences have been specifically provided. This is also because the applicant for a compulsory licence may have to discharge a higher burden and may be subject to specific terms and conditions, which may not be true where the defendant is a beneficiary of the court's refusal to deny an injunction. However, if courts deny injunctions on grounds where a compulsory licence can be invoked, the conceptual distinction between injunctive relief as an equitable remedy and a compulsory licence will not exist.].

be considered as factors for denying injunctive relief. The courts have held that while grounds for a compulsory licence, such as non-working, does not prove lack of prima facie case for the plaintiff, it could definitely be factored in the analysis of public interest.[50]

Furthermore, unlike in the European Union and the United States, the relationship between availability of injunctive relief and competition law has not emerged in the context of SEP investigation initiated by the Competition Commission of India (CCI).[51] However, the CCI has concluded in a different case that the use of fraudulent practices in obtaining injunctions for violation of IP rights is an abuse of dominance.[52]

A denial of an injunction where it is rightly due can upset the careful bargain structured by the property rights framework underlying patent system.[53] Furthermore, calculation of damages is the most vexing question for resolution of IP disputes.[54] Non-availability of injunctions in certain cases could lead to substantial erosion or loss of value in the market for innovative control.[55] There is a view that the mismatch between exclusionary rights and remedies in property law 'is protected with a remedy typical of the domain of accidents in the law of torts'.[56] The argument is that property owners must be entitled to 'propertised compensation' in the real meaning of what the right to exclude must entail instead of 'market compensation' based on some objective ex-post assessment.[57] It is also observed that there are several evidentiary tools at the disposal of the court to discover propertised compensation.[58] Obfuscation over the relationship between 'right to exclude' and exclusionary remedy aspect of patent law

---

50. *Cipla Limited v. Novartis AG*, 2017 SCC OnLine Del 7393 (Del. High. Ct.).
51. *Huawei Technologies v. ZTE Corporation*, ECLI:EU:C:2015:477 (European Court of Justice 2015).
52. *M/s. Bull Machines Pvt. Ltd. v. M/s. JCB India Ltd. and M/s. J.C. Bamford Excavators Ltd.*, MANU/CO/0032/2014 (2014 Comp. Commission of Ind.).
53. See Epstein & Kayyan, *supra* n. 43.
54. Thomas F. Cotter, *Patent Damages Heuristics*, 25 Tex. Intell. Prop. L.J. 159 (2018). *Also see*, J. Gregory Sidak, *Bargaining Power and Patent Damages*, 19 Stan. Tech. L. Rev. 1 (2015) [arguing that a 'surplus division principle' is the way forward for calculating damages in patent infringement cases for complex products]. Daniel A. Crane, *Bargaining in the Shadow of Rate-Setting Courts*, 76 Antitrust L.J., 307, 307 (2009) [arguing that regulatory compensation is more often than not prone to error].
55. Daniel Spulber, *How Patents Provide the Foundation of the Market for Inventions*, 11(2) J. of Competition Law & Economics, 271 316 (2015) [a patent system that creates a 'market for innovative control helps determine the value of inventions, selects the best inventions, and allocates inventions to the highest-value users']. A commentators in India based on anecdotal evidence has argued that price erosion was not witnessed in certain patented drugs where competing infringing drugs were available in the market due to the denial of injunction or on the drug that was granted a compulsory license granted in India. The argument is that prices were never reduced by patent holders and hence there is no price erosion. There may be several reasons why this happens in the pharmaceutical industry, including the fact that they are ethical drugs which makes consumers price insensitive. *See* Balaji Subramanian, *Interim Injunctions in Pharma Patents: Busting the Price Erosion Myth* (https://spicyip.com/2015/05/interim-injunctions-in-pharma-patents-busting-the-price-erosion-myth.html) (accessed 31 Jul. 2018).
56. Gideon Parchomovsky and Alex Stein, *Reconceptualizing Trespass* (2009) Faculty Scholarship Paper 249. (available at http://scholarship.law.upenn.edu/faculty_scholarship/249).
57. *Ibid.*
58. *Ibid.*

('no relational view'), is born out of a conceptual confusion over normative justifications of IP as a property right.[59]

Although Indian courts accepts patents as a property right,[60] so far attempts to explain the conceptual relationship between section 48 and section 108 have at best been superficial.[61] None of the decisions by Indian courts have attempted to answer the deeper question of the conceptual relationship between rights and remedies. In noting the existence of rights of the patentee under section 48, perhaps the closest that any Indian court has come in construing any conflict, was when it observed that 'the patentee has a right to get an injunction but that right is not an absolute right and a mandatory right. It has to be read in the larger scheme of the Act and section 108 of the Patents Act also deals with the reliefs in a suit for infringement which clearly lays down that the court may grant, in a suit for infringement, an injunction subject to such terms, if any, as the court may think fit at the option of the plaintiffs... A conjoint reading of the aforesaid two Sections would clearly show that though the patentee has prima facie a right to obtain an injunction but that injunction is not necessarily to be granted as a matter of course. It can be refused in case a party can adequately be compensated in terms of money or the court can sufficiently protect the interest of the plaintiffs by passing certain other directions'.[62]

Of course, as long courts in India have the judicial authority to grant an injunction, there is complete regulatory autonomy to deny injunctions on a case-by-case basis.[63] It is pertinent to note that the TRIPS Agreement provides ample flexibility in the context of remedies, such as grant of an injunctive relief.[64] Hence there are arguments that developing countries like India could leverage this flexibility from a geo-strategic perspective.[65] In a situation where Indian statute clearly recognizes injunctive relief as a discretionary remedy, along with accounts for profits or damages, there is a danger that simplistic notions about the supposed normative objectives of patent system and its role in the market system could be internalized and applied to evaluate the equitable factors in granting or denying injunctive relief.

---

59. Eric Clayes, *The Conceptual Relation Between IP Rights and Infringement Remedies*, 22(4) Geo. Mason L. Rev. 825 (2015). *See* Michael Mattioli, *Power and Governance in Patent Pools*, 27 Harv. J. L. Tech, 421 (2014) [For a view that such propertised compensation based on a voluntary exchange as beset with difficulties, unlike in case of contract damages].
60. *F. Hoffmann La Roche Ltd. v. Cipla Limited*, 148 (2008) DLT 598 (Del. High Ct 2008) at para. 63.
61. *See Vringo v. India Mart*, supra n. 15.
62. Ibid.
63. For an argument that such a flexibility could be helpful for developing countries, *see* Shamnad, supra n. 22.
64. *TRIPS Agreement*, Art. 44. *See* Andrew C. Mace, *TRIPS, eBay and Denials of Injunctive Relief: Is Article 31 Compliance Everything?*, 10 The Columbia Science and Technology Law Review, 232 (2009) [noting that 'If eBay is TRIPS compliant, developing countries can now cite the case as precedent for implementing their own compulsory licensing systems with their own notions of equity and the public interest'].
65. Ibid.

§9.03 STATUTORY FOUNDATIONS OF PATENT INJUNCTIONS IN INDIA

The right of the patent holder in section 48 of the Patents Act, 1970 has been clearly subject to other provisions in the statute.[66] Remedies for infringement of a patent forms the essential core to preserve such a right. Section 108 of the Patents Act, 1970 provides for 'Relief in suit for infringement,' wherein it states: '(1) The reliefs which a court may grant in any suit for infringement include an injunction (subject to such terms, if any, as the court thinks fit) and, at the option of the plaintiff, either damages or an account of profits'.[67] It is pertinent to note that remedies in themselves do not pose any specific restrictions or define per se situations where injunctions may be granted or denied.

The discretionary power vested in the court to grant an injunction is exercised at two levels-one, whether or not an injunction should at all be granted; two- if the court indeed grants and injunction, it may subject it to 'such terms, if any, as the court thinks fit'. Although, the Patents Act statutorily recognizes injunctive relief as a remedy that can be granted in appropriate cases, there is sufficient discretion vested in the courts to tailor the remedies. Hence courts have evolved to grant remedies by frequently invoking equitable principles. This provision in section 108 has remained in the statute without any changes in the subsequent amendments made in 1999, 2002 and 2005. However, clause 2 of section 108 was added in 2002 which deals with seizure, forfeiture or destruction of infringing materials, with or without compensation.[68] Interestingly, while the statute palaces restriction on the power of the courts in awarding damages,[69] a statutory restriction on the power of the courts to grant an injunction was omitted by the Patents Amendment Act, 2002.[70] Such an omission was specifically owing to the withdrawal of the 'licence of rights regime' in Sections 87 and 88 of the original Act due to the constraints imposed by the TRIPS Agreement.[71] There is very little in the Patents Act per se that can guide this discretion. This discretion,

---

66. The Patents Act 1970, s. 48 (is a non-obstante clause which starts with '[S]ubject to the other provisions contained in this Act...').
67. Farbewerke *Hoechst v. Unichem Labs.* (1969) AIR 255 (Bom. High Ct.); *Mahesh Gupta v. Tej Singh Yadav* (2009) 41 PTC 109 (Del. High Ct.). *See* Basheer, *supra* n. 6 (The authors state that the provision leans toward the UK approach, wherein proof of infringement is sufficient to obtain an injunction.).
68. (2) The court may also order that the goods which are found to be infringing and materials and implements, the predominant use of which is in the creation of infringing goods shall be seized, forfeited or destroyed, as the court deems fit under the circumstances of the case without payment of any compensation.
69. Section 111 exempts innocent infringement from the remedy of damages or accounts for profit. It states if on the date of the infringement the defendant was not aware and had no reasonable grounds for believing that the patent existed.
70. The original s. 112 dealing with 'Restriction of power of Court to grant injunction in certain cases' read: 'If in proceedings for the infringement of a patent endorsed or deemed to be endorsed with the words "Licences of right" (otherwise than by the importation of the patented article from other countries) the infringing defendant is ready and willing to take a licence upon terms to be settled by the Controller as provided in section 88, no injunction shall be granted against him, and the amount if any recoverable against him by way of damages shall not exceed double the amount which would have been recoverable against him as licensee if such a licence had been granted before the earliest infringement'.
71. *See* Jayashree Watal, *Patents: An Indian Perspective, in the Making of the TRIPS Agreement Personal Insights from the Uruguay Round Negotiation* 295, Ch. 16 (Editor Jayashree Watal,

however, is limited by the patent statute only in certain limited situations, which leads to a definitive conclusion about the parliamentary intention to provide the courts with clear indications that the broader public policy goals for limiting remedies have been statutorily provided and that the courts should not double count the policy objectives in specific cases.[72]

Much of the discretion in awarding an exclusionary remedy is governed by the case-law jurisprudence developed in the context of Specific Relief Act, 1963 and the Code of Civil Procedure, 1908 that forms the general law on civil remedies. The grant of injunctions has its foundations in the principles of equity in India's pre-independence period, which were codified in the Specific Relief Act, 1887.[73] In the post-independence period, the Law Commission in its 9th report suggest sweeping reforms and hence the Specific Relief Act, 1963 came into force. Injunctions in civil proceedings are governed by Chapters VII and VIII of the Specific Relief Act and Rules 1 to 5 of Order XXXIX of Code of Civil Procedure.[74] Section 36 of the Specific Relief Act states that preventive relief is granted at the discretion of the court by injunction, temporary or perpetual. Section 37 notes that a temporary or an interim injunction can be granted at any stage of the suit and can subsist till further orders of the court.[75] It may be noted that the Supreme Court of India has stated that 'a temporary injunction can be granted only if the person seeking injunction has a concluded right, capable of being enforced by way of injunction'.[76]

Like most jurisdictions, the patent holder has two broad remedies: to sue for damages or apply for a perpetual injunction to restrain the infringer from carrying on with the act.[77] However, to preserve the equities before a permanent injunction can be issued, Rule 1 to 5 of Order XXXIX of the CPC grant courts the power to grant interim injunctions. Section 94(c) and (e) of the CPC empowers to court to grant interlocutory reliefs in the form of interim injunctions and other interim orders to prevent the ends of justice from being defeated as may appear to the Court to be just and convenient in the given circumstances. Rule 1 to 5 of Order XXXIX regulate grant of Interim injunctions in India, specifically Rule 1(a) allows court to grant an injunction wherein any property in dispute is in danger of being wasted, damaged or alienated by any party to the suit. However, Court's power is not limited to Order XXXIX. Section 151, provides for inherent powers of the Court to grant injunctions in cases not covered by these Rules.[78] Rules 2(2) allows the court to grant injunctions 'on such terms as to the

---

WTO, 2015) (available at https://www.wto.org/english/res_e/booksp_e/trips_agree_e/chapter_16_e.pdf) [for an excellent exposition on why India had to strike off the provisions on licence of rights from its patent statute].
72. Notwithstanding, the courts have never dwelt into any harmonious construction of the statute based on any doctrinal distinctions.
73. Law Commission of India, *Ninth Report on The Specific Relief Act, 1877*, available at http://lawcommissionofindia.nic.in/1-50/Report9.pdf (accessed 31 Jul. 2018).
74. Ananth Padmanabhan, *Intellectual Property Rights Infringement And Remedies* (Lexis Nexis 2012) at 5.
75. Specific Reliefs Act 1963, s. 38.
76. *Agricultural Produce Market Committee v. Girdharbhai Ramjibhai Chhaniyara* (1997) AIR SC 2674 (Ind. Supreme Ct.).
77. Ibid.
78. *Tanusree Basu v. Ishani Prasad Basu,* 4 SCC 791 (Ind. Supreme Ct. 2008).

duration of the injunction, keeping an account, giving security, or otherwise, as the Court thinks fit'. This in a way allows the court to require cross-undertaking in damages by the plaintiff.

Rule 3 of Order XXXIX requires that the Court before granting an injunction must give notice of the injunction application to the opposite party, however this does not mean that the Court cannot grant ex parte injunctions. Rule 3 also creates an exception wherein if the Court is of the opinion that the object of granting the injunction would be defeated by delay, a court may grant an injunction without giving notice to the other party. Rule 3 does provide safeguards, first, the Court must record reasons for its opinion that the object of granting the injunction would be defeated by delay. A second safeguard is that the applicant has to deliver to the opposite party a copy of the application, the plaint and all documents relied on and file an affidavit evidencing the same on the day or the next day when any such ex parte injunction is obtained.

While dealing with the contours of Rule 3 in the context of ex parte injunctions, the Hon'ble Supreme Court has noted that '[T]he Parliament has prescribed a particular procedure for passing of an order of injunction without notice to the other side, under exceptional circumstances. Such ex parte orders have far-reaching effect, as such a condition has been imposed that [sic] court must record reasons before passing such order. If it is held that the compliance with the proviso aforesaid is optional and not obligatory, then the introduction of the proviso by the Parliament shall be a futile exercise and that part of Rule 3 will be a surplusage for all practical purposes. Proviso to Rule 3 of Order 39 of the Code, attracts the principle, that if a statute requires a thing to be done in a particular manner, it should be done in that manner or not all'.[79]

Further, once an injunction is awarded, the defendant under Rule 4 can apply to the same court for relief to vacate the order of injunction. It requires that courts vacate an ex parte order, wherein the same has been obtained via a false or misleading statement, and that an ordinary injunction granted after hearing both parties can only be vacated if there has been a change in the circumstances which has caused hardships to that party.[80] Commentators have noted that gross injustice has been caused in some cases

Additional protection has also been granted in the form of Rule 3A which requires that once an ex parte injunction has been granted, the Court should dispose-off the application within 30 days and record its reasons in case of failure to resolve the dispute. However, in several cases, the Court may take additional time or delay the proceedings, thus to protect the defendant, the Supreme Court has noted that no party can be made to suffer for the inaction of the Court and may file an appeal under Order XLIII, which is not permitted in case of an interim injunction.[81] As we shall see in a host of patent decisions, courts have been generally indifferent in applying the established standards or have given contrary view points, thus making it difficult to essentialise the case law development and the way forward.

---

79. *Shakir Khan v. Chameli Dass*, 4 ADJ 1769 (2018 All. High Ct.).
80. The Civil Procedure Code 1908, Rule 4.
81. *A. Venkatasubbiah Naidu v. S. Chellappan*, 7 SCC 695 (Ind. Sup. Ct. 2000).

§9.04 STANDARDS FOR GRANTING PATENT INJUNCTIONS

The law relating to injunctions in cases of patents is analogous to any other civil cases. The Supreme Court in several judgments has clarified the three essential elements which must be looked at while deciding an application for interim injunctions.[82] These factors are: first, the existence of a prima facie case, second, the ability of the applicant to establish a balance of convenience in his favour and third, establishing that irreparable loss may be caused to the plaintiff, if the court does not grant an order of injunction. The origin of application of equitable factors in determining injunctive relief can be traced to the celebrated decision of the English Court in American Cyanamid,[83] which required the courts to assess the following factors in awarding interim injunctions: (i) whether the plaintiff has a prima facie case; (ii) whether the balance of convenience is in favour of the plaintiff; and (iii) whether the plaintiff would suffer an irreparable injury if his prayer for interlocutory injunction is disallowed.[84] Indian courts have at times included 'public interest' as an additional factor in denying injunctive relief.[85] These principles have been invoked in a host of cases.[86] The following is an analysis of patent injunction cases by various Indian courts.

[A] Interim Injunctions

In Gujarat Bottling case,[87] the Hon'ble Supreme Court of India noted the need for granting interim injunctions in limited situations and explored the possibility of requiring cross-undertaking in damages to be furnished by the plaintiff. It stated:

> The decision whether or not to grant an interlocutory injunction has to be taken at a time when the existence of the legal right assailed by the plaintiff and its alleged violation are both contested and uncertain and its alleged violation are both contested and uncertain and remain uncertain till they are established at the trial on evidence. Relief by way of interlocutory injunction is granted to mitigate the risk of injustice to the plaintiff during the period before that uncertainty could be resolved. The object of the interlocutory injunction is to protect the plaintiff against injury by violation of his right for which he could not be adequately compensated in damages recoverable in the action if the uncertainty were resolved in his favour at the trial. The need for such protection has, however, to be weighed against the corresponding need of the defendant to be protected against injury resulting from his having been prevented from exercising his own legal rights for which he could not be adequately compensated. The court must weigh one need against another and determine where the 'balance of convenience' lies. .... In order to protect the defendant while granting an interlocutory injunction in his favour the Court can require the plaintiff to furnish an undertaking so that the

---

82. For a background, *see* Ananth Padmanabhan, *supra* n. 74, at 12.
83. *American Cyanamid Co. v. Ethicon Ltd.*, 1975 AC 396 (House of Lords 1975).
84. *See* Gujarat Bottling, *supra* n. 8.
85. *See* Roche v. Cipla, *supra* n. 60.
86. *National Research and Development Corporation of India v. Delhi Cloth & General Mills Co. Ltd.*, 1980 AIR. Del 132, 135 (Del. High Ct.).
87. *See* Gujarat Bottling, *supra* n. 8.

defendant can be adequately compensated if the uncertainty were resolved in his favour at the trial.

It may be noted that the existence of a prima facie case in favour of the plaintiff is not sufficient to award an interim injunction if the injury suffered by the plaintiff is not irreparable.[88] The Hon'ble Supreme Court has also noted that 'temporary injunction being an equitable relief, the discretion to grant such relief will be exercised only when the plaintiff's conduct is free from blame and he approaches the court with clean hands'.[89] It must be emphasized that court must take a balanced approach in granting various forms of interim injunctions. The need for an interlocutory injunction has to be weighed against the injury that can be caused to the defendant, wherein he may be prevented from exercising his legal rights for which no adequate compensation could be granted. The Supreme Court has admonished the practice of extended litigation in the interim phase, which results in most cases getting delayed and not decided at all.[90]

[1] Prima Facie Case

The House of Lords in *American Cyanamid*[91] authoritatively stated that all that an applicant needs to prove a prima facie case was that 'the claim was not frivolous or vexatious: in other words, that there was a serious questions to be tried'. Since *American Cyanamid* Indian courts have continuously cited and relied on this case for prima facie analysis of an interim injunction application.[92] Thus prima facie case requires the applicant to satisfy the Court that there exists a serious question to be tried at the hearing. However, the courts have stated that the ratio in American Cyanamid will not apply in matters of interim injunction to show prima facie validity of the patent since there is no presumption of validity in the patent statute.[93]

Over the years courts in different cases have given varying interpretations as to what constitutes a prima facie case. From case law set forth below three distinct standards of what satisfies a 'prima facie' case have emanated from Indian courts.[94] The first line of cases require that the plaintiff only prove that there is a serious question to be tried, and that the case was not frivolous or vexatious.[95] This is based on the correct interpretation of American Cyanamid and the standard it set. Some cases

---

88. *Best Sellers Retail India (P) Ltd. v. Aditya Nirla Nuvo Ltd*, 6 SCC 792 (Ind. Sup. Ct. 2012).
89. *Seema Arshad Zaheer & Ors. v. Municipal Corporation of Greater Mumbai & Ors.*, 5 SCC 263 (Ind. Sup. Ct. 2006).
90. *Bajaj Auto v. TVS Motor Company*, 3 SCC(Civ) 882, para. 4 (Ind. Sup. Ct. 2009).
91. *See* American Cyanamid, *supra* n. 83.
92. *Gobind Pritamdas Malkani v. Amarendranath Sircar*, 50 Comp.Cas 219 (Cal. High Ct. 1980); *Amal Kumar Mukherjee v. Clarian Advertising Service Ltd.*, 52 Comp.Cas. 315 (Cal. High Ct. 1982); *Amar Talkies v. Apsara Cinema* (1982) JLJ 812 (MP High Ct.); *See* Aditya Swarup, *supra* n. 27 (for a discussion of Indian cases explicitly relying on this case.).
93. *Biswanath Prasah Radhey Shyam v. Hindustan Metal Industries*, 1982 AIR 1444 (Ind. Sup. Ct.).
94. *See* Aditya Swarup, *supra* n. 27, at 22.
95. *Rajesh Kumar v. Manoj Jain*, 47 DRJ 353 (Del. High. Ct 1998); *Prasanta Kumar Ganguly v. Ashir Chandra Sen* 2012 SCCOnline Cal 10192 (Cal. High Ct.); *Supreme General Films v. Durgaprasad* 1984 AIR Bom 131 (Bom. High Ct.).

require that the applicant establishes a probability that he would be entitled to relief,[96] which is a requirement stricter than what has been elaborated in American Cyanamid, thus the applicant needs to satisfy the court that probability dictates that the suit will be decreed in his favour. A third line of cases, requires that the applicant prove a strong prima facie case, this must be established via affidavit evidence and the Court may decide after analysing the pleadings and documents on record,[97] turning the interim application proceedings into a mini-trial. This is notwithstanding the Supreme Court's observation that it is not appropriate for any court to hold a mini-trial at the stage of grant of temporary injunction.[98] Thus, there is a lack of clarity on what constitutes prima facie case.

The Indian Supreme Court has ruled that the grant of a patent by a Controller does not guarantee the validity of the patent, the same has been reiterated under section 13(4) of the Patents Act, 1970.[99] However, according to the 'six-year' rule, a patent can be treated as valid after expiry of six years from the date of grant. This has caused considerable confusion in determining the grant of an interim injunction. This rule finds no mention in the statute but has been consistently cited in various cases. It was first laid out in *Manicka Thevar v. Star Ploro Works*[100] wherein the Madras High Court observed that the patentee should show unchallenged possession of the enjoyment of the patent for at least a period of six years. The rule was applied by other courts as well.[101] However in the case of *F. Hoffmann La Roche Ltd. v. Cipla Limited*[102] the rule came under criticism. The Court observed that the six-year rule is to caution courts while dealing with infringement suits which stand on a different footing. A patent can be challenged even in defence and thus the Courts should not grant an injunction automatically. Thus, the six-year rule must be seen as a rule of caution rather than a rigid mathematical formulae for application. However, the rule has not lost its relevance, as the Delhi High Court in 2013 again applied the six-year rule while adjudicating an interim injunction claim. It is relevant that the same was an ex parte injunction that was granted and Court in that case did not take into consideration the decision in *Roche v. Cipla*, thus raising doubts as to its precedential value.[103]

In some other cases, the courts have noted that since there is no presumption of validity in the Indian Patents Act, the patentee plaintiff needs to 'prima facie prove that the infringer is using the same technology which is patented by them and not the

---

96. *Colgate Palmolive Ltd. v. Hindustan Unilever Ltd.*, 7 SCC 1 (1999, Ind. Supreme Ct.); *Dalpat Kumar v. Prahlad Singh* 1 SCC 719 (1992, Ind. Supreme Ct.); *Sreedhara Shenoy v. K Thanumalayam* 1952 AIR Ker 90 (Ker. High Ct.).
97. *J T Stratford & Son Ltd v. Lindley* (1965) AC 269 (House of Lords); *Shiv Kumar Chadha v. Municipal Corporation of Delhi*, 3 SCC 161 (Ind. Supreme Ct. 1993); *Uniply Industries v. Unicorn Plywood* 5 SCC 95 (Ind. Supreme Ct. 2001).
98. *Anand Prasad Agarwalla v. Tarekeshwar Prasad*, 5 SCC 568 (2001 Ind. Supreme Ct).
99. The Patent Act 1970, s. 13(4), *see* Biswanath Prasad, *supra* n. 93.
100. *V. Manika Thevar v. Star Plough Works*, 1965 AIR Mad 327 (Mad. High Ct.).
101. *NRDCI v. Delhi Cloth & Heneral Mills Co. Ltd.*, 1980 AIR Del 132 (Del. High Ct.).
102. *See Roche v. Cipla*, *supra* n. 60 at para. 63.
103. *3M Innovative Properties Company v. Venus Safety and Health*, 215 DLT 317 (Del. High Ct. 2014) (available at https://spicyip.com/2014/01/resurrecting-the-6-year-rule-in-indian-patent-law.html).

respondents'.[104] It has also noted that registration of a patent alone is not sufficient and that it has to do something more to show a prima facie case. The court went on to state 'most cogent evidence for this purpose is either that there has been a previous trial in which patent has been held to be valid or that the patentee has worked the patent and enjoyed the same without dispute, either from the defendants or anyone'.[105] It is pertinent to note that the patentee-plaintiff must not only show that it has a prima facie case for infringement, but also of validity upon a counterclaim made by the defendant. Court have looked into conduct of the parties at times to ascertain a *prima-facie* case of infringement. By looking into assertion made by a defendant at the Competition Commission that there are no non-infringing alternatives, the court stated that the defendant was claiming that they were using the essential patents.[106]

Indian patent scholars have emphatically noted that the use of the prima-facie standard is pregnant with problems in complex patent cases where the validity of patent is regularly under challenge. Depending on whether or not the patent has been subject to a previous challenge, either in a pre-grant or post-grant opposition at the patent office, they have suggested moving straight to the trial stage and decision on merits by avoiding the interim stage.[107] However, some recent commentators have examined the issue deeply and noted that mini trials are reflection of huge procedural delays and the need for timely justice, although litigants may be willing to sacrifice the use of procedure for correct judgment.[108] Hence it is noted that until the problems of judicial backlog are systematically solved, interim injunctions will remain part and parcel on Indian remedial system.[109]

[2] Irreparable Injury

There is a great debate on the question of irreparable harm in the context of patents since every loss caused to the patentee-plaintiff can be compensated through damages. The Hon'ble Supreme Court has observed that the Court while granting an injunction has to satisfy that non-interference by Court would result in irreparable injury or loss to the party seeking the injunction, that there is no other remedy available to the party except one to grant injunction and that he needs protection from the consequences of apprehended injury.[110] Irreparable injury or loss, however, the Court noted, does not require that there must be no physical possibility of repairing the injury, but only that the injury must be a material one, namely one that cannot be adequately compensated by way of damages or the plaintiff cannot be brought into the same situation.

In a recent high-profile pharmaceutical dispute between Merck and Glenmark, a division bench of the Delhi High Court has noted 'irreparable market effect in cases of a sole supplier of a product' and held that

---

104. *See Vringo v. India Mart, supra* n. 15.
105. *Ibid.*
106. *See Ericsson v. Intex, supra* n. 15.
107. *See* Shamnad Basheer, *supra* n. 6.
108. *See* Aditya Swarup, *supra* n 27.
109. *Ibid.*
110. *Dalpat Singh v. Prahlad Singh*, 1 SCC 719 para. 5 (Ind. Supreme Ct. 1992).

[t]he Court must be mindful – especially in a case where a strong case of infringement is established, as here – there is an interest in enforcing the Act. It may be argued that despite this no injunction should be granted since all damages from loss of sales can be compensated monetarily ultimately if the patentee prevails. This argument though appealing, is to be rejected because a closer look at the market forces reveal that the damage can in some cases be irreparable. This in turn leads to the third principle, which is where an infringer is allowed to operate in the interim during the trial, it may result in a reduction in price by that infringer since it has no research and development expenses to recoup – most revenue becomes profit. The patentee however can only do so at its peril. Importantly, prices may not recover after the patentee ultimately prevails, even if it is able to survive the financial setback (or 'hit') during the interim, which may take some time. The victory for the patentee therefore should not be physic but real. ... Equally, granting the injunction would not prejudice Glenmark to an equal extent since – if the suit is dismissed – it may return to a market that is largely variable.[111]

Even in the context of FRAND commitments, the courts have held that there would be irreparable loss (to mean irreparable harm) if FRAND agreement is not signed by the defendant or royalty is not paid since 'it would have impact of other 100 licensors who are well-known companies in the world who are paying the royalty'. The court has indicated that irreparable injury would be caused due to erosion of the licensing ecosystem. However, instead of granting an interim injunction, the court has quickly moved to award interim royalties.[112] The failure to pay these royalties could lead to the operation of the injunction. In other FRAND disputes, the courts have refused interim injunctions in case a party can adequately be compensated in terms of money if the court can sufficiently protect the interest of the plaintiffs by passing certain other directions.[113] No further analysis has been provided on why monetary damages are themselves sufficient owing to FRAND obligations, which practically doesn't tell us much about the impact of FRAND on injunctive relief.

Interim injunction could be denied if the defendant could not be adequately compensated through a cross-undertaking in damages.[114] Although interim royalties were granted in a large number of SEP cases, the courts have required the plaintiff to 'furnish surety bonds for the amount received on quarterly basis with advance copies'.[115] In other situations, cross-undertaking have been of limited use from the point of view of infringing defendants, who were able to raise it when asking for a declaratory remedy.[116]

---

111. *Merck Sharpe and Dohme v. Glenmark Pharmaceuticals*, 201 DLT 126 (Del. High Ct. 2013).
112. See *Ericsson v. Intex*, supra n. 15.
113. See *Vringo v. India Mart*, supra n. 15.
114. *Hindustan Pencils v. India Stationery Products*, AIR 1990 Delhi 19 (Del. High Ct. 1990).
115. *Telefonaktiebolaget LM Ericsson v.Mergury Elegtronigs and Ors*, MANU/DE/2127/2017 (Del. High Ct. 2017).
116. *Micromax v. Ramkumar*, 44 PTC(P&H) 408 (P&H High Ct. 2010).

[3] Balance of Convenience and Public Interest

The balance of convenience factor requires the court to analyse whether the refusal or grant of an injunction will cause an adverse impact on any of the parties before the court. Here the court will assess whether or not comparative mischief or inconvenience will be caused to any of the party either by granting or denying the injunction. It is pertinent to note that the public interest factor has emerged in the Indian context by the court's willingness to incorporate it in the analysis of balance of convenience.

In one of the earliest pharmaceutical patent dispute,[117] wherein the applicant sought injunction against a lifesaving drug, the Court observed that huge price differential between alternate drugs and the public interest in access for the people to a lifesaving drug would tilt the balance in favour of the defendant.[118] However, it must be noted that while the single judge decision relied on public interest as a factor to refuse an injunction, the division bench rather focused on the element of irreparable harm being caused to several lives.[119] The order passed by the single judge bench of the High Court was later also approved by a division bench.[120] The court in this case seemed to have been concerned with the fact that withdrawing supply of the drug may cut off access and could have immense implications for the general public who were not parties to the suit.

The Supreme Court while discussing balance of convenience has observed that an interim injunction is granted to mitigate the risk of injustice to the plaintiff during the period while the suit is pending. [121] However, this injustice needs to be weighed against the need of the defendant to be protected from the injuries resulting from a grant of injunction preventing him from exercising his own legal rights, for which he cannot be adequately compensated. Thus, the Court needs to look at these factors while adjudicating balance of convenience. Therefore, this determination is very fact-specific and differs from case to case.

In denying an injunction based on evaluation of balance of convenience, the Division Bench of the Delhi High Court has noted '[s]tultification of defendants investment, loss of employment, public interest in the product (such a life-saving drug), product quality coupled with price, or the defendant being smaller in size, may go against the plaintiff. Cases of a Bridgehead (only a short period to go before expiry of plaintiff's patent), parties being of equal size, – may go in favour of plaintiff. Case of

---

117. *Roche v. Cipla*, 148 DLT 598 (Del. High Ct. 2008).
118. *Roche v. Cipla* The single judge noted: 'this Court is of the opinion that as between the two competing public interests, that is, the public interest in granting an injunction to affirm a patent during the pendency of an infringement action, as opposed to the public interest in access for the people to a lifesaving drug, the balance has to be tilted in favor of the latter. The damage or injury that would occur to the plaintiff in such case is capable of assessment in monetary terms. However, the injury to the public which would be deprived of the defendant's product, which may lead to shortening of lives of several unknown persons, who are not parties to the suit, and which damage cannot be restituted in monetary terms, is not only uncompensatable, it is irreparable. Thus, irreparable injury would be caused if the injunction sought for is granted'.
119. *F. Hoffmann-La Roche Ltd. v. Cipla* (2009) 159 DLT 243 (DB).
120. Ibid.
121. *Hindustan Petroleum Corp. Ltd. v. Sriman Narayan*, 2002 5 SCC 760 at para. 8.

snowball (more future infringements) may not till the balance in favour of plaintiff... Again, even delay of a few months in some cases has led to refusal of injunction'.[122] Ergo, although some courts have viewed public interest as a separate factor, this case stands for the proposition that public interest may be evaluated in the context of applying the test of balance of convenience.

It is interesting that the balance of convenience almost relies on the fact of defendant being in the market and selling her product. The idea is that an interim injunction could lead to the defendant having to shift production, causing loss of revenue and employment. But it does not answer a situation where production lines are situated outside the country, and if at all, harm may be caused to the party without backward vertical integration, i.e., only a distributor. This can be witnessed in a large number of FRAND cases where the defendants are a large number of distributors with practically no manufacturing done in India. Some other courts have held that finding the balance of convenience is a case specific inquiry where the plaintiffs will have to establish 'whether it is marketing the product in the Indian market, whether it has approached the court with clean hands without concealment of material facts and whether there has been any delay in approaching the court, etc'.[123]

The Supreme Court noted that the 'first ingredient is about the use of the patent by the applicant and the respondent. It is true that in cases where the use of the applicant's patent is recent in origin or the patentee has not even used or commenced to release its product, then such patentee is not entitled for the grant of injunction'.[124] The court noted that since the defendant was in the market, the balance of convenience was in its favour because the patentee could be monetarily compensated through a cross-undertaking by any of the party since both sides were able to pay any damages which would be awarded against it after completion of the trial.[125] In this matter involving FRAND-encumbered patents, the single judge noted acquiescence of infringement by Nokia before it assigned its patents to the current plaintiffs, nor have other licensees of the plaintiffs (who the court assumes could be direct competitors) have claimed infringement. It further observed that the fact of commercial working of the patent based on a licence by the plaintiff was not mentioned in the plaint (but in a rejoinder) and hence the balance of convenience was in favour of the defendant.

In India, this requirement can be traced back to two cases.[126] In both these cases injunction was refused on the ground that the patent was not being worked in India. The Court took into consideration the economic disadvantages of granting injunctions for patents invented abroad, which are only registered in India and not worked. Thus, it is now well settled that if patent has not been sufficiently exploited in India and there is no user of the said patent in commercially viable form in India, the court may refuse to grant an injunction.[127]

---

122. Franz Xaver Huemer.
123. See *Vringo v. India Mart, supra* n. 15.
124. See *Bajaj Auto v. TVS, supra* n. 90.
125. See *Vringo v. India Mart, supra* n. 15.
126. *NRD Corporation of India v. DC & G Mills* 1980 AIR Delhi 132 (Del. High Ct.) and *Franz Xaver Huemer v. New Yash Engineers* 1997 AIR Delhi 79 (Del. High Ct.).
127. *Sandeep Jaidka v. Mukesh Mittal & Anr*, 50 PTC 234 (Del. High Ct. 2014).

Further, Delhi High Court has recently summarized the equitable principle while dealing with public interest and injunctions. [128] It held that Courts must look at the public interest in granting an injunction. In this case it was access to drugs used for treatment of diabetes, a disease highly prevalent in India. Courts can in some cases overlook the public interest to prioritize maintaining the integrity of the patent system itself, so that a legitimate monopoly is not distorted. This is because, in cases where an infringer is allowed to operate in the interim during the trial, it may result in a reduction in price by that infringer since he has no R&D costs to recover and almost the entire revenue becomes profit.

In a decision with far-reaching impact, court refused to grant an injunction against a defendant which was manufacturing for export a drug for treatment of erectile dysfunction, which was viewed from the perspective of public interest. [129] The Court expanded the scope of public interest departing from cases such as *Roche* wherein the drugs were lifesaving ones to lifestyle drugs. Rather than relying on threat to public health, Court focused on the public interest in form of the socio-economic factors such as 'loss of employment at Ajanta' and 'the loss of revenues to the state'.[130] However, the precedential value of the above mentioned case is narrow due to another later decision of the Delhi High Court, where it did not hold that export of non-life-saving drugs are in public interest. [131] It refused the argument that export is in public interest as they earn foreign exchange and encourage economic activity, and observed that the order in the Ajanta case is only an ad-interim order and hence does not qualify as precedent.[132]

Assessing the balance of convenience in the grant of interim injunctions in the agro-biotech sector have played out differently because of the interplay between existence of earlier licence between the parties and regulatory price controls imposed by the government on BT cotton seeds. In a situation where Monsanto terminated its technology licensing agreement covering a patent granted on BT gene due to its non-acceptance of depressed royalties from the licensee based on price control, the Delhi High Court vacated the ad-interim injunction.[133] It noted that an injunction operated only with reference to sale of seeds manufactured at risk after the termination of the contract. But since it instead chose to restore the contract by granting an injunction for specific performance under the Specific Relief Act, the interim injunction was nullified. It was Monsanto's claim that an injunction to restore its contract was unwarranted since monetary damages would be sufficient if a breach of contract was ultimately found.

---

128. *Merck Sharp and Dohme Corporation and Anr. v. Glenmark Pharmaceuticals*, 6 SCC 807 (Ind. Supreme Ct. 2015).
129. *Bayer Intellectual Property GmbH v. Ajanta Pharma Ltd*, available at http://delhihighcourt.nic.in/dhcqrydisp_o.asp?pn=4898&yr=2017 (accessed 31 Jul. 2018) (Del. High Ct. 2017).
130. *Ibid* at para. 11. *Also see,* Ashish Bharadwaj, *Patent Injunction and the Public Interest in India*, 40(1) EIPR 55 (2018).
131. *Bayer Intellectual Property v. BDR Pharmaceuticals International* (Del. High Ct. 2017), available at http://delhihighcourt.nic.in/dhcqrydisp_o.asp?pn=30334&yr=2017 (accessed 31 Jul. 2018).
132. *Ibid.*
133. *Monsanto v. Nuziveedu*, 239 DLT 599 (Del. High Ct. 2017).

Although this decision was briefly stayed by the Division Bench, it created a situation where the contract had terminated, but the patentee was left with no interim remedy against an infringing defendant (seed company), notwithstanding its prima-facie validity being upheld by the court. This situation was cured only when the court finally revoked Monsanto's patent for invalidity and noted that 'a negative obligation, implied to honour the existing law, binds the parties' and hence parties could be coerced in to performing the contract.[134] The court also highlighted public interest and access to cotton seeds for India's farming community and noted that 'the denial of a positive order... results in the violation of provisions of the Essential Commodities Act'.[135] The implication of this decision is clear since a revocation of a patent was not sufficient to ensure supply of off- patented technology underlying the seeds. The court had to resort to mandatory injunctions by demanding specific relief under a technology licensing contract which does not exist due to its termination and expiry of the patent which formed the subject matter.

[B] Ex Parte Injunctions

While CPC provides for issuance of ex parte interim injunctions,[136] courts have noted the scope for its abuse and cautioned on steps it must take before issuing an ex parte injunction.[137] A requirement that an ex parte must be granted only in exceptional circumstances, and that they must be vacated within thirty days failing which the court must cite reasons in writing is the law laid down by the Supreme Court.[138] The Supreme Court has also held that an ex parte which fails to follow processes can be vacated in appeal and action against erring judicial officers could be taken.[139] Courts have observed that 'granting of ex-parte injunction along with appointment of Local Commissioner has become a routine process' and that plaintiffs avoid trial on merits and that '[a]ll kinds of excuses are used to seek adjournments once a party gets ex parte injunction'.[140]

The Supreme Court has laid down guidelines, which if implemented in letter and spirit, could improve the system. [141] Since it noted the abuse of injunctions based on forged documents to create pressure on the other side, the Supreme Court observed that the Court must be extremely careful in granting ex parte ad-interim injunctions and should take an undertaking from the plaintiff to pay mesne profits and costs in case of dismissal of the interim application.[142] The court noted the trouble in vacating interim injunctions and efforts made by plaintiff to prolong the effect of an interim injunction by causing delays.

---

134. *Nuziveedu v. Monsanto*, 2018 SCC OnLine Del 8326 (Del. High Ct.).
135. *Ibid*.
136. *See supra* n. 79.
137. *Microsoft Corporation v. Dhiren Gopal and Ors.*, 42 PTC 1 (Del. High Ct. 2010).
138. *Venkatasubbiah Naidu v. S. Chellappan and Ors.*, 2000 AIR SC 3032 (Del. High Ct. 2000).
139. *Ibid*.
140. *Microsoft Corporation v. Dhiren Gopal and Ors*, 42 PTC 1 (Del. High Ct. 2010).
141. *Ramrameshwari Devi v. Nirmala Devi*, 8 SCC 249 para. 44–46 (Supreme Ct. 2011).
142. *Ibid*.

The Supreme Court has observed that as a matter of principle an 'ex parte injunction could be granted only under exceptional circumstances' and laid down factors which must be taken into account.[143] It was noted that courts should look at whether irreplaceable or serious mischief will ensue to the plaintiff and whether the refusal would involve greater injustice to the plaintiff than the grant would.[144] The Court also observed that the time at which the plaintiff first had notice of the act complained is also relevant to avoid making an improper order against a party in its absence, since the plaintiff had acquiesced to the infringement.[145] In any case the injunction would only operate for a limited time, and the general principles of prima facie case, balance of convenience and irreparable injury continue to apply.[146] Courts have clearly held that if the grant of interim injunction is going to result in closure operation/business of the defendant, in such cases the injunction should not be granted.[147] Particularly, as per the court, an ex parte injunction should not be granted in cases where the plaintiff has not shown any evidence or proof of infringement. The court has taken the view the in case of process patents an ex parte should not be granted unless the plaintiff has adduced independent expert evidence who has tested the infringing product for infringement and an opportunity is given to the defendant to explain non-infringement.[148] This requirement of hearing effectively bars process patents from an ex parte injunction.[149]

However, the practice is far removed from the law as ex parte injunctions are prone to misuse because of the difficulty in getting them vacated. A commentator has noted in a recent study that in many cases of pharmaceutical ex parte injunction, the name of the defendant is masked to show as an individual instead of the company she belongs to.[150] This may be done to create an impression that the defendant is not a well-established entity or is a fly-by-night operator, which cannot be verified at the time of granting an ex parte. In another case, the courts have granted ex parte injunction on the existence of the patent grant number, without going into any details, especially on account of patentee amending her claims that were found to be distinct from the original.[151] In this context, the patentee was able to obtain royalties from small importers of mobile phone, until the patent was revoked by the IPAB when it was finally challenged by a telecom major Samsung Inc.[152]

---

143. *Morgan Stanley Mutual Fund v. Kartick Das*, 4 SCC 225 para. 36 (Supreme Ct. 1994).
144. *Ibid.*
145. *Ibid.*
146. *Morgan Stanley Mutual Fund v. Kartick Das*, 4 SCC 225 para. 36(Ind. Supreme Ct. 1994)
147. *FDC Limited v. Sanjeev Khandelwal*, 35 PTC 436 (Mad. High Ct. 2007).
148. *Ibid.*
149. *Ibid.*
150. Sandeep Rathod, *Injunctions in Indian Pharmaceutical Patent Infringement Actions: Some Observations* (available at https://papers.ssrn.com/sol3/papers.cfm?abstract_id=2758327) (accessed 31 Jul. 2018).
151. Saahil Dama, *Interrogating Interim Injunctions: Ramkumar's dual-SIM patent*, https://spicyip.com/2015/06/interrogating-interim-injunctions-ramkumars-dual-sim-patent.html (accessed 31 Jul. 2018).
152. *Ibid.*

Further, in several matters especially those pertaining to patents, parties often obtain an injunction and then delay the proceedings.[153] Also, ex parte orders leave dangerous scope for abuse as can be seen in the *Symed* case where two process patents were alleged to have been infringed.[154] In this case, ex parte injunctions were issued against three defendants, where only one was vacated within a period of two weeks. The defendant was able to later show through the plaintiffs lab reports that the defendant's product was not the exact process covered by the patents. However, since an ex parte was granted in this matter compounded with the difficulty of getting it vacated, there was no early scope for showing that a case may not exist. While Order 39A requires that a petition for vacation be heard expeditiously, in several matters it has been observed that ex parte injunctions and the trouble in vacating them is endemic to the system.[155] The inability of the courts to distinguish between fly-by-night operators (which may exists in some situations such as smartphone vendors, where licensing is concluded at the device level) and a manufacturing defendant (which may or may not directly compete with the patentee's invention), renders an ex parte injunction a potent weapon in the hands of the patentee.

[C] *Quia-Timet* Injunctions

It may be noted that an overwhelming number of ex parte cases in pharmaceuticals are indeed quia-timet in nature. These injunctions are granted in a number of ex parte proceedings based on the fear or threat of infringement. Again, quia-timet injunctions have a historical legacy in the English courts of equity. The English courts have stated that at least two necessary ingredients are required for such an action. (i) proof of imminent danger, and (ii) proof that the damage is substantial and could cause irreparable harm from which the plaintiff cannot protect herself if quia-timet injunction is denied.[156] Indian courts have recognized the availability of quia-timet injunction based on the decisions of the English courts of equity, but have been sceptical of granting them where plaintiffs approach with unclean hands or when there is no damage or irreparable loss shown.[157] Indian courts have also granted quia-timet injunctions in several trademark cases,[158] but have now been routinely granted in patent cases, too.[159]

---

153. *See Sandeep Jaidka v. Mukesh Mittal & Anr, supra* n. 127.
154. *Symed Labs v. Glenmark Pharmaceutical Ltd.,* 2015 SCC OnLine Del 6745 (Del. High Ct.).
155. Balaji Subramanian, *Interrogating Interim Injunctions: Ex Parte Delays In Symed And Issar*, https://spicyip.com/2015/05/interrogating-interim-injunctions-ex-parte-delays-in-symed-and-issar.html (accessed 2 Mar. 2018).
156. *Fletcher v. Bealey,* 28 Ch. D. 688 (1885).
157. *P.G. Narayanan v. The Union Of India,* https://indiankanoon.org/doc/1800024/ (Mad. High Ct. 30 May 2005).
158. *Pfizer products Inc v. Rajesh Chopra,* 32 PTC 301 (Del. High Ct. 2006).
159. Madhulika Vishwanathan, *It's raining Injunctions: Novartis Granted Injunctions Against Four Other Generic Makers over Galvus,* https://spicyip.com/2014/04/its-raining-injunctions-novartis-granted-injunctions-against-four-other-generic-makers-over-galvus.html (accessed 31 Jul. 2018).

Quia-timet injunctions have been heavily criticized since they are granted in pharmaceutical patent matter where relief is sought against generic manufacturers. The patentee plaintiffs were able to satisfy the reasonable threat of infringement by bringing to the notice of the court that both these companies had obtained a manufacturing license and permission to sell generic versions of the patented drugs. The information was obtained by filing RTI (right to information) applications with the local Drug Controller. The court agreed with patentee's argument that the manufacturers were about to launch their product and lack of an injunction would lead to irreparable harm.[160] Here the court carved an exception that acts of the defendant which were covered by section 107A (Bolar/ regulatory review purpose) were exempt from quia-timet action.[161] A quia-timet injunction was also obtained against another generic based on the threat imputed from a revocation application filed before the IPAB wherein it had sought manufacturer approval from the Drug Controller.[162] However, prior to this both the Delhi High Court and Madras High Court had refused quia-timet injunctions. The Delhi High Court refused to grant a quia-timet action as its very jurisdiction to hear the dispute was in question.[163] In the other case, the defendant had made a mere statement in a revocation petition about his intention to commercially use the patent and had also conducted clinical trials. The Madras High Court took a cautious approach and refused to grant an injunction on these grounds.[164]

Thus it appears that Indian courts have not adopted any consistency in determining the exact standard for proof of imminent danger before granting of quia-timet injunction. Further, concerns have been raised on whether quia-timet injunctions can be granted in patent-related proceedings as there exists no presumption of validity of a registered patent in India. This is coupled with the low quality of patents due to inadequate examination and opposition proceedings thus making quia-timet injunctions create a risk for abuse in the market.[165] It has also been noted that the standards for quia-timet injunctions loosely applied since a mere marketing approval obtained from the drug regulator by the defendant company or allegations of clinical trials is not an indication of imminent danger absent the proof of companies taking steps to advertise the launch.[166] It may be observed that such actions have become popular after an era when interim reliefs where denied based on application of equitable factors such as lack of irreparable harm or presence of public interest (due to lower prices and

---

160. Ibid.
161. *Novartis AG v. Cadila Healthcare*, CS(OS) 1052/2014 (Del. High Ct. 2014); *Novartis AG v. Glenmark Generics*, CS(OS) 1054/2014 (Del. High Ct. 2014); *Novartis AG v. Alembic Pharmaceuticals*, CS(OS) 1051/2014 (Del. High Ct. 2014).
162. Madhulika Vishwanathan, 'It's Raining Injunctions: Novartis Granted Injunctions against Four Other Generic Makers over Galvus'. (*SpicyIP*, 2018) https://spicyip.com/2014/04/its-raining-injunctions-novartis-granted-injunctions-against-four-other-generic-makers-over-galvus.html (accessed 1 Mar. 2018).
163. *Bristol Myers Squibb Company v. Bhutada and Ors.*, MANU/DE/3672/2013 (Del High Ct. 2013).
164. *Matrix Laboratories Limited v. F Hoffman-La Roche* 1 CTC 381 (Mad. High Ct. 2012) (1).
165. Aparajitha Lath, "*Analysing the Pitfalls of Indian Patent Injunctions based on Fear of Infringement,*" 19 JIPR 253 (2014).
166. Ibid.

access issues), and at risk launches had become popular.[167] However, quia-timet injunctions practically foreclose the at-risk launches and may delay the entry of infringing drugs, although their patent validity may be suspect.[168]

[D] Permanent Injunctions

In India, suits rarely reach the stage of a permanent injunction, as it can only be granted after a full completion of trial. Since India's compliance with the TRIPS agreement, there are very few cases where trial has been concluded and a permanent injunction has been awarded. The factors for granting a permanent injunction are the same as in case of interim injunctions, except that the plaintiff does not need to establish a prima facie case any longer. Instances can arise wherein a permanent injunction might not be granted even though the court finds that the valid patent was infringed.

One of the first celebrated cases, the Delhi High Court granted a permanent injunction against Glenmark for infringing Merck's patent on the pharmaceutical compound Sitagliptin for the treatment of diabetes. It may be noted that the court did not evaluate factors for granting the permanent injunction. This could be because of the fact that the Division Bench of the Delhi high court had made an elaborate analysis of why Merck was entitled to an interim injunction,[169] although the Supreme Court had later stayed the interim injunction and ordered an expedited trial. The Supreme Court had noted that since there was no stay for a long time, it was perfectly reasonable to have few more weeks without an injunction by allowing Glenmark to sell existing stocks. It may be noted that the trial was concluded in six months when compared to the interim phase which had taken more than two years. The trial judge however noted that since the issues for damages were not framed, it was not justifiable to quantify damages and proceeded to award actual costs of the proceeding in favour of the plaintiff.

In another case, a division bench of the High Court while holding that the Roche's patent was valid and infringed by Cipla refused to grant a permanent injunction as only a few months were left for the expiry of the patent and that no interim injunction had been granted earlier.[170] As noted by a commentator, '[w]hether or not the final ruling in *Roche v. Cipla* will be tantamount to a compulsory licensing order will turn on the final quantum of damages awarded to Roche'.[171] The argument is that if Cipla is liable to repatriate all profits made by it by selling the infringing drug, it would be higher than a rate fixed by way of a compulsory licence.[172] This some believe would act as a

---

167. Jayati Ghose, *In India Copycat Drug Firm Get Off Lightly Compared with US* (available athttps://www.financialexpress.com/archive/in-india-copycat-drug-firms-get-off-lightly-compared-with-us/1130380/) (accessed 31 Jul. 2018).
168. The validity problem is acute in pharmaceuticals since s. 3(d) provides a layers of exclusions, which have been misapplied in a large number of cases. Thus secondary patents in pharmaceuticals in India may be largely suspect. *See* Feroz Ali, *supra* n. 28.
169. *Merck v. Glenmark*, 2015 SCC OnLine Del 8227 (Del. High Ct.).
170. *F. Hoffmann-La roche Ltd v. Cipla Ltd.*, 225 DLT 391 para. 134 (Del. High Ct. 2015).
171. *See* Basheer, *supra* n. 5.
172. *Ibid.*

deterrent for further infringement.[173] But in a country where exemplary damages in patents are not routinely granted,[174] it remains to be seen if the courts would factor in the price erosion factor in evaluating damages. It may be noted that non-grant of a permanent injunction and delay caused in trial could severely effect patent holders right to exclude.

The first SEP trial concluded in July 2018 provides an indication on the evidentiary factors and the burden to be discharged by parties in an infringement suit involving FRAND obligations. A permanent injunction was not granted because the patent had expired in February, 2015.[175] The court has held that 'reasonable royalties for standard essential patents are not only in terms of FRAND but also the incremental benefit derived from the invention'.[176] It proceeded to award royalties based on what was demanded during informal negotiations in the absence of any counter-offer by the defendant which could have provided indications on a different methodology. The award of damages in this case has the same effect of granting an injunction since the patentee's FRAND offer has been considered as basis for awarding of damages. In effect, the decision will push parties towards good faith negotiations, including the need for a counter-offer from the defendant.

§9.05 CONCLUSION

It is clear from the above discussion that the law on patent injunctions in India is in a state of deep flux because of obscurity arising from principles and practice. First, while global debate on normative objectives of the patent system and its impact on injunctive relief may have had some influence on the availability of injunctions in India, the case law in India has developed in remarkably different ways. The lack of presumption of validity, existence of both pre-grant and post-grant opposition mechanisms at the patent office, broader provisions for revoking patents and availability of compulsory licences, including working requirements, and external price controls could distinguish outcomes from other jurisdictions, where equities have to be solely managed through tailoring injunctive relief. However, the existence of distinct normative basis factored in the public interest provisions of the patent system in India has perhaps not been factored into patent injunction analysis. The grant of ex parte patent injunctions in a routine manner leads one to conclude that courts in India have overstepped. This is particularly so because many of such orders do not even assign sufficient reasons for granting such strong remedies.

Interim injunctions have also remained controversial since many of them have been granted by conducting mini trials. This almost leaves the parties to settle the dispute under the shadow of an injunction due to prolonged litigation take may take

---

173. Ibid.
174. Pratibha M. Singh, *Damages in Patent infringement* (available at http://apaaindia.org/docs/presentations/Damages%20in%20Patent%20infringement.pdf) (accessed 31 Jul. 2018).
175. *See Phillips v. Rajesh Bansal, supra* n. 11.
176. Ibid.

years in India. It has played differently in different sectors. In case of FRAND-encumbered patents, which are largely in the ICT sector, courts have drawn interim injunction by holding defendants as unwilling licensees. But the way in which it operates is based on interim royalties being granted by using comparable licences. The courts have noted that irreparable harm could be caused if the plaintiff was left with no remedy in FRAND cases since it could have an impact on the entire licensing ecosystem. Hence if the defendants do not agree to pay up, the interim injunction would come in to force. In other cases, particularly in the area of pharmaceuticals, the spate of at-risk launches has been substantially deterred by the grant of ex parte quia-timet injunction purely based on the apprehension of infringement.

The way in which balance of convenience has played out along with public interest attached to the requirement of the patentee to 'work' her invention provides another counter narrative. As a developing country with the need to provide access to medicines, this may not be actually surprising. However, the inability of the courts to distinguish between immediate public interest and overall public policy is striking since it has refused injunctions even in cases of lifestyle drugs. Furthermore, the deeper conflation in the instrumentalities between patents, contract law and essential commodities law has led to a unique situation in bio-tech area because a mandatory injunction has been issued to supply technology to seeds companies (previously licensees) on an off-patented invention keeping in mind the unique public interest in the farming sector. Lastly, permanent injunctions have not seen the light of the day since only few cases have been adjudicated, that too at the near end of the patent term or even post-expiry.

The basic claim made in this chapter is that Indian courts have contributed to the law of injunction by adopting a heuristic approach since infringement trials take years to conclude. Pendency of litigation pushes the courts to grant strong interim remedies. All that can perhaps be said is that while the continued availability of injunctions in specific cases is important for preserving the balance between incentives for innovation and for securing greater technology diffusion in India, the way in which courts have awarded injunctions without sufficient analysis leaves much to be desired. Overall, the courts could do well to avoid generalist presumptions about the supposed normative objectives or patent system in the grant of remedies since it would amount to double counting of the policy objectives underlying the patent system.

CHAPTER 10
Patent Injunctions in South Korea

Yoonhee Kim & Hui Jin Yang

Korean patent law provides patent owners a right to seek injunctive relief against accused infringers. When faced with a preliminary or permanent injunction in the court, the accused infringer in Korea may raise the "abuse of rights" defense on three different, but related, fronts – (1) civil law, (2) patent law, and (3) competition law – apart from typical patent law defenses, such as non-infringement and invalidity.

The IT sector is the key industry driving South Korea's economic growth and global integration. As product interoperability is critical to developing and manufacturing IT products, the "Fair, Reasonable, And Non-Discriminatory" (FRAND) commitment, which was designed to promote interoperability through standardized technology, comes under the spotlight in Korea. Not surprisingly, Korean authorities have shown significant interest in interpreting and enforcing the FRAND commitment to license standard-essential patents (SEP).

For example, the Korean court in *Samsung v. Apple* granted injunctive relief enjoining Apple from infringing Samsung's asserted SEPs and in doing so rejected Apple's FRAND defenses based on contract law and abuse of rights defenses. In 2014 and 2016, the Korea Fair Trade Commission (KFTC) revised its Guidelines on Unfair Exercise of Intellectual Property Rights (IPR Guidelines) to offer guidance on how to interpret and enforce the FRAND commitment.

With this background, this chapter presents an overview of Korean jurisprudence on patent injunctions with particular emphasis on SEPs and the FRAND commitment.

§10.01 INJUNCTIVE RELIEF UNDER KOREAN LAW

[A] Preliminary Injunction

Patent owner seeking preliminary injunctions in Korea must meet the requirements under Article 300(2) of the Civil Enforcement Act, which provides:

A provisional disposition may also be effected in order to fix a temporary position with respect to a right in dispute. In this case, such a provisional disposition shall be effected specially in case where it was intended to avoid a significant damage on a continuing right or to prevent an imminent danger, or where there exist other necessary reasons.

This provision governs provisional enforcement of the "right in dispute" and is the basis upon which the courts in Korea have granted temporary remedies for patent infringement. Under Article 300(2), a court hearing a petition for preliminary injunction largely looks to two aspects of the case: (1) whether there is an infringed right for which relief is to be granted and (2) whether there is a need to preserve such right.

Korean courts typically find the first requirement to be satisfied if the patent owner has established present or imminent infringement of patent rights. The required level of proof may be slightly lower than in permanent injunction proceedings. With respect to the second requirement, the courts in Korea have ruled that the following factors should be collectively considered to determine whether there is a need to preserve the patent rights being infringed:

(1) whether the patent owner has established a substantial likelihood of success on the merits (typically, the validity of a patent);
(2) whether the patent owner has established that it will suffer irreparable harm if a preliminary injunction is denied;
(3) whether the hardships the patent owner would suffer in the absence of an injunction outweigh the harms an injunction would cause to the accused infringer; and
(4) whether and how the grant or denial of a preliminary injunction would affect the public interest.

As such, Korean courts would address the public interest in deciding on preliminary injunctions, for example, whether granting a preliminary injunction would disrupt a "national export strategy."[1] In practice, however, the validity of a patent in the first factor has played the most important role, while the third and fourth factors have been rarely recognized in court decisions. For example, in two occasions, Korean courts dismissed the alleged infringers' argument that preliminary injunctions should be dismissed because the asserted patents covered only a small part of the accused products.[2] Further, there is no apparent court decision in which a preliminary injunction claim for patent infringement was dismissed solely based on public interest considerations.

---

1. Supreme Court of Korea, 93Ma2022, decided Nov. 10, 1994.
2. Busan District Court, 2007GaHap2316, decided Dec. 30, 2009; Daegu District Court, 2010Ga-Hap238, decided Sep. 16, 2010.

[B] Permanent Injunction

Korean courts in permanent injunction proceedings do not follow a "flexible" approach adopted in the United States post *eBay Inc. v. MercExchange, LLC*.[3] An injunction order would typically issue upon a showing of patent infringement, provided that the accused infringer fails to establish affirmative defenses.

This may be a natural outcome under the Korean legal system. Article 22(2) of the Constitution of Korea provides that the rights of authors, inventors, scientists, engineers, and artists shall be protected by an "Act." Article 37(2) of the Constitution further provides that the freedoms and rights of citizens may be restricted by an "Act" only when necessary for national security, the maintenance of law and order, or for public welfare. In this context, an "Act" means a law enacted by the National Assembly. Accordingly, courts have long interpreted these clauses of the Constitution to mean that an individual right so rooted in the Constitution can be restricted only when and to the extent which a law enacted by the National Assembly specifically and clearly allows such restriction.

With respect to a patent owner's right to injunction, Article 126(1) of the Korean Patent Act simply provides that a patent owner or an exclusive licensee may seek an injunction for, or prevention of, infringement against a person who infringes, or is likely to infringe, its patent rights. Such statutory language does not provide equitable considerations or limitations Korean courts may take into account in determining whether to grant or deny injunctive relief. This stands in sharp contrast to 35 U.S.C. § 283, which provides that U.S. courts may grant injunctions "in accordance with the principles of equity."

Bound by such constitutional limitations, the Patent Act does not accommodate much room for judicial discretion to consider non-statutory factors such as social order or public interest. For example, Korean courts have not been attentive to the accused infringer's argument that injunctive relief should be dismissed because the asserted patent covers only a small part of the accused devices.[4] No apparent cases were found where courts considered the public interest in determining whether to grant injunctive relief for patent infringement. Instead, courts have only considered statutory defenses such as an abuse of rights defense.[5]

However, there is an academic discussion that the law does not preclude courts from considering such factors as in *eBay*. In practice, the abuse of rights defense in the Korean statutory civil law is general enough to harbor the same defenses under patent law and under competition law. As such, it would be more plausible for courts to elaborate a legal theory, analogous to *eBay* factors, as a general restrictive rule on injunctions in the form of an abuse of rights defense.

---

3. *eBay Inc. v. MercExchange, LLC*, 547 U.S. 388 (2006).
4. *See* note 2 *supra*.
5. Korean jurisprudence has not yet explicitly recognized Art. 44(2) the TRIPs Agreement that allows Members to limit the application of injunctive relief under certain conditions. The TRIPs Agreement is not a first and direct source of law that individuals and entities in Korea look to in their causes of action.

§10.02 ABUSE OF RIGHTS DEFENSES TO CLAIMS FOR INJUNCTIVE RELIEF

Accused infringers in Korea may raise three types of abuse of rights defense, rooted in civil law, patent law, and competition law, respectively. Embodied in all three defenses is the rule of "trust and good faith." Under this principle, the courts may limit the exercise of patent rights as contrary to the duty of good faith. Each abuse of rights defense sets forth different requirements for what may constitute a breach of the duty of good faith.

[A] Civil Law

Article 2 of the Korean Civil Code provides that "the exercise of rights . . . shall be in accordance with the principle of trust and good faith. . . . *No abuse of rights shall be permitted.*"[6] Broad enough to cover other areas of law, this provision serves a statutory basis for the abuse of rights defenses in patent law and in competition law. For an exercise of rights to constitute an abuse of rights under civil law, the Supreme Court of Korea ruled that such exercise must not only be "subjectively" intended to gain no benefit but to harm the opponent, but also be "objectively" viewed as violating the social order.[7] Therefore, the accused infringer must prove both "subjective" and "objective" elements of the defense, but the mere fact that the harm suffered by the accused infringer is "significantly" greater than the benefit the patent owner would obtain from exercising its rights would not be sufficient to constitute an abuse of rights under civil law.

[B] Patent Law

The Supreme Court of Korea ruled that an abuse of rights defense is available to accused infringers if the asserted patent is shown to be "clearly invalid" for anticipation or obviousness.[8] The Court further held that a civil court presiding over such a patent infringement case may dismiss the case before a final judgment of invalidity by the Korean Intellectual Property Office (KIPO). This is significant because in the Korean legal system, while only civil courts have jurisdiction over patent infringement, validity issues are primarily adjudicated by the KIPO. The Court's holding rested on public policy that if the claimed invention belongs to the public domain for lack of novelty or non-obviousness, granting a monopoly to that invention "squarely undermines the legislative purpose of the Patent Act," and recognizing a right of action for infringement would also run counter to "the principles of substantive justice and equity."

Korean courts have expanded the reach of an abuse of rights defense beyond invalidity of patents. For example, the Supreme Court sought to define the limits of a

---

6. Civil Code, Art. 2 (emphasis added).
7. Supreme Court of Korea, 2011Da12163, decided Apr. 28, 2011.
8. Supreme Court of Korea, 2010Da95390, decided Jan. 19, 2012.

legitimate exercise of intellectual property rights.[9] The Court ruled that an exercise of intellectual property rights, even if done in the appearance of legitimacy, may amount to an abuse of rights, if it exceeds the legislative purpose or function of intellectual property law by "disrupting the order of fair competition and commercial transactions" and "violating the principle of good faith." Unlike in civil law, an abuse of rights defense in patent law does not require that such exercise is "intended" to gain no benefit but to injure the accused infringer.

[C] Competition Law

Accused infringers in Korea may raise a competition law defense against patent owners seeking an injunction in "unjust" manners. Article 59 of the Monopoly Regulation and Fair Trade Act (MRFTA) provides that "this Act does not apply to a *just exercise* of rights under the Patent Act."[10] The difficulty resides in defining the boundaries of a "just exercise" of patent rights. Any disposition necessarily entails striking a balance between promoting innovation by granting limited monopolies to the innovation and protecting the marketplace from competitive harms. Grappling with the meaning of "just exercise," the courts hearing a patent infringement case in Korea have typically addressed an abuse of patent rights defense under Articles 3-2(1) and 23(1) of MRFTA.

Article 3-2(1) prescribes abusive use of dominant market position and defines "abusive conduct" by monopolists, with its section (iii) prohibiting "unjustly hindering the business undertaking of others." This provision requires a showing of market power or dominant market position. Article 23(1), in contrast, does not require market power and sets forth a list of unfair trade practices, including "unjustly refusing to deal or treating a trading party in a discriminatory manner." As a tool to examine competitive harms from patent enforcement, these provisions involve a similar analysis with respect to whether an accused infringer's business is 'unjustly' hindered by the patent owner's seeking of injunctive relief.

Since Article 3-2(1) requires a showing of market power, an abuse of patent rights defense necessarily turns on abusive use of market dominance, and its section (iii) accordingly provides that it shall be an abuse of dominant market position to "unjustly" hinder the business undertaking of others. And the KFTC Guidelines in relevant part provide that it may be an abuse of dominant market position to hinder the business undertaking of others "by unjustly using patent litigation, patent invalidity trial, or other judicial or administrative proceedings with respect to intellectual property rights."[11] To establish a violation under Article 3-2(1), the defense must prove both anticompetitive "intent" and anticompetitive "effect."[12] In other words, for a patent infringement action to constitute an abuse of market dominance, the patent owner must engage in conduct, with the "intent" to restrain competition, that generates, or has an "objective probability" of generating, anticompetitive "effect."

---

9. Supreme Court of Korea, 2005Da67223, decided Jan. 25, 2007.
10. Monopoly Regulation & Fair Trade Act, Art. 59 (emphasis added).
11. Guidelines for the Abuse of Market Dominant Position, § IV(3)(D)(6).
12. Supreme Court of Korea, 2008Du17707, decided Apr. 8, 2010.

Korean courts have taken a comprehensive approach to evaluating anticompetitive effect, inquiring not only into competitive impacts to the relevant market, but also into its upstream and downstream markets.[13]

A typical section of Article 23(1) that the accused infringer may base an abuse of rights defense upon is section (i), which prohibits "unjustly refusing to deal or treating a trading party in a discriminatory manner." To constitute a violation under that section, "discrimination" must rise to a "significant" level, as the Enforcement Decree of the MRFTA defines "price discrimination" to be "transacting at a significantly favorable or unfavorable price depending on a trade region or a trading party."[14]

The Korean antitrust agency's interpretation of "unjust exercise" of patent rights under Article 59 of the MRFTA is embodied in its Review Guidelines on Unfair Exercise of Intellectual Property Rights (IPR Guidelines). Supplementing Article 3-2(1) with a type of "abusive" patent litigation, section III.2 of the IPR Guidelines provides that it is likely to be an "abuse of patent rights" to bring an infringement action (1) on a fraudulently obtained patent with the knowledge of such fraudulent manner; (2) on a patent its owner knows to be invalid or otherwise not infringed; or (3) on a patent for which infringement is objectively baseless in light of social norms. The Guidelines add, however, that no patent litigation will be presumed abusive based on the patent owner's failure to prevail in the litigation alone.

§10.03 SAMSUNG V. APPLE: THE KOREAN COURT'S PERSPECTIVES ON SEP INJUNCTIONS

All three types of abuse of patent rights defense under civil law, patent law, and competition law are available to standard implementers accused of infringing FRAND-encumbered SEPs. However, the Seoul district court in *Samsung v. Apple* rejected each defense primarily because the court was not convinced that Apple was a "willing" licensee.[15] This section reviews the court's reasoning that Samsung was entitled to injunctive relief against Apple for SEP infringement.[16]

[A] FRAND Commitments from a Contract Law Perspective

In *Samsung v. Apple*, Samsung sought injunctive relief against Apple's smartphones and tablet PCs for alleged infringement of SEPs owned by Samsung. Samsung had

---

13. Supreme Court of Korea, 2007Hu2827, decided Sep. 24, 2009.
14. Supreme Court of Korea, 2004Du4703, decided Dec. 7, 2006.
15. *Samsung Elecs. Co. v. Apple Korea Ltd.*, Seoul Central District Court, 2011GaHap39552, decided Aug. 24, 2012. Yoonhee Kim, a co-author of this chapter, previously discussed the relevant fact findings and conclusions in *Samsung v. Apple* in: Sang-Seung Yi & Yoonhee Kim, *Patent Pledges: Korean Perspectives* in Jorge L. Contreras & Meredith Jacob (eds), *Patent Pledges: Global Perspectives on Patent Law's Private Ordering Frontier* (Edward Elgar 2017), 209, and in: Sang Seung Yi & Yoonhee Kim, *FRAND in Korea* in Jorge L. Contreras (ed.) *The Cambridge Handbook of Technical Standardization Law: Competition, Antitrust, and Patents* (Cambridge Univ. Press 2017), 319.
16. No appellate court opinions exist in *Samsung v. Apple* as the parties settled before a final decision on appeal.

declared to license the asserted SEPs on FRAND terms as essential to ETSI's 3G UMTS mobile wireless standard. Faced with a possibility of injunctions after the court found the asserted SEPs valid and infringed, Apple countered that Samsung was not entitled to injunctive relief, arguing that a contract was formed under ETSI's IPR Policy because Apple had "accepted" Samsung's "offer" to license by implementing the ETSI standard.

Applying French law that was designated as governing law in ETSI's IPR Policy, the court rejected that Samsung's FRAND commitment constituted an "offer" to license.[17] The court concluded that under French contract law, an agreement to royalty rates is "material" to formation of a contract; however, there was no such agreement manifested in the FRAND commitment, and nor was there a basis to determine FRAND rates in ETSI's IPR Policy. The court also rejected Apple's argument that it "accepted" an offer by implementing the ETSI standard.[18] The court ruled that unilateral implementation of the standard alone did not constitute acceptance and Apple did not present a proper basis to show that acceptance was communicated to Samsung. The court further rejected that Samsung's FRAND commitment to ETSI created a third party beneficiary claim for Apple.[19] Interpreting Article 1121 of the French Civil Code, the court ruled that a third party beneficiary claim is allowed only in such limited circumstances as where a promisor makes a "stipulated condition for itself." The court found no such contractual relationship between ETSI and Samsung.

Notably, the court interpreted "FRAND" from a contract law perspective as imposing a "duty to negotiate in good faith."[20] In doing so, the court noted the lack of textual support for relevant details of FRAND terms in the FRAND declaration itself as well as in ETSI's IPR Policy and disagreed with a liberal interpretation of FRAND that could be tantamount to allowing de facto "compulsory" licenses.[21]

[B] The Duty to Negotiate in Good Faith and Abuse of Rights Defenses

Having found that Apple had no enforceable contract with Samsung, the court examined whether Samsung abused its patent rights. The court first ruled that the duty of a SEP holder to negotiate in good faith extends only to "willing" licensees and determined that both parties breached their duty to negotiate in good faith.[22] The court viewed that the parties were both "unwilling" participants interested more in the outcome of the litigation than in substantive negotiations on FRAND terms. Nevertheless, the court went on to find for Samsung that its initial offer was not "excessively high."[23] The court ultimately held that Samsung did not abuse patent rights in violation of its FRAND commitment.

Addressing the civil law abuse of rights defense, the court did not find that Samsung's action of seeking an injunction was "intended" to gain no benefit but to

---

17. Seoul Central District Court, 2011GaHap39552, at 173–74.
18. *Id.*, 174–175.
19. *Id.*, 175.
20. *Id.*, 177–180.
21. *Id.*, 179.
22. *Id.*, 183–186.
23. *Id.*, 186–190.

harm Apple.[24] Although it was found that Samsung could have brought this action as a counter to Apple's lawsuit filed against Samsung in the United States for alleged infringement of design and utility patents,[25] the court stressed that Apple had caused harm to Samsung by infringing the patents-in-suit. It also reasoned the technical and financial value of utility telecommunications patents cannot be taken lightly just because they were encumbered with FRAND commitments.

With respect to the patent law abuse of rights defense, the court examined whether the fact that Samsung did not negotiate in good faith could justify Apple's abuse of rights defense.[26] The court declined to rule that Samsung's conduct amounted to "disrupting the order of fair competition and commercial transactions" or to "violating the principle of good faith." It reasoned that:

- It was not clear that seeking an injunction against an unwilling licensee may run against the purpose or function of SEP/FRAND regimes, considering that a responsibility for determining the specifics of FRAND conditions resides with a party negotiation.
- Apple was presumably aware of the essentiality and any royalty base of the patents-in-suit, but nevertheless had practiced them without a license or requesting one.
- Apple's royalty proposals to Samsung were not based upon the premise that the patents-in-suit were valid and infringed.
- Apple did not move to escrow a putative FRAND royalty as it did in other jurisdictions such as the Netherlands and Japan.
- Apple's royalty proposal departed significantly from customarily proposed initial FRAND rates.
- Apple's royalty bases rested on a significant underappreciation for telecommunications-related SEPs.
- Apple asked Samsung for a disclosure of the terms with other SEP licensees, but it refused to sign a non-disclosure agreement necessary for the negotiation to proceed.

On similar reasons and findings as above, the court rejected Apple's abuse of rights defense in competition law. Addressing the allegations under Article 3-2(1) of the MRFTA, the court found that Samsung possessed market power in the product market consisting of handsets and tablet PCs that support 3GPP telecommunications, and that the patents-in-suit were an "essential facility" under competition law.[27] However, the court was not persuaded that Samsung's bid for injunctions was "subjectively" intended to restrain competition in the relevant market with an "objective probability" of generating anticompetitive harm.[28] The court also dismissed the charges under

---

24. *Id.*, 191.
25. *Apple, Inc. v. Samsung Elecs. Co.*, No. 11-cv-01846 (N.D. Cal.).
26. 2011GaHap39552 at 191–96.
27. *Id.*, 201–203.
28. *Id.*, 203–206.

Article 23(1) of the MRFTA, concluding that Samsung's initial proposal was not "significant" price discrimination against Apple.[29]

The court's refusal of all three abuse of rights defenses raised in *Samsung v. Apple* indicates that the court could have been more open to a breach of the FRAND commitment by the SEP holder had the accused infringer shown "good faith" effort to reach an agreement. The question of good faith was asked to both Samsung and Apple, and the court found both parties in breach of the duty to negotiate in good faith. What cleared Samsung from the charges after all could be the findings that its proposed rate was not "excessively high" and that Apple was an "unwilling" licensee.

[C] FRAND Negotiation under Scrutiny

As discussed above, the Korean court examined closely how Samsung and Apple negotiated a FRAND royalty rate. In *Samsung v. Apple*, it was Samsung, in reply to Apple's request for a quote of FRAND terms and for a disclosure of the terms with other SEP licensees, that made a first offer based on the sales price of the accused devices.[30] Apple counteroffered to license Samsung's portfolio of SEPs,[31] and there was a "significant" gap between their respective proposed rates. Negotiations to close this gap continued in parallel with the litigation, but no compromise was reached on FRAND terms through the end of trial. The court found that neither party made a "good faith" effort to close this gap in royalty rates.

Notably, the court suggested that a standard implementer who made a formal request to license or agreed to pay royalties without contesting patent validity and infringement could be an example of willing licensee.[32] In the court's view, however, Apple was not such example. After finding both parties in breach of their duty to negotiate in good faith, the court proceeded to compare each proposed FRAND rate with the rates disclosed by several SEP holders in the telecommunications sector, and concluded that Samsung's offer was not "excessively" high while Apple's counteroffer was "significantly" low.[33] The court declined to rule Samsung's offer "excessive" because it was within the range of FRAND rates – 0.8% to 3.25% – that the court found other SEP holders in the telecommunications sector typically proposed to potential licensees. The court acknowledged that the numbers in the range were "unilaterally disclosed" and actual FRAND rates drawn from individual negotiations are usually confidential; however, the court found that both Samsung and Apple insisted on their respective initial offers despite the possibility of compromise, and did not even advance the negotiation as they failed to sign a confidentiality agreement.[34] *Samsung v. Apple* thus illustrates that in evaluating the willingness of potential licensees, Korean courts will consider initial FRAND rates proposed by each party, together with how they

---

29. *Id.*, 206–208.
30. *Id.*, 184–186.
31. *Id.*, 185–186.
32. *Id.*, 183–184.
33. *Id.*, 186–189.
34. *Id.*, 187–189.

participated in subsequent negotiations and whether any agreement on FRAND terms was reached.

Since the parties reached no agreement on FRAND conditions, the court in *Samsung v. Apple* was not in a position to inquire into what may ultimately constitute "fair and reasonable" terms within the meaning of "FRAND." While not explicit, however, the court seems receptive to the idea that an agreed-upon royalty between sophisticated parties reflects their judgments as to what terms are fair and reasonable, so long as the parties negotiated in "good faith." Instead of offering guidance on fair and reasonable terms, the court discussed basic premises for parties to negotiate a FRAND royalty upon. The court repeatedly pointed that Apple did not negotiate a royalty rate on the premise that the asserted SEPs were valid and infringed. In addition, the court viewed that a confidentiality agreement, which Samsung and Apple could not agree to sign, is a prerequisite to FRAND license negotiations. Finally, the court gave close attention to whether a proposed royalty base was commensurate with established industry practice. It rejected Apple's proposed royalty base – Samsung's share of total industry 3GPP patents – as not supported by evidence.[35] Apple also proposed a per-chip rate, arguing that the infringing use of the chip installed in the accused devices was only one aspect of the features serving consumer needs.[36] However, the court found Samsung's proposed royalty base – per-handset rate – more plausible in view of established industry practice.

Samsung v. Apple indicates that a standard implementer in Korea cannot establish itself as a willing licensee by merely expressing intent to become a FRAND licensee. Instead, a standard implementer must show that it negotiated a FRAND license in "good faith." Likewise, SEP holders do not owe a duty to negotiate in good faith to "unwilling licensees."[37] One way of showing good faith could be to escrow a putative FRAND royalty. That was missing in *Samsung v. Apple*, which the court found against Apple because it was shown that Apple moved to escrow in other jurisdictions such as the Netherlands and Japan in anticipation that Samsung's patents could be found valid and infringed.[38]

In sum, *Samsung v. Apple* hints a type of behavior that may be viewed as tending to show *unwillingness* of potential licensees to take a FRAND license:

- a potential licensee unilaterally practices a SEP without an official request for a FRAND license.
- a potential licensee's proposed rate is not based on the premise that the patent is valid and infringed.
- a potential licensee does not deposit a putative FRAND royalty into escrow.
- a potential licensee's proposal marks a significant departure from customary royalty proposals in the relevant sector.
- a potential licensee refuses to sign a non-disclosure agreement before starting a negotiation.

---

35. *Id.*, 190.
36. *Id.*, 189–190.
37. *Id.*, 183–184.
38. *Id.*, 205.

Samsung v. Apple also illustrates a FRAND dispute where the court looked not only into the willingness of a potential licensee, but also into whether a SEP holder negotiated in good faith. In this light, the court made clear that enforcing a FRAND commitment hinges on an individual negotiation between a SEP holder and a potential licensee to determine relevant details of FRAND conditions. However, it was not clear to the court that Samsung's initial proposal was "excessive" relative to typical initial proposals. In 2012, Apple petitioned the KFTC to investigate whether Samsung's act of seeking an injunction in the Seoul district court was a competition law violation. The KFTC reached the same conclusion as the court, that there was no clear showing that Samsung's proposed FRAND rate was "excessively high."[39] Rather, the KFTC found that, while it was not clearly shown that Samsung did not negotiate in good faith, Apple's conduct shown in the course of the FRAND negotiations was a typical example of "reverse hold-up."[40]

On this competition law question, however, the Seoul district court seems open to the possibility that seeking an injunction for SEP infringement may constitute a competition law violation where the facts so warrant. The court in *Samsung v. Apple* appears to pave that way by finding that Samsung had market power and the asserted SEPs were an "essential facility" within the meaning of competition law,[41] and therefore did not rule out the possibility that seeking injunctive relief for SEP infringement may "unjustly" hinder the business of others in violation of competition law. The court was not convinced, however, that Apple's business was "unjustly" hindered because Apple was found an *unwilling* licensee in Korea.

Later in 2017, the KFTC in *In re Alleged Abuse of Market Dominance of Qualcomm Inc.*[42] stated that potential licensees can dispute the validity and infringement of patents during negotiations with SEP holders. Building upon the principle articulated in *Samsung v. Apple* that SEP holders must negotiate in good faith with willing licensees, the KFTC signaled that it is likely to be anticompetitive for SEP holders to seek an injunction against willing licensees.[43] In doing so, the KFTC consulted approaches that the courts and antitrust agencies in the European Union and the United States took with respect to FRAND-encumbered SEPs.[44] Notably, noting that many SEPs are found to be invalid or not standard-essential, the KFTC viewed that a potential licensee shall be guaranteed an opportunity to dispute the validity and essentiality of the SEPs and the extent to which they are embodied in the accused product.[45]

---

39. KFTC, Press Release, *Determination That Samsung Does Not Violate the Monopoly Regulation & Fair Trade Act by Seeking Injunctive Relief Against Apple for SEP Infringement in Korea* (Feb. 25, 2014).
40. *Ibid.*
41. 2011GaHap39552 at 201–03.
42. KFTC, 2015SiGam2118 (Jan. 20, 2017).
43. *Id.,* 162–164.
44. *Ibid.*
45. *Id.,* 160.

§10.04 THE IPR GUIDELINES: THE KFTC'S PERSPECTIVES ON SEP INJUNCTIONS

In 2014 and 2016, the KFTC revised the IPR Guidelines to address SEP injunctions, FRAND negotiations, and non-practicing entities (NPE). Notably, during the revision process, distinctions between SEPs and de facto SEPs emerged in the IPR Guidelines.

[A] SEP Injunctions and FRAND Negotiation

The 2014 IPR Guidelines provide that "an act of filing for an injunction against willing licensees by a SEP holder who promised to license its SEP on FRAND terms can be regarded as behavior that restricts competition in the relevant market as it exceeds the reasonable extent of exercise of patent right."[46] The IPR Guidelines suggest the following factors in determining a SEP holder seeking injunctive relief may be viewed as not negotiating in good faith:

- whether a SEP holder officially proposed negotiations to a potential licensee;
- whether the period of negotiation was appropriate;
- whether the proposed terms to a potential licensee were reasonable and non-discriminatory;
- whether a SEP holder agreed to a third party determination of FRAND terms by a court or by an arbitrator where no agreement is reached.

The 2014 IPR Guidelines also present two examples in which a standard implementer can be viewed as an *unwilling* licensee:[47]

- a potential licensee refuses to enter a license agreement on FRAND terms adjudicated by a court or through arbitration.
- obtaining money damages is unlikely as, for example, a standard implementer is near bankruptcy.

Further, to clarify a type of conduct that may violate FRAND commitments, the 2014 IPR Guidelines state that "demanding unfair conditions after being designated as technical standard" can be viewed as restricting competition in violation of "just exercise" of patent rights.[48] Examples of such conduct include:[49]

- avoiding or circumventing licensing on FRAND terms to strengthen market dominance or to exclude competitors (§ III.5.A(3));
- unfairly rejecting the licensing of a standard essential patent (§ III.5.A(4));
- unfairly imposing discriminatory conditions when licensing standard essential patents or imposing an unreasonable level of royalty (§ III.5.A(5)); and

---

46. 2014 IPR Guidelines, § III.5.B.
47. *Ibid.*
48. 2014 IPR Guidelines, § III.5.A.
49. *Ibid.*

- imposing conditions unfairly restricting the exercise of patent rights held by licensees or unfairly imposing conditions of cross licensing of non-standard essential patents held by licensees (§ III.5.A(6)).

Also, the IPR Guidelines provide a list of factors to consider in determining whether a level of royalty rates is fair and reasonable. The list includes:[50]

- an objective technological value of the patent;
- a level of royalties a licensor receives from other licensees;
- a level of royalties a licensee pays for the use of comparable patents;
- the nature and scope of a license;
- the duration of a license; and
- the profitability of a licensed product reading on the patent.

Notably, the IPR Guidelines state that single-firm conduct is subject to the Guidelines "only when a firm with market dominance independently exercises IPRs."[51] In particular, refusing to trade or imposing a considerably excessive royalty is subject to the Guidelines only when the firm has "overwhelming market dominance."[52] In this respect, the KFTC's primary objective is to provide criteria to decide whether an exercise of patent rights by a "dominant firm" falls within the scope of "unjust exercise" of patent rights.

[B] NPEs and Jurisdictional Reach

The 2014 revisions to the IPR Guidelines include the addition of section III.7, which specifically addresses NPEs. While acknowledging that NPEs may encourage incentives to innovate, the Guidelines recognized the possibility that NPEs could be more likely to abuse patent rights than typical patent holders because NPEs "do not engage in manufacturing activities" and "have more incentives and capabilities to impose excessive royalty than usual patent holders." In this regard, section III.7 identifies five types of potentially abusive or unreasonable conduct by NPEs that may go beyond "just exercise" of patent rights:

- imposing markedly unreasonable levels of royalties in light of customary trade practice (§ III.7.A);
- imposing royalties at an unreasonable level in conflict with FRAND terms on patents acquired from a third party who was subject to FRAND terms (§ III.7.B);

---

50. 2014 IPR Guidelines, § III.7.B. These factors are listed in section III.7.B dealing with NPEs (*see* Part 10.04[B] *infra*); however, the 2014 IPR Guidelines state that section III.7.B equally applies to "other patentees which are not an NPE."
51. 2014 IPR Guidelines, § II.2.B.
52. *Ibid.*

- setting up a consortium acting as an NPE with multiple firms and then unjustly refusing to grant licenses to or agreeing to grant licenses on discriminatory terms to non-members (§ III.7.C);
- filing a lawsuit or sending a cease and desist letter for patent infringement using deceptive means to mislead, conceal, or omit as to important information necessary for the opposing party to defend against infringement claims (§ III.7.D); and
- transferring patents to an NPE and having such NPE engaging in one or more acts above (§ III.7.E).

As such, sections III.7.A and III.7.B are concerned with NPE's act of demanding an "unreasonable" level of royalty rates, and section III.7.B provides that FRAND commitments travel with SEPs. With respect to section III.7.A, the Guidelines further state that "in case of a royalty for a FRAND-encumbered patent, it is more likely to be determined as unjust." The new IPR Guidelines therefore provide for standard implementers a competition law defense against a claim of injunction by NPEs.

With respect to the geographical scope of a license and jurisdiction, section I.2.B states that the IPR Guidelines "shall apply to any contract, agreement, or other act of foreign firms that affects the domestic market whether it occurs inside or outside of Korea. Such application may not depend on whether a foreign firm maintains a domestic business operation in Korea or whether its business counterpart is a domestic firm or consumer." The KFTC's expansive approach to jurisdiction indicates that NPEs may be subject to jurisdiction so long as harmful local effect resides in Korea, and the KFTC would hinge an intervention more on local harm than on the geographical scope of a license.

[C] The 2016 Amendment: Distinctions Clarified Between SEPs and "De Facto" SEPs

In 2016, the KFTC further revised the IPR Guidelines and clarified that "de facto" SEPs do not fall within the same ambit as SEPs. Notably, section I.3.A(5) of the pre-2016 version of the IPR Guidelines defined the term "standardized technology" to originate in the standard-setting process *or* in a "de facto" standard. Along those lines, the 2014 IPR Guidelines incorporated into sections III.5.A(4)–(6)[53] the language that equated de facto SEPs to FRAND-encumbered SEPs, stating "this applies not only to standard technologies set by standards organizations, but also to technologies widely used as de facto standard technologies in related areas, such as technology selected as must-use technology when bidding for public organization projects."

The 2014 IPR Guidelines' view of de facto SEPs, however, was set aside in the 2016 IPR Guidelines. The KFTC was receptive to the distinctions that monopoly power of SEPs is "artificially" gained in exchange for FRAND commitments in the standard-setting process, whereas de facto SEPs become a standard as a result of "market

---

53. *See* note 49 *supra.*

competition."[54] Thus, the 2016 amendment to the IPR Guidelines lends support to the proposition that de facto SEPs are placed outside the bounds of the IPR Guidelines as applied to SEPs.

This agency action does not necessarily mean that firms accused of infringing de facto SEPs are left with little recourse in the face of injunctions. An abuse of rights defense under patent law or civil law may be brought against the holder of a patent encumbered with "public" pledges, e.g., patent pledges made to government officials, because both doctrines demand that a patent holder exercise its rights in compliance with "good faith" and "social norms." For example, the accused infringer can assert the patent law abuse of rights defense, if the patent owner's exercise of patent rights gives rise to "disrupting the order of fair competition and commercial transactions" and to "violating the principle of good faith." Also, the accused infringer may ground the competition law defense in section III.2 of the IPR Guidelines[55] addressing "abusive" patent litigation, for example, that asserting infringement of a patent encumbered with a public pledge is "objectively baseless in light of social norms."

§10.05 CONCLUSION

The court and competition authority in Korea expressed divergent views on the availability of injunctive relief for SEP infringement and the duty of SEP holders and standard implementers to negotiate in good faith. While the court in *Samsung v. Apple* focused on how a standard implementer and a SEP holder participated in FRAND negotiations and rejected the FRAND and abuse of rights defenses raised by the implementer, the KFTC shored up the IPR Guidelines to curb potential abuse by SEP holders asserting infringement and seeking injunctive relief. Despite this difference, the common message is clear—the key question of good faith will be asked to both parties and the antitrust agency and courts in Korea will scrutinize how the parties negotiated a FRAND license to discern their good faith efforts to reach a consensus.

---

54. Global Antitrust Inst., George Mason Univ. Sch. of Law, *A Conversation with Former Federal Trade Commissioner Joshua D. Wright and Korea Fair Trade Commission Vice Chairman Kim Hack-hyun* (Apr. 8, 2016).
55. *See* Part 10.02[C] *supra*.

CHAPTER 11
Injunctive Relief in Japan

Christoph Rademacher

§11.01 LEGAL FRAMEWORK AND COURT SYSTEM

Japan started to establish a system of protection of patents when it introduced its first patent law during the Meiji period in the late nineteenth century. The current patent act was adopted in 1959,[1] and amended frequently throughout the last decades. Recognizing a need to promote the interests of patentees in order to promote innovation, the Japanese government adopted a number of mainly procedural revisions during the late 1990s and early 2000s, mainly aiming to streamline enforcement procedures and to facilitate evidence collection.

One of the procedural revisions implemented during this period was to concentrate patent litigation at specialized divisions at the Tokyo District Court and Osaka District Court. Appellate litigation was concentrated at the newly established Intellectual Property High Court in 2004. The IP High Court also hears appeals on validity decisions made by the Japan Patent Office. Finally, decisions issued by the IP High Court can be appealed to the Supreme Court.[2]

Every year, about 150–200 patent infringement cases are filed at the two competent district courts in Japan, and about fifty appellate cases are filed at the IP High Court. One of the main objectives of the civil procedure and patent law reform mentioned above was to increase the speed of proceedings. These days, infringement proceedings are comparatively fast in Japan; as of 2016, the average time for the resolution of intellectual property infringement lawsuits has been about thirteen

---

1. Tokkyo Hō [Japanese Patent Act], Law No. 121 of 1959.
2. *See* overview, e.g., at Toshiaki Iimura, Ryu Takabayashi & Christoph Rademacher, *The Binding Nature of Court Decisions in Japan's Civil Law System*, https://cgc.law.stanford.edu/commentaries/14-iimura-takabayashi-rademacher/ (accessed 31 Jul. 2018).

months for first instance proceedings and about eight months for appellate proceedings.[3]

§11.02 REMEDIES

Both the patentee and the exclusive licensee have standing to bring a patent infringement claim and are entitled to the same remedies.[4] For simplicity, this chapter will refer to the patentee and the exclusive licensee as 'patentee'. Upon prevailing in a patent infringement proceedings, the patentee is entitled to the following type of remedies:

- injunctive relief;
- destruction of infringing goods and means used for productions;
- monetary damages.[5]

[A] Permanent Injunctive Relief

The claim for injunctive relief is the primary remedy that a patentee will request in almost all cases when asserting infringement. Unlike in the US, there is no separate test for equitable relief, and the court will almost always grant an injunction upon a showing of infringement. Since 1959, the claim for injunctive relief has been codified in Article 100 Patent Act. That said, courts had awarded injunctions against patent infringers already under earlier patent law before 1959, holding that a registered patent right contained sufficient similarity to a real right that entitles the right's owner to exclude third parties from unauthorized use.[6]

[1] Requirements

Pursuant to Article 100 of the Japanese Patent Act, a claim for injunctive relief requires a showing of a current infringement or a likelihood of a future infringement.[7] In cases where the claim is based on a likelihood of future infringement, the court has to recognize an objective likelihood that the infringing conduct will occur in the future, which has to be supported by specific factual evidence.[8] Such likelihood of infringing conduct is assumed by the courts if the defendant has the ability to resume the

---

3. *See* statistics published at the IP High Court website: http://www.ip.courts.go.jp/eng/vcms_lf/2017_E_stat03.pdf (first instance proceedings; accessed 31 Jul. 2018) and http://www.ip.courts.go.jp/eng/vcms_lf/2017_E_stat01.pdf (appellate proceedings; accessed 31 Jul. 2018).
4. For such reason, the remedies provisions in the Japanese Patent Act usually mention both the patentee and the exclusive licensee as entitled entities.
5. For a discussion on Japanese patent damages *see*, e.g., Christoph Rademacher, *Patent Damages in Japan: Why do Japanese Courts award so little?*, 47(3) Patents & Licensing 9 (2017).
6. Nobuhiro Nakayama, *Tokkyohō [Patent Law]* (3rd ed., Koubundo 2016), at 357.
7. Ryu Takabayashi, *Hyōjun Tokkyohō [Patent Law from the Ground Up]* (6th ed., Yūhikaku 2017), at 296.
8. Tokyo District Court, Decision of August 26, 2011, Case No. Hei 20 (wa) 831, published in 1402 Hanrei Times 344 (2011) – '*Dōbutsu-yō hainyō shori-zai*'.

infringing conduct, which can be demonstrated, for example, by showing that the defendant has the know-how to resume manufacturing the infringing product or by the fact that the defendant disputes that the allegedly infringing products falls within the scope of the invention protected by plaintiff's patent.[9] Also, a likelihood of infringing conduct will be assumed by the courts if the defendant declares that he would resume conduct as long as the court dismisses the infringement action.[10] The claim for injunctive relief does not require any degree of fault by the defendant.[11]

[2] Scope

The party entitled to a claim for injunctive relief can request the defendant to cease the infringing conduct (*kyōgi no sashitome seikyūken*) and to refrain from such conduct in the future (*yobō*). In addition, the plaintiff can request the defendant, pursuant to Article 100(2) Patent Act, to destroy the equipment used to produce the patent infringing goods.[12] To declare the claim for destruction of the equipment, the court needs to specify the nature of the patent infringing goods and of the infringing conduct. Thus, the details of the infringing conduct have to be investigated and recorded, and the product names, product details, technical drafts, and serial numbers have to be confirmed by the courts.[13] The claim for the destruction of equipment used to produce patent infringing products must be tailored to what is objectively necessary to prevent future infringement and cannot be overly broad.[14]

The claim for injunctive relief typically encompasses only the infringing conduct identified by the court. Accordingly, the injunction orders issued by the courts are usually concise and very specific. A patentee has to bring a new action to again assert the patent if a defendant modifies the previously infringing device or process but nevertheless still falls within the scope of the asserted patent.[15]

---

9. Osaka District Court, Decision of January 24, 1975, Case No. Sho 48 (wa) 3834, published in 323 Hanrei Times 270 (1975) – *'Plastic film'*.
10. Tokyo District Court, Decision of December 22, 1969, Case No. Sho 41(wa) 11570, published in 1 Mutaishū 396 (1969).
11. Takabayashi, *supra* n. 7, at 297; Nakayama, *supra* n. 6, at 357.
12. Shunji Miyamaū & Nobuo Matsumura, *Chitekizaisanken Soshō: Jitsumu kaisetsu [Intellectual Property Right Litigation: Practical Commentary]* (2nd ed., Sekai Shisosha 2005), at 493; Takabayashi, *supra* n. 7, at 297.
13. Osaka District Court, Decision of November 25, 1987, Case No. Sho 59 (wa) 7127, published in 19-3 Mutaishū 434 (1987) – *'Wood Work'*.
14. *See* Supreme Court, Decision of July 16, 1999, Case No. Hei 10 (o) 604 – *'Physiologically Active Substance Measurement Method'*, in which the court denied the patentee's requests to dispose drugs and to effectively revoke the drugs approval only because they were tested by a patent-protected quality standard testing process.
15. Tokyo District Court, Decision of January 18, 1984, Case No. Sho 58 (wa) 8056, published in 1101 Hanrei Jihō 109 (1984) – *'Porno Disneyland'*; Sapporo High Court, Decision of March 27, 1974, Case No. Sho 48 (ra) 58, published in 308 Hanrei Times (1976), 227 – *'Misono Azumusushi'*; Yoshiyuki Tamura, *Chitekizaisanshingaisoshō ni okeru kajyōsashitome to chūshōteki sashitome (Ge)[Excessive and Abstract Injunctions in Intellectual Property Infringement Litigation (Part 2)]*, 1125 Jurist 129, 130 (1997).

[3] Compulsory Enforcement of Injunctions

In order to seek enforcement of the injunction, a prevailing plaintiff can request the court to order compulsory enforcement of the decision. That said, a permanent injunction issued by a district court cannot be enforced against the infringer if the infringer has filed an appeal at the IP High Court and such an appellate procedure is still ongoing. In this case, the claim for permanent injunctive relief can be enforced after it has been confirmed by the IP High Court.

After prevailing at the district court level, the plaintiff can request a declaration of provisional execution (*karishikkōsengen*), which in principle would entitle the plaintiff to enforce the permanent injunction before conclusion of the appellate proceeding. However, the defendant can stop the provisional execution by posting a security bond in an amount set by the court.

[B] Preliminary Injunction

Preliminary injunctions are generally considered as an important instrument to enforce patents at least in situations where the infringement is clear.[16] Different than in case of regular injunctions, the compulsory enforcement of preliminary injunctions cannot be stopped by posting a bond.[17] Thus, preliminary injunctive relief can be very effective in preventing further infringing activity, as it can prohibit an infringer from continuing the production or sale of an infringing good and thus can lead to substantial interruptions of the business activities of the defendant.[18]

[1] Requirements

Pursuant to Article 23-2 of the Civil Preservation Act, a preliminary injunction requires a showing of immediate harm or substantial damages. To show such a requirement is met, the courts require the plaintiff to show the necessity (*hitsuyōsei*) of the preliminary injunction, which has to be established by a balance of hardships between the

---

16. Toshiaki Iimura & Shin Sano, *Chitekizaisanjiken to Karishobun [Intellectual Property Cases and Preliminary Injunctions]*, 17 *Law & Technology* 14 (2002).
17. Ryuichi Mimura, *Tokkyo shingai soshō no genjō to taisaku – shōrai no shingai soshō o misueta kigyō katsudō no ari kata [Current Situation and Development of Patent Litigation: Corporate Activities in Anticipation of future infringement litigation]*, 62-12 Patent, 100, 107 (2009).
18. Toshiaki Iimura & Shin Sano, *Chitekizaisanfunsō ni okeru karishobun no katsuyō nitsuite [About the Use of Preliminary Injunctions in Intellectual Property Disputes]* in Toshiaki Nagai, Kuniharu Yasue & Sachikuni Iwasaki (eds), *Chiteki zaisanken: Sono keisei to hogo: Akiyoshi Michihiro sensei kiju kinen ronbunshu* (Shin Nihon Hōki Shuppan (Insatsu) 2002), 34, 37.

plaintiff and the defendant.[19] A showing of necessity is facilitated in cases of infringement likely to result in damages which would be difficult to compensate monetarily.[20] Examples are imitations of a major product line of the patentee,[21] imitations of a product designated to be sold only during a short period of time, or imitations of a product which is designated to be introduced in the distant future supported by a substantial marketing campaign. Another factor supporting the necessity of a preliminary injunction would be a possible lack of financial means of the defendant limiting the defendant's capability to compensate potential claim for damages.[22]

On the other hand, courts have denied the necessity for a preliminary injunction in cases where the injunction would have severely impacted the defendant's business, likely to result in bankruptcy, while the plaintiff only incurred slight damages by the infringement. Also, necessity has been denied in cases where the plaintiff had not made use of the intellectual property right in questions.[23] Other cases where the courts have followed the plaintiff's reasoning and accepted necessity include the following scenarios:

- concise preparation for the production and sale of a patent-protected product;[24]
- concise marketing activities introducing the product by the patentee;
- concise preparations to reintroduce a patent-protected product into the market;
- showing of infringement while the patentee/plaintiff is conducting license negotiations with a third party;[25]
- infringement affecting the core product of the plaintiff;[26]
- widespread publication of promotion material by the defendant incorrectly asserting non-infringement;[27]
- infringement in a very small market with only a few participants and substitutes in which an infringement inevitably results in substantial damages for the patentee and its licensees;[28]
- existence of substitute products manufactured by the defendant which are not IP-infringing;

---

19. Shogo Nakamura, *Tokkyo jitsuyō shin'an-ken minji karishobun ni okeru 'hozen no hitsuyō-sei'* [About the 'necessity of preservation' through preliminary injunctions in patent and utility model cases], 57-10 Patent 39 (2004); *see also* Kazuhiko Yoshida, 1062 Hanrei Times 59 (2001), who argues for raising the bar for accepting necessity in the context of preliminary injunctions.
20. Toshiaki Iimura & Shin Sano, *Current State of Preliminary Injunction Cases Involving Intellectual Property Rights*, 1 Journal of the Japanese Group of AIPPI, 12, 19 (2003).
21. Shizuoka District Court, 6 Nov. 1973 Mo 442.
22. Iimura & Sano, *supra* n. 18, at 41.
23. Nagoya District Court, 20 May 1985, Sho 59 (yo) No. 318.
24. Kyoto District Court, 26 Jun. 1967, Sho 42 (yo) No. 56.
25. Gifu District Court, 14 Apr.il 1971, Sho 44 (yo) No. 53.
26. Shizuoka District Court, 6 Nov. 1973, Sho 48 (mo) No. 442.
27. Osaka High Court, 8 May 1969, Sho 42 (ne) No. 1104.
28. *Ibid.*

- contributory infringement by an object which can only be used for patent infringing purposes.[29]

[2] Procedural Overview

The preliminary injunction can be decided in a trial hearing (*kōtōbenron*) or a court hearing of the defendant (*saimusha shinjin*),[30] the latter being more common in practice.[31] The court usually grants the defendant a preparation period of three weeks until the court session.[32] Rendering a preliminary injunction without hearing the defendant is very rare and generally only possible in situations where infringement is easy to prove and where the scheduled court hearing and the accompanied warning of the defendant would obviously run against the purpose of the injunction.[33]

A patentee will only be able to obtain a preliminary injunction against clear infringement conduct. Thus, in a case of multiple infringement actions by one defendant, the patentee should move for preliminary injunctions only in those cases where prima facie evidence for an injunction can be presented. Such separation of equitable claims can also be done after filing for preliminary injunction.[34] Frequently, the defendant will not be interested in a quick resolution of the dispute. Nevertheless, he is expected to – at least in theory – contribute to an efficient and smooth resolution of the dispute and should refrain from any measures delaying the proceedings.[35] If the defendant was aware of the fact that his conduct was likely to cause infringement and had obtained expert opinion examining the legal and factual situation, he is obliged to provide the court with such expert opinions.[36]

The patentee often moves for a preliminary injunction and files for the main proceedings at the same time.[37] In many cases, the decision regarding the preliminary injunction will be announced roughly around the time of the closing argument of the main proceedings.[38] As the outcome of the preliminary injunction will heavily influence the main proceedings, especially in situations where the factual circumstances are legally and technically unambiguous, the patentee should prepare the motion for preliminary injunctive relief very carefully. In uncomplicated cases, the motion for

---

29. Aomori District Court, 22 May 1972, Sho 46 (yo) No. 2.
30. Article 23-4 of the Civil Preservation Act; *see also* Kato, 41(9) Hoso Jiho 2621 (1989); Mamoru Hanari, *Kari sashiosae karishobun no hōritsu sōdan* (2004), 12.
31. Iimura and Sano, *supra* n. 18, at 39.
32. *Id.*, 39.
33. *Id.*, 40; one of the rare cases of obtaining a preliminary injunction without a hearing of the defendant is described in Eiji Katayama & Takayuki Hirose, *Senryaku toshite no chizai Karishobun to kanzeitetsuzuki no yuukou katsuyou*, 29 *Law & Technology* 57, 59 (2005).
34. Iimura & Sano, *supra* n. 18, at 42.
35. *Id.*, 43.
36. Tokyo District Court, 20 Sep. 1999, Hei 11 (yo) No. 22125, published in 1696 Hanrei Jihō 76 (1999) – '*iMac*'.
37. Iimura & Sano, *supra* n. 18, at 43.
38. *Ibid.*

initiating the main proceedings and the motion for the preliminary injunction can often be seen to have basically the same content.[39]

[3] Damages for Wrongful Injunctive Relief

Japanese case law allows defendants who incurred damages due to a wrongful preliminary injunction to claim compensation of such damages from the plaintiff who moved for the preliminary injunction.[40] In 2005, the Osaka High Court confirmed the applicability of such general civil law claim for damages, which is based on Article 709 of the Civil Code, in patent law cases.[41] According to the court's decision, the defendant could claim damages for the wrongful preliminary injunction, as the underlying patent had been ruled invalid after the court issued the injunction order. The court considered the hardship for the plaintiff, who is held accountable for the examination errors of the JPO in possibly complex and unclear technical circumstances.[42] But at the same time, the court concluded that the party moving for the preliminary injunction should be in the best position of all parties, including the JPO, to provide a final evaluation of the infringement and validity situation and its underlying technical parameters. The court's decision provided a legal basis for compensating the party who might have incurred substantial and far-reaching damages caused by an unjustified preliminary injunction. Having said so, in the precedent case the court only awarded damages of one million JPY caused by the market confusion and reputation damage incurred by the preliminary injunction, plus attorneys' fees and other costs.[43]

§11.03 DEFENCES AGAINST INJUNCTIVE RELIEF

As mentioned above, a claim for permanent injunctive relief is usually granted automatically upon a finding of infringement of a valid patent. In order to prevent an injunction, a person who desires to use patented technology can apply for a compulsory license. Also, in recent years, courts have denied injunctive relief in situations in which they would have considered an injunction to constitute an abuse of rights under the Japanese civil code.

[A] Compulsory License

Under Japanese patent law, a patentee can be forced to grant a compulsory license to the patented technology in case:

---

39. Ibid.
40. Confirmed by the Supreme Court in S. Ct. 22—13 Minshu 3428 (1968).
41. Osaka High Court 1912 Hanrei Jihō 107 (2005) – 'Damage Claim for Wrongful Injunction'.
42. Id., 113.
43. Id., 118.

(1) the patentee hasn't practiced the patent for at least three years (Article 83 Patent Act);
(2) public interest commands the grant of the license (Article 93 Patent Act); or
(3) the patent covers a senior technology and blocks a dependent invention (Article 92 Patent Act).

In each of the above constellations, the applicant for a license has to consult with the patentee regarding the grant of a regular license. Only in case such discussions are not successful, the respective applicant can seek grant of a compulsory license. Also, an ongoing attempt to obtain a compulsory license does not constitute a viable defence in an infringement proceeding and thus would not bar an injunction. If an implementer wants to rely on a compulsory license pursuant to Articles 83, 92, or 93 Patent Act, it would have to obtain such compulsory license prior to working the patent to avoid liability for infringement.

[1] Lack of Practice

Pursuant to Article 83 (1) Patent Act, a license can be sought in case the patentee hasn't practiced the invention covered by the patent for the last consecutive three years. If the patentee refuses to grant a license, the applicant can request the Japanese Patent Office to resolve the dispute and determine the terms of the license. In this context, it has been discussed what kind of conduct by the patentee would qualify as 'practicing' the invention. An implementation guideline issued by the Ministry of Economics, Trade and Commerce held that 'nominal use' of the patented technology shall not be sufficient to avoid the patentee's obligation of granting a license under Article 83 Patent Act.[44] After implementation of the system of compulsory license under Article 83, uncertainties remained to whether importing of a product covered by a patent could fall under the scope of 'nominal use', and thus would expose the patentee to the risk of having to grant a compulsory license. The official view continues to state that importation would be considered as nominal use and not constitute a sufficient practice of the invention pursuant Article 83.[45] At the same time, the vast majority of influential commentators are challenging this official view, reasonably arguing that it would be an out-dated requirement to have a patentee to practice the patent through manufacture in every country in which patent exclusivity is sought.[46] Given that also Japanese industry often imports patent-protected products from overseas manufacturing plants, it seems unlikely that importation would not be considered as sufficient patent practice under

---

44. *Saitei Seido No Unyō Yōryō* (Implementation Outline of the Arbitration System), issued 1 Dec. 1975, and revised 24 Apr. 1997, http://www.jpo.go.jp/shiryou/toushin/shingikai/pdf/strategy_wg07/paper12.pdf (accessed 31 Jul. 2018).
45. Implementation Guidelines, *Id.*, 2. See also Hiroyuki Morisaki & Norie Matsuyama, *Commentary on Article 83 Patent Act*, in Nobuhide Nakayama & Naoki Koizumi (eds), *Shin Chūkai Tokkyohō [New Patent Act Commentary]* (2nd ed., Seirin Shoin 2017), at 1528.
46. Nakayama, *supra* n. 6, at 527. Takabayashi, *supra* n. 7, at 207; Kazuhiko Takeda, *Tokkyo no chishiki: riron to jissai* (8th ed., Diamond 2006), at 474.

Article 83 Patent Act if the Implementation Guidelines would be reviewed again in the future.

Only in case the patentee can demonstrate legitimate reasons for not practicing the invention, the JPO would refrain from granting a compulsory license.[47] A review of legitimacy has to be conducted on a case-by-case basis. The implementation guideline, however, refers to sample cases such as:

- patentee being in concise preparation of commercialization;
- a natural disaster resulting in destruction of the production facilities of the patentee; or
- patentee having difficulty in obtaining raw material required for production process.

Under the above criteria, it seems unlikely that a non-practicing entity which would not practice its patent through manufacturing, import and sales of technology covered by the patent, but which would rather commercialize its patent through licensing programmes, could escape the obligation of granting a compulsory license under Article 83 Patent Act.

Practice requirements which a patentee has to satisfy in order to avoid obligations under Article 83 (1) Patent Act are also extended to the licensee after obtaining a compulsory license. Accordingly, if the licensee does not assume practicing the patent in a reasonable amount of time after having obtained the license, the patentee or any other interested party can request cancellation of the compulsory license. In such cancellation proceeding, the licensee can similarly assert above 'legitimate reasons' of not having practiced the invention which are available to the patentee under Article 85 (2) Patent Act.

[2] Dependent License

Article 72 of the Patent Act prohibits practicing a patented invention if practicing such invention would infringe another party's senior patent or other registered intellectual property right. In order to be eligible to use the patented invention, the patentee has to obtain a license from the patentee holding the senior patent.

In case both parties cannot agree on a license, Article 92 provides the holder of the patent covering the dependent invention with a claim for a compulsory license.

[3] Public Interest License

In case the exclusive effect of a patent would be in contrast to public interest rights, Article 93 Patent Act allows for application of a compulsory license to use the patented invention. Such showing of public interest seems, however, rather difficult. According

---

47. Article 85 (2) Patent Act.

to the Implementation Outline of the Arbitration System,[48] public interest would command the grant of a compulsory license pursuant to Article 93 Patent Act if:

- there is a specific need in a field directly related to national life, such as the lives of Japanese citizens, preservation of property, or construction of a public facility; and
- if the act of not granting a non-exclusive license on the patented invention hinders the healthy development of the entire industry, and substantial harm is found to be caused to national life as a result.

Other sample scenarios in which public interest would require granting a compulsory license have been mentioned in a report issued by an expert committee of the Foreign Capital Council.[49] Accordingly, a compulsory license should be granted if the exclusive effect of the patent results in confusion (e.g., corporate failures) in:

(1) a industry in which the patented invention is expected to be used, and is likely to result in large-scale unemployment;
(2) a industry in which the patented invention is expected to be used, and extremely valuable existing facilities, which could have been used if the patented invention could be practiced, are likely to become useless as a result; or
(3) a Japanese key industry, such as important export industry, or industry in the area of advanced technology, in which the patented invention is expected to be practiced, and if the lack of such practice is likely to considerably obstruct the healthy economic or technological development of these key industries.

Other than in case of seeking a compulsory use for the patentee's lack of practice of the invention (pursuant Article 83 Patent Act) or for being able to use a dependent and patented invention (pursuant to Article 92 Article), a compulsory license for public interest concerns has to be requested by the Minister for Economy, Trade and Industry, as the determination and assessment of public interest concerns is considered to be beyond the responsibility of the JPO. However, while the above framework has been available for more than thirty years, there are no reported decisions where a compulsory license for public interest reasons has been applied for.

[B] Abuse of Rights Defence

Article 1 of the Japanese Civil Code provides for three basic principles that govern the exercise of private rights and that reads as follows:

---

48. *Ibid.*
49. Published in Jurist No. 399, at 123; the key points of the report are also re-printed in a more recent report published by the Japanese Patent Office *Wagakuni ni okeru Saitei ni tsuite [About the Japanese Arbitration System]*, http://www.jpo.go.jp/shiryou/toushin/shingikai/pdf/strategy_wg07/paper08.pdf (accessed 31 Jul. 2018), at 7–8.

(1) Private rights must conform to the public welfare.
(2) The exercise of rights and performance of duties must be done in good faith.
(3) No abuse of rights is permitted.

The doctrine of good faith and fair dealing stipulated in paragraph (2) and the doctrine against abuse of rights stipulated in paragraph (3) are sometimes invoked by courts in order to justify equitable approaches that the court could not reach otherwise.[50] While the doctrine of good faith and fair dealing is usually applied to adjudicate contractual claims, the doctrine against abuse of rights is used in situations where no contract exists between the parties involved.

The doctrine against abuse of rights stems originally from discussions amongst French academics and French case law,[51] but also resembles the German civil code prohibition of chicanery[52] and the Swiss civil code doctrine against abuse of right.[53] Classical cases on the Japanese doctrine against abuse of rights often concerned unfair business practices amongst landowners and users.[54] The first very notable Japanese patent infringement case that involved the abuse of right doctrine was the litigation resulting in the *Kilby* decision. While the patentee could successfully show infringement of the patent, the defendant was unable to show the invalidity of the asserted patent due to the fact that invalidity could only be asserted at the Trial and Appeals Board of the JPO. In a series of influential decisions, the courts held that enforcing a claim for injunctive relief in light of a likely invalidity of the asserted patent would constitute an abuse of right.[55] After the Supreme Court affirmed the lower courts' decisions in 2000,[56] Japanese courts started to accept an invalidity defence in the infringement proceedings and thus abolished the German-style bifurcation between infringement and validity proceedings.[57]

The only pattern in which the abuse of rights defence has been successfully raised in a patent law infringement context after *Kilby* was in case of technology standard-essential patents (SEP).[58] In 2013, the Tokyo District Court held in a declaratory

---

50. Hiroshi Oda, *Japanese Law* (3d ed., Oxford Univ. Press 2009), 119.
51. Teruaki Tayama et al., *Minpō Sōsoku [General Civil Code]* (4th ed., Seibundo 2010), 55.
52. Article 226 German Civil Code: 'The exercise of a right is not permitted if its only possible purpose consists in causing damage to another'.
53. Article 2(2) Swiss Civil Code: 'The manifest abuse of a right is not protected by law'.
54. A textbook case often cited is the *Unazaki Hotspring* case decided by the Supreme Court on 5 Oct. 1935, Minshu 14-1965. A pipeline connecting a hot spring resort through a small piece of land. The plaintiff in the case had purchased the land and requested the operator of the hot spring resort to purchase the land at inflated cost. When the operator refused, the plaintiff brought a case and demanded the removal of the pipeline. The Supreme Court held that such claim for removal of the pipeline would be an abuse of right.
55. Tokyo District Court, Decision of August 31, 1994, Case No. Hei 3 (wa) 9782; Tokyo High Court, Decision of September 10, 1997, Case No. Hei 6 (ne) 3790.
56. Supreme Court, Decision of April 11, 2000, Case No. Hei 10 (o) 364; English discussion available.
57. The gist of the *Kilby* decision was subsequently codified in Art. 104-3 Patent Act. *See* an English translation and discussion of the Kilby decision by Ichiro Nakayama, *Recognizing the Abuse of Rights Defense and the Invalidation Defense* in Kung-Chung Liu (ed.), *Annotated Leading Patent Cases in Major Asian Jurisdictions* (City University of Hong-Kong Press 2017), 20–32.
58. The defence has not been successfully raised in the context of NPE litigation or in case of infringement of a small component of a complex product, i.e., situations in which US courts

judgment action brought by Apple against Samsung that the enforcement of an SEP against a willing licensee could constitute an abuse of right.[59] In the appeals proceedings, the grand bench of the IP High Court partially confirmed the District Court, holding that seeking an injunction against a party that has demonstrated a willingness to obtain a license would be an abuse of right.[60] Specifically, the IP High Court reasoned that allowing a SEP owner to obtain injunctive relief against a willing licensee[61] would constitute excessive protection of SEP owner. It would further discourage the dissemination of the technologies of the patented invention, and consequently hinder the 'development of industry' being the primary objective of the Japanese patent system.[62] The court set forth three factors that it referred to when reviewing the abuse of right defence:

- obligation to good-faith negotiation / willingness to obtain license;
- timely disclosure of patent and details of infringement claim;
- obligation arising under FRAND-declaration.[63]

In a non-related subsequent proceeding, the Tokyo District Court relied on the IP High Court's decision when confirming that even threatening to enjoin an implementer from using technology protected by a SEP in the course of a licensing negotiation would constitute an abuse of right that could theoretically lead to damages claims for unjust warning.[64]

---

would likely refuse to grant injunctive relief. The author contends that it would be successful in case of routine NPE litigation as Japanese courts would not be convinced that the business model of the patentee would be relevant in deciding an infringement case. It may in theory be a successful defence against an injunction due to an infringement of a small component of a complex product where the injunction would threaten removal of an important product from the Japanese market. That said, the rather conservative stance of Japanese courts in calculating damages in this kind of infringement situations may be one reason for scarcity of this type of patent assertions. Another scenario in which the abuse of right defence might in theory be effective is cases in which an implementer would also be entitled to a compulsory license for public interest reasons pursuant to Art. 93 Patent Act; *see* discussion here at Nakayama, *supra* n. 6, at 534.

59. Tokyo District Court, Decision of February 28, 2013, Case No. Hei 23 (wa) 38969; English version available on the IP High Court website under http://www.ip.courts.go.jp/eng/vcms_lf/23_wa_38969.pdf (accessed 31 Jul. 2018).
60. IP High Court, Decisions of May 16, 2014, Case No. Hei 25 (ne) 10043, Case No. Hei 25 (ra) 10007, and Case No. Hei 25 (ra) 10008. English versions available on the IP High Court website under http://www.ip.courts.go.jp/eng/vcms_lf/25ne10043full.pdf, http://www.ip.courts.go.jp/eng/vcms_lf/25_ra_10007zenbun.pdf, and http://www.ip.courts.go.jp/eng/vcms_lf/25_ra_10008zenbun.pdf (accessed 31 Jul. 2018).
61. In the specific case, the court mainly focused on formal conduct requirements and found Apple to be a 'willing licensee', given that Apple made several specific royalty rate proposals showing a calculation basis and engaged in intensive licensing discussion with its counterparty Samsung. The court recognized the 'material discrepancy' on the appropriate license rate between the two parties, but found such discrepancy to be somewhat natural given the conflicting interests between the patentee and the implementer. Without engaging in further discussion on the content of the proposals, the court found Apple's proposals 'fairly reasonable'.
62. *Ibid.*
63. *Ibid.*
64. Tokyo District Court, Decision of February 18, 2015, Case No. Hei 25 (wa) 21383, published (in Japanese), e.g., in 1412 Hanrei Times 323 (2015).

§11.04 CONCLUDING THOUGHTS

The claim for injunction relief is firmly rooted in the tradition of Japanese patent law. Japanese courts will continue their practice to grant injunctive relief upon a finding of infringement. The absence of jury trials and the scarcity of NPE litigation create an environment in which there is little policy pressure to change this general rule.

The one type of patents in which the Japanese government is considering to introduce tools that may further impact the availability of injunctive relief is SEPs. Following the IP High Court decision in *Apple v. Samsung* in 2014, the Japan Fair Trade Commission slightly revised their 'Guidelines for Use of Intellectual Property under the Antimonopoly Act' and basically referenced the IP High Court decision.[65] More substantive change was envisioned when the Japan Patent Office started discussing to introduce a new compulsory licensing system for SEPs in 2017. Encouraged by the 'Connected Industries' initiative of the Ministry of Economy, Trade and Industry (METI) and by certain groups of implementers, the JPO suggested a system in which implementers could obtain fast and inexpensive licenses to SEPs.[66] Following the intervention of certain patent-heavy industry representatives and a routine change of leadership at the JPO, the JPO moved away from such initial proposal, and established a system to seek non-binding advisory opinions by JPO on whether or not patents declared as standard-essential are really essential for a specific technology standard. Further, following extensive outreach to the industry and other interest groups, the JPO released a final version of a Guide to Licensing Negotiations involving Standard Essential Patents in June 2018.[67] However, even in this field, the policy goal of the JPO is to enhance transparency and to aid parties in finding the right compensation for use of SEPs in an efficient fashion. If an implementer fails to compensate the patentee, an injunction will remain to be the applicable remedy.

---

65. For a short discussion of the JFTC guideline amendments *see*, e.g., Kei Matsumoto, Christoph Rademacher & Tsugihiro Okada, *Amendments to Japan's IP Guidelines*, Intellectual Property Magazine, October 2015, https://www.intellectualpropertymagazine.com/patent/amendments-to-japans-ip-guidelines-111893.htm (accessed 31 Jul. 2018).
66. *See*, e.g., presentation material by Izumi Hayashi for the METI SEP Study Group, 7 Jun. 2017, on file with author.
67. *See* the English version of the Guide at https://www.jpo.go.jp/torikumi_e/kokusai_e/files/seps-tebiki_e/guide-seps-en.pdf https://www.jpo.go.jp/iken/pdf/180308_hyoujun/sep_guide_draft_en.pdf (accessed 28 Sep. 2018). The Guide encompasses forty-seven pages and includes extensive references of international SEP case law. It aims to be an industry guidepost on the process and the content of FRAND negotiations. That said, the Guide will not be a binding document for Japanese courts.

PART III Conclusions

CHAPTER 12
Between Automatism and Flexibility: Injunctions in Twenty-First Century Patent Law

Rafał Sikorski

§12.01 PATENT EXCLUSIVITY AND INJUNCTIVE RELIEF: TWO SIDES OF THE SAME COIN

Inventions are immaterial goods. As such, in contrast to their traditional tangible counterparts, they are both non-rivalrous and non-excludable.[1] Any invention can be used at the same time by an indefinite number of users. The fact that one user practices it does not preclude another user from practicing the same invention at the same time. Non-rival and non-excludable character of immaterial goods makes them susceptible to free-riding by others willing to use the invention. Whereas innovation is often costly, time-consuming and risky, free-riding is easy, quick and comes at little or no cost. The nature of immaterial goods creates an incentive to free ride and at the same time a disincentive to innovate and create.

To address this market failure, innovators are granted exclusive rights which enable them to exclude others from practicing a patent-protected invention.[2] The prospect of patent exclusivity provides the necessary incentives to engage in innovation in the first place. By being able to exclude others, patentees can be rewarded for

---

1. *See* basic discussion of these concepts in: Marco Ricolfi, *The new paradigm of creativity and innovation and its corollaries for the law of obligations*, in: Peter Drahos, Gustavo Ghidini, Hanns Ullrich (ed.), Kritika: *Essays on intellectual property* (Edward Elgar Publishing 2015), 137; Joseph William Singer, Bethany R. Berger, Nestor M. Davidson, Eduardo Moses Panalver, *Property Law. Rule, Policies and Practices* (Wolters Kluwer 2017), 175–176.
2. Mark A. Lemley, *Ex Ante versus Ex Post Justifications for Intellectual Property*, 71 The University of Chicago Law Review (2004), 129.

their innovation. Finally, exclusivity also opens the door to successful commercialization of inventions.

Injunctions and exclusivity are in fact two sides of the same coin. Injunctions are a necessary corollary to exclusive intellectual property rights. Injunctive relief protects patent exclusivity against unauthorized use by third parties. That is why generally once the boundaries of patent have been trespassed by an unauthorized user, the patentee should be entitled to a remedy that reinstates the state of exclusivity.

Importantly, injunctive relief plays a crucial role in ensuring that the patentee is properly rewarded for his investment in innovation.[3] Patentees may reap their reward effectively also because they act in the shadow of injunctive relief.[4] When a patentee decides to practice an invention himself and thus maintain a technological advantage over other market participants who lack access to a given invention, injunctive relief will be helpful in safeguarding patentee's market position and the technological edge over others.[5] Here, patentee's reward would result from the competitive advantage enjoyed by the patentee on the market where the patent-protected invention is implemented. If, on the other hand, a patentee decides to commercialize his invention by way of licensing in order to collect the reward for innovation via royalties, potential licensees will usually be interested to prohibit the use by unauthorized third parties, either to eliminate use by those who were not granted a license or those who were unwilling to conclude a licensing agreement.

When patent remedies, including injunctions, enable patent holders to reap the rewards that reflect the value of the protected inventions, the patent system may properly fulfill its role as a stimulator of innovation.[6] It also leads to efficient allocation of innovators' resources and produces socially desirable innovation. The consumers are better off as they gain access to new products capable of satisfying their needs more efficiently and the overall welfare increases.[7] When the remedies overcompensate, the resources of innovators will be diverted towards areas which guarantee such excessive profits.[8] Needs of consumers might be neglected, prices are likely to be higher and consumers will very likely be worse off.[9]

Patent holders may also use injunctions to obtain royalties that grossly exceed the value of their inventions. Indeed frequently, a mere threat of an injunction will suffice. The ability to obtain excessive royalties for the use of patent-protected inventions, referred to in the legal and economic literature as hold-up, has been a growing concern on various markets.[10] Hold-up occurs when an implementer invests to implement a given technology. Typically, as a result of his investment the implementer incurs certain costs. Such costs are very often tied exclusively to the implementation of a given

---

3. Federal Trade Commission, *The Evolving IP Marketplace. Aligning Patent Notice and Remedies with Competition* (March 2011), 138.
4. Ibid.
5. FTC, *supra* n. 3, at 143.
6. FTC, *supra* n. 3, at 141.
7. FTC, *supra* n. 3, at 140.
8. FTC, *supra* n. 3, at 146.
9. FTC, *supra* n. 3, at 145.
10. Mark A. Lemley, Carl Shapiro, *Patent Holdup and Royalty Stacking*, 85 Texas Law Review (2007), 1991, 1993.

technology. Thus, the implementer incurs a certain amount of sunk costs. If he decides to move to another technology these costs will be lost. Consequently, because of the investment and costs incurred the investor becomes locked-in to a certain technology. The costs of moving to another technology, the so-called switching costs, may be high. Sometimes, as is the case with standard essential patents, there will be no technology to switch to.

In the above described circumstances, the patentees can demand royalties that exceed the value of the invention. Not surprisingly, the implementers will usually be willing to pay more in such circumstances because they face the prospect of losing all the costs already incurred and they also face the costs of switching to another technology. Implementers are likely to accept an increase in the royalty rate as long as that increase does not exceed the amount of the switching costs. Switching costs thus will serve as a ceiling on the amount of royalty rate's increase. In case of licensing standard essential patents, there will be no such ceiling because the technology implementers have no alternatives to turn to.

On the markets where technologies are complex and often are covered by hundreds if not thousands of patents hold-up may occur rather frequently. To navigate through such dense thickets of numerous patents is cumbersome.[11] The likelihood of infringement is very high. Full pre-clearance is also hardly possible.[12] Manufacturers of complex products use components delivered by third parties. To expect these manufacturers to pre-clear all possible patents possibly involved in particular components is not only unrealistic but could also be stifling for innovation, hamper introduction of new products and result in less consumer choice.

Injunctions in so far as they allow patent holders to extract hold-up value rather than the market value of an invention are problematic. They result in overcompensation of the patentee and inefficient allocation of resources. Additionally, the harm to the implementer may be disproportionately high when compared with the gain of the patentee resulting from obtaining an injunction. When an implementer has already incurred costs associated with implementing a given technology, moving to another technology would require adaptation, possibly entering into another licensing agreement or designing around. This indeed might be costly. At the same time if a patent holder does not operate on the market where his invention has been implemented, or if the invention is only minor and must be used with other inventions that together make a more complex technology, an injunction would not necessarily benefit the patentee more than would the payment of royalties.

While admitting that hold-up might have negative consequences and disproportionate harm, one also has to admit the dangers that result from the phenomena called

---

11. On the concept of patent thickets *see*, Carl Shapiro, *Navigating the Patent Thicket: Cross License, Patent Pools, and Standard-Setting*, in: Adam B. Jaffe, Josh Lerner, Scott Stern (ed.), *Innovation Policy and the Economy* (MIT Press 2001), 119–122.
12. William F. Lee, Douglas Melamed, *Breaking the Vicious Cycle of Patent Damages*, Stanford Law and Economics Olin Working Paper Series Paper No. 477 (2015), http://ssrn.com/abstract=2 577462 (accessed 30 Jul. 2018), 17.

reverse hold-up or hold-out.[13] Hold-out usually refers to a situation where an implementer refuses to engage in good faith negotiations with the patent holder hoping that he would avoid paying royalties for the use of the patented invention or that he would pay less than the value of the invention.[14] Authors discuss the hold-out phenomena predominantly in the context of standardization. These authors also suggest that weakening of the bargaining position of the standard essential patent holders vis-à-vis standard implementers results from depriving SEP holders of the right to seek injunctive relief.[15] When the negotiations between SEP holders and SEP implementers are conducted in the shadow of injunctive relief the position of the SEP holder is significantly stronger. On the other hand, when that shadow is gone, SEP implementers' bargaining position is significantly strengthened and is likely to result in undercompensating the patentees which in turn undermines the foundations of the patent system as the stimulator of innovation.

All this leads to a conclusion that exclusivity and injunctions are important components of a properly functioning patent system. They are crucial in enabling the patent system to properly fulfill its role of incentivizing innovation and ensuring adequate reward once a patent is commercialized. However, as technologies and products have become increasingly complex, in the sense that it is not unusual for them to be protected by hundreds of patents, injunctions have become much more susceptible to abuse.[16] There has never been a more a compelling need to achieve a balance between the interests of right holders, patent implementers and the public interest both in maintaining a patent system capable of incentivizing innovation while at the same time also receptive to various public needs.

It is generally accepted that injunctive relief should be available to right holders whose patents were infringed. Indeed, there seems to be a presumption in favor of granting an injunction in case of infringement in most if not all patent systems. However, there is also a growing consensus that injunctions should be denied when they are anticompetitive, (grossly) disproportionate or contrary to the public interest.

§12.02 CASES FOR FLEXIBILITY

The discussion as to when the courts should consider denying injunctive relief concentrates on four types of cases. First, it is usually assumed that an injunction

---

13. On the concept of reverse hold-up or hold-out *see*, Damien Geradin, *Reverse Hold-ups: The (Often Ignored) Risks Faced by Innovators in Standardized Areas*, available at: http://ssrn.com/abstract=1711744; Colleen V. Chien, *Holding Up and Holding Out*, 21 Michigan Telecommunications & Technology Law Review 1 (2014).
14. Colleen V. Chien, *supra* n. 13, at 21–22.
15. Damien Geradin, *supra* n. 13, at 14.
16. For a thorough analysis of injunctive relief in patent law, particularly in the context of complex products, *see*, Norman V. Siebrasse, Rafał Sikorski, Jorge L. Contreras, Thomas Cotter, John M. Golden, Sang Jo Jong, Sang, Brian J. Love, David O. Taylor, *Injunctive Relief*, in: Brad Biddle, Jorge L. Contreras, Brian J. Love, Norman V. Siebrasse (eds.), *Patent Remedies and Complex Products: Toward a Global Consensus* (Cambridge University Press, 2018, forthcoming) available at SSRN: https://ssrn.com/abstract=3249058.

should not be granted if sought by a SEP holder who has committed during standard-setting process to license its SEPs on FRAND terms against a licensee willing to license on such terms. Second, it is believed that courts should be able to deny injunctions to entities that do not practice patents themselves and are only occupied with licensing or engage in aggressive patent litigation usually with a purpose of obtaining excessive royalties. Third, it is also suggested that courts should also be able to deny an injunction when it is sought by a patentee whose patent covers only a minor feature of a complex product. Fourth, courts should also be free to deny injunctive relief when granting an injunction would be against public interest. Comparative analysis of injunctive relief in patent cases shows that courts also deny injunctions in other cases. This is the case, for example, when the patentee has knowingly tolerated use of a patented invention over a longer period of time or when the infringement ceased and there is no likelihood that the infringement would commence again. In some jurisdictions an injunction could also be denied when the parties negotiate, and the licensee has already implemented the patented invention acting in good faith.

The most interesting however are the four types of cases listed above. This is so because these cases raise systemic questions on the relationship between the exercise of patents on the markets where technologies are highly complex and frequently subject to voluntary standardization. Standards that are already widespread will become even more pervasive with the rise of IoT and implementation of 5G telecommunications standard. Similarly, products that are already complex, in the sense that they already implement hundred or even thousands of protected inventions, are unlikely to become less complex.

[A] Standardization and Standard Essential Patents

Standardization has been crucial to the development of such industries as telecommunications (mobile telephony) or consumer electronics (video and audio recording) and is also vital for automotive or electricity grid industries.[17] Standards are often if not predominantly developed within standard-setting organizations (SSOs).

Frequently, standards are protected by numerous patents rights belonging to multiple patent holders. SSOs adopt intellectual property policies in order to ensure that the standards may develop smoothly in order to become widespread.[18] For that purpose, SSOs require that participants in the standard setting process to disclose their patents or patent applications that might read on a technological standard prior to

---

17. *Patents and Standards. A modern framework for IPR-based Standardization*, Final Report. A study prepared for the European Commission Directorate-General for Enterprise and Industry (2014), 57–108.
18. *See*, for example, Common Patent Policy ITU-T/ITU-R/ISO/IEC (version 2012) applied by CEN (European Committee for Standardization) and CENELEC (European Committee for Electrotechnical Standardization), available at: ftp://ftp.cencenelec.eu/EN/EuropeanStandardization/Guides/8_CENCLCGuide8.pdf; ETSI (European Telecommunications Standards Institute) Intellectual Property Rights Policy, available at: https://www.etsi.org/images/files/IPR/etsi-ipr-policy.pdf.

adopting a standard[19] and that the holders of patents essential to the practice of a standard undertake to license their patents usually on fair, reasonable and non-discriminatory terms to any implementer willing to take a license.[20]

Markets such as telecommunications or consumer electronics are characterized by strong network effects.[21] Standardization is typical for such markets. The value of a standard depends on the number of those who apply it. Once the number of users reaches a certain level the markets tips in favor of a given standard with the effect that other technologies lose their appeal to possible implementers. This means that to be able to compete on a market for which a given standard has been adopted, access to that standard is necessary.

In order to ensure that the standard is accessible to all willing implementers, the SSOs require patentees participating in the standard-setting process to commit themselves to license on fair, reasonable and non-discriminatory terms. A FRAND commitment is an undertaking: (1) to conclude a licensing agreement with all those who are willing to license on FRAND terms; (2) not take advantage of the patent hold-up; (3) to avoid royalty stacking; and (4) to set the royalty at the level proportional to the invention's contribution to the standard technology overall.[22] A FRAND declaration by no means aims at lowering the royalty rate below what is required for the patent law to fulfill its primary function. By becoming a part of a standard, a FRAND-encumbered patent only expands its licensee base and the potential to generate royalty revenue. At the same however encumbering a patent with a FRAND commitment aims at ensuring that the privileged position on the technology market is not abused.

FRAND commitments are motivated in two ways.[23] First, they are required to secure the effectiveness of the standard setting process. Confidence in technological standardization would be severely undermined, if the SEP holders could obstruct the proliferation of a standard by denying access to their standard essential patents or by offering licenses on non-FRAND terms. Second, their purpose is to alleviate competition concerns that the patentees could exercise their rights in order to foreclose access to product markets where standards are implemented. Neither of the two motivations lying behind encumbering patents with FRAND commitments demands the patentee to waiver rights to injunctive relief. The integrity of voluntary standard setting will not be undermined when the patentee retains his right to injunctive relief against unwilling SEP implementers. Nor will the goals of competition be compromised in such cases. To maintain competition on product markets it is enough to target the patentees when they seek injunctions against implementers willing to negotiate a FRAND license.

---

19. *See*, for example, ETSI IPR Policy, s. 4.
20. *See*, for example, ETSI IPR Policy, s. 6.
21. On markets with network effects and standardization *see*, Peter S. Menell, *Economic Analysis of Network Effects and Intellectual Property*, available at: https://ssrn.com/abstract=3072633.
22. Norman V. Siebrasse, Thomas F. Cotter, *The Value of The Standard*, Legal Studies Research Paper Series Research Paper No. 15-21, 101 Minnesota Law Review (2017), 1159, 1160–1163.
23. For thorough analysis of the motivations behind FRAND commitments as well historical origins of FRAND please *see*: Jorge L. Contreras, *A Brief History of FRAND: Analyzing Current Debates in Standard Setting and Antitrust Through a Historical Lens*, 80(1) Antitrust Law Journal (2015), pp. 39–120; Rafał Sikorski, *Funkcjonowanie zasobów patentowych* (C.H. Beck 2013), at 43–44, 70, 74–75, 83, 88.

Thus, under the private ordering regime as envisaged by the SSOs, the negotiations between licensees and licensors take place under the shadow of injunctive relief. Generally, this mitigates concerns over hold-out, because an injunction would be available if the implementer does not negotiate in good faith or rejects FRAND offers by the SEP holder, nor comes up with FRAND counter-offers of his own within a reasonable period of time. Similarly, hold-up concerns are also addressed because a licensing offer that would include the value of hold-up would not be FRAND. However, the private ordering regime established by SSOs will only work well when the rights and obligations of both SEP holders and implementers are properly distributed. Only then will the shadow of injunctive relief be neither too imminent – so as to lead to hold-up – nor too elusive – so as to result in hold-out. The negotiation frameworks differ among jurisdictions. These differences are not immense but still capable of favoring one or the other party.

[B] NPEs, PAEs, Patent Trolls and Privateering

The terms: non-practicing entities (NPEs), patent assertion entities (PAEs), trolls and privateers all refer to entities that do not practice their patents.[24] Such entities do not manufacture goods. They are primarily engaged in patent licensing and asserting their patents against infringers. NPEs are entities that apart from being engaged in the licensing of their patents may also be involved in significant research & development activities.[25] Universities, institutes or research labs are examples of such NPEs. PAEs are a subcategory of NPEs. They are not involved in any R&D. Rather they license their patents or assert these patents in the courts in litigation when the negotiations fail.[26] Patent trolls is another term used for PAEs. PAE are not necessarily involved in dubious activities, the terms "patent trolls" is generally a pejorative term to name those entities that are involved in particularly aggressive litigation strategies.[27] Privateers are a special subset of PAEs. They are linked to practicing entities operating on the product markets. Their primary purpose is to target competitors of a practicing entity on the downstream product markets by targeting them and raising their costs.[28]

PAEs' patent portfolios are often composed of SEPs.[29] Typically, PAEs will be interested in exploiting their position on the technology markets in order to obtain royalties that exceed the market value of their SEPs. This is also the purpose of the

---

24. For comprehensive studies on NPEs, PAEs, trolls and privateers *see,* Nikolaus Thumm, Garry Gabison (ed.), *Patent Assertion Entities in Europe,* JRC Science for Policy Report (2016); Federal Trade Commission, *Patent Assertion Entity Activity* (October 2016).
25. Damien Geradin, *Patent Assertion Entities and EU Competition Law,* George Mason University Law and Economics Research Paper Series, 16-08, available at: ssrn.com/abstract = 2728686, 5.
26. Ibid.
27. Ibid.
28. Ibid.
29. See Jorge L. Contreras, *Assertion of Standards Essential Patents by Non-Practicing Entities* (2016), available at: ssrn.com/abstract = 2700117.

so-called privateers. Since they are tied to practicing entities operating on downstream product markets they are usually interested in raising rivals' costs.[30]

SSOs often require that FRAND commitments be binding on those who have not taken part in standard setting process but have acquired SEPs later on. The fact that SEP acquirers have not committed themselves to FRAND licensing should not allow such SEP holders to exclude willing licensees from access to SEPs. With respect to SEPs the ability to obtain an injunction is, as has already been pointed, limited. PAEs – like other SEP holders – will be able to obtain an injunction only against unwilling licensees.

Outside of the standardization context, non-practicing entities should not be generally deprived of injunctive relief. Generally, it is true that NPEs monetize their patents through licensing and are also usually interested to license as many licensees as possible. However, NPEs that develop their own technologies, are often interested in concluding exclusive license agreements, rather than entering into numerous non-exclusive licenses with all willing licensees. Here, availability of injunctive relief will be essential for supporting the licensing strategy of the NPE.

[C] Complex Products

Many products manufactured and marketed today are highly complex. Often hundreds, if not thousands of patents read on such technologies. As has already been observed full pre-clearance of patents granted, and patent applications is rarely a viable option for the manufacturer. Individual patents usually read on minor features of the technologies implemented and as such individually are hardly drivers for the demand of a product in which they are implemented.[31] Even though the protected features are minor, when a patentee seeks an injunction, it is likely to be highly disruptive for the manufacturer of such a product. The costs of designing around even a minor patent might be significant. More importantly however an injunction is likely to throw such a complex product out of the market for the time necessary to design around.

Granting injunctive relief in complex products cases can be particularly disproportionate. The harm of the manufacturer will usually be very significant, and will normally include sunk costs, costs of switching to another technology and lost profits. The patentee on the other hand is unlikely to benefit from an injunction, unless the patentee is a competitor and the feature protected by his patent drives the demand for the product on the market. Comparison of the harm and the elusive benefits of an injunction would strongly favor monetary compensation in lieu of an injunction or at least tailoring of injunctive relief that would allow for designing around while allowing the manufacturer to stay on the market for the time necessary to switch to a new technology.

---

30. Ann Layne-Farrar, *A Theoretical Framework for Empirical Research on PAEs and Privateers*, available at: ssrn.com/abstract=2728390, 6.
31. Marco Ricolfi, *supra* n. 1, at 165.

[D] Public Interest

Injunctions granted in patent infringement disputes affect the parties to the proceedings. An injunction is an order directed to the infringer who, as a result, is supposed to cease the infringing activities. However, in some cases an injunction given in a private dispute might influence third parties and sometimes even the public at large. This would be the case if an injunction had an impact on security of highly popular software,[32] access to lifesaving medical devices[33] or led to an immediate closure of a factory resulting in unemployment of a large group of workers.[34]

Public interest concerns should be treated with caution and they may weigh against granting injunctive relief in exceptional cases only. After all one must remember that there is always a competing public interest in having a patent system capable of stimulating innovation[35] and that availability of injunctive relief is an important element of that system. In such cases tailoring should also be considered. Public interest concerns may not necessarily justify complete denial of injunctive relief. If it is sufficient to stay an injunction for the period necessary to switch to an alternative technology, tailoring of injunctive relief should be the preferred option.

§12.03 LEGAL FRAMEWORK

[A] International Law Framework – The TRIPS Agreement

The TRIPS Agreement – unlike previous intellectual property conventions – contains extensive rules relating to IP remedies and enforcement procedures.[36] Part III of the TRIPS Agreement is based on the idea that protection of IP rights requires effective enforcement procedures and remedies. Part III however rather than harmonizing remedies and enforcement procedures introduces a set of standards and requirements.[37] Unsurprisingly, the TRIPS Agreement requires members to ensure that their courts have the authority to grant injunctions ordering the infringing party to cease infringement.[38] Though members are required to grant their judicial authorities the competence to issue permanent injunctions, members may also set the conditions for granting injunctive relief.[39] The Agreement does not demand that permanent injunctions be granted in each and every case of patent infringement.

---

32. *Z4 Technologies, Inc. v. Microsoft Corp.*, 434 F. Supp. 2d 437 (E.D. Tex. 2006).
33. *Edwards Life Sciences LLC v. Boston Scientific SCIMED INC*, [2018] EWHC 1256 (Pat).
34. *Bayer Intellectual Property GmbH v. Ajanta Pharma Ltd.*, IA No.86/2017, Hon'ble Mr. Justice R.k.Gauba, Order 4.01.2017.
35. *Polara Engineering, Inc. v. Campbell Co.*, 237 F. Supp. 3d 956 – Dist. Court, CD California 2017.
36. Justin Malbon, Charles Lawson, Mark Davison, *The WTO Agreement on Trade-Related Aspects of Intellectual Property Rights. A Commentary*, Edward Elgar 2014, 615.
37. *Ibid.*
38. Article 44 TRIPS Agreement.
39. Justin Malbon, Charles Lawson, Mark Davison, *supra* n. 36, at 648.

The TRIPS Agreement was concluded well before the era of excessive patent litigation in industries such as telecommunications or consumer electronics.[40] Therefore, the drafters did not contemplate whether permanent injunctions should be available to holders of standard essential patents or whether they should be granted to patent assertion entities nor did they consider potential negative implications of granting injunctions against manufacturers of complex products.

Interestingly however, the TRIPS Agreement contains quite a number of provisions that seem to favor flexible approach towards of injunctive relief. These are both provisions which establish general standards for the application of enforcement mechanisms, as well provisions containing detailed rules.

First, the TRIPS Agreement requires that remedies be *fair and equitable* (Article 41.2 TRIPS). In the context of international agreements, this is usually a reference to proportionality, good faith, due process and non-discrimination.[41] Second, it also requires that remedies be applied in a manner that *avoids creation of barriers to legitimate trade and provides for safeguards against their abuse* (Article 41.1 TRIPS). Both provisions ensure that members have significant discretion for adopting injunctive relief to the circumstances of a particular case.

The TRIPS Agreement however also contains more detailed rules on granting injunctive relief. For example, Article 44(1) provides that TRIPS members are not required to grant an injunction against those who order or acquire a protected subject matter prior to knowing or having reasonable grounds to know that dealing with such subject matter would entail infringement. This provision allows for alternative measures such as Article 12 Directive 2004/48. Additionally, Article 44(2) provides that an injunction may be denied when granting it would be inconsistent with Member's laws, however only when a declaratory judgment and adequate compensation are available. This opens the doors to denying an injunction on grounds of abuse of rights or on grounds of proportionality. Finally, Article 40 recognizes that when the exercise of intellectual property rights has adverse impact on competition, either as a result of licensing practices or unilateral actions, an intrusion via competition/antitrust regulations is possible, when consistent with the TRIPS Agreement.

[B] Permanent Injunctions at National Level

The legal frameworks for administering injunctive relief in patent law vary between the jurisdictions analyzed in this book. First, there are quite substantial differences between the legal systems analyzed. In the jurisdictions where injunctive relief originates with equity certain degree of discretion in granting injunctions is natural. Flexibility and the ability to respond to new phenomena such PAEs or privateering is just a matter of applying the tests, principles or standards already known to the courts. Second, some jurisdictions are more popular *fora* for patent litigation than others. This may result from the level of economic development, characteristics of the patent

---

40. Justin Malbon, Charles Lawson, Mark Davison, *supra* n. 36, at 615.
41. Justin Malbon, Charles Lawson, Mark Davison, *supra* n. 36, at 628.

system or civil procedure rules. Naturally, courts in countries with more patent cases are more experienced in dealing with patent disputes, including the remedies.

What seems striking is that these different legal systems effectively come to very similar or even the same conclusions, namely that there are cases when injunctive relief should be denied. There seems to be a growing consensus that in the case of standard essential patents, patent assertion entities, complex products and when there is a compelling public interest, injunctions may, in certain circumstances, be denied. It is then just the matter of tools that are available to the courts in various jurisdictions. Some will deny an injunction upon finding that an injunction would be disproportionate, others will resort to the general abuse of right, still others will address the problem via competition/antitrust law.

Though the legal tools employed to make injunctive relief more flexible differ between jurisdictions it seems that the role of proportionality is on the rise. In fact, proportionality seems to have become a bridge between jurisdictions where injunctions are an equitable remedy and jurisdictions where granting injunctive relief was considered a logical consequence of finding infringement of a valid patent. Here, Directives 2004/48 and 2016/943, both play an important role, as both have rooted their remedies in the principle of proportionality. Indeed, the Directive 2016/943 has greatly contributed to the development of the concept of proportionality in the field of IP remedies.

[C]   Preliminary Injunctions

The authors in various chapters deal with circumstances when permanent injunctions should be denied since patentees should not be allowed to use injunctive relief in order to obtain royalties that grossly exceed the market value of the protected invention. As has been shown such unjustified overcompensation of the patentee will harm implementers, consumers, and is also likely to negatively affect allocation of resources, innovation and the general welfare. While ensuring that there are properly functioning safeguards against abuse of permanent injunctions, one should not forget about the anticompetitive potential of interim injunctions.

As the authors have shown, many patent disputes end with settlement once a preliminary injunction has been issued. Interim injunctions immediately affect the alleged infringer. Conducting negotiations in the shadow of interim injunction will often be much more problematic for the alleged infringer than conducting such negotiations under the threat of a permanent injunction. When interim injunctions are granted without considering the interests of the implementer, they may lead to far greater hold-up than permanent injunctions.

It is therefore extremely important to balance at the interim relief stage the conflicting interests of the right holder and the implementer. Whereas the right holder must be allowed to obtain an interim injunction so as to avoid irreversible consequences of patent infringement, including the irreparable harm, the implementer rights of defence must also be safeguarded. It is particularly visible in the ex parte proceedings. It is not a problem that a patentee has a right to obtain an interim injunction *inaudita altera parte*. In such cases it is important however that the implementer may be heard within a reasonable period of time upon granting an interim measure. In ex parte proceedings after all, the court only has a chance to see the dispute from one perspective.